Supervision and Clinical Psychology

Increased attention is now being paid to the role of supervision in both pre-qualification and post-qualification practice in clinical psychology in the UK. This definitive text addresses the issues of central concern to supervisors in clinical psychology.

Senior trainers and clinicians draw on relevant research and their own experience, covering:

- Historical development of supervision and a review of worldwide literature on supervision.
- Supervisory and therapy models.
- Maximizing supervisory resources.
- Supervisory training and effectiveness.
- Cultural and gender issues in supervision.
- Measuring the effectiveness of supervision.
- Future perspectives for supervision in clinical psychology.

Supervision and Clinical Psychology provides practical advice essential for clinical psychology supervisors, as well as those in psychiatry, social work and psychotherapy.

Ian Fleming and **Linda Steen** are joint Clinical Directors of the doctoral Clinical Psychology training programme at the University of Manchester. They have considerable experience of all aspects of training and a particular interest in supervision. As clinical psychologists in the NHS for over twenty years they have a wealth of experience of supervising others, including trainee clinical psychologists.

Supervision and Clinical Psychology

Theory, practice and perspectives

Edited by
Ian Fleming and Linda Steen

Brunner-Routledge
Taylor & Francis Group

HOVE AND NEW YORK

First published 2004
by Brunner-Routledge
27 Church Road, Hove, East Sussex BN3 2FA

Simultaneously published in the USA and Canada
by Brunner-Routledge
29 West 35th Street, New York NY 10001

Brunner-Routledge is an imprint of the Taylor & Francis Group

Typeset in 10/12pt Times NR
by Graphicraft Limited, Hong Kong
Printed and bound in Great Britain by
TJ International Ltd, Padstow, Cornwall
Paperback cover design by Hybert Design

British Library Cataloguing in Publication Data
A catalogue record for this book is available from the British
Library

Library of Congress Cataloging-in-Publication Data
Supervision and clinical psychology / [edited by] Ian Fleming and
Linda Steen.
   p. cm.
Includes bibliographical references and index.
   ISBN 1-58391-254-1 (hdbk) – ISBN 1-58391-255-X (pbk.)
   1. Clinical psychologists–Supervision of. I. Fleming, Ian.
   II. Steen, Linda.

RC467.7.S87 2003
616.89′023–dc21   2003010098

ISBN 1-58391-254-1 (hbk)
ISBN 1-58391-255-X (pbk)

Contents

Figures

* Every effort has been made to trace copyright holder and obtain permission to reproduce Figures 8.2 and 8.3. Any omissions brought to our attention will be remedied in future editions.

Tables

Boxes

Contributors

Gill Aitken works as Lead Consultant Clinical Psychologist – Women's Services, across a high and a medium secure psychiatric service. Alongside team members, she has a commitment to developing and providing more (timely) gender and culturally appropriate (psychological) services to women. Like many others working towards social inclusion, Gill attempts to put and keep women's issues and issues of equality on institutional and professional agendas. In her non-work time she can be found socializing, rock climbing, with a rucksack in warm climes, and being on the back of a motorbike.

Helen Beinart is Clinical Director of the Oxford Doctoral Course in Clinical Psychology and works clinically with children, young people and their families in a primary care setting in Oxfordshire. She has worked in the NHS for the past 22 years as a clinician, service manager, supervisor and trainer. Over the past 8 years, she has been involved in clinical psychology training and supervisor training. She has recently completed a doctorate exploring factors that influence the quality of supervisory relationships.

Delia Cushway is Director of the Coventry and Warwick Clinical Psychology doctorate. During the 14 years she has worked in clinical training her main teaching, research and clinical interest have been in helping us to help ourselves so that we might more effectively help others. Her Ph.D. was in stress and its management in mental health professionals. Clinically, Delia espouses a humanistic philosophy and is interested in Gestalt therapy and working with dreams and nightmares. She has a particular interest in clinical supervision.

Maxine Dennis is a consultant clinical psychologist at South West London and St George's NHS Trust. She manages a primary care team and is involved in the teaching, training and supervision of psychologists, psychotherapists and counsellors. She has been chair of the British Psychological Society's 'Race' and Culture Special Interest Group.

Ian Fleming is joint Clinical Director of the University of Manchester doctoral Clinical Psychology training programme and has a clinical post in Rochdale working with people with learning disabilities. He is involved in training supervisors and also practises as a regular supervisor for local training programmes. He has been co-author of past books about work with older adults (*Goal Planning with Elderly People* and *Positive Approaches to Assisting Older People*) and people with learning disabilities (*People with Learning Disability and Severe Challenging Behaviour*).

David Green has been Clinical Tutor on the Clinical Psychology training programme at the University of Leeds since 1988. His responsibilities include both supervisor training and the organization of a wide range of post-qualification training opportunities for clinical psychologists in Yorkshire. He completed his doctoral research using qualitative methods to investigate the core skills of clinical supervision in 1998.

Jacky Knibbs is a lecturer/practitioner with the Coventry and Warwick Clinical Psychology programme. She trained and worked in London before moving to the West Midlands. Jacky set up the Child and Adolescent Clinical Psychology and CAMHS teams in South Warwickshire, which is where she works for the rest of the week. Jacky has a long history of enthusiasm for working with trainees, and is keen to develop effective supervision practice.

Shane Matthews is Clinical Director for the Bristol Clinical Psychology programme and a consultant clinical psychologist for Avon and Wiltshire Partnership Mental Health Trust. He has completed a diploma in supervision and works clinically as a systemic psychotherapist. Current interests include developing supervision training and researching supervision-related therapist change.

Nimisha Patel is a chartered consultant clinical psychologist, currently employed as a senior lecturer at the University of East London on the doctoral degree programme in Clinical Psychology and as head of Clinical Psychology at the Medical Foundation for the Care of Victims of Torture, a human rights non-governmental organization.

Peter Rajan works for Nottinghamshire Healthcare Trust. He is a consultant clinical psychologist in adult mental health and manages a multi-professional psychological service to adults in Central Nottinghamshire. He is interested in supporting links between NHS and university departments in the development of Clinical Psychology training and sits on the commissioning subgroup for Clinical Psychology of the East Midlands Workforce Confederation.

Joyce Scaife is Director of Clinical Practice for the Doctor of Clinical Psychology training course at the University of Sheffield and a consultant clinical psychologist with Chesterfield Primary Care Trust. She is author of *Supervision in the Mental Health Professions*, published by Brunner-Routledge in 2001.

Linda Steen is joint Clinical Director of the Manchester University Clinical Psychology training programme and a consultant clinical psychologist at Manchester Mental Health and Social Care Trust, where she works within the Adult Primary Care Service. She has a long-standing interest and involvement in training and supervising both trainee clinical psychologists and other health professionals.

Andy Treacher has worked for many years in the south-west of England as a family therapist and trainer. He has written extensively both on Clinical Psychology and Family Therapy, including *Introducing User-friendly Family Therapy* (Routledge, 1995). Currently he is involved in developing an accredited supervision course for clinical psychologists in the South West.

Graham Turpin is Director of the Clinical Psychology Unit at the University of Sheffield. He has a long-standing interest in clinical psychology training, having established the D.Clin.Psy. course at Sheffield some 12 years ago. He has served as chair of the BPS accreditation committee (CTCP) and also the Group of Trainers in Clinical Psychology. He has been closely involved in developments in training, including the introduction of doctoral programmes, expanding government support and funding for training, and career development needs of clinical academic staff.

Sue Wheeler is Professor of Counselling and Psychotherapy at the University of Leicester. She is a BACP accredited counsellor and fellow, and a UKCP registered psychotherapist. She has been a practising counsellor, psychotherapist and supervisor throughout most of her career, as well as organizing and delivering counsellor training courses. She is the author of several books, including *Supervising Counsellors: Issues of Responsibility*, published by Sage (2001), co-edited with David King, and a series of articles about supervision. In recent years she has been providing workshops on good practice in supervision for clinical psychologists.

Foreword

Clinical Psychology has come of age. One has only to attend a conference or read current government policy to realize just how far the therapies that clinical psychologists have developed have come in recent years. British clinical psychologists have played a valuable role in this march forward. To illustrate, at the recent annual conference of the British Psychological Society, Phillipa Garrety of the Institute of Psychiatry in London provided an overview of progress in our work with people who experience psychotic phenomena. She had been asked to prepare a systematic review for the relevant government body, the National Institute for Clinical Excellence (NICE), and had located over twenty control-led trials of cognitive behavioural therapy (CBT) for this potentially distressing experience. The great majority of these trials have been conducted in the UK by clinical psychologists, and the review indicated that CBT was effective. Similar signs of progress are evident if one reads policy documents produced by the Department of Health (e.g. the National Service Frameworks).

Given the advances that the profession has made on the therapy front, it becomes especially critical that comparable progress is made in relation to the systems that support therapists. For many years, clinical supervision has served as the firm foundation of clinical practice. It is timely that this foundation is now developed, so that advanced practice can be supported appropriately. This book is just such a development. It offers a rare combination of the scientific literature and clinical experience, designed explicitly to enhance supervision for clinical psychologists in the UK.

According to the authors in this book, the goals of clinical supervision are to encourage reflection, understanding and self-awareness in the supervisee, and to enable problem-solving. Principally, the aim is to enhance clinical practice, and its effectiveness, in the best interests of the client. Lastly, but in keeping with such quality control priorities, supervision serves as a 'gatekeeping' procedure, designed to ensure that those who qualify as clinical psychologists are indeed suitably fit to practise.

Given such important goals, it is indeed surprising that so little attention has been given to the topic, whether this is in terms of the training and development of the supervisors' relevant research, or the formal requirements placed upon supervisors. Indeed, such has been the parlous state of the clinical supervision enterprise that one author has even taken the view that supervision 'like love, cannot be taught' (Scott, 1999: 756). Clinical psychology is a precocious, growing profession and, partly because of its success in demonstrating the effectiveness of psychological therapies, the NHS has dramatically increased its demand for properly trained clinical psychologists. There is also an accompanying demand for supervision, not just in the period of initial training but also as a career-long basis for the kinds of practice-enhancing goals that are outlined above. In this context, it would be strange indeed if a book of this kind were to subscribe to Scott's position. Rather, the authors provide an impressive range of material to suggest that, to contradict Scott, 'like therapy, supervision can be taught'.

To illustrate this optimistic view, consider the contributions that are contained in the pages that follow:

- A historical summary is provided, to afford perspective (Wheeler, in Chapter 2).
- Evidence-based models are identified and refined (Chapter 3, Beinart).
- A local analysis of the quality and quantity of training placements is presented (Chapter 4, Turpin, Scaife and Rajan).
- The training courses in the UK are surveyed and a reflexive, psychologically informed approach clarified (Chapter 5, Fleming).
- Sound reasoning and a distillation of a professional consensus on the factors that contribute to successful supervision is provided (Chapter 6, Green).
- Ways of enhancing practice through such methods as facilitating reflection and critical thinking are noted (Chapter 7, Patel).
- The importance of the socio-political context for the effective conduct of supervision is recognized (Chapter 8, Dennis and Aitken).
- Rich information from workshops and surveys of both supervisors and supervisees is furnished to yield a refined list of what works in supervision (Chapter 9, Cushway and Knibbs). A summary of four different models for providing supervision, emphasizing an integrative approach and the six 'modes' needed to make supervision successful is provided (Chapter 10, Matthews and Treacher).
- Implications for the future training and accreditation of supervisors, and the links to continuing professional development, are teased out (Chapter 11, Fleming and Steen).

One cannot help but be impressed by such a wide-ranging, well-grounded and upbeat account of what is possible in the name of clinical supervision. Indeed, I would suggest that, in addition to the aims of the book as outlined by Fleming and Steen in Chapter 1, the book also has an implicit aim. It is to foster supervision from a rare base in the crystallization of exceptionally relevant experience (the assembled team of authors) and the intelligent use of key literature. This is not to deny the value of their identified aims – namely, to provide a focus on the particular concerns of UK clinical psychologists and to document supervision practice within the National Health Service. These are indeed valuable aims, and are sufficient to arouse the interest of those working in this field on these islands. However, my reading of this book suggests that this rare blend of pragmatism and professionalism will invite a wider readership.

So far I have discussed the goals and methods inherent within this account of clinical supervision. I wish to close by identifying what I similarly perceive to be the (at times) implicit outcomes of the accounts that follow. I then want to link these outcomes to a particular orientation to our work, for which these authors are also to be congratulated. By the outcomes I refer to the following qualities that struck me: the emphasis of the chapters is unfailingly pro-supervision in that the authors, while recognizing the many obstacles and challenges inherent in providing effective clinical supervision, are biased towards finding solutions and giving issues a positive spin. The book is also highly accessible and applicable, clearly informed by many years of practice. This arises perhaps from working at one moment in the NHS 'trenches' where fundamental issues about supervision arise regularly, and at the next moment rubbing shoulders with those of a more academic institution in the host training courses. A further rare quality is that the book, based on this theory–practice integration, provides genuinely and unstintingly helpful guidance. Unlike the typical book of this kind, we are not asked to be persuaded by a vast array of recent literature but rather by material carefully selected for its relevance. This gives greater weight to this sifted material and shows much more clearly how such 'theory' links to the authors' practice.

In conclusion, and to their great credit, it would seem to me that this group of authors have addressed the issue of clinical supervision as 'reflective educators'. Reflective educators treat the education and training of clinical psychologists as a profession in itself (Peterson, 1995). Just as their clinical colleagues adopt the scientist–practitioner model, these trainers of the next generation of clinicians seem to have adopted the appropriately parallel reflective educator approach to their duties. Specifically, they exemplify the approach that Peterson put forward so powerfully in a prestigious American journal. He argued that, whether we are trainers or clinicians,

> every one of us needs to engage in a continuing process of reflection in action as we go about our educational duties . . . We need to take a close, critical look at our programmes, to question everything about them, and to come as near as we can to rational answers to the questions, before inserting, removing or sustaining various features of our programmes.
>
> (Peterson, 1995: 981)

Once you've had the pleasure of reading the richly informative, theory–practice integrated material that follows, I'm sure that you will join with me in applauding these authors, under the guidance of the editors, Ian Fleming and Linda Steen, for approaching the educational duty of organizing supervision appropriately as true reflective educators. They have helped clinical supervision to come of age.

Derek Milne
Newcastle upon Tyne
April 2003

Chapter 1

Introduction

Ian Fleming and Linda Steen

> The process of supervision like all human relationships is fraught with hazards.
>
> (Dryden, 1991: 69)

Supervision is held to be an essential requirement for learning and professional development, especially within professions working with other individuals. In their review of psychotherapeutic interventions, Roth and Fonagy (1996: 373) conclude that supervision is 'an essential prerequisite for the practice of psychotherapy'. Similarly Holloway and Neufeldt (1995: 207) state that 'supervision, as a psychotherapy training method is considered critical by educators . . .'

It is important and exciting to consider how people experience acting as a supervisor. What are the highs and lows? What causes excitement and anxiety? What are the intrinsic rewards? Also, how are these skills and attributes acquired and learned?

Some professions have mandatory requirements concerning all aspects of supervision. The British Association for Counselling and Psychotherapy (BACP, 2002), for example, requires all its members 'to have regular and ongoing formal supervision/consultative support'. In midwifery, there has been a statutory requirement, since 1902, for practising midwives to receive regular supervision. As will be discussed below, whilst there is a growing recognition of the role of supervision in post-qualification practice in clinical psychology, at present there is no statutory requirement for clinical psychologists to receive supervision for their clinical work, once qualified.

What is supervision?

Before proceeding, it is important to consider what is meant by the term 'supervision'. To supervise is to 'oversee the actions or work of [a person]' (*The Concise Oxford Dictionary of Current English*, 1990).

Within the literature on clinical supervision, the term 'supervision' has been interpreted and defined in numerous competing ways. Some professions have produced their own definitions of 'supervision'. The United Kingdom Central Council (UKCC), the professional body for nursing in the UK, for example, states that 'clinical supervision brings practitioners and skilled supervisors together to reflect on practice. Supervision aims to identify solutions to problems, improve practice and increase understanding of professional issues' (UKCC, 1996: 3).

The British Association for Counselling and Psychotherapy (BACP) defines supervision as:

> a formal arrangement for counsellors to discuss their work regularly with someone who is experienced in counselling and supervision. The task is to work together to ensure and develop the efficacy of the counsellor/ client relationship. The agenda will be the counselling work and feeling about that work, together with the supervisor's reactions, comments and confrontations. Thus supervision is a process to maintain adequate standards of counselling and a method of consultancy to widen the horizons of an experienced practitioner.
>
> (BACP, 1996: 1)

One of the crucial elements of this definition is the idea that the role of supervision is to protect the best interests of the client.

As will be discussed later in the book, other definitions of supervision derive more from specific orientations to clinical practice or explicit models of supervision than from professional ethos.

The Division of Clinical Psychology (DCP) of the British Psychological Society (BPS), whilst recognizing the importance of supervision throughout a clinical psychologist's career, stops short either of providing a definition or of endorsing any one particular model of supervision. The recently published DCP guidance on clinical supervision states: 'there is no one model or style of supervision that will apply to all clinical psychologists in all settings and at all times in their career' (BPS, 2003: 2).

In the absence of an agreed definition of supervision within clinical psychology, one which seems to cover many of the relevant factors is that of Bernard and Goodyear:

> An intervention that is provided by a senior member of a profession to a junior member or members of that same profession. This relationship is evaluative, extends over time and has the simultaneous purposes of enhancing the professional functioning of the junior member(s), monitoring the quality of professional services offered to the clients that she, he or they see(s), and serving as a gatekeeper for those who are to enter the particular profession.
>
> (Bernard and Goodyear, 1992: 4)

This definition relates particularly well to supervision during pre-qualification training, referring as it does to 'a senior member of the profession', 'junior members of that same profession' and the functions of evaluation and gatekeeping 'to enter the profession'. In view of the increasing recognition of the importance of post-qualification supervision within the profession, however, it is pertinent to consider how much of Bernard and Goodyear's definition translates to this context, where there is likely to be a greater emphasis on peer and cross-professional supervision and where there is increased onus on the supervisee to be self-evaluative. These themes will be considered throughout the book and are drawn together in the final chapter.

Clinical psychology: the service context

Within clinical psychology in Britain, increased attention is being paid to the role of supervision in both pre-qualification training and post-qualification practice. The factors that have contributed to this are discussed later after an overview of the context in which the profession of clinical psychology operates in the UK.

It is pertinent at this time to examine these issues. Initially a small and possibly precocious profession within the National Health Service (NHS), clinical psychology has grown rapidly since 1980. The membership of the Division of Clinical Psychology (of the British Psychological Society) has grown from 966 in 1980 to 4,514 in 2001. In the past 30 years there has been an almost continuous growth in both the number of clinical psychology training programmes[1] (29 in the UK currently) and the number of clinical psychologists being trained (for example, up from 189 in 1993 to 390 in 2000 in England). To illustrate this point, the Manchester programme had an annual intake of nine people when we started in post as clinical tutors in 1994; the intake in 2002 was 21. This growth is expected to accelerate over the next few years on the back of manpower forecasts and identified roles for clinical psychology within the different National Service Frameworks in NHS planning (for example, DH, 1999).

Alongside expansion and increasing demand for clinical psychologists across all areas of the NHS, there is an increasing requirement for the scrutiny of clinical practice, most recently manifested in *clinical governance* (DH, 1998a).

This immediately raises the issue of the *effectiveness* of practice, and in turn of the role played in this by supervision. It also means that the training of people in the supervisory process needs to be examined.

Why another book about supervision?

There exists already an extensive and growing library devoted to supervision in the broadest sense, and a significant 'stack' to supervision in clinical professions in the mental health trade. Key texts include Bernard and Goodyear (1992), Watkins (1997b), Kadushin (1992), Hawkins and Shohet (1989, 2000) and Carroll (1996). Why, you might ask, should there be any reason, other than author vanity, for an additional text?

Our starting point for this book was the absence of any text dedicated specifically to supervision in clinical psychology in the UK. This is despite the requirement for all *trainee* clinical psychologists to receive supervision of clinical work on placements. This requirement has been in place for many years.

More recently it has been accompanied by recommendations for *qualified* practitioners to also undergo supervision as part of good practice and professional development. Both the Division of Clinical Psychology's *Professional Practice Guidelines* (BPS, 1995b: 9) and the DCP *Guidelines for Clinical Psychology Services* (BPS, 1998c: 31) state that supervision should be organized for clinical psychologists at 'all levels and grades of experience'. In a similar vein, the DCP *Guidelines for Continuing Professional Development* (DCP, 2001a: 8) acknowledge that 'all qualified clinical psychologists **whatever their level of experience** should have access to and be prepared to make constructive use of some appropriate supervisory facility to support their work'.

This 'gap' in the literature became apparent to us when, as clinical tutors on the Manchester University Clinical Psychology (Clin.Psy.D.) programme, we began to organize training for people who would supervise the programme's trainees. In the process of developing training for supervisors on the Manchester programme we became aware of some important issues. These are outlined below and support the value of the contribution that will be made by this book.

First, most of the books devoted to supervision within mental health professional practice are focused on counselling, social work and psychotherapy. Although much can be learned from this body of work, this book will be focusing on the particular concerns of clinical psychologists. The forms of supervision that have developed within clinical psychology, and their relationships to the psychological models that make up the dominant practice of clinical psychology in the UK, will be examined within the book.

Second, it seemed to us then that there was a need to document the experience of supervision in clinical psychology within the National Health Service. This would not be opposed to that mentioned above, but would complement it. In the process of finding out what was happening, clinical psychologists could be both consulted and informed.

Third, much, but not all, of the existing literature is from North America. Whilst we are at pains to deny any parochialism, we feel that there are limitations to how much this work will generalize to working in the National Health Service in the UK. Therefore this book will have a UK focus. This is certainly not for narrow chauvinistic or parochial reasons but because the majority of clinical psychologists in the UK work in the National Health Service and we wish the book to reflect the common constraints and opportunities for supervision within the particular culture of this system. It can be argued that the NHS, through its dominant funding position for clinical psychology training in the UK, is the profession's *sponsor*; therefore national directives about practice within the general NHS will affect clinical psychology practice and professional development. The editors are unsure, however, as to how generalizable is much of the experience derived from other organizations of health care.

Supervision and clinical psychology: a growing relationship

As mentioned earlier, the importance of, and requirements for, supervision varies across different health and social welfare professions. It is fair to say that only in recent years has it been accorded significance within mainstream clinical psychology.

In recent years, professional bodies representing clinical psychologists in the UK have placed increasing emphasis on continuing professional development and the role that supervision can play in this. In part this has been a response to public concerns and a perceived need to demonstrate the requirements for *professionalism*. This has been augmented by concerns and initiatives at a government level for a public health service, actuated in demands for *clinical governance*.

With the planned introduction of statutory registration for all applied psychologists in the UK, the importance of supervision within the profession is likely to increase further.

What will the reader gain from the book?

Supervision and supervisor training usually require objectives and goals so, for the sake of consistency, we include some here.

It is hoped first that the reader will be excited by the possibilities contained within supervision. This book provides a collection in one work of chapters on important aspects of supervision written by leading practitioners and trainers, all of whom have been chosen for their experience in the field of supervision.

A second aspiration is that readers will gain knowledge about the most developed forms of practice in the UK and adapt these to their own practice.

Third, the book as a whole is intended to help ease the concerns of clinicians with respect to continuing professional development (CPD). It is intended that the book will help the reader to clarify the links between supervision, CPD and clinical governance as the last takes root within the NHS. The relevance of supervision to practise will be addressed. It is also hoped that readers will recognize the value to their practice of *supervising*.

A fourth goal involves those concerned in the organization of clinical psychology pre-qualification training. If successful in one of its objectives this book will act as a useful source for considering training issues. By design, contributors to this book are senior members of doctoral training programme teams.

Fifth, it is hoped that this book will enable readers to decide whether they need to have and use an explicit model of supervision in order to practise effectively both as a supervisor and as a clinician.

Sixth, it is hoped that the reader will be alerted to the important ways in which individuals' social and cultural history and features and their gender influence their supervision.

A final aspiration is that the content of this book can generate research that will enable the training community in clinical psychology (and in other related professions) to identify the key tasks involved in preparing clinicians to become supervisors.

What are the critical issues in supervision?

A survey of the literature suggests that there are a number of important questions still to be answered. These include the following:

Is there agreement on what tasks are involved in supervision?

Authors have developed a range of different models of supervision. In this book, these are introduced in the chapter by Sue Wheeler and developed further in Helen Beinart's chapter where she reviews different models of supervision and the research evidence that supports them. While there are many differences between the models of supervision, it can be argued that there is some common ground concerning the demands or tasks involved in supervision. In her chapter, Sue Wheeler cites the work of Carroll (1996) who identifies seven main tasks of supervision – namely, the relationship task, the teaching/learning task, the counselling task, the monitoring task, the evaluation task, the consultative task and the administrative task. Following a review of five social role models of supervision, Carroll (1999) concludes that there are some tasks, such as teaching, which are universally agreed, whereas others are particular to individual models and authors. Within clinical psychology, whilst there may not have been much explicit discussion of supervisory *tasks*, as reported in Chapters 5 and 6 of this book, developments in supervisor training would suggest that there is broad agreement amongst clinical psychologists on what the content of supervisor training should be.

Do we know what factors influence effective or 'good' supervision?

Throughout the history of supervision there has always been an assumption that it can be effective (see Chapter 2 for a brief history of supervision). There have been numerous attempts to evaluate this and many brave research studies have floundered on methodological rocks in the process. In part, this is because of the difficulties of accounting for or controlling the array of interpersonal variables that exist in any supervisory and therapeutic relationship involving a supervisor, a supervisee therapist, and a client.

In addition, there is the question of what would constitute a 'successful' outcome; this has been addressed by many writers, for example, Wampold and Holloway (1997). This issue is expanded upon in the current book by several of the contributors, notably Delia Cushway and Jacky Knibbs, David Green and Helen Beinart.

In a recent systematic review of this area of research, Ellis *et al.* (1996) analysed 144 studies and concluded that much of the empirical research on clinical supervision was not methodologically rigorous. This led Ellis and colleagues to set out criteria for future empirical research on clinical supervision (Ellis *et al.*, 1996; Ellis and Ladany, 1997).

It has been argued that in seeking to demonstrate effectiveness, past researchers may have been asking the wrong questions. This is reassuring, and for a number of years in the UK Derek Milne and co-workers have been considering effectiveness with one eye on the conclusions of Ellis *et al.* and another on what are the essential factors to demonstrate in effective supervision (Milne and James, 2002).

In much of the research on supervision, the supervisory *relationship* has come in for scrutiny, and interpersonal variables have been found to play a central role. This is reflected in the current book by its coverage in several of the chapters, for example those by Sue Wheeler, Helen Beinart, Delia Cushway and Jacky Knibbs, and Shane Matthews and Andy Treacher.

Can we effectively train people to be good and effective supervisors?

Following on from the question about whether supervision can be effective, we ask whether training can ensure effective supervision. An answer to this question precludes two other questions: can training be effective, and do we know what to train? Both these questions are considered in some depth in the current book in Chapters 2, 5 and 6.

Training supervisors should incorporate elements from the body of research demonstrating the effective ways of teaching skills. It is not enough to presume that a qualified therapist possesses the necessary skills for supervision, however, and the profession of clinical psychology needs to address how to enable, promote and value supervision in the way that other professions, such as counselling and social work, have done already.

With respect to the second part of the question, the answer can be a positive one. Many educationalists subscribe to Kolb's (1984) model of experiential learning, in which new skills are acquired by encouraging the learner to work through an experiential cycle. Milne and his co-workers (Milne and James 2002; Milne and Howard, 2000) describe the application of this model to supervisor training. At present, it is not known how widely or systematically this model is used by others in the training of supervisors; this is discussed more fully in Chapter 5.

How do 'race', culture and gender impact on supervision?

Suggestions have been made (e.g. Fleming and Burton, 2001) that clinical psychology historically has ignored social context in favour of intra-personal space in its determinations of psychological distress. If there is substance to such an accusation then it would not be surprising to find an omission of social and contextual factors in supervision. Indeed, Carroll, a major figure in UK counselling psychology, has complained about UK supervision texts: 'All almost totally ignore the cultural dimensions of supervision, spending together approximately 3 pages on the topic' (1996: 36).

In the USA, work examining the influence on supervision of culture and gender has increased in the past 20 years and is now extending to Britain, despite Carroll's rather pessimistic observation. Clearly, as cultural, gender and class issues are important in human interaction then they may be critical in supervision with its implications for trust, observation and evaluation.

In this book, there are chapters describing the influence in supervision of gender (Maxine Dennis and Gill Aitken) and 'race' and culture (Nimisha Patel). Furthermore, it is interesting to note (Chapter 5) how many training programmes for clinical psychologists are addressing these issues in the training provided for supervisors.

Whose responsibility is the training of supervisors and why?

Bernard and Goodyear (1998), with reference to the traditional lack of training for supervisors, use Hoffman's (1994) description of it as the mental health profession's 'dirty little secret'.

It is pleasing to know that there has been a significant change both in the importance accorded to supervision *and* to the training of supervisors in the skills deemed important for the activity.

There remains an important discussion about who has the responsibility for providing the training of supervisors. In this book, these issues are taken up by several of the contributors. Sue Wheeler's chapter is concerned with the wide range of available supervisor training in the UK. In Chapter 5,

Ian Fleming focuses specifically on supervisor training for clinical psychologists, giving a detailed description of the training currently provided by Clin.Psy.D. programmes in the UK. In Chapter 6, David Green too considers the issues involved in training clinical psychologists in the tasks of clinical supervision and reviews the research in evaluating the effectiveness of such training.

In addition to training supervisors, many writers are now recognizing that effective training in supervision should also involve training supervisees to use supervision (Inskipp, 1999). As Inskipp notes, 'the supervision alliance is a facilitative relationship which requires active and intentional participation by both parties' (1999: 186). That this is an increasingly important issue is illustrated by the fact that it is taken up by several of the contributors to this book, notably in Chapters 2, 4 and 6.

Multi-professional training is being accorded prominence within the NHS at the time of writing. Many clinical psychologists are involved in both supervising and receiving supervision from members of other professions. Taken together these suggest that both inter-professional training in supervision and training for the supervision of members of other professions may become important issues in the near future. As such they serve to emphasize the importance of identifying whose responsibility it is to fund, resource and provide training for supervisors, and ongoing supervision for those supervisors.

What can we learn about different forms/models of supervision (e.g. group supervision)?

This is likely to become an increasingly pertinent question as qualified clinical psychologists view supervision as a necessary part of their clinical practice rather than as an 'optional extra'. Inevitably this will have resource implications, and traditional one-to-one models of supervision are likely to be neither feasible nor necessarily desirable. In relation to pre-qualification training, the BPS Committee on Training in Clinical Psychology (CTCP) paved the way for a move towards using models of supervision other than one-to-one when, in 1995, the then revised *Guidelines on Clinical Supervision* (BPS, 1995a) formally introduced the option of team supervision for trainees. The revised *Criteria for the Accreditation of Postgraduate Training Programmes in Clinical Psychology* (BPS, 2002a) take this one step further by explicitly stating that 'a variety of supervisory arrangements is acceptable. These include trainee to supervisor ratios of 1:1 and 2:1 and various forms of team supervision for groups of trainees' (section 8.4).

Models of group, team and peer supervision are reviewed extensively in Hawkins and Shohet's (2000) text on supervision.

In the current book, a number of contributors comment on future arrangements for supervision within clinical psychology. Graham Turpin, Joyce Scaife and Peter Rajan, for example, in their discussion of clinical psychology training placements, suggest having one main supervisor working alongside other supplementary supervisors. In her chapter, Sue Wheeler introduces the concept of group supervision, pointing out some of the benefits and pitfalls of this form of supervision. This is likely to be of increasing relevance to qualified clinical psychologists as they consider models of peer supervision (DCP, 2001a).

Is there a need for congruence of models between practice and supervision?

As both Sue Wheeler (Chapter 2) and Helen Beinart (Chapter 3) describe in their chapters in this book, early models of clinical supervision were direct extensions of psychotherapy models. These later gave way to supervision-specific models.

In Chapter 10, Shane Matthews and Andy Treacher review a number of different models of supervision, each one linked to a therapeutic model. They then go on to describe their particular approach to supervision. Early in their chapter they describe how their selection of a model for supervision was guided more by theory than by the scientist practitioner paradigm. They argue that this form of practice provided them with confirmation of its value.

For the purposes of writing her chapter, for example, Sue Wheeler (Chapter 2) asked a panel of experts for their views about the importance of having congruence between clinical practice and supervision and found that there were some very mixed views about this.

This issue is addressed in several of the chapters, but, as will be seen from the discussion therein, there is currently no clear picture about the need for congruence between therapy and supervision models, although, unsurprisingly perhaps, there is some evidence that supervisors cite their preferred therapeutic model as the most significant factor influencing their supervisory behaviour (Putney *et al.*, 1992).

Post-qualification supervision and its relationship to continuing professional development

Accreditation for supervisors has been under discussion for some time. As an aspiration it forms an important part of quality assurance for clinical psychology training programmes. Alongside this there is a recognition that accreditation of individual supervisors or of supervising departments will require both explicit criteria against which judgements can be made and an apparatus for carrying out the process, as well as agreement by those to be accredited. These factors may well delay the aspiration becoming a reality.

Another lever acting upon individual practice in order to ensure quality is continuing professional development (CPD). Later in the book, the relationship between supervision and CPD is discussed, as is their link to accreditation.

Mention above of CPD and clinical governance ensures that readers consider the supervision that they receive after qualification or provide to others who are already qualified. This requirement is of recent origin and it is of interest to know about the quality and quantity of supervision qualified clinical psychologists are currently receiving.

In a recent survey of all clinical psychologists working in the NHS and universities in the north-west of England, 86 per cent of respondents reported that they received regular supervision, on average every two weeks (Golding, 2003). This usually took the form of either peer or clinical supervision. Seventy-eight per cent reported being supervised by another clinical psychologist. Whilst the response rate of 49.7 per cent (224 clinical psychologists) suggests that these data should be interpreted with a degree of caution and that this may be an overestimate of the true state of affairs (cf. Gabbay *et al.*, 1999), the results certainly suggest that post-qualification supervision is on the agenda for clinical psychologists in the north-west of England. There is no reason to suppose that the picture in this part of Britain is any different from that elsewhere in the country.

In a smaller survey of 22 newly qualified clinical psychologists carried out in the north-west of England almost ten years previously (Verduyn *et al.*, 1994), 23 per cent reported receiving no supervision at all. Whilst it is not possible to compare these findings directly with those of the Golding (2003) survey, it is interesting to reflect on whether the situation has changed over the past ten years, particularly with regard to newly qualified clinical psychologists. In our experience as clinical tutors, newly qualifying clinical psychologists certainly see supervision as an important (if not crucial) factor when choosing a first post, and it is likely that the percentage not receiving supervision would be much lower now than it was ten years ago.

Related to the above, in addition to the information about supervision received, the Golding (2003) survey also found that supervision was the most frequently listed CPD training need for the year ahead. Moreover, both *receiving* and *providing* supervision were frequently cited as examples of CPD activity. Finally, in keeping with the findings of other similar studies carried out elsewhere in the UK (e.g. Knight and Llewelyn, 2001; Lavender and Thompson, 2000), *availability of good and regular supervision* was found to be one of the key factors most likely to keep staff in their posts.

Clinical psychologists are more familiar with pre-qualification (training) supervision and it is interesting to consider similarities and differences between this type of supervision and that required after qualifying. According to Hawkins and Shohet (2000), there are at least four main categories of supervision – namely, tutorial supervision, training supervision, managerial supervision and consultancy supervision. Additionally, within consultancy supervision, the relationship between supervisor and supervisee can be either *vertical* or *horizontal* (as in peer supervision). In a similar vein, Milne and Howard (2000) refer to Hart's (1982) three categories of supervision – namely, 'apprentice-master', 'client-therapist' and 'collegial'. Post-qualification supervision is most likely to involve either consultancy ('collegial') or managerial supervision.

In much of the literature there is little distinction made between the supervision that is used within pre-qualification training and that for post-qualification practice. Arguably, one clear distinction involves the *evaluative* and managerial components of the former.

However, as CPD takes root and becomes a crucially important feature of clinical governance and individual development, this distinction can be seen to recede. Although any trace of real evaluation may be far from current practice in peer supervision within clinical psychology, there is no clear reason to presume that it will not be present in future forms of supervision. That it may be of a different form, and involve a requirement for clear definition and boundaries, does not preclude its existence.

In all types of supervision, a clear contracting process is considered essential (see, for example, Chapter 2 of this book) for making explicit the expectations of both/all parties.

The editors: where does our interest in this area derive?

The editors' own perspective may be of interest. We trained together some 20 years ago on separate and distinct training programmes in the north-west of England. Our experience of supervision during training was (like that of many people we have interviewed) variable. As our careers progressed in different specialist areas (adult mental health, LS; people with learning disabilities, IF), we *became* supervisors (Pickvance, 1997). This development constituted promotion (in the sense that it seemed to confer on us by our profession seniority and competence), but was not accompanied by much.

After qualifying, LS worked in a Clinical Psychology department in which the head of department was closely involved in the organization of one of the North West's clinical psychology training courses,[2] and where several of the psychologists were regular contributors to both the course teaching and trainee supervision. Within this context, becoming a supervisor after having been qualified for two years was viewed as an inevitable part of one's career progression. At that time, whilst the course did organize regional supervisor training days and there was an active supervisors' group that met regularly to discuss issues of mutual concern, attendance of both was optional.

On qualification, IF worked for eight years in a large department that occasionally provided placements for local training courses. Learning about supervision came about from informal discussions with colleagues and the local Special Interest Group for clinical psychologists working with people with learning disabilities. He received no 'training' in supervision during these years. This picture remained basically unchanged during subsequent moves to two other services, although in the first of these he remembers receiving specific input from a clinical tutor attached to the training programme from which trainees were on placement with him. He can draw on memories of very helpful supervision during his own clinical training.

So the years (and the trainees) went past. Opportunities for supervision *as qualified clinicians* grew slowly and varied considerably depending on the department and employing organization. It is accurate to say that developments in supervision elsewhere rather passed us by.

In 1994 LS joined the University of Manchester's clinical psychology training programme as a senior clinical tutor, and IF joined in a similar capacity in the next year. In the following years, the training programme underwent and enacted a number of changes. Both active and passive tenses are appropriate: the programme responded to a number of external pressures and made decisions about changes to improve the quality of training.

One of the general issues concerned the recruitment and retention of adequate numbers of high-quality clinical training placements and supervisors. From this there developed an increased interest in the process of supervision and the training of supervisors to achieve levels of competency. This interest has been supported by the other members of the Manchester programme team, and by the collegial culture of the Group of Trainers in Clinical Psychology (GTiCP) whose members are always willing to share ideas and experience in a most constructive way.

About the book

This book aims to provide the reader with an overview of the issues directly relevant to supervision within the profession of clinical psychology.

Chapter 2 begins with a historical overview of clinical supervision and sets the scene for the remainder of the book by describing supervision and supervisor training in the helping professions in general. The chapters that follow are all concerned with specific issues relevant to supervision in clinical psychology. The final chapter draws together the main themes of the book and considers future perspectives.

As with much of the writing on clinical psychology supervision to date, the emphasis in the book is on supervision of trainee clinical psychologists. As will be seen, however, many of the chapters cover issues of relevance to both pre-qualification and post-qualification supervision, and these themes are revisited in the final chapter.

Finally, whilst acknowledging the role of *research* supervision for both trainee and qualified clinical psychologists, the emphasis in this book is on supervision of *clinical* work. Consideration is given to research supervision in the last chapter.

About the contributors/authors

From amongst the Group of Trainers in Clinical Psychology (GTiCP), we have learned a lot about supervision. Many, but not all, of the contributors to this book are members of the GTiCP and major innovators in supervision developments in their own areas. In addition, we are extremely grateful to have contributions from Sue Wheeler who is a major figure in the counselling profession in the UK and an academic with a justly high reputation for research into supervision, and from the clinical psychologists, Gill Aitken, Maxine Dennis and Peter Rajan. Each of these has a wealth of experience of supervision and teaching.

Notes

1 Throughout this book, the word 'programme' will be used to describe the organization of clinical psychology training in the UK. The word 'course' will be used to describe supervisor training courses.
2 This was before they became programmes.

Chapter 2

A review of supervisor training in the UK

Sue Wheeler

Introduction

There have been many changes in the National Health Service in recent years, but perhaps the most dramatic change is the impact of clinical governance on the day-to-day work and professional development of everyone employed by the service. The government has responded to notorious cases of malpractice by establishing the National Institute for Clinical Excellence (NICE), which sets standards of service through the National Health Service Frameworks. Accountability to patients, organizations and the profession is currently a high priority for all clinicians. It is through clinical governance that organizations ensure good practice, by making individuals accountable for setting and monitoring performance standards.

While clinical supervision has always been a requirement for clinical psychologists in training, the demands for accountability are now such that supervised practice is becoming more prevalent amongst health professionals, including nurses and other medical practitioners. The Department of Health has defined supervision as

> a formal process of professional support and learning which enables individual practitioners to develop knowledge and competence, assume responsibility for their own practice and enhance consumer protection and safety of care in complex clinical situations.
>
> (DH, 1993)

Butterworth (2001) summarizes the value of clinical supervision to clinical governance:

> Clinical supervision focuses on matters of central importance in the provision of safe and accountable practice. The concept of clinical supervision is focused on: organisational and management issues, clinical case-work, professional development, educational support, confidence building and interpersonal problems.
>
> (Butterworth, 2001: 319)

For many years the British Association for Counselling and Psychotherapy (BACP) (formally British Association for Counselling, BAC) has made supervision a requirement for all practising counsellors and therapists, regardless of their length of experience (BACP, 2002). While the British Psychological Society (BPS) encourages professional development, accountability and regular use of supervision, it is not a requirement. Indeed, in response to a question about chartered psychologist status and supervision, the frequently asked questions page of their website replies that,

> Once you have completed an accredited training course in Clinical psychology you are fully qualified to practise without supervision, therefore eligible to apply for Chartered Status. You might need further experience under supervision if you want to specialise say in Child psychology, but this is not a requirement for Chartered Status.
>
> (BPS, 2002b)

The UKCP (United Kingdom Council for Psychotherapy) also stops short of making supervision a requirement for psychotherapists. However, the practice of supervision is of considerable interest to professions. Kilminster and Jolly (2000) see clinical supervision as having a vital role in postgraduate medical education, but acknowledge that a limited amount of medical literature addressing supervision currently exists. Clinical supervision has an important role to play in safeguarding the interests of patients and clients, and is increasingly being recognized and valued by professional groups who did not previously see it as necessary. These new groups of health professionals, in particular, are exploring the existing literature and research on supervision in order to develop their own models of supervision and find ways of promoting it.

This chapter sets the scene for the rest of this book by looking at the historical development of clinical supervision and the provision of training for supervision, and then by reviewing research literature relevant to the training of supervisors. While the intention is not to provide a blueprint for supervisor training, a syllabus for such a course could probably be constructed from the information presented. Standards for supervisor competence are discussed, including the question of 'What makes a good supervisor?', followed by a debate about how such standards can be developed through training. The numerous considerations of a training programme, such as models of supervision, contextual issues, theoretical orientation, the supervisory relationship, teaching methods, ethics, contracts, gender and equal opportunity issues, group supervision, evaluation and assessment of competence, are reviewed, incorporating research evidence to support suggestions wherever possible. It should be noted that much of the research discussed has been conducted in North America and the subjects have almost invariably been trainee counsellors and therapists. However, both trainees and experienced therapists, psychologists or counsellors can benefit from good supervision, and training supervisors to be competent in that role will benefit all the professionals that use their services, as well as the clients for whose benefit such provisions exist.

History of supervision

The supervision of clinical practice has had a place in the training of analysts, therapists and social workers particularly, since almost the beginning of therapeutic practice (Jacobs *et al.*, 1995). In his report of the case of Little Hans, Freud describes how he worked with the boy's father, who was conducting the therapy with his son. Max Graf, the father, had his own ideas about the development of his son's neurosis, but Freud used the relationship with Max Graf to further develop his own views on childhood sexuality. The supervision that is described is chaotic and intrusive, and there is a lack of clarity about the relationships fostered between father, son and analyst/supervisor. When thinking about Freud and his work, it seems inevitable that other therapists would wish to consult him and discuss their cases. Much of the communication was through letters and personal meetings, nothing that resembles the formal structures of supervision that are to be found today. As the demand for training in psychoanalysis grew, it became more important to move beyond the old apprenticeship model. Formal training courses were developed by an organizing body, with the development of a syllabus, admissions criteria, criteria for assessment and other systematic education procedures. In the early days of therapy training it was custom and practice for trainees to discuss their cases with their own analyst. In 1924, the Congress of the Berlin Institute published the requirement that candidates have at least two years of clinical work as part of their education. The idea of supervision arose as analysts became tired of hearing about their patients' patients. Karl Abraham, Max Eitingon and Georg Simmel were some of the first supervisors at the Institute, but others soon followed (Jacobs *et al.*, 1995).

By the 1930s the practice of social work as a professional activity had become established, and case-work had a more therapeutic aim than appears to be the case today. The clients' individual psychodynamics were seen to contribute towards their current difficulties and were the focus of attention. In 1936, Robinson described the supervisor's task, which was to pay attention to ways in which the client and the supervisees were relating, in order to understand more about the client's interpersonal difficulties, rather than focusing on the personal history of the supervisee, as analysts had previously. Kadushin (1968) and Mattinson (1977) developed their own ideas about supervision, within the context of social work, which were not widely influential with other professions at the time.

In 1987, Hess articulated ways in which the practice of therapy and supervision are different and require different skills. He asserted that supervisors must be good therapists, but they need training to be good supervisors as the focus of the endeavours are different. During the last three decades, interest in supervision has grown. In their classic text, *The Teaching and Learning of Psychotherapy*, Ekstein and Wallerstein (1972) describe the practice of supervision:

> The supervisor is directly related to the student but has a quasi-indirect relationship to the patient. On one hand his responsibility is to teach psychotherapeutic skills to the student, but there is an additional responsibility in maintaining clinical standards and seeing that patients benefit from the service which is being extended.
>
> (Ekstein and Wallerstein, 1972: 12)

With the exception of the work of Janet Mattinson, who worked with the Tavistock clinic in London, the development of supervision in Britain seems to have followed on from research and practice developed in the USA. Many models of supervision have been derived by American researchers (Fleming, 1953; Hogan, 1964; Littrell *et al.*, 1979; Stoltenberg, 1981; Loganbill *et al.*, 1982), and it is only in recent years that British texts have appeared to provide models of supervision for British audiences. Hawkins and Shohet (1989) published their classic text, *Supervision in the Helping Professions*, which offered a process model of supervision. Page and Wosket (2001) followed on with their cyclical model of supervision. Carroll (1996) offered an alternative model of supervision based on his doctoral research. Meanwhile, Inskipp and Proctor (2001a, 2001b) have been writing about, and teaching, supervision for two decades.

In a recent review of supervision research (Wheeler, 2002), over four hundred research articles were found related to supervision, of which only 11 boasted British authors. Hence when addressing the topic of supervision in Britain, reference is always being made to American research literature which informs our practice. Supervision is still predominantly only a requirement for counselling and psychotherapy trainees in the USA, hence most research literature refers to supervision with trainees.

Supervision training in the UK

Having established that supervision is a good thing for trainee psychotherapists, psychologists and counsellors, the question is raised of whether all supervisors are competent. There is some evidence to suggest that training in supervision has a positive effect on supervisor behaviours (Stevens *et al.*, 1998; Borders *et al.*, 1996; Nordlund, 1999). However, the training of supervisors is a relatively recent activity in counselling and psychotherapy and particularly in clinical psychology. In an attempt to trace the history of supervisor training in Britain for the purpose of writing this chapter, and in the absence of any documentary evidence, in 2002 I asked ten expert supervisors in the field of counselling and psychotherapy to complete a short questionnaire. These experts have all been involved in supervisor training, have written extensively about supervision, or have engaged in supervision research. The first question asked when they had become aware of courses in supervision. On average, respondents replied that they had become aware of supervision training about 12–15 years ago. One respondent mentioned the late 1970s and another 1983. One person was involved with a special project with the Department of Education, training school counsellors and supervisors between 1972 and 1974. In 1989, Hawkins and Shohet were advocating that supervisor training be provided, ranging from introductory to advanced level. Inskipp and Proctor started CASCADE, an organization promoting supervisor training and publishing materials related to supervisor training in 1988. At about the same time, the Westminster Pastoral Foundation also began supervisor training courses, with a psychodynamic emphasis. In relation to clinical psychology, Milne and James (2002) claim that training and monitoring of clinical psychology supervisors has been a part of good practice for more than a decade. This training is most commonly provided by pre-qualification clinical psychology training programmes (see Chapter 5). To date clinical psychologists have infrequently participated in extensive training that is rapidly becoming a continuing professional development expectation of counsellors and psychotherapists.

Standards for supervision

Supervisors' training courses for counsellors and psychotherapists now proliferate, and are to be found in universities and training agencies that offer substantial training courses in counselling or psychotherapy. There are generic supervisor training courses that attract other professional groups, such as nurses, occupational therapists, doctors, managers, social workers, as well as therapists and psychologists. A brief look at publicity related to supervisor training courses reveals that training may be offered for anything between one day and two years, and may lead to an attendance certificate, undergraduate or postgraduate certificates, diploma or even a Masters degree. The array of courses is confusing and no recognizable standards are set for supervisory practice. The British Association for Counselling and Psychotherapy (BACP, 2002) has an accreditation scheme for supervisors of counsellors and psychotherapists that has specific requirements, including the following:

- The candidate has an individual BACP membership.
- Complies with the *Ethical Framework for Good Practice in Counselling and Psychotherapy*.
- Is a BACP Accredited Counsellor or the equivalent.

- Has undertaken not less than 600 contact hours over three years with clients.
- Has demonstrated in counselling supervision a capacity for safe and effective counselling practice.
- Can show evidence of continuing professional development.
- Has satisfactorily completed a substantial structured training programme in supervision, *or* has followed a programme of learning with a supervisor.
- Is currently practising as a counselling supervisor.
- Has had a minimum of two years' practice as a counselling supervisor.
- Has had regular supervision from an experienced counselling supervisor.
- Has completed a minimum of 180 contact hours with supervisees over a maximum of three years, immediately prior to application.
- Can provide evidence of a range of experience, i.e. work with trainees and experienced counsellors.
- Can provide evidence of the way in which he/she uses his/her authority as a counselling supervisor to promote the safety of the client.
- Can provide evidence of an identified theoretical framework in his/her practice.
- Can demonstrate an awareness of the values, beliefs and assumptions which underpin his/her work.
- Can provide evidence of a capacity for self-regulation.

This is an evidence-based approach to accreditation and does not set standards. A second question asked of the ten experts was how much experience therapists should have before becoming supervisors or embarking on supervisor training. Responses varied, but the typical response was as follows: 'I think people should have experience of working as a psychologist, counsellor or social worker for a minimum of three years, full-time, before taking on the mantle of supervision. This allows them some time after qualification to gain experience and allow the knowledge and skills required through training to be consolidated.' 'Potential supervisors must have had the experience of being supervised themselves for a minimum of five years, preferably with several different supervisors.'

   Supervisor training courses have varied requirements in terms of previous experience of supervising others. Some courses require that trainees already have experience of supervision and stipulate a minimum number of hours of supervision as an entry requirement. Some courses require trainees to have had a minimum amount of experience of being a supervisor with consultative support before they achieve the final qualification. Other courses take the view that training in preparation for supervision should be open to anyone with sufficient experience of being a therapist. The panel of experts were divided in their views, but agreed that experience as a therapist was essential. Several people suggested that very experienced therapists might take on supervisees before having training, but relatively inexperienced practitioners should definitely have training first to ensure that they are fully conversant with codes of practice and legal issues at the very least. Another commented that 'many of the people on my training course have already started supervising before they begin training and they are hungry for information, bring questions and are ready for learning'. Another respondent suggested that 'potential supervisors attend a brief introduction and read relevant literature on supervision before embarking on a course, but have a course firmly in view'. Emphasis was also placed on trainee supervisors having a consultant for supervision, who was prepared to take on an inexperienced supervisor and monitor them closely.

How much training in supervision is enough?

When asked how many hours of training supervisors should have, responses varied between a minimum of 45 hours of theory and 45 hours of practice as supervisors, to a maximum of 200 hours. There was general agreement that they should have roughly the same amount of theory and practice with consultant supervision. Some respondents stressed that the basic supervision course would not necessarily prepare people to work with groups, in specific contexts, or with organizations. One person commented that training should be staggered over a period of time and should not be concentrated in one block. 'Supervisor training interspersed with practice, with periods of time for reflection between training sessions, seems to be a more reflective way to learn than in intensive training blocks.'

The BACP Directory of Counselling and Psychotherapy training courses in Britain (2001) advertises a range of supervisor training courses that offer diverse qualifications. Most respondents to the survey suggested that supervisor-training courses should be postgraduate level, or at least something that could be described as a professional training level. Some were concerned that supervision does not necessarily require academic competence: 'I would be concerned about someone who passed the academic requirements of a course who was poor at facilitating the clinical work of others.' Another said: 'Normally it should be postgraduate level, but some excellent training courses concentrate on the practice, skills and personal awareness needed in supervision, without high academic demands.'

Contextual issues

Recently the CPC (Counsellors in Primary Care Association) has been concerned about the standards of supervision offered to practitioners in primary care settings. Drawing on the research of Burton *et al.* (1998), sometimes there was a lack of congruence between supervisor and supervisee when the supervisor did not have experience of working in primary care settings. In response to this concern a division of the organization has been established that addresses itself to supervisory issues.

Whether supervisors should have experience in the context of their supervisees is a debatable topic. The experts consulted were again divided in their responses to the question of whether supervisors should have direct experience of the context in which their supervisees are working. One respondent said: 'No. I feel strongly about this, we need plurality. It would be sad if all supervision became context-specific because it would inhibit the fertilization of ideas and the opening up of new perspectives.' On the other hand, another said: 'I think supervisors should have direct experience of the context and client group of their supervisees if their supervisees are in training. Trainees need someone who knows the context well. It is not necessary for qualified workers.' The special point was made that, in working with some groups, it is essential that supervisors have direct experience. For example, 'supervisors who are working with children must understand enough about the law related to children and ethical issues'. The final pertinent comment on this issue: 'This is where the length and content of the training becomes important. The supervisor must be able to orientate themselves to the supervisees' context and circumstances and have the ability to fill in contextual gaps rather than having the exact experience of working with a particular client group.'

Theoretical orientation

Some supervision courses are set up to work with potential supervisors within specific theoretical orientations. A course offering psychodynamic supervision training will be very different from one offering generic supervision open to a range of professionals. There is some evidence that congruence of theoretical orientation between supervisor and supervisee enhances the supervision alliance (Putney et al., 1992). However, given the plethora of therapy models, if every supervision training course were specific to theoretical orientation, there would be more courses than students. When asked whether supervisor training courses should offer a specific theoretical orientation, the expert group were again divided between those who saw theoretical congruence as essential and those who believed in diversity. 'I believe that supervision should be regarded as a profession in its own right, with the principles, theory and skills being clearly connected to practice. There can be a richness in working with people from other orientations.' On the other hand: 'I strongly believe that it is important that supervisor training is provided in the theoretical orientation of potential supervisees. At the same time I believe that all supervisors should have a strong understanding of the three main theoretical paradigms influencing psychotherapy, behavioural, humanistic and psychoanalytic, and the application of theory to practice in each of these modalities.' Considering the supervision of trainees, another respondent said that 'theoretical congruence between supervisor and supervisee in training of the therapist is crucial. Supervision has such a crucial role to play in training therapists, the supervisor must be able to offer very specific feedback about skills and practice.' It seems that candidates looking for supervisor training courses will have considerable choice between courses that offer a specific therapeutic modality and others that offer plurality.

Supervision as profession?

There are certainly practitioners in Britain whose professional identity is specifically related to supervision. For example, Peter Hawkins and Robin Shohet, Michael Carroll and Brigid Proctor have developed their careers to provide not only clinical supervision to psychotherapists but also consultancy to individuals and organizations. The panel of experts was asked whether a specific professional identity should be developed for supervisors in organizations and professional associations to which they might belong. Most respondents were not in favour of the suggestion, although some thought it was inevitable: 'all supervisors should be practising therapists. I do not think that supervision should have a specific separate professional identity. The two roles of therapists and supervisors should be delineated clearly but not in a hierarchical manner.' 'I think supervision will become something of a profession in its own right eventually (as it is in mainland Europe), for it is strongly connected to organizational consultancy, coaching and mentoring, and is relevant to a variety of professions. Supervisors will be seen as skilled facilitators of reflection.'

Experiences of supervisor training

The panel of experts was asked about their experiences of supervisor training and their satisfaction with it. In general, supervisor training has been experienced as helpful. Specific mention was made of 'supervisor training providing a greater understanding of organizational and personnel management issues, which are useful in supervising counsellors working in various agency settings rather than private practice'. Another commented on the generic training they had taken, which 'meant I could benefit from seeing other people of different orientations at work while integrating core skills into my own approach'. Criticisms included the following: 'I had one very eminent supervisor trainer who was very able, but he told me what to do and what to say'; 'courses can be too rigid'. 'There is a danger that courses can be too theoretical and not look carefully enough at actual supervisory work'; 'courses must encourage the supervisor to be a facilitator of learning, rather than an expert'. 'The training was good but there were many areas that were missed such as cross-cultural supervision and organization dimensions.' 'Supervision training should include a strong element of training in ethical thinking and decision-making, along with some systematic training about how to deal with inappropriate practice by supervisees and the supervisor's role in relation to complaints.'

What makes a good supervisor?

There are many perspectives on what makes a good supervisor. Personal characteristics, the experiences of supervisees, the impact of supervision on therapeutic work, contextual or cultural issues that impact on supervision and the supervisor, theoretical orientation and the knowledge base of the supervisor, as well as issues such as age, gender and experience. Weaks (2002) reported on her qualitative enquiry into what supervisees think makes for good supervision. Three key constituents were identified as 'core conditions', which were necessary for an effective supervision relationship to become established: equality, safety and challenge. Shanfield *et al.* (1992), assessed the behaviour of supervisors, and found a high level of agreement about the use of empathy, focus on the supervisees' immediate experiences and making in-depth comments that facilitate understanding of the client. In a study involving the supervision of nurses who were asked what they found most helpful about their supervisors, it was the ability to form supportive relationships that was most important. Having relevant knowledge/clinical skills, expressing a commitment to providing supervision, and having good listening skills were also important characteristics of their supervisor. They viewed their supervisor as a role model, someone they felt inspired them and looked up to, and had a high regard for their clinical practice and knowledge base (Sloan, 1999).

The supervisory relationship

Evidence concerning the effectiveness of supervision and the satisfaction of supervisees, in clinical psychology, counselling, nursing, occupational therapy and psychiatry, regardless of theoretical orientation, points to the relationship between supervisor and supervisee as being the most important factor (Kilminster and Jolly, 2000; Ladany *et al.*, 1999a; Magnuson *et al.*, 2000b; Sweeney *et al.*, 2001).

Not surprisingly, supervisees respond to a climate of trust, understanding and acceptance when making themselves vulnerable by presenting their therapeutic work for scrutiny. While in training, supervisees look to the supervisor to provide them with support, guidance and encouragement, but anxiety about exposing potential mistakes to an authority figure is ever present. The supervisory relationship is influenced by personal characteristics (White, 2000), some of which are fixed and others dynamic. Constant factors include gender and sex-role attitudes, and the supervisor's style, age and race. Relationship dynamics such as power and intimacy, as well as stages of the relationship, are examples of dynamic sources. Uncertainty about supervisory expectations and methods of evaluation, or ambiguity and role conflict (Ladany and Friedlander, 1995), as student, therapist or colleague, also affect relationship dynamics.

The Supervisory Alliance Inventory (Efstation *et al.*, 1990) is frequently used in supervision research. Patton and Kivlighan (1997) found that the supervisory alliance was significantly related to the client's perception of the counselling alliance. This implies that the supervisory relationship has an influence on the outcome of counselling, as the alliance is a predictor of outcome (Marziali, 1984). Ladany *et al.* (1999a) found that, although the supervisory alliance over the course of supervision did not predict supervisory outcomes, trainees were more satisfied with supervision the greater the emotional bond between them and their supervisor. Supervisees become less dependent on their supervisors' overtime (Kauderer and Herron, 1990).

Clinical psychology graduates were surveyed and 38 per cent of trainees reported a major conflict with their supervisor, which inhibited their ability to learn from supervision (Moskowitz and Rupert, 1983). Therapeutic orientation, style of supervision and personality issues were the main areas of conflict. While theoretical orientation can be a source of conflict, similarity in theoretical orientation and interpretive styles contributes to good supervision experiences and a positive relationship (Kennard *et al.*, 1987). Supervisors were found to be able to repair ruptures in the supervisory alliance more easily when they take into account the developmental level of the trainee involved (Burke *et al.*, 1998).

Disclosure in supervision

Given that supervision is charged with ensuring that clients get the best possible service from the therapist, the relationship must be one within which supervisees are able to disclose their most intimate thoughts, fantasies and experiences with the client. Yourman and Farber (1996) suggest that while usually presenting an honest picture of the work with patients, they consciously distort and/or conceal some material at least some of the time. Numerous studies have investigated disclosure in supervision on the part of both the supervisor and the supervisee. The relationship is seen to be enhanced when the supervisor shares his/her own experiences (Ladany *et al.*, 2001) and the supervisory style is interpersonal, sensitive and task oriented. Supervisor nondisclosures can be very unhelpful. Ladany and Melincoff (1999) found 12 categories of nondisclosure for supervisors, the most frequently cited being the negative reactions to the trainee's counselling and professional performance, as well as negative reactions to the trainee's supervision performance. The conclusion is that supervisors' use of disclosure, to some extent, strengthened the working alliance.

Webb and Wheeler (1998) investigated what supervisees find difficult to disclose in supervision. They concluded that erotic thoughts and feelings about supervisor or client and difficulties in the supervisory relationship will be hard to discuss. Also there is less disclosure with supervisors who are imposed or who have an assessment function, rather than those that are chosen. Supervisees were likely to disclose more in individual rather than in collective supervision and when they were supervised independently of the setting in which they practised as counsellors. Negative reactions to the supervisor were the most frequent type of nondisclosure. Other reasons for nondisclosure of issues included perceived unimportance, material being too personal, and a poor working alliance with the supervisor.

Preparation for supervision

The effects of a role-induction procedure on beginning counsellor-trainees' perceptions of supervision, using a ten-minute audiotaped summary of Bernard's model of supervision, were examined. Trainees evaluated supervision more negatively over the time period before the role induction. Following role induction, trainees reported a clearer conceptualization of supervision and a greater willingness to reveal concerns to their supervisors (Bahrick *et al.*, 1991). Olk and Friedlander (1992) developed a Role Conflict and Role Ambiguity Inventory and found that beginning trainees reported higher levels of role ambiguity than more experienced trainees, but that role conflict was only problematic for advanced trainees who experience little ambiguity.

Effectiveness of supervision

Ultimately, supervision is expected to have an impact on the therapeutic work between therapist and client. Demonstrating that this is the case has many methodological difficulties. There is as yet scant evidence to support the effectiveness of supervision. Lenihan and Kirk (1992) monitored clients of trainees in close supervision who adopted prescriptive techniques, and found that clients progressed and that therapeutic changes occurred. Couchan and Bernard (1984) found that follow-through from supervision to counselling, as measured by counsellor behaviour, was greatest when supervision was given four hours before the therapy session. Milne and James (2000) conducted a systematic review of effective cognitive behavioural supervision and found 28 empirical studies of change processes occurring between participants in what they describe as the educational pyramid: consultant and supervisor, supervisor and supervisee, and supervisee patients. They describe close monitoring of the supervisee, providing a model of competence, specific instructions, goal-setting and feedback on performance as the main methods of supervision, which seemed to benefit the supervisees. Their final conclusion was that cognitive behavioural supervision is valuable in the support and training of practitioners.

Training supervisors

Given the substantial evidence that suggests that supervisors can enhance their skills and practice through training (Milne and James, 2002; Russell and Petrie, 1994; Holloway, 1997), but in the absence of any verified template for training supervisors, what follows are suggestions, based wherever possible on empirical evidence, of what might be included in a supervisor training course. Traditionally supervisors learn skills through the experience of being supervisees, taking on the model presented to them by their supervisor, or by adapting the therapeutic skills learned in their training as therapists. While these methods have some merit they also have considerable limitations. Bad practice can easily be handed down from generation to generation without some new import from an external source.

Models of supervision

Supervision has its own theory and practice associated with it. Models of supervision provide a reference point, a structure or framework that gives the work coherence, and makes sense of common difficulties. A model might indicate which behaviours are appropriate at a particular time with particular supervisees, or might prescribe a range of tasks or functions that need to be fulfilled in order to provide adequate supervision. Some models describe how supervision should be conducted with respect to a particular model of therapy. There are many models to choose from and new ones emerge all the time. Supervisors might be trained in the particular model chosen by the course directors, or they might be encouraged to review existing models and develop their own. Whichever path is chosen, supervisor competence will be enhanced if the supervisor knows and understands which model they are using and why. Similarly, when it comes to evaluation or assessment of supervisor competence, a model of supervision provides a frame of reference by which performance can be judged. Scott *et al.* (2000) surveyed training courses in supervision accredited by the American Psychological Association and found that 20 per cent of supervision training courses have no formal or informal methods to evaluate supervision competence.

Effective supervision requires the supervisor to have good communications skills. Kilminster and Jolly (2000: 840) reviewed literature on the skills and qualities of effective supervisors and concluded the following:

- Supervisors need to be clinically competent and knowledgeable, and have good teaching and interpersonal skills.
- The relationship between the supervisor and trainee changes as the latter gains experience.
- Helpful supervisory behaviours include giving direct guidance on clinical work, linking theory and practice, joint problem-solving, offering feedback, reassurance and role models.

- Trainees need clear feedback about their errors; corrections must be conveyed unambiguously so that trainees are aware of mistakes and weaknesses they may have.
- Ineffective supervisory behaviours include rigidity, low empathy, failure to offer support, failure to follow the supervisees concerns, being indirect and intolerant and emphasizing negative aspects in the evaluation process.

Ronnestad *et al.* (1997) investigated levels of supervisory activity and confidence in relation to a number of therapist characteristics, and reported that supervising work of other therapists is a normal part of professional development. They noted that supervisory confidence increases noticeably with early supervisory experiences and thereafter progressively and slowly. There is no substitute for experience when guidance and feedback are to be given to trainee therapists, but interpersonal skills required to communicate such guidance can be enhanced through training. Stevens *et al.* (1998) examined the influence of experiencing training on supervisory stance, supervisory confidence, and self-efficacy, and found that training was positively associated with more positive, less critical, dogmatic approaches to supervision but that experience was not. They found no support for the notion that experience alone is sufficient to enhance the supervisor's development.

Methods and teaching

Numerous authors have offered suggestions for a curriculum for training supervisors. Inskipp and Proctor (2001a, 2001b) have produced a comprehensive manual for training supervisors that provides a wide range of creative suggestions for experiential learning. Holloway (1999) offers a framework for supervisor training. Bradley and Whiting's model of supervisor training has four major goals:

1   To provide a theory or knowledge base relevant to supervisory functioning;
2   To develop and refine supervisory skills;
3   To integrate theory and skills into a working supervisory style; and
4   To develop and enhance the professional identity of the supervisor.
                                                      (Bradley and Whiting, 2001: 363)

The syllabus for a supervision course might include all or some of the following: ethics, law, organizational issues, supervisory relationships, supervision models, supervision skills, evaluating trainees, contextual issues, equal opportunities issues, using authority, supervision process, research, managing complaints and mistakes, contracts, creative techniques and group supervision.

Inevitably the range of topics requires a range of teaching and training methods. Scott *et al.* (2000) found that methods of conducting training in supervision vary across institutions and include didactic instruction, individual supervision, group supervision and assigned reading. They found that reviewing audio or videotapes of supervision sessions were used to a lesser extent. Using audiotapes or videotapes in supervisor training can be a valuable resource when used to explore and enhance relationship skills, given the importance of the relationship to supervisory practice.

Supervisor trainers need to be very careful about what they offer in a training programme, with thought given to the model of supervision they are teaching and the way that good teaching mirrors that model. Didactic teaching will reinforce the notion that supervision is a didactic experience, modelling a relationship in which one person knows, and the other needs to learn. If supervisees are to become reflective practitioners (Schon, 1986), then both supervisors and trainers need to model those skills.

Ethics

A critical role of the supervisor is to ensure the ethical practice of supervisees; hence training in supervision must include close attention to ethical issues. The relevant ethical codes relating to specific professions need to be reviewed critically to ensure that they are clearly understood. Understanding ethical codes, however, is relatively straightforward in theory but not so easy to put into practice. For example, Erwin (2000) measured supervisors' responses to sensitive case studies, and found that the majority of supervisors received low moral sensitivity scores for a case involving breach of confidentiality and dual relationships. Miller and Larrabee (1995) surveyed counsellors about intimacy in counsellor education and supervision, and found that 16 per cent of respondents reported sexual encounters with supervisors or educators while involved in counsellor training programmes, a lower percentage than was found in studies of female psychologists and supervisors (Glaser and Thorpe, 1986; Pope, 1989). This suggests that supervisors have a lot to learn about ethics and need to apply them to their own practice. An investigation of psychiatric residency training directors revealed that their faculty supervisors were not familiar with issues of accountability and that little effort was made to rectify this (Schulte *et al.*, 1997). In Britain, King and Wheeler (1999) consulted expert supervisors about the responsibility they consider themselves to have for their supervisees, particularly those in private practice. Most expressed reluctance to take action against supervisees who were in breach of their ethical codes. Ladany *et al.* (1999b) investigated supervisor ethical practices and found that 51 per cent of the supervisees sampled reported at least one ethical violation by their supervisors. The most frequently violated guidelines involved inadequate performance evaluation, confidentiality issues, and ability to work with alternative perspectives of the supervisees' work.

As a result of their study, Nickell *et al.* (1995), investigating sexual attraction with clients, recommended that supervisor training programmes should address gender differences, using touch therapy, sexual attraction issues, and codes of ethics. There is a difference between bad supervision (ineffective supervision) and harmful supervision (that traumatizes the supervisee). Supervisor training must seek to ensure that supervisors who are deemed to be competent as a result of training are unlikely to be either bad or harmful in their supervisory practice.

Contracts

An aspect of ethical practice that has received little empirical investigation is the use of contracts for supervision. Osborn and Davies (1996) highlight the importance of written contracts for supervision and suggest five principles to be addressed in such contracts:

1   clarify the methods, goals and expectations of supervision;
2   clarify the mutuality of the relationship;
3   clarify ethical principles;
4   detail practical issues related to the service provided;
5   ally supervision with counselling and consultation.

Proctor (1997) highlights the need for a working agreement to underpin the supervisory relationship. She says, 'the initial contracting weaves a container for the work together and also sets markers by which both parties can guide and prioritize their direction at points of choice or confusion' (1997: 190). Carroll (1996) described seven supervision tasks as a result of his research inquiry into roles and tasks reported by experienced supervisors. These tasks include creating a learning relationship, teaching, counselling, consulting, evaluating, monitoring professional ethical issues and working with administrative/organizational aspects of clients' work. All of these tasks can be negotiated and included in a working agreement. One crucial aspect of contracts, particularly when working with trainees, is a clear understanding of the methods of assessment or evaluation of the work. The contract is not only with the supervisee but also with the training agency that takes responsibility for the supervisee's work (Izzard, 2001).

Training supervisees

While training supervisors, time should be found to stress the importance of training supervisees to fulfil their role and make the best use of supervision. In a study by Bahrick *et al.* (1991), trainees were found to evaluate their experience of supervision more negatively before they were given some training in using supervision effectively. The training programme introduced them to the model of supervision to be used, and following the session they reported a clearer conceptualization of supervision and a greater willingness to reveal their concerns to their supervisors. Inskipp (1999) suggests three main reasons why supervisees should be trained to use supervision: (1) It is empowering for the supervisee, (2) they need to take an active part in negotiating a working alliance, a relationship that enables them to learn, and (3) they need to take an active part in negotiating the working agreement, including the contract. She suggests that supervisees need to be empowered to use the supervisory relationship in a way that increases their confidence and enables them to engage actively with their side of the contract and working agreement.

Supervising and evaluating trainees

It has already been noted that most research literature refers to inquiries conducted in the USA, usually with trainees. Hence most research referred to in this chapter relates to supervision with trainees. However, there are some important points that need to be noted with respect to trainees when training supervisors in Britain. Probably the most important and stressful issue is assessment. Samec (1995) studied the experiences of supervisors who failed the clinical work of candidates, and stresses that supervisors need support when they decide to fail a candidate's clinical work, as the process may be traumatic for both supervisor and supervisee. Supervisors tend to judge candidates according to their ability to make use of supervision. This is always complicated because, if a supervisee finds it difficult to engage in supervision, they are not always consciously aware of what impedes them. The impact of the supervisor on the relationship cannot be underestimated. Carey et al. (1988) demonstrated that the supervisor's expertness, attractiveness, and trustworthiness were related to supervision outcome measures.

Criteria for the evaluation of competence needs to be clearly defined. Overholser and Fine (1990) define five domains as contributing to clinical competence: actual knowledge, generic clinical skills, orientation-specific technical skills, clinical judgement and interpersonal attributes. Bernard and Goodyear (1998) advise that evaluation must be conducted sensitively and offer the following conditions that supervisors should remember:

1 The relationship between supervisor and supervisee is unequal.
2 A clear contract is needed.
3 Supervisee defensiveness should be taken into account and addressed.
4 Individual differences need to be discussed.
5 Evaluation procedures and processes should be clearly defined.
6 Evaluation should be a formative as well as a summative process that is present throughout supervision.

7 Life events external to the supervisory relationship should be taken into account for the final evaluation.
8 The evaluation must be institutionally supported. Supervisor decisions need to be trusted and honoured, while respecting the supervisee's right to reply.
9 Avoid rushing to conclusions at an early stage of the supervision.
10 Supervisors should invite feedback on their own performance.
11 Attention must be paid to the supervisory relationship. If it falters, evaluation becomes questionable.
12 Supervisors should enjoy supervision.

Finally, on the topic of assessment in supervision, the benefits of self-assessment in conjunction with supervisor assessment should not be underestimated. Dowling (1984) and Hilderbrand (1989) both found that supervisees tend to assess themselves and their peers accurately, and self-evaluation helps to develop the reflective practitioner. However, such positive findings should be viewed with caution, particularly as Steward *et al.* (2001) found that the self-evaluations of novice supervisees depended on their perceptions of supervisor style. The more attractive they perceived their supervisors to be, the lower they rated themselves.

Contextual and organizational issues

'Organizations have their own cultures, some of which are supportive of counselling, some of which tolerate it and some of which are embarrassed by it' (Carroll, 1996: 125). Supervisors need to be prepared to deal with the complex dynamics of institutions that impinge on therapeutic work. The dynamics of the patient, therapist and supervisor triad are interwoven with the dynamics of the institution itself, of the staff team and of the relationship between the supervisor and the service. The supervisor has to balance the needs of trainees, the dynamics of the team and the organization, which can be contradictory and confusing (Anastasopoulos and Tsiantis, 1999). Copeland (1998) investigated the dilemmas that supervisors experience when working in organizations, which are different depending on whether the supervisor is an employee of the organization or contracted externally. The roles, responsibilities and contracts need to be carefully defined in order to ensure clarity in the supervisory relationship and clear lines of accountability. It is also crucial that supervisors have some understanding of the context in which they are contracted to work. For example, as mentioned earlier, Burton *et al.* (1998) investigated primary care counsellors' experiences of supervision, and found that supervisees were sometimes dissatisfied with their supervisor's understanding of the complex dynamics of the primary care environment.

Supervision process

Potential supervisors need an understanding of the process of supervision, particularly the parallel process. It is through the parallel process that supervisors can come closest to understanding the experience that the therapist has in the presence of the client. Searles (1955) first described it as the reflection process in his writings on psychoanalytic supervision. Mattinson (1977) analysed interactions between therapists and clients and supervisors and therapists and observed that thoughts and feelings that were unspoken in the therapeutic relationship sometimes seemed to surface in the supervisory relationship. At times, the supervisor's response to the supervisee mirrors the supervisee's response to the client. An awareness of this reflection or parallel process can provide insight into the unconscious processes of the client in the relation to the therapist. If it remains out of awareness, a vital clue is missed and a misjudgement of the supervisee is possible. Raichelson et al. (1997) investigated the degree to which parallel process existed in supervision, and found that in a review of 300 therapists studied few denied the existence of parallel process. They found that there were some differences in therapeutic orientation, with the psychodynamic therapists consistently reporting the importance of parallel process. Doehrman's (1976) research revealed that parallel process is bi-directional. In other words, just as the counsellor may unconsciously imitate the client in supervision, the counsellor may unconsciously imitate the supervisor in their therapy with the client. Hence, when the dynamics of the supervisor/supervisee relationship do not match that which is expected, attention to parallel process may solve the problem.

Issues of difference in supervision

In modern Britain attention to issues of difference is crucial to all aspects of supervision and therapy. Issues of race, culture, gender and sexual orientation may have an impact on the supervisory relationship and need to be considered. Research findings on the impact of difference in supervision are inconsistent. Gardner (2001) studied cultural perspectives of the supervisory relationships, and found no significant differences between race and supervisees' perceptions of empathy, respect and congruence. On the other hand, racial identity interaction predicts aspects of the supervisory alliance. When supervisory pairs are similar in racial identity they are more likely to agree about the supervision process (Ladany et al., 1997). Evidence that supervisors need training in issues of difference is found in the work of Duan and Roehlke (2001), who noted that, in cross-racial supervision dyads, supervisees were more sensitive to cultural/racial issues than supervisors, and supervisors reported making more efforts to address cultural issues than supervisees perceived.

Race and gender are often investigated together. For example Wells (2001) investigated gender roles, and racial and gender attitudes, and found that, as therapist experience increased, more emphasis was placed on gender and race in the therapeutic relationship. However, many supervisors had not received training in multicultural counselling or indeed in clinical supervision. Gatmon *et al.* (2001) found that when discussions in supervision include cultural variables, supervisees report enhanced supervisory working alliances and increased satisfaction with supervision. The power relationship in supervision, when the interaction is between male supervisors and female supervisees, needs to be carefully monitored. An investigation into the effects of gender in group supervision highlighted that, on average, male supervisees were asked for their opinion more than twice as often as female supervisees. Male supervisees were given less direction than their female counterparts (Granello *et al.*, 1997). Nelson and Holloway (1990) similarly found subtle and highly complex differences between the way that male and female supervisees were encouraged to communicate in supervision. Female trainees tended to relinquish power to the supervisor.

Creative techniques in supervision

Evidence for the use of creative techniques in supervision is lacking, but, nonetheless, including sessions on the use of creativity in supervision can be an asset to any supervision training course. Numerous authors have contributed their ideas of creative supervision, including Inskipp and Proctor (2001a, 2001b) whose supervisor training manuals are a rich source of exercises and teaching materials. Houston (1995) draws on her experience as a Gestalt therapist to produce some exciting and unconventional methods of reaching the heart of the client. Wilkins (1995) suggests creative methods of working with supervision groups, which Proctor (2000) extends in her book on group supervision.

Group supervision

Supervisors are often called on to provide supervision in groups and they need preparation to fulfil this role. An awareness of group dynamics will be a good start. Bernard and Goodyear define group supervision as

> a regular meeting of a group of supervisees with the designated supervisor, the purpose of which is to further the understanding of themselves as clinicians, or of clients with whom they are engaged, or service delivery in general, aided in this endeavour by their interaction as part of the group process.
>
> (Bernard and Goodyear, 1998: 111)

Prieto (1996) reviewed the literature on group supervision and confirmed the lack of hard evidence supporting its effectiveness. However, there are perceived to be many advantages of group supervision, including an economy in time, money and expertise, less supervisee dependence, opportunities for vicarious learning, exposure to a broader range of clients, diversity of feedback and greater opportunity to use action or creative techniques. Limitations also exist, such as individuals being overpowered by the group, concerns about confidentiality, group dynamics impeding learning, and the potential for scapegoating in the group. Jones (2000) investigated damaging incidents in group supervisions and noted many complaints from group members about the treatment they had received in such groups. Complaints included the lack of congruence of theoretical orientation with the group facilitator, who was perceived to favour supervisees who were sympathetic to her theoretical position, and being assessed negatively in front of other group members. Aronson (1990) claims that the effectiveness of supervisory groups depends on the contributions of the leader, the group members' interaction with the each other and with the leader, and group identity that leads to members valuing being a member of the group.

Conclusion

There is now a vast literature on supervision that can be consulted when a training programme for supervisors is planned. There are also many incentives to provide supervisor training, given the importance and complexity of the task and the imperative to ensure that professions providing psychological therapies are seen to be self-regulating and working towards offering high standards of care that adhere to strict ethical codes. The apprenticeship model has something to offer potential supervisors and learning from experience is valuable, but it is arguable that the weight of responsibility that the supervisor carries warrants a good foundation through comprehensive, in-depth training. Supervisors bear some of the responsibility for the future development of professional practice; they need to be prepared.

Chapter 3

Models of supervision and the supervisory relationship and their evidence base

Helen Beinart

Most clinical psychologists are unaware of the large body of literature on clinical supervision, and most of us, as beginning supervisors, rely on our existing knowledge of psychotherapy models and our transferable therapeutic relationship skills. This situation is not entirely surprising because the supervision literature is largely based on psychotherapy and counselling and there is very little written about clinical supervision for clinical psychologists in the UK. Hopefully, this book will make a difference.

This chapter focuses on models of supervision that are generic; that is, not based on psychotherapy models but developed to aid our understanding of supervision and the learning and training of supervision in its own right. Selected models are described and their evidence base examined. Models of the supervisory relationship are then described as the evidence points towards the overriding importance of the supervisory relationship in understanding supervision. The complexity of developing an evidence base for supervision and methodological issues that have beset this field are discussed, followed by some suggestions for methodologically competent studies. The author then briefly describes her research on the supervisory relationship and her own (evidence-based) model. This leads to general discussion about what supervisors (and supervisees) can do to enhance the effectiveness of their supervision.

Models of supervision can be divided into two broad categories: those based on psychotherapy theories and those developed specifically for supervision. Early supervision models were direct extensions of psychotherapy theories. The earliest of these were based on psychodynamic theories (e.g. Ekstein and Wallerstein, 1972), followed by humanistic or person-centred supervision (e.g. Rice, 1980; Patterson, 1983), behavioural (e.g. Boyd, 1978), cognitive behavioural (e.g. Liese and Beck, 1997), systemic (e.g. Liddle *et al.*, 1997) and narrative (e.g. Parry and Doan, 1994). Authors such as Lambert and Arnold (1987) have suggested that research on the effectiveness of supervision is tied to knowledge about the effectiveness of psychotherapy. Bernard and Goodyear (1998) argue that whilst there are clear influences between supervision and therapy, there are substantial drawbacks to using therapy models for conceptualizing supervision. As supervision differs from therapy, therapeutic models have proved too narrow to explain the complexity of supervision and have possibly restricted the evidence base by offering few directions for research and practice in supervision (Bernard and Goodyear, 1998). Schon (1983) suggests that professional training draws on two different realms of knowledge: theory and research that forms the basis of an academic programme and knowledge derived from practitioner experience. The recent growth of the therapy professions has led to an increasing emphasis on practitioner-led supervisor training, and much of the writing on supervision, particularly in the UK, reflects the realm of knowledge based on practitioner experience (e.g. Proctor, 1997; Scaife, 2001a). Psychotherapy-based models do not provide a framework for training beginning supervisors as opposed to therapists. This has led to a shift from therapy-based models to the development of generic or supervision-specific models. This chapter will focus on the main generic models that have been specifically developed to explain the complex phenomenon of supervision. These can be divided broadly into the developmental models (e.g. Littrell et al., 1979; Loganbill et al., 1982; Stoltenberg, 1981; Hess, 1986; Stoltenberg and Delworth, 1987; Stoltenberg, et al., 1998) and social role models (e.g. Bernard, 1979; Friedlander and Ward, 1984; Hawkins and Shohet, 1989; Williams, 1995; Carroll, 1996). Recently, Holloway (1995) developed the Systems Approach to Supervision – a more contextually based model which developed from the social role models.

Developmental models

Developmental models attempt to explain the complex transition from inexperienced supervisee to master clinician (Whiting et al., 2001). There has been a great deal of model development and research into the developmental models, such that they have been called the 'zeitgeist of supervision thinking and research' (Holloway, 1987: 209). Most developmental models share the fundamental assumptions that supervisees develop through a series of different stages on their journey towards competence and that supervisors need to adjust their supervisory style and approach to match the supervisee's level of development as a counsellor/therapist (e.g. Stoltenberg, 1981). Worthington (1987), in his comprehensive review of the developmental literature, suggested that models and studies can be divided into those that address the supervision of the developing supervisee (e.g. Loganbill et al., 1982) or those that address the development of the supervisor (e.g. Hess, 1986).

Early developmental models (e.g. Littrell et al., 1979; Stoltenberg, 1981) proposed stage-based models – for example, it was assumed all supervisees developed through the same stages, from novice to master counsellor, for a range of different clinical skills regardless of previous experience or individual difference. In response to criticisms of the early models and the growing literature base, Stoltenberg and Delworth (1987) and Stoltenberg et al. (1998) developed the Integrated Developmental Model (IDM) of supervision. This model will be discussed in some detail here.

Integrated Developmental Model (IDM)

Stoltenberg *et al.* (1998: 1) state, 'understanding change over time in one's ability to function as a professional is fundamental in the practice of clinical supervision'. The IDM developed by Stoltenberg and Delworth (1987) suggests three overriding structures to monitor supervisee development over three developmental levels across various domains of clinical training and practice. These three structures are self- and other awareness (cognitive and affective), motivation, and autonomy. Level one supervisees are seen as anxious, highly motivated and dependent on their supervisors for advice and guidance. The primary focus is on the self while dealing with anxiety about performance and evaluation. Level two supervisees have acquired suffi-cient skills and knowledge to focus less on themselves and to increase their focus on the client. Motivation and autonomy vary at this stage depending on levels of confusion and ambivalence. Level three supervisees develop the ability to balance the client's perspective appropriately whilst maintaining self-awareness. Motivation stabilizes as the supervisee begins to function as a relatively autonomous professional.

The Integrated Developmental Model (IDM) recognizes that develop-mental levels might vary across different types of professional activity. The following categories are used to describe professional tasks or domains: intervention skill competence, assessment techniques, interpersonal assess-ment, client conceptualization, individual differences, theoretical orientation, treatment goals and plans, and professional ethics. The IDM allows for skills to develop differently – for example, a trainee might reach level three in the area of assessment techniques but be operating at level two for client conceptualization.

In addition to addressing supervisee developmental need the IDM also identifies different tasks for supervisors at each development level. At level one the supervisor provides structure and encourages the early development of autonomy and appropriate risk-taking. The supervisor's tasks include containing anxiety and providing a role model. At level two the supervisor provides less structure and encourages more autonomy. Tasks include clarifying trainee ambivalence, modelling and providing a more facilitative and less didactic focus. At level three the supervisor focuses more on personal/professional integration. The supervisor's task is to ensure consistency in per-formance across domains, identify any deficits and work towards integration and refining a professional identity.

Evidence base of the developmental models

The developmental models have stimulated much supervision research. However, there are few research studies that explicitly investigate supervisee development over time; to do this in a meaningful way, longitudinal studies are needed. Despite this, on the basis of their review, which takes into account the conceptual and methodological rigour of the studies, Ellis and Ladany (1997) tentatively conclude that supervisees may increase in autonomy as they gain experience and that beginning supervisees may prefer structured supervision. However, the need for structure appears important across all levels of experience if dealing with a clinical crisis (Tracey *et al.*, 1989). Rabinowitz *et al.* (1986) found that the needs for structure and support were present at the beginning of new supervisory relationships regardless of experience. Friedlander and Ward (1984) suggest that supervisory style and attitude outweigh specific factors such as structure and format of supervision. There is some support for the developmental models from one study (Borders, 1990), which found some increase in trainee autonomy over one semester. Although there have been studies that have specifically tested Stoltenberg and Delworth's IDM (1987) poor methodologies lead Ellis and Ladany to conclude that the IDM has not been adequately tested and 'no tentative inferences from the data to the models seems justifiable given the inadequate rigour of the studies' (1997: 483).

Although the developmental models make intuitive sense there is very little research evidence to support them. Most studies have methodological problems – for example, the use of cross-sectional designs that do not answer questions about development over time. However, there is some research evidence to support the concept of increasing trainee autonomy over time and also some evidence that beginning trainees benefit from more structured supervision experiences. Given the number of theories and studies in this area, these findings are disappointing. Early developmental theories assume the supervisory relationship; however, more recent publications (Stoltenberg *et al.*, 1998) suggest that good supervisory relationships encompass warmth, acceptance and understanding, and create an atmosphere of experimentation. The supervisory relationship provides a learning context in which the supervisee matures regardless of stage of development.

Social role models

The fundamental assumption underlying social role models is that the supervisor undertakes a set of roles that establish expectations, beliefs and attitudes about what functions the supervisor will perform. Several models of supervision include the tasks and functions (role) of the supervisor – for example, Friedlander and Ward (1984), Williams (1995) and Carroll (1996). The most comprehensive of these models, which will be discussed in detail here, was developed by Bernard in 1979 and developed by Bernard and Goodyear in their 1992 and 1998 texts.

The Discrimination Model

Bernard developed the Discrimination Model as a teaching tool in order to provide a map for supervisor training. It is called the Discrimination Model because it assumes flexibility on the part of the supervisor to respond to specific supervisee needs. There are two axes (roles and foci) within the model, consisting of three basic supervisor roles (therapist, teacher and consultant), and three basic foci of supervision (process, conceptualization and personalization). Using this model there is thus a matrix of nine choices for supervisor intervention. Bernard (1997) describes the Discrimination Model as atheoretical in that it can be used across any model of psychotherapy. The roles of therapist, teacher and consultant are relatively self-evident and will not be described in detail here. The three foci or learning dimensions are described as the primary functions of a competent therapist. Process skills are the basic psychotherapy techniques and strategy such as engagement and interviewing skills. Personalization refers to the personal or feeling elements of the supervisee's experience, such as the ability to manage the client's feelings as well as their own within a therapy session. Conceptualization is a more covert cognitive skill that involves the tasks of thinking, analysis and theory–practice links involved in formulation. All of these learning dimensions are thought to be key within any one supervision session. However, the emphasis between foci is likely to vary according to the theoretical orientation of the supervisor and the supervisee's level of development. For example, supervisors of beginning supervisees are likely to focus more on specific process skills such as interviewing, whereas supervisors of more experienced supervisees are likely to focus on self-reflection (personalization) and refining formulations (conceptualization).

Evidence base of the Discrimination Model

Bernard and Goodyear (1992) acknowledge that the Discrimination Model is rooted in technical eclecticism. The strength of this is that it provides a means of training flexible and responsive supervisors; however, it fails to address important issues such as evaluation and the supervisory relationship. There is some evidence to support elements of the model. Stenack and Dye (1983) found that supervisees were able to differentiate different supervisor behaviours within the three supervisor roles of teacher, consultant and counsellor. Ellis *et al.* (1988), in two well-designed studies, explicitly tested the three-by-three model using supervisee judgements of dissimilarities between the nine role-function combinations. They found that supervisee perceptions were similar to supervisor perceptions and consistent with the model. However, it was also suggested that Bernard's model was simplistic as relationship issues were not included.

The Discrimination Model is thus a testable model in which to conceptualize supervisor roles in relation to supervisee needs. There has not been a great deal of research to test the model; however, there is some evidence to support a shared understanding between supervisors and supervisees that these roles occur during supervision. A major criticism of the model is the failure to take account of the role of evaluation within the supervisor roles and the failure to address the relationship dimension within supervision. The model could thus be seen as partially useful but incomplete in that it over-simplifies a complex area.

The Systems Approach to Supervision

The Systems Approach to Supervision (SAS) was developed as a dynamic model capable of assisting supervisors in a systematic assessment of super-visee learning needs and supervision teaching interventions (Holloway and Neufeldt, 1995). Holloway's (1995) model builds on social role models but sees the supervisory relationship as core and takes into account a range of contextual factors. These contextual factors include the client, the trainee, the supervisor and the institution. Holloway presents her model diagram-matically with the relationship at the centre. The role of the supervisor, or the task and function, is identified in the foreground and the four contextual factors are represented in the background. It is proposed that these seven dimensions or components of the model (relationship, client, trainee, super-visor, institution, tasks and function) are part of a dynamic process in that they mutually influence one another (hence, systems approach). Each factor can also be examined independently.

The SAS model addresses the complexity of the process of supervision and provides a map for analysing a particular episode of supervision in terms of (a) the nature of the task, (b) the function the supervisor is performing, (c) the nature of the relationship, and (d) the contextual factors relevant to the process.

Holloway (1995) has identified three elements within the relationship: (a) the interpersonal structure of the relationship, including the dimensions of power and involvement; (b) the phase of the relationship referring to the development of the relationship specific to the participants; (c) the super-visory contract which includes establishing a set of expectations regarding the tasks and functions of supervision.

Holloway defines the tasks of supervision as 'the body of professional knowledge requisite of the counsellor role' (1995: 12). She divides these into five broad areas: counselling skills, case conceptualization, professional role, emotional awareness and self-evaluation. The functions of supervi-sion are defined as the specialist or professional activity of the supervisor. The five main functions that the supervisor carries out during supervision are: monitoring/evaluating, instructing/advising, modelling, consulting, and supporting/sharing. Similar to the Discrimination Model, Holloway depicts the tasks and functions of supervision as a grid. She describes the inter-action of deciding what to teach (task) with how to teach it (function) as the process of supervision.

The supervisory relationship and the tasks and functions of supervision are influenced by contextual factors relating to the supervisor, the client, the supervisee and the institution. Supervisor factors include the supervisor's previous professional experience, their expectations regarding roles of supervisor and supervisee, their theoretical orientation, and cultural elements, including race, ethnicity, gender and self-presentation. Supervisee contextual factors include previous experience in counselling and use of supervision, theoretical orientation, supervisee learning style and needs, cultural characteristics and supervisee self-presentation. Client contextual factors include client characteristics, identified problem and diagnosis and the counselling relationship. Institutional contextual factors include organizational structure and climate, and professional ethics and standards.

Evidence base of the Systems Approach to Supervision

Unlike the previous two models described, the SAS cannot be criticized for simplicity. It is the first supervision-specific model that has attempted to place development and social role within the context of a supervisory relationship that is influenced by a range of contextual factors.

Holloway has based the model on existing evidence. However, as yet, there are no studies that have tested the whole model. The strength of the Holloway model is that she attempts to integrate the complexity of the supervisory relationship into her theory. This goes some way to respond to the plea from Ellis and Ladany (1997: 466) 'that until the unique qualities of the supervisory relationship are both acknowledged and integrated into theorising about the supervisory relationship our understanding will continue to falter'. However, there is still a long way to go to develop an evidence base that fully describes the supervisory relationship. In part, this is due to a lack of adequate instruments to measure the relationship in supervision.

There is some evidence to suggest that the structure of the relationship is predictable (Holloway, 1982), that social influence factors may have some impact on supervisor perceptions of supervisee performance (Carey et al., 1988), and that supervisees expect supervisors to be trustworthy, expert and attractive (Friedlander and Snyder, 1983). Trustworthiness accounted for the largest proportion of the variance in judgements about the relationship and was related to trainee performance with clients. In one of the few studies of clinical psychology trainees in Britain, D. R. Green (1998), using a qualitative research methodology, found that 'special knowledge', 'credibility' and 'integrity' were terms used by trainees to describe influential supervisors. He argues that these combined characteristics of sapiential authority are similar to the construct of trustworthiness. There is also some evidence to suggest that trainees who reported positive supervisory experiences were evaluated more highly by their supervisors (Kennard et al., 1987).

A series of microanalytic studies which use content analysis to understand the detailed interactions within supervision sessions draw the following conclusions: (a) supervision and counselling processes are distinct, (b) there are significant changes in discourse across the relationship, (c) there is a predominant pattern of verbal behaviours which resembles teacher/student interactions, and the structure of the supervisory relationship has hierarchical characteristics (Holloway and Poulin, 1995). There is also some recent evidence to suggest that goal-setting and providing specific instructions are associated with benefits to supervisees (Milne and James, 2000). The above findings provide some support for the hierarchical nature of the supervisory relationship, the role of social influence and the importance of a supervisory contract.

In summary, the SAS is the most comprehensive model of supervision to date but has not yet been fully tested. Each element of the model is based on existing research, but it is not clear how these various variables are interrelated. The strength of this model is that it provides an account of the supervisory relationship, which was missing in earlier models. There is mounting evidence to suggest that the supervisory relationship is key to supervisee experience of supervision, and possibly to performance in the workplace (Olk and Friedlander, 1992). The next section will explore models of the supervisory relationship, and their evidence base, in more detail.

Theoretical perspectives: models of the supervisory relationship

Hess (1987) stressed the importance of the supervisory relationship but clarified that it was not the supervision. The supervisory relationship is unique in that it comprises at least three people, client(s), therapist (supervisee) and supervisor. This has led to the concept of parallel process, which has its roots in psychodynamic supervision in the concepts of transference and counter-transference. Parallel process refers to the process or dynamics in the supervisory relationship replicating or mirroring those in the therapeutic relationship (Hawkins and Shohet, 1989). The concept of parallel process has been developed and expanded by systemic family therapists into isomorphism, which refers to relational and structural similarities between therapy and supervision rather than intrapsychic parallels. Although these concepts have been widely adopted in the practice of supervision within their respective psychotherapeutic traditions, there is very sparse empirical support for them (Bernard and Goodyear, 1998). The models of the supervisory relationship discussed in detail below refer to supervision specifically and are generic with regard to psychotherapeutic model.

Bordin's model of the supervisory working alliance

Bordin (1983) defines the working alliance as 'a collaboration for change' consisting of three aspects:

1   Mutual agreements and understanding of the goals.
2   The tasks of each of the partners.
3   The bonds between the partners.

Bordin suggests that the clarity and mutuality of the agreement contributes to the strength of the working alliance. Once goals are mutually agreed the tasks by which each of the participants may achieve those goals needs to be part of the mutual understanding. Bonds are associated with carrying out a common enterprise and sharing experience. Bordin argues that time spent together, mutual liking, caring and trusting, and the public/private dimension of the relationship influence the development of bonds. Bordin (1983: 38) lists the goals of the supervisory working alliance as follows:

1   Mastery of specific skills.
2   Enlarging understanding of clients.
3   Enlarging awareness of process issues.
4   Increasing awareness of self and impact on process.
5   Overcoming personal and intellectual obstacles toward learning and mastery.
6   Deepening understanding of concept and theory.
7   Providing a stimulus to research.
8   Maintaining the standards of service.

Bordin identifies three main tasks for the supervisee that include preparation of oral or written reports of their work, objective observation of therapeutic work (either direct, sound or videotaped recordings), and selection of problems and issues for presentation. The supervisor's tasks include coaching, giving feedback, focusing on areas of difficulty or gaps for the supervisee, and deepening theoretical or personal understanding. The supervisory process is managed through establishing the contract and providing mutual ongoing feedback and evaluation.

Evidence base of the supervisory working alliance

The main construct underlying the working alliance model is mutuality between supervisor and supervisee perceptions of the supervisory relationship. This has resulted in the development of useful measurement tools that explore both sides of the supervisory relationship; however, researchers have operationalized the supervisory working alliance differently. Efstation *et al.* (1990) define and measure the alliance as client focus, rapport, and identification from the supervisor's perspective and client focus and rapport from the supervisee's perspective. The supervisory working alliance was operationalized by Ladany and Friedlander (1995) as mutual agreement on the goals and tasks of supervision and emotional bond between supervisor and supervisee. Efstation *et al.* (1990) found that the supervisory working alliance was related to supervisor style (attractiveness, interpersonal sensitivity and task orientation) and supervisee self-efficacy. Ladany and Friedlander (1995) found that it was related to supervisee role conflict and ambiguity; that is, the supervisee experiencing competing or unclear role expectations. Ladany *et al.* (1996) found that the working alliance was also related to satisfaction with supervision.

Holloway's model of the supervisory relationship in a Systems Approach to Supervision

Holloway (1995) describes the relationship of supervision in more detail than any other current author. She also attempts to base it on available evidence:

> In the systems approach to supervision, relationship is the container of a dynamic process in which the supervisor and supervisee negotiate a personal way of using a structure of power and involvement that accommodates the supervisee's progression of learning. This structure becomes the basis for the process by which the supervisee will acquire knowledge and skills – the empowerment of the trainee.
>
> (Holloway, 1995: 41–42)

Holloway identifies three essential elements of the supervisory relationship:

1 Interpersonal structure of the relationship – the dimensions of power and involvement.
2 Phases of the relationship, relational developments specific to the participants.
3 Supervisory contracts – the establishment of a set of expectations for the tasks and functions of supervision.

Interpersonal structure

Supervision is seen as a formal relationship in which the supervisors' tasks include imparting expert knowledge, making judgements of trainees' performance and acting as gatekeepers to the profession. The supervisory relationship is hierarchical in the sense that these tasks suggest that power rests with the supervisor. The SAS interpersonal structure of the supervision relationship is based on Leary's (1957) Theory of Interpersonal Relations. This is described as power through involvement. Each individual brings to the relationship interpersonal histories that influence the level of involvement or attachment within the supervisory relationship. Affiliation influences the exercise and effect of power in the supervisory relationship and creates more individualized rather than role-bound relationships. Both supervisor and supervisee influence the distribution of power or the degree of attachment to one another.

Phases of the relationship

Based on the socio-psychological literature, Holloway argues that supervisory relationships develop over time from formal to informal interpersonal relationships. In the early phase participants rely on general sociocultural information about roles. However, as more information is gathered the relationship becomes more individualized and predictable. As the supervisory relationship evolves to a more interpersonal one there is reduced uncertainty and participants become more open and vulnerable and are more likely to self-disclose. Although supervision provides a general set of expectations, as the relationship develops it is individualized according to the learning needs of the supervisee and the teaching approaches of the supervisor. Each participant needs to learn the idiosyncratic reciprocal rules in interactive process. Holloway uses Mueller and Kell's (1972) conceptualization of the beginning, mature, and terminating phases of the supervisory relationship. The beginning phase consists of clarifying the relationship, establishing a supervision contract and working on specific competencies and treatment plans. During the mature phase the relationship becomes more individualized and less role-bound, which allows greater social bonding and influence. It also deals with developing formulation skills, working on self-confidence and exploring the personal/professional interface. The terminating phase allows increased autonomy and the need for less direction from the supervisor. The development of theory practice understanding in relation to specific clients is characteristic of this phase.

The supervisory contract

The supervisory contract is seen as important as a way of negotiating both goals and tasks but also parameters of the relationship. This clarifies both content and relational characteristics and establishes mutual expectations of the supervisory relationship. The evidence base of the Systems Approach to Supervision was discussed earlier and will not be repeated here.

Methodological issues

It is evident that research into supervision is complex and in its early stages. There have been several recent review papers that look at the effectiveness of supervision (Holloway and Neufeldt, 1995; Ellis *et al.*, 1996; Ellis and Ladany, 1997; Neufeldt *et al.*, 1997; Lambert and Ogles, 1997).

Holloway and Neufeldt (1995) argue that although there is evidence to support supervision enhancing psychotherapeutic skills in supervisees few studies exist which relate the role of supervision to client change. Ellis *et al.* (1996) provide a methodological critique of supervision research from 1981 to 1993. They examined 144 clinical supervision studies and concluded that the majority of the studies were not based on theory, did not test clear hypotheses, used unvalidated measures and were beset with Type 1 and 2 errors. They found that investigations of supervision were unlikely to detect true effects and very likely to find spurious significant results. They also identified features of a well-designed supervision study for use in future research.

Ellis *et al.* (1996) suggest that methodologically sound studies should aim to test specific theories or models of supervision and develop clear research questions and hypotheses informed by these theories or models. Methodologies should attend to the representativeness of the sample, use longitudinal designs to test developmental models, use psychometrically sound measures appropriate to the supervision context and attend to statistical power; that is, control Type 2 error. They also stress the importance of internal consistency of aims, hypotheses, method and analyses. Data analyses should ensure that the assumptions of statistical tests are met and that the tests relate directly to the hypotheses. The interpretation of results should attend to the strengths as well as the weaknesses of the study, explore alternative explanations and discuss the generalizability of the results.

Clearly this advice falls into the positivistic and quantitative research tradition, but the issues raised about good-quality research are equally valid for qualitative research methodologies, which should be rigorous within their own context.

Lambert and Ogles (1997), in their comprehensive review of the effectiveness of psychotherapy supervision, conclude that it is tempting to assume on the basis of psychotherapy research that training and supervision are effective. They warn that there are no good outcome studies that make a clear connection between training and therapy outcome. In particular, it is not known how elements of training programmes such as teaching, supervision or practice contribute to the development of effective practitioners.

The methodological issues inherent in this field of research are complex. Ellis and Ladany (1997) conclude that the overall quality of research over the past 15 years has been 'sub-standard'. There is a general lack of replicated studies and huge conceptual and methodological problems within the studies. Although there are many theories and many studies, much of the research is atheoretical or does not explicitly test theory. Ellis and Ladany found that only seven theories had been explicitly tested, and only two of those on more than two occasions. The absence of replication studies makes it difficult to establish the value of the theories or previous findings. A final methodological issue within supervision research is the lack of viable measures specific to clinical supervision. There are very few measures that assess supervisee competence, evaluate supervisee performance or measure the quality of the supervisory relationship. Although new measures are beginning to be developed their psychometric properties are as yet unclear.

Until recently (for example, D. R. Green, 1998; Milne and James, 1999, 2000), there has been very little research about the evidence base for clinical supervision for clinical psychology in the UK. Much of the theory and research discussed above stems from the USA and is based on the psychotherapy, counselling and counselling psychology literature. It is unclear how generalizable findings from counselling and psychotherapy are to clinical psychology; for example, Lawton and Feltham (2000), suggest that supervision in counselling is more process-focused than supervision in clinical psychology; which tends to be more goal-oriented. Similarly, training methods and routes in the USA (Cherry *et al.*, 2000) are dissimilar to those in the UK, particularly with regard to the way clinical placements are structured, supervised and monitored, and hence findings may not be generalizable.

A grounded theory of the supervisory relationship

Recent research by the author (Beinart, 2002) explored the factors that predict the quality of the supervisory relationship and attempted to meet the qualities of a methodologically sound study, as described above. The study tested aspects of the two models of the supervisory relationship described earlier (Bordin, 1983; Holloway, 1995). The study used both quantitative and qualitative methodologies to answer the main research question that asked supervisees to rate and describe the characteristics and qualities of the supervisory relationships that had contributed most and least to their effectiveness as a clinical psychologist. A sample of clinical psychology trainees and newly qualified clinical psychologists (up to two years post-qualification) from the South of England was used. Data was collected on just under a hundred supervisory relationships.

The quantitative study found that satisfaction with supervision, rapport between supervisee and supervisor, and the supervisee feeling supported by the supervisor were the main qualities of supervisory relationships perceived to be most effective by supervisees.

A grounded theory analysis of the qualitative data, derived from written answers to open-ended questions about the quality of the supervisory relationship, suggested that there were nine categories that described the supervisory relationship. These were: boundaried, supportive, respectful, open relationship, committed, sensitive to needs, collaborative, educative and evaluative.

A grounded theory was developed that proposed that a framework for the supervisory relationship needed to be in place for the process or business of supervision to occur. The main aspect of the framework was the development of a boundaried relationship. This included both structural boundaries, such as time, place and frequency of supervision, and personal/professional boundaries that enabled the supervisee to feel emotionally contained within the supervisory relationship. The other aspects of the framework were the development of a mutually respectful, supportive and open relationship, where the supervisee felt that the supervisor was committed to the supervision, and regular two-way feedback. The model was adapted from Rogers's (1957) concept of necessary and sufficient conditions of therapeutic change. In supervision certain optimal relationship conditions seem necessary for the more formal process of supervision to take place effectively.

Clinical psychology supervisees described a strong preference for collaborative supervisory relationships where both parties were involved in setting the agenda and the goals of supervision. A certain amount of flexibility of both approach and therapeutic model seemed to aid the collaboration. The two tasks of education and evaluation were helped if the supervisor was sensitive to the supervisee's needs, both in terms of their previous experience and stage of training and the personal impact of the work. Unlike previous studies (e.g. D. R. Green, 1998) the wisdom and experience of the supervisor seemed less important than opportunities to observe the supervisor's work and have curious and stimulating discussions. The most important aspect of the educative code seemed to be collaborative work on formulation, which included theory–practice links. Again, flexibility was important to supervisees who found didactic supervision or inflexible adherence to models less helpful. Interestingly, the evaluative aspect of supervision was only an issue in poorer-quality supervisory relationships. Supervisees valued and appreciated feedback and challenge in good collaborative relationships, and the formal elements of evaluation did not seem to impact on this.

Implications and conclusions

This chapter has described a selection of generic models of supervision and the supervisory relationship in some detail. It has presented the evidence base for the models and the complexity and difficulties of supervision research, which raise a range of methodological issues. A brief discussion of the author's recent research followed. What are the implications of these discussions and findings for clinical psychologists, supervisors and supervisees? Clearly, and as always, there is a need for more good-quality research and better theory development based on this research. There is an enormous amount of practitioner experience that can and does add to the existing body of knowledge.

Findings are beginning to emerge about what is and is not helpful in supervisory relationships. Unsurprisingly, helpful supervisory relationships seem to be rather similar to other good relationships and are based on mutual trust and respect. The research described above suggests that it is worth taking the time at the beginning of the relationship to establish rapport. Contracting and the exploration of expectations and hopes are helpful in the development of effective supervisory relationships. Setting clear boundaries, both in terms of structure and what can be brought to supervision, is helpful. The supervisor maintaining interest and curiosity and showing some commitment to making the process work seems necessary for good relationships to develop. Conversely, it is not helpful to display a lack of interest or commitment to supervision, often displayed by turning up late and not maintaining the structural boundaries that might be expected. Neither is it helpful to ignore the power relationship inherent in the supervisory relationship, which can make it difficult for supervisees to address issues such as persistent interruptions or lateness. It is worthwhile to set aside time at the beginning of a new supervisory relationship to address the needs of a particular supervisee and clarify expectations on both sides. It is not helpful to assume that supervisees will be similar and will find similar support or interventions equally helpful.

Supervisees need to take responsibility for taking an active part in supervision. This involves playing a part in a collaborative relationship, showing interest and enthusiasm, identifying needs clearly, arriving at a supervision meeting properly prepared having thought through issues and priorities, being open and receptive to feedback and being prepared to give clear and honest feedback to the supervisor. It is not helpful when supervisees fail to raise issues that they are struggling with, get defensive when offered feedback or do not take the advice of their supervisor without good reason or discussion.

The findings on the supervisory relationship described above also have implications for clinical psychology training courses and the content of supervisor training programmes. Courses may benefit from paying attention to the development of effective supervisory relationships by providing training for supervisors and supervisees and specifically monitoring the development of these relationships. Hopefully the developing evidence base will provide some guidance to tutors who undertake these tasks on behalf of courses.

This chapter began by suggesting that many supervisors depend on their existing and transferable relationship skills when they begin supervising. Hopefully, this chapter has provided some models and evidence to help guide supervision practice. What is encouraging about the research described, for a profession in the midst of rapid expansion, is that supervisees do not necessarily find expert supervision most effective, they perceive boundaried and collaborative supervisory relationships to be most helpful and most psychologists are good at these.

Chapter 4

Enhancing the quality and availability of clinical psychology training placements within the NHS[1]

Graham Turpin, Joyce Scaife and Peter Rajan

Acknowledgements

Much of the thinking within this chapter has emerged following the Trent Region Placement Project commissioned by the Trent NHS Workforce Development Confederation. We are particularly grateful to Jane Johnson and Di Bulter from the Confederation in supporting this project and also to local clinical psychologists for co-ordinating and participating within the research. We are also grateful for permission to quote from the North & Central London NHS Workforce Development Confederation Clinical Psychology Placement Project Report.

Introduction

The last decade has witnessed major changes to the training of clinical psychologists within both the health service and higher education sectors. There has been a universal shift to three years of postgraduate training resulting in the award of a professional doctorate in clinical psychology. Both the size and number of doctoral training programmes have increased and the divide between university-based education and in-service training has disappeared, with all programmes being based within universities and supported by a system of resourcing and contracting by the NHS. The importance and sophistication of workforce planning within the NHS has also developed, evolving from educational contracts (Working Paper 10, 1989) through education consortia (NHSE, 1995) to workforce confederations (DH, 2000a, 2002).

This has all culminated in major opportunities for the profession of clinical psychology to develop and expand, and in doing so to attempt to meet the needs for psychological health care within the NHS. At the same time, the demand for psychological health care from the service has also increased, resulting in psychological care being emphasized within many recent National Service Frameworks and the National Plan (DH, 1998b). The demands have also diversified so that clinical psychology is no longer synonymous with the provision of adult mental health services but also makes major contributions to services for children and adolescents, older people, people with a learning disability, the brain-injured, and a broad spectrum of clinical health psychology services ranging from oncology through to cardiac rehabilitation. These increased demands have consequently led to a chronic undersupply of qualified clinical psychologists to the NHS, and the resulting vacancy rates of around 25 per cent have become a long-standing feature of the profession's employment profile (MAS, 1989). Various initiatives have been suggested in the last decade (e.g. BPS, 1995c) to meet this supply problem and to expand the training capacity of programmes. Although the resources to fund these new initiatives have not always been forthcoming, developments in workforce planning within the Department of Health have led to a slow improvement in the availability of resources to support expansion. Indeed, we have now achieved a doubling of training numbers from around 180 places for England in the early 1990s to around 400 in 2001 (Turpin, 1997; BPS, 2001a). Moreover, the implementation of National Plan targets for the Allied Health Professions workforce would suggest further dramatic expansion in training places. A recent BPS consultation paper, based on discussions with the Department of Health (BPS, 2001a; Gray, 2001), suggested possible targets of between 550 and 680 training places by 2003. Similarly, the BPS (2001b) has also published general guidance on methods of workforce planning for clinical psychologists at a local level. Hopefully, the better integration of service planning with workforce development through the establishment of workforce action teams (DH, 2001a) will likely lead to increased forecasts in the demand for qualified professional psychologists.

We have arrived, therefore, at a situation whereby resources alone are not the major barrier to course expansion and professional development. As was pointed out recently by the BPS (2001a), the real obstacles to further expansion in training are placement availability and supervision resources, physical resources for programmes (e.g. teaching rooms) and scarcity of clinical academic staff. If future expansion is to go ahead as planned, it will become necessary to consider how the provision of clinical psychology training might be adapted in order to achieve these substantial increases in training numbers. Other issues may also be identified which may impact upon training programmes within the next decade. These include the development of occupational standards across the whole of applied psychology (BPS, 1998b, 2001c), developments in e-learning and continuing professional development (DH, 2001b), the shortage of clinical placements within the NHS generally (Cheesman, 2001; ENB/DH, 2001), the modernization agenda (DH, 2000b) and the increasing importance of inter-professional learning (DH, 2001b, 2001c; Miller et al., 2001). The purpose of this chapter is to focus on the impact of increasing training demands on the provision of clinical placements and supervision, and to identify the barriers to placement provision and how these might be resolved in order to enhance both the availability and quality of supervised clinical placements.

Finally, we should acknowledge that whilst the reports and policy documents published by the BPS are relevant to the UK generally, differences exist in the organization of health services across the home nations. We have tended to focus on Department of Health policies and procedures, which only directly influence England.

Nevertheless, the issues discussed here have relevance across the home nations of the UK and may also be of interest to the Irish Health Boards. For psychologists working outside England, various reports and reviews have been commissioned by the Scottish and Welsh Assemblies, and these would clearly be of relevance (e.g. NHS Scotland, 2002). In particular, the recent and comprehensive *Clinical Psychology Workforce Planning Report* for the NHS in Scotland (NHS Scotland, 2002) makes a range of recommendations on how the psychology workforce can be strategically developed at both national and local levels. Various innovative initiatives have been identified and include assessing psychological need and its workforce implications at a local planning level, special circumstances of rural communities, retraining other psychologists or professions, etc., and clearly merit careful consideration outside Scotland.

Constraints on placement availability

Clinical psychology training within the UK has stressed the importance of theory–practice links, and the design of programmes has always been heavily influenced by the necessity of trainees undertaking a series of clinical placements supervised by a qualified clinical psychologist. Requirements and standards for placement experience are determined by the Committee on Training in Clinical Psychology of the BPS and are published as the Criteria for Programme Accreditation (BPS, 2002a). Prior to the widespread introduction of three-year training programmes in the early 1990s, placements within the traditional two-year M.Sc. university programme were usually around three months in duration and mandatory experience included work with adults, children and people with learning disabilities. With the standardization of training to three years and the revision of the CTCP criteria in 1989, an additional mandatory area of supervised experience working with older people was included within the criteria reinforcing the lifespan development basis around which the criteria had been originally established. Clinical placement experience was expected to constitute between 50 and 60 per cent of programme time and was usually arranged as two five-month placements each year, constituting three days a week within the NHS. Minimum criteria were also developed for placement experience within each of the 'core placement areas' (e.g. adult mental health), although it was agreed that core experience need not be obtained within a single placement but could be acquired throughout the three years of training.

Until recently, most training programmes operated a system of clinical placements constrained by the above criteria. The content of placements was frequently organized to integrate with university teaching. For example, at the North Trent/University of Sheffield programme, trainees would undertake placements with adults and older adults in the first year, children/adolescents and people with learning disabilities in the second year, and elective placements which they choose individually within the third year. Nearly all supervisors would be qualified (i.e. at least two years) clinical psychologists and supervision would normally be one-to-one. Placements would be identified by clinical tutors and were individually planned directly with the supervisor on a voluntary basis. The work provided by the trainee was seen as supernumerary.

What are the constraints of the present system as described above? The major problem that has arisen concerns the shortage of qualified staff within some of the specialities that are considered as mandatory or core within the criteria. Although the pattern of shortages is not universal and some courses may experience unique local shortages in some clinical specialities, the general pattern of placement provision is oversupply of adult placements, around adequate supply of child and adolescent placements, and major shortages within placements in services for either people with learning disabilities or older people. For example, as part of the BPS Options Project, courses were surveyed in 1994 about their ability to provide adequate numbers of placements, together with questions regarding how accreditation criteria might impact on availability. This work was subsequently published (Turpin, 1995). At that time programmes within England identified 1,970 potential supervisors of whom 1,310 (66 per cent) were regular supervisors. For Scotland and Wales the numbers were between 69 and 187, but the percentage uptake of supervisors was about the same. At that time, the annual intake size for programmes in England was between 189 and 224 depending on the year. It would appear, therefore, that there were around 700 trainees at any one time, and that around 1,400 placements would, therefore, be required. Assuming that supervisors might provide two placements per year, overall there was a potential supervisory resource of 3,950 placements of which 2,620 might regularly be provided. Superficially this would suggest that there was spare capacity within the supervision system and that there was potential to double the number of training commissions. Unfortunately, these figures do not take account of the availability of placements across each of the core areas of placement experience. The distribution of regular supervisors across specialities is very uneven: adults (38 per cent), children (26 per cent), learning disabilities (21 per cent) and older people (15 per cent). Despite the fact that a much higher proportion of supervisors in both older adults and learning disabilities supervise, and many offer two placements a year, the scarcity of staff and placements within these specialities constrains the overall capacity of the training system, assuming that all trainees are required to undertake mandatory placements/experience within these clinical specialisms. Indeed, 91 per cent of courses identified placements for older adults as being the major obstacle for course expansion within the UK. A follow-up survey conducted by Gray (1997) two years later reported very similar findings with respect to overall capacity and the availability across specialisms.

Although these surveys were conducted over five years ago, the situation has changed very little. In several recent placement projects, which will be highlighted in the following section, placements working with older people represent the speciality in shortest supply. An adequate number of placements can only be realized if all supervisors provide placements, continuously and with more than one trainee being supervised. Even with this level of commitment, it is unlikely that sufficient placements would be available to meet the demand for training places identified by some work force planning models under the National Plan.

Realizing the potential

Recently the training community has been carefully exploring options whereby continuing expansion might be achieved. The process commenced in 1995 with the Options Project (BPS, 1995c), which examined different models of training and sources of funding. Among the options that were considered by the profession in 1995 were the following: in-service training, part-time modular courses, student bursaries, distance learning, assistant psychology training and accreditation, etc. Since 1995 the CTCP criteria have been amended to allow non-clinical psychologists to be involved in supervision, to allow for supervision models other than 1:1, to shorten the minimum requirement for supervision to one year post-qualification in certain circumstances, and to re-emphasize the flexibility of organizing core experience throughout training rather than restricting it to a single placement (Ashcroft and Callanan, 1997; Ashcroft *et al.*, 1998). More recently, the BPS discussion document *Expanding Clinical Psychology Training* (BPS, 2001a) identified several different strategic directions: these included expanding programmes around the existing training model, developing new courses, optimizing programmes around a new more flexible model of placement provision, and developing a second tier of professional practice. The latter solution concerns the employment and training of assistant or associate psychologists who would deliver limited psychological interventions under the supervision of a qualified psychologist.

The solution which was considered to be the most appropriate and also most likely to impact on training capacity quickly was the proposal to reorganize training around the 'competence-based' model. This model is essentially a radical approach to specifying the learning outcomes in which trainees should have demonstrated competence when graduating from a programme. This is in contrast to the current (2002) system whereby trainees 'serve their time' and are assessed as performing adequately within a particular speciality but where there is little detailed assessment of specific learning outcomes within that speciality. Such models have been around for a long time in vocational education and skills training and typify National Vocational Qualifications (Bartram, 1995) and the development of occupational standards across different professions (DH, 2001a). This is particularly the case for generic standards for mental health workers as represented by the work of the Sainsbury Centre for Mental Health and Healthwork UK (DH, 2001a; SCMH, 2001). These ideas have also been applied within psychology with respect to both NVQs and Occupational Standards (BPS, 1998b, 2001a), although the ease with which these concepts can be transferred to a doctoral/post graduate level professional training programmes is a source of some continuing debate (Hingley, 1995). For example, the NVQ model has really only been tried and tested against vocational skills and lacks sufficient emphasis on knowledge and the application of higher order skills involving more abstract levels of analysis and action. The use of skills assessments and competency checklists has also been considered inappropriate for the measurement of professional skills performed at a higher level of abstraction and application of knowledge. Hence, there is some scepticism within the profession as to whether these models can adequately account for professional and therapeutic skills and roles.

At the same time as 'competence-models' were being entertained as a better basis for organizing and assessing clinical experience, a growing dissatisfaction with the traditional 'four core placements model' was growing. Programmes were keen to remove the CTCP constraints, which limited the size of intakes by the minimum availability of core placements, usually placements working with either older people or people with learning disabilities. Staff in newly emergent specialisms such as clinical health psychology or psychosocial rehabilitation (Ledwith and Stowers, 2001) questioned whether they should also be involved in providing compulsory core experience alongside the existing four. Even within core specialisms, supervisors were finding it increasingly difficult to provide the minimum core experiences since their jobs had become more specialized and clinically focused. Indeed, there was a sense that core experiences were forcing the profession to adopt a model of placement experience that was constrained and based upon job descriptions designed some 20 years ago. Moreover, the ever-increasing diversity of clinical psychology services led some to question whether core experience in particular specialisms was any longer feasible. Instead, it has been suggested that there should be an emphasis on the application of psychological skills and knowledge generically to clinical problems and not constrained directly by different clinical specialities. Trainees would be required to apply their knowledge across ranges of ages, disabilities and service models, rather than to serve their time within a fixed number of core placements.

The desire to overhaul the accreditation criteria surrounding placement experience led to the establishment of a BPS Working Group, chaired by Malcolm Adams (Adams, 2001), with the task of re-examining the criteria around a competence-based framework and to consult widely within the profession about the acceptability of any changes. A final set of criteria have recently been endorsed by the Society (BPS, 2002a). As a result of some of the criticisms of competence-based models, the newly proposed criteria were formulated around a matrix of learning outcomes which specify the know-ledge and skills to be acquired by a trainee in order to meet, on graduation, the occupational standards for the profession. The new criteria describe a framework for various pathways through training, delineating client popula-tions, clinical contexts and learning outcomes which contribute to a generic training in Clinical Psychology. A flavour of this framework is provided by the following selective quotation from the criteria:

> Clinical experience will be gained in service delivery systems that offer a coherent clinical context. This will usually be a setting oriented towards a population defined by age (e.g. child, adult, older people) by special needs (e.g. learning disabilities, serious mental health prob-lems, health-related problems, substance abuse) or by a service delivery focus (e.g. psychological therapy). In addition, clinical experience will be gained in a range of service contexts (primary, secondary and tertiary care, in-patient, out-patient, community), with service delivery models ranging from independently organised work through to integrated inter-professional working.
>
> (BPS, 2002a: 7)

There have also been some doubts about the appropriateness of the new criteria and how they might work in practice. The major concern has been from the Older People and Learning Disabilities Special Interest Groups who are determined to preserve compulsory training experiences with these often poorly resourced client groups. Concerns have also been raised about moving away from generic training, difficulties recruiting trainees to these under-represented and staffed specialities within the NHS, and the organiza-tional and practical difficulties that might be encountered if formal placements were disbanded (see Adams, 2001).

A compromise solution has been carefully negotiated which seeks to main-tain the usage of all 'core placements' and to ensure that placements in either learning disabilities or older adults are not under-used. It is likely that individual programmes will have sufficient leeway to determine the extent to which they wish to embrace the 'competence-based model'. Different courses might evolve different approaches, some relying on detailed schemes of competence-based placements and assessments, others perhaps just extend-ing their definitions of core placements to also include health psychology, neuropsychology, forensic, psychosocial rehabilitation, etc.

It needs to be emphasized that the adoption of a 'competence-based model' for clinical placements may also have a profound effect on how trainees are assessed and on the structure of the curriculum. The present traditional system of fixed mandatory placements possessed the advantage that teaching usually preceded placement experience and hence was oriented at preparing trainees for work with specific client groups. Greater flexibility of placement provision will mean that programmes will have greater difficulty providing a uniform curriculum in order to prepare trainees for their forthcoming placements. Courses that are considering fully embracing the 'competence-based model' are likely to have to introduce major changes in the design of their curriculum.

We hope that we have introduced the background underlying placement availability issues and some of the more recently discussed solutions. Before suggesting which of these might be usefully developed within training courses, we would like to report the results of some studies which have empirically investigated these issues further. From the data that has already been presented, it is clear that just above 60 per cent of the profession are engaged in supervision. This raises the question as to why the remaining 40 per cent are not so engaged. Is this lack of involvement due to lack of placement resources, lack of training, incompatible job roles, negative attitudes, poor management practices, etc? In order to maximize our supervisory potential, not only do we need to free up flexibility around core placements but we must also ensure that we maximize the involvement of the qualified clinical psychology workforce. Moreover, we need to consider not only the quantity of available supervision resources but also its quality! What resources and training are required to provide good quality and effective supervision to trainee psychologists? Are these quality standards being met within the NHS and, if not, what management practices might be preventing their attainment? Questions such as these have been addressed in a number of local research projects designed to look at factors surrounding placement provision. The following section will summarize some of the themes emerging from this work; finally we will examine the recommendations for good practice emerging from this work.

Lessons from the placement projects

With the planned expansion of clinical psychology training resulting from the NHS National Plan (BPS, 2001a), the training community within England began to consider how it might achieve a significant increase in training numbers. During 2000/01 a number of projects were developed and funded by the NHS Workforce Confederations to consider methods for expanding training whilst maintaining or improving quality by identifying obstacles to developing placement capacity and methods for resolving them.

In this section we will outline some of the issues highlighted by two such projects: the Trent Clinical Psychology Placement Project (Rajan *et al.*, 2002), hereafter called the Trent Project, and The North & Central London Workforce Confederation Clinical Psychology Placement Project (Dooley *et al.*, 2002), hereafter called the London Project (covering the London region, Kent, Surrey and part of Sussex). Although the two projects adopted differing methodologies, both included university and service staff on their project teams, emphasizing the collaborative nature of clinical psychology training. They both sought to identify the placement resource available to the several programmes, which provided training within the Workforce Confederation areas under consideration, and surveyed supervisors concerned, in order to identify obstacles to expanding placement provision. Additionally both projects sought the views of managers and clinical psychologists with regard to possible ways in which placement availability might be enhanced.

The Trent Project initially utilized questionnaires asking all clinical psychologists identified on a pre-existing database maintained within the region about their availability to provide placements in the next academic year. Respondents were also asked to identify their perceived barriers to placement provision. The survey was able to account for 95 per cent of the 347 clinical psychologists registered on the database. A second phase of the project employed local clinical psychologists to interview supervisors and managers about their attitudes towards and knowledge of clinical psychology training using a semi-structured interview. The London Project, covering seven confederation areas, intended to make telephone contact with all potential supervisors. This method proved unworkable because staff couldn't be recruited to do this work, so postal contact was used to supplement the data collection. Both projects included services which vary considerably in size, which emphasizes the fact that there is no standardized unit of clinical psychology service organization. This may give rise not only to a methodological consideration for the studies but also indicates that many clinical psychology services have recently been or are in the process of reorganization. This is partly due to the development of new provider organizations such as Primary Care Trusts and specialist Mental Health Trusts. The days of the 'District Department' are now gone, and thus there is no simple process by which programmes are able to access high-quality information regarding the workforce and available supervisors.

Availability of core placement experience

The London Project identified whole-time equivalents in their area (see Table 4.1). These data mirror the national picture in as much as there are many more clinical psychologists potentially available to provide adult and child core placement experience than is the case for older adult and learning disability placements. Similar findings were gathered in the Trent Project

Table 4.1 The London Project: whole-time equivalents

Speciality	Adult*	Child and adolescent	Older adult	Learning disability
Whole-time equiv.	398	266	112	105

Note: * The category 'Adult' refers generally to adult mental health work but might include some specialist work (e.g. HIV) if supervisors worked within a large adult speciality but excluded specialist areas in larger trusts where these were in a different unit/directorate. Hence the figures might be an underestimate depending on the definition of 'adult'.

confirming that with the usual model of core placement experience and one-to-one supervision, the availability of older adult and learning disability supervisors is a major limiting factor. Both projects also identified that these supervisors provide almost twice as many placements per supervisor than their colleagues in other specialities. This is due to supervisors in older adults and learning disabilities frequently supervising 'back-to-back' and sometimes taking more than one trainee at a time.

Attrition

The theoretical size of the supervisor pool does not in practice match the availability of placements. In the London Project, across all NHS trusts and specialities, 54 per cent of the potential supervisor pool is lost due to a combination of factors, including vacancies (15 per cent), clinical psychology posts filled by non-qualified or non-fully qualified staff (14 per cent), staff not yet eligible to supervise (11 per cent), and other factors such as sickness and staff holding managerial posts (14 per cent). The Trent Project revealed a similar finding of 45 per cent, and this was made up of staff who had left the service or were absent through ill health (9 per cent), those unavailable for supervision (31 per cent) and non-responders (5 per cent). The reasons for the lack of availability of supervisors identified within the Trent Project will be discussed later. Interestingly, the London Project did not attempt to estimate the numbers of potential supervisors who in practice refused to supervise.

In addition, the Trent Project assessed attrition by following up those supervisors who had said that they would be available to provide placements, but subsequently withdrew the offer, and found a loss of between 15–20 per cent of potential supervisors. All in all it seems that potential placement availability is compromised by a range of factors and there is no simple relationship between number of potential supervisors and the availability of placements. Indeed, it would appear that we can predict that around 50 per cent of supervisors, due to various reasons, are unavailable to provide placements at any one time.

Barriers to placements

The Trent Project asked potential supervisors who said they were unavailable to provide placements to indicate the factors that prevented them from doing so. They were provided with three categories (i.e. practical, personal and organizational) and asked to indicate which of these were relevant. Organizational issues such as job descriptions, managerial roles and/or work pressures provided relatively few barriers. Personal factors such as lack of years' service for eligibility to supervise, lack of supervision training and/or personal plans provided additional barriers. However, out of the three categories it was practical problems such as lack of office and clinical space that figured most highly. Supervisors who were able to offer placements also indicated barriers to effective placement provision, and when these two groups were combined, a total of 27 per cent of respondents cited lack of office space, 17 per cent a lack of clinical space and 9 per cent a lack of clerical support. Similarly the London Project cited lack of accommodation as a 'serious impediment', resulting in an estimated loss of 10–20 per cent of potential placements in the adult speciality.

Attitudes to training

Both projects considered the views of clinical psychologists and managers towards training and any potential expansion. Within Trent these views were identified by a stakeholders' conference, followed by semi-structured interviews with a sample of managers (including chief executives) and a sample of clinicians. These interviews were carried out by local clinicians who were recruited to link to local services in order to promote the identification of the project with their services. In the London Project telephone interviews were held with professional heads of psychology services representing 41 NHS trusts.

In Central & North London 78 per cent of services were going through or had just experienced major organizational change. Within Trent, it was felt that the reorganization of trusts, together with the implementation of the various National Service Frameworks, was dominating senior managers' thinking, and although these managers had some knowledge of the general move to modernize clinical psychology training it did not figure very highly on their agendas. Although general managers expressed support for clinical psychology as a profession, they seemed to have little specific knowledge of the size of the workforce they employed or issues relating specifically to clinical psychology training. Within Trent, some psychologists were concerned that changing from the current core experience model with one-to-one placements would lead to a loss of quality in training, although there was some support for the notion of redefining what constitutes core placement experience, especially the possibility of using specialist supervisors to provide 'core placements'. Both projects identified the need for NHS management to consider the impact of training on resources such as accommodation and clerical support. They also identified the need for both psychology and general managers to find ways for supervisors to accommodate the additional workload of trainee supervision within their workplans. This might require consideration of reducing the clinical caseloads of supervisors taking trainees on placement.

The projects highlighted the need to formalize the procedures for planning and utilising the placement resource. Suggestions included service level agreements, better co-ordination by having confederation-wide placement planning in order to avoid competition for placements between programmes, employing local training co-coordinators within NHS trusts, more use of part-time staff not currently used by having one main supervisor working alongside other supplementary supervisors to provide a component of the experience. Within Trent the potential for the development of 'accredited training units' formed from several small or a single larger department(s) was also raised.

Quality

A concern for quality was also indicated by clinicians who recommended, for example, more supervisor training, using group supervision in addition to but not instead of one-to-one supervision, and a desire to take change one step at a time and evaluate what works. Both projects considered developing standards for placements, and the London Project specifically built upon the BPS accreditation criteria, together with recommendations from an earlier study conducted by the Salomons Clinical Psychology Training Programme. The following criteria were recommended to be adopted within the London region:

1   Access to (at least) a shared office space (i.e. use of a shared desk and telephone).
2   Provision of local, accessible and lockable storage space, e.g. one drawer of a filing cabinet in which to keep client records (when appropriate) and other clinical or placement material.
3   Access to a computer for word processing as required for writing reports, letters, etc. This may be shared with others and may need to be booked.
4   Clinical rooms for client work that can be booked on a regular basis. These should be adequately furnished, safe, private and with a suitable reception facility. The amount of time needed will vary between specialities and placements.
5   Secretarial/administrative support for work not done on word processing; e.g. appointment letters, urgent client matters, booking of rooms and other administrative activities linked to the placement activity.

Although establishing standards for placements was an objective of the Trent Project, consultation with supervisors indicated that although there was agreement that this was needed there was some reluctance to take this forward at this point in time. This was due to concern that at a time of potential expansion, placement capacity could be lost rather than gained if significant numbers of placements could not fulfil these standards. Rather, staff recognised the existence of the BPS standards, which could be referred to as necessary.

Summary

It is clear from these projects that resolving one issue alone will not be sufficient to solve placement availability problems. There are a set of inter-connected issues that need to be dealt with adequately. These include:

*   Revising the model of core placement experiences and the competence framework.
*   Perceived location of responsibility for placement provision.
*   Arrangements for placement planning and co-ordination.
*   Agreements between universities and the service regarding placements.
*   Practical resources to support trainees and departments whilst trainees are on placement.

Whilst the profession has responsibility to develop best-practice training models, the Workforce Development Confederations (WDCs) within the NHS have the responsibility to provide support and resources in a number of key areas. The major recommendations reached by the Trent Project were that WDCs might:

*   Raise awareness about clinical psychology training issues for managers of NHS trusts and Primary Care trusts.
*   Establish confederation-wide structures for the planning and co-ordination of placements. Supra-confederation structures might be necessary for co-ordinating placements within small professions such as clinical psychology.
*   To provide resources targeted at supervisors to support placements (i.e. a non-medical equivalent of SIFT whereby NHS trusts and hospitals providing resources for medical education were funded specifically for taking on these additional responsibilities).
*   To make resources available to local Special Interest Groups to work with programmes on developing and revising core placements in order to facilitate more placements alongside the proposed revision of the curriculum.

Conclusions and recommendations

What can be done to maximize supervisory resources?

The studies described above identify a number of key issues that are crucial to the development and expansion of supervisory resources for clinical psychology training in the UK. Some require a more radical approach than others and all rely on the co-operation of the stakeholders in the training process. Purchasers need to identify additional resources in order to facilitate the provision of placements in NHS trusts; programmes need to be prepared to restructure not only placement organization but the nature of the curriculum and the way in which it is taught. NHS clinical psychology departments and supervisors need to acknowledge the central role that they play in training and that they are the ultimate beneficiaries in having a well-trained workforce from which to recruit.

Keeping track of potential placement supervisors

With the expansion in numbers of qualified clinical psychologists working within the NHS, repeated reorganization of NHS trusts and their arrangements for employing staff, plus changes in regional boundaries, it has become increasingly difficult for programmes to keep up to date with staff who constitute the potential supervisory resource. The University of Sheffield maintains a database on behalf of the former Trent region, funded by the Trent NHS Workforce Development Confederation and accessible by local clinicians, the Confederation, trainees and the regional DCP. It is updated on an *ad hoc* basis and from information provided by programme administrators, trust departmental secretaries and local representatives on programme training committees and special interest groups. It is invaluable in helping programmes to plan placements. Confederations elsewhere could be encouraged to fund the establishment and maintenance of such a resource.

Future developments in the profession of clinical psychology

The expansion of clinical psychology, both in terms of the numbers of people entering the profession and in the roles and tasks that its members undertake, has meant that there is now a great diversity of specialism and role. New applications of psychology in health care settings continue to evolve and even without the impetus to expand training numbers, congruent models of training need to be developed to ensure that recruits fit professional requirements.

The traditional core specialisms of the profession have become multiple specialisms. For example, a child placement could now be with a CAFTS team, in a Child Development Centre, in a Home Start programme, working with looked-after children, or in a tier 4 specialist in-patient unit. Each of these involves significantly different work, and a trainee in one setting will gain a very different experience and learn some different skills from a trainee working in another. The number of people in post working with physical health problems may well exceed those in some of the traditional core specialisms, and these changes need to be reflected in the manner in which practice placements are provided for new recruits. An advantage of the 'competence-based model' is that it emphasizes commonalities in the skills and knowledge required to practise both across and within particular specialisms rather than a progressive differentiation of skills for particular client groups. It is hoped that this approach might give rise to a less fractionated and more integrated curriculum, which might facilitate trainees extending knowledge acquired in one service context and with a particular client group to a new client group or emerging service demand (e.g. asylum seekers) not previously anticipated.

Finally, clinical psychologists also need to be mindful of more general developments in applied psychology and particularly how professional psychology practice is emerging within the European Union. Within the UK, the increasing numbers of other applied psychologists (e.g. counselling and health psychologists) working within the NHS will provide opportunities for supervision across the family of applied psychologists but may also give rise to greater pressures due to competition between training these other applied psychologists and the existing demands of the supervision system. Within Europe, the distinction between different types of applied psychologist is less prominent and there is a pressure to harmonize higher education qualifications around five years of training, resulting in a masters level of qualification. Such a trend would raise fundamental problems with the UK system of differential applied psychologists, many of whom are now trained to doctoral level.

The importance of overseas developments, particularly within the European Union, should not be underestimated. The NHS progressively looks to recruitment from other countries in order to resolve its workforce supply problems (DH, 2001a). Traditionally, many overseas clinical psychologists have been trained for the NHS via the BPS Statement of Equivalence route. This route to qualification is particularly important in areas of the UK with major staffing shortages and also specialisms such as learning disabilities that have experienced difficulties in recruitment. Within both placement projects, but particularly the London Project, the provision of placements for Statement of Equivalence candidates, or qualified posts filled with overseas-qualified staff not eligible to supervise, has had a significant impact on the overall availability of placements.

The presence of overseas-qualified staff within the NHS places particular pressures on training and placement provision. However, it should be emphasized that the employment of clinical psychologists trained and qualified abroad also enhances the diversity of the profession and the NHS and offers a wider range of experiences and models of psychology relevant to health care. It also deserves recognition that the Statement of Equivalence route to qualification is exacting in its BPS requirements and is often completed without the usual academic input and support for someone training via a university programme. Indeed, concerns have been expressed about viability and quality assurance methods of the BPS Statement of Equivalence route (Wilner and Napier, 2001). Accordingly, several programmes (e.g. University of Leeds and Salomons, Canterbury Christchurch University College) have organized formal courses for these candidates (McGuire *et al.*, 2001; Whittington and Burns, 2001). Ongoing developments within the BPS will also allow university programmes to assess the training requirements for the Statement of Equivalence as laid down by the BPS Committee for the Scrutiny of Individual Clinical Qualifications (CSICQ). Any overall plan for placement supervision should take into account the needs and opportunities afforded by overseas-qualified psychologists.

Attitudes and values of supervisors and psychology departments

Who has responsibility for providing placements for clinical psychologists in training? We would contend that this is shared between universities, clinical psychology departments in NHS Trusts and the purchasers of the programmes. Whilst there may be little contention in this assertion, in practice it has been the programmes that have carried out the task of finding sufficient placements for the agreed number of training commissions. This process has relied on good will, of which there has been plenty, and it worked well when the profession was small. With expansion in the workforce it is much more difficult to maintain the personal knowledge of each other that is required in order for the goodwill model to work. In the absence of well-developed personal relationships it is much easier for a busy clinician to turn down a request for a placement, and programme team staff have no managerial responsibility for the supervisors on whom training relies.

Under the conditions in which the profession now functions, the responsibility for finding placements must shift, with a greater emphasis on shared responsibilities between the major stakeholders. It may also be necessary for more formal arrangements to give structural support to the placement planning process. There are a number of models through which this might be encouraged. These range from the incorporation of supervision responsibilities within job descriptions, the creation of Service Level Agreements between service providers, and courses to ensure a minimum supply of placements, the creation of accredited Training Units through to a radical internship model recently proposed by Kinderman (2001). However, it is unlikely that organizational and structural changes will be sufficient by themselves to bring about changes in the attitudes and aspirations of individual supervisors.

One of the striking findings of the placement projects described above was that the ratio of placements provided to number of staff in post varied significantly according to the particular specialism and by individual department. Clinicians working with people with a learning disability and with older adults provided, on average, a greater number of placements than those working in adult mental health and child and family services. Traditionally, posts in learning disability and older adult services have been harder to fill. With unfilled posts, these clinical psychology departments have used their funding creatively, employing assistant psychologists who have been factored in to the ongoing service provision. Qualified clinicians have become used to supervising a continuous supply of junior staff and these skills readily translate to the supervision of trainees. In contrast, the lone psychologist in a multidisciplinary team may feel less skilled and experienced in the supervision and management of junior staff, and hence less willing to volunteer placements.

The data from the Trent Project also showed great disparity between departments in number of placements offered, irrespective of speciality. Those that provided large numbers of placements to staff in post were characterized by heads of department who were themselves enthusiastic about training and supervision, often taking trainees back to back on placement themselves and modelling enthusiasm about the role to other staff in the department. This enthusiasm was in some cases also in evidence where departments or specialities within departments were particularly engaged in the process of supervision for qualified staff, seeing it as an entitlement rather than an imposition.

It has been suggested (Dooley *et al.*, 2002) that professional heads of service ensure the formalization of supervision as a role in jobs through internal structures and procedures. This should ensure acknowledgement of the demands of the role, the provision of supervision time and an appropriate reduction in other activity. On its own, however, it would not ensure that less willing staff undertook the role. Positive approaches to changing attitudes and values are likely to be more productive, and the single most important factor associated with successful supervision has been identified as the interest of the supervisor in the task (Nelson, 1978; Engel *et al.*, 1998).

These findings suggest a number of approaches which might encourage a change of attitudes and values within the profession leading to an expansion in the placement resource:

- The encouragement of a greater sense of responsibility for placement provision within psychology departments in NHS trusts. This can be achieved through a number of measures such as placement projects which involve stakeholders in ongoing discussion and debate about training and the practice components.
- This sense of responsibility can also be formalized by the recruitment of staff in NHS trusts to posts attached part time to the university on a substantive or honorary basis with a brief to take some responsibility

for placement provision and co-ordination within the trust. These may be designated honorary clinical tutors or associate tutors.

• Clinical psychologists can be encouraged to value the process of super-vision more highly through the notion of career-long supervision as an entitlement in post-qualification training. The clinical governance agenda requires such mechanisms to be in place. An aspiration would be that supervision of trainees becomes an expected component of a clinical psychologist's role. Only in certain circumstances (e.g. newly qualified, very part-time working, managerial post, specialist research post) would a qualified psychologist not have or expect to have a trainee.

• Programmes could introduce training in supervision as a core skill throughout the three-year doctoral training, giving new qualifiers well-developed skills and positive expectations in their role as a supervisor.

• As the knowledge and skill base of supervision has developed apace, this could be reflected in the development of more formal post-qualification training programmes for supervisors. Well-trained and qualified staff are more likely to feel confident in the role of supervisor and to enjoy the role.

• Programme staff could develop supervisor training programmes that encourage a positive attitude to the role. These could be individually designed for particular departments and specialisms, and targeted at those who have traditionally offered a low ratio of placements to qualified staff. (See Scaife, 2001a, for key topics that might contribute to the curriculum for such a programme.)

Core experience and flexibility

The recent review of the accreditation criteria for clinical psychology pro-grammes (Adams, 2001) frees core experience from core placements. Under the new proposals, each trainee could have an individualized training pro-gramme within parameters that ensure that they gain experience in work across the age span, with people with chronic and enduring health needs and with people with a disability. These proposals have been generally welcomed within the profession with the proviso that the strengths of the current training model should not be lost.

With this increase in flexibility it will be possible to include placements traditionally designated as 'specialist' as suitable for trainees in the first two years of their training. Such a move would also reflect the changes that have taken place in the profession as it has expanded into increasingly diverse health and social care settings. Implementation of this change will take time. It requires programmes and supervisors to review the manner in which skills, knowledge and experience are designated core. It will also be crucial to ensure the full involvement of local clinical psychology special interest groups in this process.

Alongside this review will be the need to redesign formal recording methods of placement experience, assessments of clinical competence and aims and activities plans. Where the programme curriculum is designed around core placements, a major reorganization and review will be required. A number of options are possible. Core teaching at the university site would need to be relevant across specialisms in modules such as assessment, formulation, working with difference, interviewing skills, psychological therapies, research skills, etc. Indeed, continued work undertaken by the BPS on occupational standards might help further to shape a revised curriculum. The redesign of the curriculum would allow for the development of module options, possibly undertaken by distance learning in order that trainees could study individual topics best fitted to their current placement experience. It would be essential to retain the sense of a learning community and systems of support were trainees to be in less frequent contact with the university base.

Resources

The third general area in which there were identified constraints to the expansion of the placement resource was that of inadequate resources. These were largely in regard to clinic space, office space and administrative and clerical support. This inadequacy meant that in many cases clinicians who were willing and able to supervise were unable to offer placements.

The problem is by no means confined to the profession of clinical psychology or to the issue of training. It has resulted from the drive towards greater efficiency and the widespread reduction in hospital beds and accommodation that took place in the latter part of the twentieth century. It has left staff in substantive posts with inadequate resources for the job. In such a context it is difficult to make a case for resources for trainees, particularly if they are not seen as making a substantial and ongoing service contribution. Attempts to deal with these problems have also been identified in various interdisciplinary reports (ENB/DH, 2001; Cheesman, 2001).

The Trent study showed that many general managers have a very inadequate knowledge of the profession of clinical psychology, and in a climate of recurrent reorganizations and resource shortfall they are unable to prioritize the provision of resources to support training placements. Since general managers are unlikely to seek knowledge of the profession themselves, members of the profession need a strategy to educate and inform. Such a strategy can be undertaken at the level of the workforce confederations and by local service heads.

Workforce confederations have a major role to play here within their brief to provide a well-trained workforce to meet the projected requirements of the NHS. The trusts are represented on confederation boards and are the route for a wider dissemination of the blocks to placement provision that currently exist and of the potential solutions. Confederations need to stress the interdependence between service size and development, provision of training, and staff recruitment and retention. Programmes can facilitate this process by making available the data and the studies that demonstrate the major constraining factor that a lack of resources present.

Recent reviews of funding policy for training in the health professions may suggest a way forward as regards resourcing placements (NAO, 2001; DH, 2002). For many years medical training has been supported by the SIFT system. In order to reflect the need for additional resourcing for placement provision across all forms of health professional (HP) training, and also to ensure equality in the way that resources are distributed, a recent consultation document (Universities UK/DH, 2002) has recommended the merging of all levies and the use of such funds to support placement provision across all health care professions.

It is also likely that the differences in both the organizing and funding of training across the different health care professions will be radically diminished. The NAO report (NAO, 2001), together with the recent universities UK/DH (2002) consultation document, points to a system of standardized fees nationally agreed but locally implemented at the institutional level. Such a system would reduce the need for an administrative infrastructure whereby each individual HP training programme has to engage in protracted contract negotiations. At the same time, there are also major developments in the systems of quality assurance for the health professions. The recent establishment of common benchmarks for undergraduate courses by the QAA and Health Professions Council further underscores the joint working across professional bodies (QAA, 2001a). Similarly, the QAA has also established standards for work experience and placements (QAA, 2001b). It is likely that contract monitoring and quality assurance might take place at an institutional level across a range of health professions. The quality of placement experience, the availability of resources on placement, and the accountability of any 'SIFT-like' support to NHS trusts or training units, would all come under scrutiny. Clinical psychology programmes need to monitor these important policy changes both nationally and locally, and will need to establish good working relationships with the training bodies of the medical and allied health professions. Indeed, not only is greater co-operation required between professional bodies but the current NHS agenda is generally to encourage shared learning within the education of health professionals. At the undergraduate level, several innovative schemes are being established to support inter-professional learning across medical, allied health care professions and social work education.

Although the focus of this chapter has been on placement provision, the continuing development of clinical psychology training requires that adequate resourcing of the training system be achieved across the board. The shortage of clinical academic staff to run clinical psychology programmes based within universities and to supervise the research projects of clinical psychologists in training is recently being acknowledged (Davey, 2002; Thomas *et al.*, 2002; Turpin, 2002) as a critical problem. Similarly many courses based in universities are limited and constrained by teaching accommodation established for small group teaching rather than accommodating the increased numbers being demanded of the service. The provision of capital costs for new buildings and teaching resources will be critical for the future expansion of clinical psychology programmes.

In conclusion, universities and clinical psychology training programmes, together with WDCs, need to consider the following developments:

- A model of accredited training units akin to those adopted by the medical profession would allow departments providing placements to benefit from additional resources and to obtain recognition for their efforts. Such units might be accredited and provided with additional training funds.
- Transferring training from the university to placements, especially for specialist skills or client/services knowledge, would encourage supervisors to be more directly involved in training and for their skills to be more positively valued.
- Ensuring that adequate teaching accommodation exists for university-based programmes.
- Ensuring that support and remuneration exists to attract clinical academic staff into programme teams.
- Opportunities for interdisciplinary learning would allow the profession to draw upon the knowledge and skills of staff in other disciplines where this was considered relevant and appropriate in the training of clinical psychologists.

Conclusion

The expansion in the number of substantive posts and training places, and the increasing diversity of work carried out by the profession, is testament to the success of clinical psychology during the latter part of the twentieth century. Current indicators suggest that the profession will continue its successful development into the foreseeable future. This development is contingent on a continuing supply of adequate numbers of good-quality placements. This chapter has reported on studies of blocks to such placement provision and makes suggestions as to the measures that would facilitate an expansion in the placement resource. The commitment of all stakeholders in the training process is a necessary condition. There is every indication that the resourcefulness of the stakeholders, the willingness of the profession to seek flexible solutions, and the ongoing goodwill of supervisors will secure such an optimistic future.

Note

1 To Mr Jinks for 18 years of non-judgemental feline supervision.

Chapter 5

Training clinical psychologists as supervisors

Ian Fleming

> As few clinicians undertake any formal training in supervision prior to assuming the role, considerable variation may be expected, and is often found, between supervisors concerning the ways in which they function and perceive their role . . . In practice, supervisors often function within the same professional discipline or organisation, in very different ways.
>
> (Edwards, 1997: 14)

> There are those who have natural ability to supervise productively, and there are those who make a pig's ear out of it, no matter how many books they read or courses they go on.
>
> (Laing, 1965, quoted in Fowler, 1998: 82)

What can we deduce from these selected quotations? What is the role of training in the acquisition and assurance of high-quality supervision? Can it make a difference to supervisory practice? This chapter will attempt to shed some light on these issues through an examination of the current training of clinical psychology supervisors in the UK.

Earlier chapters in this book have addressed the functions of supervision both in general and within clinical psychology in particular. In this chapter we wish to report on the current situation with regard to clinical psychology in Britain concerning the training of clinical psychologists as supervisors, and to discuss the data collected in a survey with respect to the current state of knowledge about supervision. The data concern supervision of pre-qualification practice (i.e. of trainee clinical psychologists), although the relationship that this may have with post-qualification supervision will be discussed.

Although there are a variety of courses in the UK providing training in supervision, the focus will be on the supervisor training that is provided by doctoral clinical psychology training programmes. The information derives from a survey of UK clinical psychology training programmes carried out in the summer of 2001. Before reporting and discussing these data it will be helpful to consider the professional and service contexts in which supervision operates.

Turpin *et al.* in Chapter 4 of this book have described the service context that has seen, and will continue to see, significant growth in the numbers of clinical psychologists being trained in the UK. Green in Chapter 6 reports on a study that described the content of supervisor training that clinical psychologists want to see. This chapter will make links with both of these contributions.

The historical importance of supervision in clinical psychology

Clinical psychology is a small but rapidly growing profession in the UK (see data in Chapter 1). The National Health Service (NHS, the state health care provider in the UK) is the major employer of clinical psychologists and commissions and pays for their training via workforce planning (see Chapter 4 for more details). There is currently an excess (estimated at 25 per cent) of vacant clinical psychology posts, and there are continuing difficulties in filling posts in particular clinical and geographical areas.

In an attempt to meet this shortfall there has been an expansion in the number of training places in England from 189 in 1993 to 390 in 2000. In Scotland, Wales and Northern Ireland this rise has been less pronounced. (In Eire the expansion has also been less pronounced.) The expansion is influenced by the explicit and positive references to the role of clinical psychologists and psychological approaches in different aspects of health care, such as the National Service Frameworks published in 1998.

At the time of writing (October 2002), there are 29 clinical psychology training programmes in the UK (compared to 24 in 1990), and two in Eire. All UK programmes are required to achieve accredited status from the British Psychological Society's Committee on Training in Clinical Psychology (CTCP). There are explicit criteria that must be met to achieve accreditation, and this is awarded for a maximum of five years. Accreditation can be withdrawn, and awarded for a period of less than five years subject to interim review.

During training, clinical psychologists are required to undertake extended periods of supervised practice. The current accreditation criteria (BPS, 2002a) reflect the move away from an earlier requirement for trainees to complete placements in specialist client areas towards the more flexible gaining of specified experience and competencies. The necessity to identify these, organize them and evaluate a trainee's performance may result in additional and more detailed input from those clinical psychologists who are supervising trainees.

Although the majority of clinical psychologists in the UK are actively involved in supervising trainees, a sizeable minority do not supervise at all regularly (some of the reasons for this have been discussed earlier in

Chapter 4). Currently there are no mandatory requirements on qualified clinical psychologists to act as supervisors.

It can be argued that the profession of clinical psychology in the UK has only recently become concerned with the role of the supervisor and the practice of supervision (e.g. Fleming and Steen, 2001). Although individuals have attended to supervisory skills, there is little evidence of clinical psychology defining, developing or evaluating supervisory practice, especially when compared with allied professions such as counselling and psychotherapy. This is illustrated in recent surveys of placements and supervisors as training resources (Turpin, 1995; Gray, 1997). In these the emphasis was on placement capacity, rather than the competencies of supervisors or their training in supervisory skills. The more recent attention paid to these issues is reflected in Chapter 4 of this volume.

One reason for this lies in the historically dominant therapeutic models in British clinical psychology (e.g. Newnes, 1996), and their lack of emphasis on supervisory relationships and processes. The origins of supervision can be traced to the training process in psychoanalysis (e.g. Page and Wosket, 1994), and, although supervision is well established in social work (e.g. Kadushin, 1992), counselling (e.g. Carroll, 1996; Lawton and Feltham, 2000), psycho-analytic psychotherapy (see Shipton, 1997), and beginning to develop in nursing (e.g. Butterworth and Faugier, 1992), it is less well rooted in clinical psychology in the UK (Gabbay *et al.*, 1999).

This has been accompanied by a historical lack of attention to the training of supervisors in clinical psychology, although the situation is now changing. Increased attention is being paid to the tasks and competencies of super-vision, and the training of people in supervisory skills. Consideration is also being given to quality issues and the accreditation of supervisors – although this does *not* exist currently. These changes have been accompanied by a small literature describing supervision in clinical psychology and supervisor training (e.g. Allen and Brazier, 1996; Bacon, 1992; Gabbay *et al.*, 1999; Hitchen *et al.*, 1997; Milne, 1994; Milne and Britton, 1994).

The impetus for this change in emphasis comes from both general health care systems and the clinical psychology profession. One reason is a general concern with the quality of health care. There were a number of clear failures of the health care system in the UK in the 1990s, and one conclusion from the resulting inquiries was that there should be improved vigilance of clinical practice with supervision at the core of this.

Clinical governance (e.g. DH, 1998a; Hall and Firth-Cozens, 2000) is another tool for promoting the development of the highest practice through increased accountability. It can be argued that good-quality supervision can provide some of the means by which clinical governance is implemented.

Another driver for an increased emphasis on supervision comes from continuing professional development (CPD) (e.g. Green, 1995). It will soon be a requirement for clinical psychologists to demonstrate their CPD activity, and it is very likely within a few years that the demonstration of suitable CPD will be requirement for professional registration (BPS, 2001a; DCP, 2001a).

There is also an increasing trend towards self-regulation within the profession of clinical psychology that contributes to the focus on most effective practice.

What does the clinical psychology profession currently require of supervisors?

The changing emphasis on supervision has been accompanied by more consideration of the training clinicians require to practise as supervisors. As mentioned previously, the CTCP is the body within the British Psychological Society that has the responsibility for awarding accreditation to clinical psychology training programmes. Guidance from the CTCP has, in general, focused more on the activities of clinical psychology training programmes than on the practice of individual supervisors, and contained little in the way of detail. Thus, although there has been increased emphasis on the need for supervisors to receive 'training', the form and content remain unspecified.

The NHS and the profession have assumed and expected that clinical psychology (pre-qualification) training programmes would be the providers of this particular form of post-qualification training, and in general this has been the case. Indeed, the BPS *Guidelines for Continuing Professional Development* (BPS, 1998a) refer to this being an obligation placed on training programmes by the CTCP (section 5.1). Some clinical psychologists attend independent courses of training in supervision skills, but the numbers seem to be small and participants are more likely to work in particular specialities. It is not inconceivable that other providers could appear in future if training in supervision skills became an identifiable component of continuing professional development (CPD), and if and when there is a requirement for the quality control of supervisory practice (perhaps via accreditation). These latter issues will be discussed later.

Fleming and Steen (2001) described the developments in supervisor training in one doctoral training programme, in which there was an attempt to increase the amount and range of training in supervision tasks that was made available to clinical psychologists who supervised trainees from that programme. Current guidance states:

> 8.7 Regular workshops on supervisory skills and other teaching events for supervisors must be organised by the Programme to ensure a high standard of supervision. Supervisors should be encouraged to attend workshops and teaching events.
>
> (BPS, 2002a: 15)

This is a minor improvement on the previous guidance dating from 1996 that required programmes to demonstrate training for supervisors, and said that 'supervisors are expected to attend workshops on supervision' (BPS, 1996: appendix 3).

Neither the number nor content of these workshops are specified. The accreditation criteria refer to (undefined) 'good quality supervisory resources'. Clinical psychology training programmes are accredited, but not individual supervisors, and data are not available to determine the extent to which this guidance is followed. BPS/DCP guidelines on supervision are, at the time of writing (autumn 2002), expected to be published soon.

The BPS *Division of Clinical Psychology Professional Practice Guidelines* (BPS, 1995b) state that 'relevant workshops' should be attended prior to undertaking supervision. Time should be allowed for supervisors to attend appropriate supervisor groups and newly qualified supervisors should be enabled to enhance their competency in supervision (section 4.3) Subsequently, the DCP *Guidelines for Clinical Psychology Services* (BPS, 1998c) state that supervisors 'will have attended at least one workshop on supervision prior to taking on a trainee' (section 1.5.2.8).

In future the development of national occupational standards (NOS) for applied psychology may include specific data about core competencies for supervision and, in turn, this may have implications for supervisor training. Requirements in future for multi-professional training (NHSE, 1995; DH, 2001c) and supervision are also likely to have a significant impact on the training of supervisors.

In view of the absence of specific guidance about training of supervisors it was decided to conduct a survey of clinical psychology training programmes to gain data about their current practices.

Data from the 2001 survey

In August 2001 the author sent a survey form to all existing doctoral clinical psychology programmes in the UK and Ireland. The survey comprised 29 questions divided into areas of organization, content, costs, evaluation, and links with CPD. By December 2001, a total of 27 programmes had returned completed survey forms, a response rate of 87 per cent.

Analysis of results

Organization

1   All 27 doctoral training programmes provided training for supervisors of trainees from their programme. Of these 19 (70.4 per cent) organized programmes of training; a minority described their training events as '*ad hoc*'.

Within these programmes the number of separate training events varied considerably from 1–10, with a mode number of 3. On average 4.6 training events had been put on during the previous 12 months, with a range of 1–9 and a mode of 3.

The average number of training events in the previous 12 months was similar, both for those organizations arranging programmes and those organizing *ad hoc* events, although there was a greater range in the number organized by the former.

There was variation in how often training was organized and repeated. The largest number of training programmes (12) indicated that the frequency was annually; other significant proportions were every six months and 'as necessary' (8). Some programmes indicated that the frequency of events varied according to content, with, for example, 'introductory' training being provided on a more regular basis.

2   The most common duration for training events was one day (16 training programmes). Five programmes organized mainly two-day events, and four mainly residential events. Those training programmes with programmes of supervisor training organized more residential and two-day events than those that organized more *ad hoc* training.

Only seven (26 per cent) programmes routinely organized events for both trainees and supervisors, although another four programmes did so on an occasional basis.

3   Twelve (44 per cent) programmes used only staff from their own pro-gramme to deliver the training. Very few training programmes used outside speakers/facilitators solely, although 12 indicated that they used both, according to the content of the training event. Clinical training programmes that organized their supervisor training on an *ad hoc* basis were more likely to utilize trainers from outside the programme team. It is not clear if there was a relationship between clinical training programmes that delivered more training for supervisors and the available internal resources (e.g. staff time, perceived competencies of staff) for the delivery of this training. Cost issues of training are discussed later.

4   Many training programmes are geographically close to others, with the result that individual clinicians may regularly supervise trainees from more than one programme. Sixteen (59 per cent) programmes organized supervisor training with other local programmes on a regular basis and only five (18.5 per cent) reported that they did not organize training events with other programmes. Some programmes indicated that this depended on the content of the training event, and that some events were organized in conjunction with other programmes but others were not. Six programmes organized with others on an infrequent basis and six did so in addition to their own training for supervisors.

Table 5.1 Content of supervisor training events using categories supplied in the survey questionnaire

Content of training event	No. of programmes organizing such training events
Supervision and learning processes	23 (85%)
Different theoretical models of supervision	22 (81.5%)
Failing trainees/placements	19 (70%)
'Race', culture and gender issues in supervision	14 (52%)
Team supervision	8 (30%)

Table 5.2 Content of supervisor training events based on respondents' own reports

Content of training event	No. of programmes organizing training events with this content
Supervising research	9
Dealing with dilemmas, conflicts and challenges in supervision	8
Teaching clinical skills in supervision (e.g. cognitive-behavioural therapy, formulation)	7
Supervision contracts; setting-up and managing placements	5
Supervising other professions, consultation skills	4
Group supervision	3
Gatekeeping	2
Dynamics of supervisory relationships	2
Taping live supervision	2
Personal and professional development	2
Trainee-facilitated workshop	1
Ethics/boundary issues	1
Developing trainees self-appraisals	1

Content

5 Programmes were asked about the content of their training events. Table 5.1 contains the responses to titles provided, and Table 5.2 their own descriptions of the content of their training events.

Attendance

6 Attendance at training events varied according to content. The majority of programmes reported average attendances of over 20, and the largest attendance was reported as 'up to 50'. Most training is organized in a workshop format with an emphasis on enactive teaching using exercises, role-play and

small group work. This mode of training has implications for resources (e.g. teaching rooms in a venue, numbers of facilitators) and the number attending. From our personal experience in Manchester, as in Newcastle (Milne and Howard, 2000), supervisors regularly attest to the value of role-play in reflection and learning during training workshops.

7   Programmes were asked what they knew about the individuals who attended their training events. Seventeen of the clinical training programmes (63 per cent) reported that they informally monitored attendance of supervisors at training events. Twenty-two (81 per cent) reported that they knew of active supervisors who rarely attended supervision training events, and 15 (55.5 per cent) programmes 'targeted' these individuals and encouraged them to attend. One programme reported that they did so 'sometimes' and, although this was not specifically asked, another programme reported that it intentionally identified newly qualified clinicians ready to become supervisors. (This is probably an underestimate of this practice across training programmes.) Of those that monitored attendance, 13 (76 per cent) considered that this targeting was generally successful, with increased attendance and participation in training.

Attempts to monitor attendance need to acknowledge that individuals may attend supervisor training events organized by neighbouring training programmes, especially where this is geographically more likely (see p. 77). In the north-west of England, for example, the Manchester, Lancaster and Liverpool clinical training programmes are in a region approximately 80 miles long and 45 wide, and a number of individual clinicians supervise trainees from more than one programme.

This situation is likely to increase in accordance with the expansion in the number of training programmes. Individual supervisors could use logbooks to monitor their attendance and participation at training events and as a tool for personal development. This is discussed on pp. 212–213.

8   Sixteen clinical training programmes (59 per cent) did *not* have a specific budget for training. Despite this, only two levied a charge for attendance at training events, and this was for residential events only.

Audit

9   Most programmes made attempts to evaluate the training for supervisors, although it was generally recognized that this was carried out in a limited way. Twenty-three (85 per cent) programmes made regular attempts to evaluate these training events and another did so 'sometimes'. Twenty-three employed written feedback from those attending the workshops. A further three used observation of supervision and another two asked supervisors to monitor their subsequent practice in supervision or use learning logs. No programmes sought reports from clinical psychology trainees.

Table 5.3 Details of the relationship between supervisor training and continuing professional development

When asked to enlarge on this relationship, the following were included:

- The situation may change in the near future as a result of increased interest locally (three programmes).
- Some supervisors' individual performance reviews take account of supervision skills (two programmes).
- The regional Post-Qualification Training Consortium organizes a CPD programme that includes supervision (two programmes).
- There is locally a 0.5wte* Regional CPD Co-ordinator, but that person is not involved with supervisor training (one programme).
- There is a requirement for supervisors to attend a three-day training event prior to supervising, and a 'refresher' event every three years (one programme).
- Supervisor training has been 'marketed' as fulfilling CPD requirements, and accreditation certificates are being sought from the university (one programme).

Note: * wte = whole time equivalent

Table 5.4 Organization of continuing professional development in the localities of Clin.Psy.D. training programmes

• Events are organized mainly by local Special Interest Groups and DCP branches.	(5 programmes)
• There is a regional Post-Qualification Training Committee or an 'active' CPD committee that organizes events.	(4 programmes)
• There is a less-active CPD committee that organizes some events.	(3 programmes)
• Arrangements are *'ad hoc'*, 'variable', left to individual trusts.	(3 programmes)
• A post-qualification doctorate.	(2 programmes)
• Mainly organized by the DCP but plans for future joint organization with the University.	(1 programme)
• CPD tutor recently appointed/survey carried out.	(2 programmes)

Continuing professional development

10   Programmes were asked if there was a specific link between continuing professional development (CPD) initiatives locally and supervision training events that they organized. Only five (18.5 per cent) programmes affirmed this link and 17 (63 per cent) indicated no link. One was unsure. Programmes were asked to elaborate on this relationship and their responses are contained in Table 5.3.

11   Three (11 per cent) training programmes reported that they have responsibilities for post- as well as pre-qualification training; 19 (70.4 per cent) indicated that they did not. Table 5.4 contains the programmes' descriptions of the arrangements for CPD in their localities.

Accreditation

12   Only one programme reported that it accredited supervisors in any way on the basis of competence. The vast majority of programmes (25) did not do so. In this single instance accreditation was given for attendance at supervisor training events.

Three programmes reported that they had plans to employ accreditation in the near future. Another reported that it 'would like to', and one thought that these plans were a possibility. Twenty-two programmes indicated that they had no plans to do so, however.

Despite this four (15 per cent) programmes (with another 'possible') have plans to use supervisor training to identify the competence of supervisors.

Discussion: what does this tell us about training people to supervise in clinical psychology?

Data have been presented that describe the current provision by clinical psychology training programmes of training for clinical psychology supervisors in the UK. Experience from attending 'external' courses in supervision is not discussed here.

The following discussion will consider aspects of the organization of training for supervisors, the content of the training provided and its perceived relevance to the tasks of supervision, and future developments of supervisor training within the changing context facing the profession of clinical psychology. It will enquire how well the profession is providing training for supervisors and what can be learned and taken forward from experience.

Why train supervisors?

The value of training for supervisors has been questioned, for instance, by Bramley (1996):

> No doubt supervision too is about to come under inspection in this regard and therapists will flock to 'recognised' training courses that will spring up all over the country to meet the demands. While welcoming any move to keep up standards and protect the public, I am worried about too much standardisation; too much concern about career prospects and making sure one is part of the professional 'in crowd' at the expense of the patient, who would benefit much more from his therapist's supervisor if she had been allowed to develop the art of supervision gradually, as her own expertise and knowledge as a practitioner increased rather than in a rushed once and for all qualifying course.
>
> (Bramley, 1996: 182)

In contrast to this there is a prima facie case made for all aspects of training to improve performance, although the empirical evidence available to support this has been subject to criticism (see Chapter 6). Other reasons for training supervisors include an increasing concern generally with the quality of supervision (as well as the quantity of supervisors); supervisors' own requests for more training; and the identification of the lack of training experience as a (lesser) barrier to individual clinical psychologists offering to supervise trainees. A further impetus may come with the European Union directives related to the qualifications and employment of applied psychologists (see Chapter 4).

What happens in supervision in the absence of training in supervision skills? If the profession of clinical psychology has underemphasized the practice of supervision in the past, has this affected what takes place?

A general argument in the literature is that in the absence of specific training, supervisors tend to apply their clinical skills to supervision. For example, Carroll (1996) says:

> Often the decision about which tasks to employ in supervision, made either consciously or unconsciously, accords with the theoretical orientation, and/or is due to the limited training and competences of supervisors.
>
> (Carroll, 1996: 52)

There is also a general presumption that training in supervisory skills is desirable, if only to impose a minimum standard. For example, Page and Wosket state: 'If supervisor training were to accomplish nothing beyond eradicating previous bad habits, it might serve some useful purpose' (1994: 174).

Blocher, with reference to counselling, identified some potential problems that could develop for untrained supervisors:

> The supervisory relationship is by its nature one in which the counsellor begins, at least, by feeling inadequate and vulnerable. The possibility always exists that an immature, inadequate, and insensitive supervisor may intimidate, bully, and even damage a supervisee. No theoretical model of supervision is idiot proof and bastard resistant. When such destructive events occur in supervision it is more likely to be due to the personal inadequacies of the supervisor than to the deficiencies in any well-thought through theoretical model.
>
> (Blocher, 1983: 30)

It is interesting to consider whether these experiences apply to clinical psychologists in the UK. Introductory supervisor training sessions in Manchester ask individuals to identify unhelpful personal experiences of being supervised. The ease with which participants can complete this exercise suggests that Blocher's remarks may not be too exaggerated.

The general view in the literature is of training being able to provide supervisors with the different skills necessary for the task, irrespective of the different supervision models (see Chapters 2 and 3).

Training provides supervisors with a grounding in the particular skills and duties involved in supervision. It can build confidence, promote enthusiasm for the task of supervising, provide skills for supervision that are additional to therapeutic clinical skills, and rid supervision of the worst forms of bad practice. Across the different models of supervision, there appears to be agreement about the importance of the relationship within supervision. Training in this area thus seems very important, and the content of training for supervisors can benefit from considering the research carried out into the supervisee's experience of supervision. The prominence given to elements of the supervisory relationship is congruent with comments made elsewhere in this volume by Beinart, Wheeler, and Matthews and Treacher.

The content of supervisor training

The survey demonstrates that the majority of clinical psychology training programmes organize training for psychologists who supervise trainees from their programmes. It is unclear, however, how the content of supervisor training has been developed, and whether it is designed explicitly to meet the tasks of supervision. There is little evidence for clinical psychology having a particular model of supervision (cf. BPS guidance referred to in Chapter 1), and this absence may have led to a more pragmatic and idiosyncratic content developing.

While this survey provides data about the content and organization of supervisor training, it fails to convey much of the detail. There are a limited number of published examples of training workshops (e.g. Allen and Brazier, 1996; Milne and Howard, 2000).

The survey data do suggest that there is a shared view about the core issues for supervision training, and therefore by extension for what constitutes effective supervisory skills, although this will reflect to some degree clinical training programmes' sharing of experience. The most prevalent training provides supervisors with an introduction to the tasks of supervision and to the particular requirements of that clinical psychology training programme. In view of the very real importance of the *evaluative* function of the supervisor this 'administrative' training is crucially important. In light of the earlier comments concerning different theoretical models of supervision it is interesting to read that this is the second most frequent area of content in training. The importance to supervisors and to training programmes, of correctly evaluating performance, and the necessity of professional gatekeeping tasks is shown in the third most frequent training content. The increasing recognition of societal factors in all aspects of clinical psychology practice is demonstrated by the organization of training for supervisors in issues of 'race', culture and gender. A simple, if slight majority, of training programmes organize such training. This issue is discussed later in Chapters 7 and 8.

These data (what is currently provided) have much in common with those discussed in Green's Chapter 6 (what it is desirable to provide). A question remains about the relevance of both of these to the tasks of supervision. Milne and James (2002) argue that research is able to help determine relevant content for the training of clinical psychology supervisors. The training should help supervisors to facilitate supervisees in experiential learning (Kolb, 1984). Taken together this information could help the CTCP to provide more detail about supervisor training in future revisions of the accreditation criteria. An implication of this might be that the profession of clinical psychology should recommend or require that supervisors be trained to competence in a specified content.

The general literature on supervision discusses the issues that training should include and is referred to by Wheeler in an earlier chapter. It is acknowledged (e.g. Lawton and Feltham, 2000) that there remains a lack of detail about the practice of supervision even in these other professions with reportedly more advanced considerations of supervision. One outcome can be the compilation of large lists of content areas, and in clinical psychology the increased emphasis on the development of competencies might be matched by a similar development of the competencies of supervisors. Clarkson and Gilbert (1991), for instance, have compiled a list of 17 topics 'essential to supervisor training'. Carroll (1996) describes six elements of a 'model curriculum' for counsellor supervisor training. Some of these are common to the supervisor training programmes surveyed here:

1   Knowledge of supervision including different models.
2   Reviewing issues to do with power, including gender.
3   Isolating and practising supervision skills.
4   Understanding and implementing tasks of supervision.
5   Being supervised for supervision.
6   Knowledge of the stages that supervisors go through.

How much can clinical psychology learn about training content from other professions? (It may be sensible to limit our focus to professions in the UK, although North American literature describes a richly varied picture of the practice and content of training provided for supervisors.) There is not a clear answer to this question. Although other professions have introduced standards for the training of supervisors the content and practice in such training is not always clear. In the UK the British Association for Counselling and Psychotherapy (BACP) has requirements for 'supervisors to engage in specific training in the development of supervision skills', and its ethical codes have consistently emphasized the importance of training in supervision-relevant practice.

In nursing, the requirement for clinical supervision was formally introduced in 1992 and expanded in 1996. The UKCC wrote a position paper that identified six statements to assist the development of clinical supervision at local levels. Education for supervisors is identified within these statements. Although not a statutory requirement (unlike for midwives) supervision for nurses is recommended.

It is very important that issues of diversity are being attended to within supervisor training (see Chapters 7 and 8). These reflect the explicit moves in the profession as a whole to embrace these issues (e.g. Patel *et al.*, 2000). The data from the survey stand up well to Carroll's critique (1996) of the lack of emphasis on culture and diversity in recent UK (counselling) texts on supervision.

The general literature often talks of supervision and training in broad terms. Is the training for post-qualification supervisors the same as that for supervisors of people who are completing their qualification into the profession? It can be argued that there are real differences – in the evaluative component for example. A further complication is presented if inter-professional supervision is considered. Many clinical psychologists supervise members of other professions or receive supervision from them in their general clinical practice. Are these requirements different to those of supervising trainee (or even qualified) clinical psychologists, and if so, how? Are we talking of generic or particular skills in supervision?

Within the clinical psychology training organizations, experiential and reflective models of learning such as that developed by Kolb (1984) are often utilized. Milne and James describe using experiential learning within supervision and their assessment of the effectiveness of training a supervisor to 'move . . . (a learner) . . . around the experiential learning cycle' (2002: 59). It is not possible from this survey to know how general is such an attempt to develop supervisor training within this model of learning

Developing standards and the accreditation of training for supervisors

How should training for supervisors be evaluated? Should the profession set standards for the training of supervisors? What is the relationship between the content of training and these standards? Should training be linked to a form of accreditation by which the quality can be controlled?

Although it is often presumed that different training programmes reflect the different therapeutic models within clinical psychology, there is little evidence of this from the survey of the content of supervisor training. This would indicate that it may be less difficult to identify a common core of content for the training of supervisors. By extension it may be possible to develop some standards for the training and the subsequent performance of supervisors.

Despite the apparent homogeneity in the content of supervisor training, it is not clear whether there is agreement about the skills required of a supervisor.

The more pragmatic approach referred to above may enable clinical psychology to sidestep some of the discussions about model-specific standards. Concerns about a lack of theory can be assuaged by reference to developments within experiential learning (e.g. Milne and James, 1999, 2002) and cognitive-behavioural psychotherapy.

Examination of the general literature suggests that it is possible to draw on this in developing standards, although attention also needs to be given to any particular requirements of clinical psychologists. An example of difference in emphasis is the supervisory relationship. Considered crucial in much of the literature, in training clinical psychologist supervisors it is considered more obliquely; for example, in training about managing dilemmas and challenges in supervision (see Tables 5.1 and 5.2). In Manchester, for example, supervisor training also draws on developmental models of supervision because there is recognition of the different demands in supervision of neophyte and third year trainee clinical psychologists. Drawing on different models in this way would also have the benefit of not discomforting any particular constituencies within the profession, and introducing possibly unhelpful allegiances to a particular training programme.

In developing standards for training of supervisors and the resulting supervisory activity it will be helpful to retain a sense of what is 'good enough' in practice. Kadushin (1992) has commented that supervision is about 'motivating towards excellence' rather than 'merely protecting against incompetence', and Wheeler, earlier in this book, referred to the difference between 'bad' and 'harmful' supervision.

The development of standards for supervisor training leads logically towards a discussion of accreditation, either of supervisory practice or supervisor training, although it is clearly preferable for the two to be related.

Accreditation of supervisors has been under discussion in recent years for a number of reasons. First, it is seen as an element of professional governance and a means of assuring the quality of supervision within clinical training. Second, within discussions about increasing the number of available training placements, the introduction of accreditation (for individual supervisors, or for supervising departments) has been seen considered as an incentive to increase clinicians' commitment to supervising trainees. Third, it is suggested that a commitment to supervision could constitute a legitimate CPD activity, thus providing mutual benefits to individuals and their profession.

As stated earlier, from the survey, only one training programme uses accreditation, and that is linked to attendance at training events. It would be useful to know more about this experience from both the point of view of the programme and from the supervisors involved.

CPD may play a critical role in linking up these different professional activities. Some of the competing pressures on clinicians' time, the requirement for clinical governance, and establishing a linkage between supervisory and clinical practice could be assured through supervision and supervisor training being established as legitimate activities to be assessed through CPD.

These issues are discussed further in Chapter 11.

In Manchester, clinical psychology supervisors often talk of a need for supervision for supervisors. As an informal method of upholding quality and sharing learning this arrangement may have much to offer. Consideration should be given to 'surgeries' at which a member of the programme team examines issues that have arisen in supervision, and the form of specific consultancy described by Milne and James (2002).

It is hoped that the enhancement of supervisory skills will have generalized effects on the therapeutic practice of supervisors. In this way supervisor training can facilitate the introduction of the governance-based measures discussed earlier. Whilst there is a prima facie case for this (improvements in, for example, skills of listening, reflecting, evaluating, giving clear feedback are consistent with professional practice), there is a lack of empirical support.

Currently, supervisors generally welcome training, although participation and attendance is voluntary. A minority of supervisors do not attend even when given particular invitations from programme staff. Some of these individuals may not supervise on a regular basis; others may be regular supervisors; occasionally they may be senior, regular supervisors. Linking supervisory activity to CPD is likely to have a significant effect on the attendance at supervisor training, is likely to change significantly if accreditation is linked to supervisory status, and if supervising is, in turn, linked to promotion and CPD.

Different clinical training programmes reflect different emphases in professional practice (for example, on therapeutic models). Although there has been a concern that supervisors who offer placements to more than one programme may experience problems in working across the 'cultures' of different training programmes, there is no evidence to support this – nor that the training of supervisors differs significantly in different programmes. Rather, supervisors have reported frustrations with the different assessment protocols than with varying demands within the supervisory process.

The profession may be only a short distance from a position where supervisor training can be clearly linked to an explicit form of quality control via clear standards, and possibly through accreditation. For that to occur there would need to be clear statements about the exact purposes and objectives for supervisor training, and its content, along with an agreed form of evaluation of its effectiveness. This could be organized within the general accreditation exercise that clinical psychology training programmes

undergo, or within the educational establishment that hosts the training programme, although there remains the issue of whose responsibility it is for
accreditation.

Organizing and providing supervisor training

All this is consistent with increased importance for supervisor training.
Any move from voluntary to mandatory will have implications for resources.
At present, the majority of training is delivered by (pre-qualification) training programmes, using programme staff mainly and free of charge to those
attending, although most programmes have no dedicated budget for this
activity. Any move towards accreditation, or any form of training linked
to identified standards, has financial and organizational implications for
clinical training programmes.

Reference was made earlier for supervisors' request for their own supervision of their own supervisory skills. Milne and James (2002) have described
the benefits of a consultancy model for the quality of supervision and its
maintenance. Establishing these will have implications for the clinical training programmes.

Would accreditation be transferable? If awarded by a training programme in the south of England would its legitimacy extend to Scotland?
Or, if awarded by a training programme with a reputation of strength in
cognitive-behavioural therapy would the supervisors' accreditation still hold
after a move to a region where the training programmes had an explicit
emphasis on person-centred therapy? One answer to this, of course, is a
nationally administered accreditation. An additional advantage could be
that the resource implications are then transferred from training programmes
to the profession.

The issue of the *costing* of supervisor training will increase in importance
as numbers increase and supervisor training becomes more established. If
supervisor training is to be linked with CPD and clinical governance then
the financial provision may need to be more formalized within the profession
or the Health Service. There are parallels with the issue of whose responsibility
it is to seek and provide training placements (see Chapter 4).

Evaluation

All of the above is based on the assumption that training has a beneficial
effect on supervision. Notice the noun *supervision*; there are different views
within the literature as to what should be the demonstrable results of supervisor training. A clearly logical model suggests (rather like the staff training
models of the 1980s) that supervisor training will only be effective if demonstrable change can be identified in *both* supervisee performance and in the
outcome of the therapy carried out by the supervisee.

Is this increased attention to supervisor training effective? An answer should consider two issues. First, is the training of supervisors able to improve their performance and make supervision more effective? Second, is supervision *per se* effective in enabling beneficial change in supervisee behaviour and in client outcome? The literature suggests that there is evidence for the former, though less for the latter (see Chapter 6). No one doubts the complexities inherent in evaluating supervision, given the many different characteristics of the supervisory dyad alone (Wampold and Holloway, 1997). Holloway (1997) concludes that there is little research that examines client change as an outcome of the supervision process. In general, although there is research that demonstrates the effects of training and supervision on the development of particular skills relevant to therapy, there is less evidence for overall effects.

Clinical psychologists in the UK (e.g. Milne and James, 1999, 2002) have reviewed the research into the effectiveness of supervision. They conclude that an evidence base for clinical supervision that can be used to promote good practice does exist. They have argued that research on supervision within counselling and psychotherapy has lacked empiricism, and that clinical psychology approaches research differently. Milne and James argue that learning and changes in supervisee behaviour can be legitimate goals of supervisor training and that an insistence on seeing therapeutic changes as well can place an unjustifiable demand on research that paradoxically makes it almost impossible to carry out because of the numerous variables that would have to be controlled. In their research various measures were used to evaluate training.

In practice the situation is rather different. From the survey it is clear that the forms of evaluation used by trainers are quite limited. Although more useful evaluation would require resources beyond those available to programme teams, it is important that more research into supervisor training is carried out.

It is noticeable that supervisor training appears to be positively welcomed by supervisors, particularly by individuals who have qualified recently. This finding is reinforced in Green's report (Chapter 6). Attendance figures are high in general, and in Manchester only two workshops in six years have had to be cancelled because of inadequate interest. This finding offers a more optimistic view of supervisors' perceptions of training than that of others in the literature (e.g. Bernard and Goodyear, 1998).

In the light of this generally favourable view of supervisor training in clinical psychology, combined with the fact that individuals are now eligible to supervise trainees one year after qualification rather than two years (which was the previous requirement), it is appropriate that more attention is devoted to using supervision in pre-qualification teaching (as recommended in Chapter 4). It is noticeable that a number of programmes organize training in supervision for supervisors and supervisees together. Clinical psychology programmes generally teach trainees to play an active role in the supervision process (for instance via negotiating placement contracts). Hitchen *et al.* (1997) describe an innovative workshop for Oxfordshire clinical psychology supervisors put on by supervisees. Despite this it is interesting to ponder Carroll's remark below, especially given the finding from the survey that clinical psychology trainees' views about the effectiveness of supervisor training are not sought generally:

> It would seem that supervisees are passive *vis-à-vis* supervision, have few expectations from which to negotiate with supervisors, and are prepared to 'fall in' with supervisor ways of setting up and engaging in supervision.
>
> (Carroll, 1996: 92)

Conclusions

If we return to the remarks quoted at the beginning of this chapter how do we assess them with regard to clinical psychology in the UK? On balance, it is difficult to deny the situation described by Edwards because there are many active supervisors who have not received any specific training in supervisory skills, and because there is a paucity of data about current practice with which to discuss variability. For a number of reasons discussed earlier this situation is changing and will continue to do so in the near future. Laing's remarks will remind us that training is only a start to change in practice and no guarantor of it. As psychologists we need to learn from the extensive literature on behaviour change, and its maintenance, if supervisor training is to have its intended effect.

Clinical psychology is a rapidly developing profession in the UK. Pre-qualification training involves spending at least 50 per cent of the training period learning clinical skills on placement and receiving supervision from a qualified practitioner.

Until recently little attention has been paid, in general, to the tasks and skills of these supervisors. Previously an apprenticeship model was used that had developed largely independently of the supervisory developments in related professions such as counselling and psychotherapy.

Possible reasons for this include a lack of attention to the therapeutic relationship and process, and an emphasis on more 'technical' therapeutic skills. In the wider supervisory literature debate continues as to whether there needs to be congruence between supervisory style and therapeutic approach (e.g. Kadushin, 1992; Lawton and Feltham, 2000). In clinical psychology, any such agnosticism to the importance of supervisory processes may have been underlined by the lack of consensus on the definition of supervision and the array of different models of supervision (e.g. the estimated 25 different developmental models alone; Carroll, 1996). An additional, contributory factor may have been that the emphasis on a scientist-practitioner model within clinical psychology rendered it difficult to assimilate some of the complexities of supervision.

There have been significant changes in many aspects of clinical psychology training in the last decade and more attention is now being directed at supervision, although this improvement may not be generalized and many clinical psychology supervisors may have received no specific training (see Chapter 10). Some of the factors associated with this include increased training numbers to accommodate the expansion of the profession, an emphasis on clinical governance, and continuing professional development. Alongside this change it is noticeable that the majority of research and literature concerning supervision derives from psychoanalysis, counselling or social work. There is a smaller, but growing, literature about clinical psychology.

The survey of UK clinical psychology training programmes reported in this chapter provides useful data about the state of supervisor training. Training is being provided on an increasingly systematic basis within an enactive framework. There is a good uptake of training by supervisors generally, although there may remain exceptions in the absence of accreditation status for supervisors.

Programme team members deliver most of the training and are well placed to do so, but would probably benefit from using the research literature to develop the most effective training and to evaluate this. Professional developments are likely to lead to the development and sharing of high-quality training materials, and the relevant professional body (the Group of Trainers in Clinical Psychology) has an active interest in these areas combined with an active spirit of co-operative enquiry. So, although it is not clear whether there exists a uniform view about the tasks and process of supervision, there is a sharing of knowledge and developments across training programmes. Whilst this might exaggerate the impression of an agreed model for training, and there is very little about this in the accreditation criteria, there appears to be a common core of issues that are deemed important for supervisor training.

It would appear that some if not most of the content of supervisor training originates in work from counselling and other disciplines. Indeed, very little has been written about supervision from the perspective of functional analysis or cognitive-behavioural therapy (Liese and Beck, 1997; Padesky, 1996; Liese and Alford, 1998; Ricketts and Donohoe, 2000). Since cognitive-behavioural therapy is a popular theoretical model within UK clinical psychology currently, this lends support for the view that supervisory models are generalizable (Holloway, 1997), and that there need not be a contradiction between supervisory and therapeutic practices. Since studies have reported that supervisors will adopt their preferred clinical approach in supervision, the important component of supervisor training may be that to do with making the learning processes most effective.

With reference to counselling in the UK Carroll makes the claim,

> The various codes of ethics for supervisors emphasise the need for supervisors to be alert to their own competency and involved in their ongoing training. This training is fast becoming a requirement for supervisors, rather than an optional extra. The days of inheriting the supervisory mantle, and requiring no initial and ongoing training in supervision, are disappearing.
>
> (Carroll, 1996: 159)

It is clear that this description may also describe clinical psychology in the UK in the first years of the twenty-first century.

What this survey does not tell us of course is much about the actual practice of supervision in clinical psychology in the UK. That research remains to be carried out. Other areas to research include the content of training, the effectiveness of training and whether training can generalize to supervisors' therapy skills. It will be interesting to investigate further whether there is a benefit in developing a cognitive-behavioural approach to both supervisor training and to supervision, and whether congruence between supervision and therapeutic models is beneficial. However, in light of the discussion of the training offered to supervisors it is hoped that the practice is effective and coherent, and yet able to accommodate differences in formulation and intervention.

Finally, the profession should use these data to develop guidance about the training of clinical psychology supervisors. It seems likely that such training will be the responsibility of clinical psychology training programmes based in universities. Development of supervisor training will benefit from further research. The degree to which learning from other professional contexts can be utilized will need evaluation. The links between supervisor training, accreditation and CPD, and the extension of training for entry to the profession to post-qualification responsibilities will need to be carefully considered, and programme teams will need the resources and confidence of the profession to carry this out.

Chapter 6

Organizing and evaluating supervisor training

David Green

Introduction

Supervision in the mental health professions is an expanding market. Therapists are increasingly expected to seek out some systematic oversight of their work as a hallmark of good practice. Those searching for a reliable supervisor to take on this critical role would be well advised to shop carefully. The wrong choice could prove expensive or worse. When faced with important decisions of this order most of us cautious consumers might like to check out the qualifications of the several potential providers that people this particular marketplace. Where was she educated? What psychotherapeutic training has he received? With what professional associations is she registered? And so on. Sooner or later we should also be asking the question which is the focus of this chapter. What specific preparation for the task of clinical supervision has he undertaken? In all probability the honest answer is likely to be remarkably little. A brief historical overview may perhaps explain how this surprising state of affairs has come to pass.

History of supervisor training

In the final chapter of *The Handbook of Psychotherapy Supervision*, the magnum opus which he edited in 1997, Watkins (1997a) expressed open puzzlement at the sorry lack of recognition of the importance of supervisor training in the available research literature in the field. Trainee psychotherapists are expensively and intensively trained. A core plank of their education is the monitoring and guiding of performance that is provided by their clinical supervisors. But these supervisors themselves typically receive little or no training in how to supervise. As Watkins candidly observed: 'Something does not compute.'

On reflection this apparently illogical commitment of resources makes some sense if seen in a historical context. The practice of psychological therapy has been given a rough ride by its critics. Eysenck (1952) famously asked whether the passage of time might be as effective a healer as an experienced psychotherapist in treating emotional disturbance, and triggered an immense investment in large-scale scientific outcome research. This battle could not be postponed. 'But does it work?' is a question that cannot be ducked. The emphasis on the efficacy of our collective product (i.e. the brand of therapy) has been at the cost of chronic inattention having been paid to the efficiency of our means of production (i.e. the 'traditional' structures of professional training). Many of our assumptions about what are the essential ingredients in the peculiar broth that we feed novice therapists remain gloriously untested (Alberts and Edelstein, 1990; Binder, 1993; Stein and Lambert, 1995). Could it be that our faith in the centrality of clinical supervision is no more than a widely held psychologists' myth (Bickman, 1999)?

There are certainly good intellectual reasons for doubting another prevalent lazy assumption – namely, that 'good therapists automatically make good supervisors', so investing in further training is a waste of everyone's time and effort. Just let them get on with it . . . There is an allied line of argument that accompanies this assertion. Psychological therapies are founded on well-articulated and researched theories of how to help human beings change and grow. This hard-won expertise should surely be made available to a psychologist's students as well as her patients. There is some merit in these arguments. One mechanism whereby professional skills and standards are passed from one generation to the next is undoubtedly modelling (Bandura, 1965). Trainees respect, identify with, and ultimately copy the ways of supervisors whose work they admire. Conversely it is very hard for a supervisor to be taken seriously as a constructive critic of another's performance if they themselves do not 'cut the mustard' in the therapy room (D. R. Green, 1998). It would also be a poor comment on our faith in the benefits of psychotherapy if we were only prepared to apply our psychological models to other people's problems but refuse to see their reflexive possibilities in better understanding ourselves. There are transferable skills that the able therapist can surely use in supervision (rapport building, empathic listening, summarizing, and so forth), but their effective application demands that he does not confuse the different goals of supervision and psychotherapy. Micro-analytic research has also indicated that clinicians tend to hold significantly different conversations with their supervisees from those they have with their patients (Holloway, 1995). Supervisor training can and should alert new supervisors to the dissimilarities as well as the similarities between psychological treatment and clinical supervision.

It would be easier to persuade sceptics that educational theory was a sounder basis for the practice of clinical supervision than psychotherapeutic models of change if the research evidence supporting its application were more convincing. Unfortunately, though there is a substantial amount of published work on the practice of clinical supervision its quality has rarely matched its quantity (Ellis and Ladany, 1997). When Ellis and his colleagues reviewed 12 years of published empirical studies in clinical supervision from 1981 to 1993 and evaluated them against a series of established scientific criteria that could threaten the validity of each experiment's findings, they were palpably unimpressed by the results (Ellis *et al.*, 1996). They concluded that the vast majority of published research that they had analysed failed to meet necessarily rigorous academic standards. Subsequently the authors concluded that there currently exists no worthwhile scientific evidence base on which the assiduous supervisor could found her practice. By the same token those presuming to train supervisors for their role cannot point to an established body of empirical knowledge to support their educational programming. If we cannot say with confidence what works in supervision, how dare we imagine we know how to prepare clinical supervisors for their responsibilities?

While other researchers (Milne and James, 2000) have found more encouragement in the available literature than Ellis and his colleagues, there remain substantial obstacles to a truly evidence-based curriculum for supervisor training. The acid test of effective supervision would be demonstrable proof that a particular form of supervisory intervention could be traced through to a positive clinical outcome for the client receiving help from the supervisee. This is the whole point of the exercise. However, the number of causal links and intervening variables that must be accounted for in testing this hypothesis is formidable. We would expect the clinical outcome of any psychological intervention to be affected by factors such as the personal characteristics of the therapist; the nature of the problem for which the client has sought help; the brand of therapy employed; the setting within which the work was conducted; extra-therapeutic life events; and so on. Unsurprisingly, therefore, no published research yet appears to have established a secure relationship between supervisor conduct and patient outcome (Holloway and Neufeldt, 1995). What chance, then, of adding yet another link to this lengthy causal chain by asking what form of specialist training would best equip the supervisor to set in train the beneficial sequence of events that would result in life getting better for the client/consumer at the end of the line? Furthermore, there are problems for any UK clinical psychologists who might wish to draw even tentative clues for good practice from the extant body of research evidence on clinical supervision for it is overwhelmingly American and conducted with counsellors, counselling psychologists and psychotherapists. Differences in professional training structures, as well as in service delivery systems, mean that we should be tentative about generalizing findings from even the best-conducted studies across very varying contexts (Carroll, 1988).

This fleeting review goes some way to explaining why supervisor training appears to have been largely overlooked as both a professional development activity and a research enterprise. It is evidently not going to be straightforward either to design a credible training programme for supervisors or to evaluate its effectiveness. Why bother?

Rationale for supervisor training

The primary justification for formalizing supervisor training lies not in its scientific foundations but in the pivotal role supervision plays in the scrutiny of trainees' evolving clinical competence. Clinical supervision is the means by which trainee clinical psychologists gain the practical skills required to deliver the therapeutic service for which most will subsequently be employed. They can learn 'about' psychotherapeutic theory and research findings in university lecture theatres and libraries (so called 'declarative knowledge'). However, the capacity to translate this book-based wisdom into effective practice requires a well-developed sense of 'how' and 'when' to intervene during a therapeutic session that requires 'procedural' and 'conditional' knowledge. These skills are acquired through experiential learning that cannot just involve exposure to more and more hapless clients until our trainee finally somehow gets the hang of it. Clinical supervisors have a responsibility to both supervisees and their patients to ensure that this educational venture proceeds as efficiently and safely as possible. Clinical work must be planned. Therapeutic sessions need to be systematically reviewed, for it is this process of considered reflection that transforms exposure into meaningful experience (Boud, 1985). Sometimes crises will have to be managed. Finally the clinical supervisor plays a crucial professional gatekeeping role in determining whether supervisees are safe to practise. Of course it is possible to fail a clinical psychology training programme on academic grounds by, for example, submitting a sub-standard research thesis. However, it is clinical supervisors alone who directly sample the quality of the face-to-face contacts that trainees have with clients. Indeed, any direct access to a novice therapist's work with clients is likely to be infrequent as we continue to rely heavily (and some would say naively) on the supervisee's self-report in clinical supervision. When qualified clinical psychologists are professionally reprimanded it is rarely because of their inadequate essay technique. In the hierarchy of competences of our profession appropriate and effective care of patients should surely top the list. Clinical supervisors are pivotal members of the training community who must both energetically promote best practice and maintain safe professional standards. Can we seriously argue that clinical psychologists do not need to be properly prepared for this essential role? Quite how they should be prepared is another question entirely.

The content of supervisor training

In the UK clinical psychology training programmes have been obliged since 1989 to provide some form of supervisor training as a condition of their continued accreditation by the British Psychological Society. However, these conditions do not stipulate either the minimum dosage or the curriculum that should be followed. Nonetheless even this level of professional guidance is more stringent than that applying to contemporary US clinical psychology training programmes (Knapp and Vandecreek, 1997). As a consequence the British training community has considerable collective experience in organizing educational modules for clinical psychologists who are about to take on supervisory responsibilities for the first time. Typically, the consumers of this training are recently qualified clinicians who are just becoming eligible for the supervisor role. Is there a way of distilling the understanding that has been acquired through the development of these modules so that a consensus on good practice might be achieved?

The movement towards competence-based training in the health professions has prompted a number of researchers to experiment with novel ways of investigating what exactly a capable clinical psychologist, speech therapist, dietician, etc. should be able to do (Caves, 1988). A popular vehicle for dissecting a large body of opinion is the 'Delphi approach' (Clayton, 1997; Stonefish and Busby, 1996). This methodology aims to consult the views of a representative panel of judges who are considered expert in a given field. It seeks to promote consensus decision-taking in two ways. Firstly, the technique involves an iterative sequence of consultations through which panel members receive written feedback, not only on their own views but also on those of all their fellow judges. Having digested this information, each panel member is invited to reconsider his or her opinion. Secondly, the Delphi process is traditionally organized using postal questionnaires. It has hence been characterized as 'how to hold a meeting with no one there'. Even if it were possible to gather hordes of experts together in a single room the developers of the Delphi approach reckoned that the resulting large group dynamics would be inimical to reflective participatory discussion. On the contrary they predicted that some voices would be dominant while others might be scarcely heard. They also feared that public debate might entrench opposing views rather than promote the gradual emergence of an agreed group position which consensus policy-making requires. Although Delphi methodology was initially developed by the US defence industry as a predictive tool, it has subsequently found ready application in the field of professional education (Green and Gledhill, 1993; Williams and Webb, 1994; White and Russell, 1995). The approach therefore might enable us to satisfy our curiosity about the collective opinion of those currently running supervisor training modules for UK clinical psychologists.

The Delphi survey

While fuller descriptions of the Delphi technique are available elsewhere for the interested reader to consult (Jones and Hunter, 1995), the simple mechanics of this particular experiment warrant a brief explanation. The goal of the project was to see if an adequate consensus on the most useful format for the basic training of clinical supervisors in clinical psychology could be constructed. The panel of 50 'experts' represented the primary stakeholders in the professional training of clinical psychologists in the UK: ten clinical tutors (who routinely organized placement rotas and supervisor training modules); ten programme directors (who had ultimate oversight of the post-graduate clinical training programmes); ten heads of department (who both employed the would-be supervisors and routinely recruited newly qualified clinical psychologists into the NHS workforce); ten experienced supervisors (who had all been providing placements for their local university training course for a minimum of five years); and finally ten novice supervisors (who were attending an introductory series of supervisor training workshops and so offered a consumers' perspective). The task set for this august set of judges was to complete a postal questionnaire by rating the importance of 45 potential elements of a basic training package for new clinical supervisors on a seven-point scale, and whenever possible write a few words to explain their thinking. The 45 items had been culled from a range of relevant sources such as professional guidelines, the curricula of specialist diploma courses in clinical supervision, and published research papers. This constituted Round One of the Delphi procedure. For Round Two panel members received both quantitative and qualitative feedback on the full range of replies given to each item during Round One. They were then asked to re-rate the initial 45 items, plus offer their opinions on five further items added as a result of Round One recommendations. All 50 of the panel completed Round One and 47 managed to last through to the end of Round Two!

The full results of this survey are available from the author, but a few essential 'headline findings' will suffice for the purposes of this chapter. Firstly, the consensus building claims of the Delphi methodology received some support. In Round Two the variance of replies was significantly less than in Round One for 26 of the 45 items. Of the remaining 19 items, 18 showed no significant difference and on one item Round Two variance was higher than in Round One. Of more practical import, the second round of consultation served to remove some troubling inter-group disagreements that emerged in the analysis of Round One replies. At this stage the novice supervisors appeared out of kilter with their more senior colleagues. Analysis of variance showed they had rated nine items as significantly less important than any of the other subgroups of judges. This pattern of scores suggested a possible mismatch between what our youthful consumers wanted from a supervisor training module and what their 'elders and betters' thought they needed! However, all these significant inter-group differences of opinion disappeared after the analysis of the Round Two questionnaires.

Overall the results of this consultative exercise indicated that there may well be a working consensus on a standard curriculum for the basic training needs of new supervisors in clinical psychology. In Round Two the mean score of the lowest rated item was 4.58 on a seven-point scale, so there was nothing here that could be classified as unimportant or irrelevant. However, even in this top-heavy distribution of scores a definite sense of priority could be detected. The most valued component was 'considering when and how to fail a placement' with a mean rating of 6.76. The next three most important elements were 'legal responsibilities of supervisors' (6.54), 'the need to ensure that the supervisee's client receives appropriate care' (6.52) and 'how to negotiate a placement contract' (6.52). The message here seems to be that novice supervisors need to be ethically sensitive and procedurally well-informed (Russell and Petrie, 1994) before assuming their new responsibilities. The lowest-rated items provide an intriguing insight into what is unlikely to get new supervisors excited. 'Bottom of the Pops' was 'require that supervisor provide audio or video recordings of actual supervision sessions' with a mean score of 4.58. This lack of enthusiasm for systematic scrutiny of the supervisor's own performance was echoed in the third-lowest scoring item 'provide formal supervision for the trainee supervisors' (4.94). The other undervalued components falling in the bottom four of the elements surveyed were 'the use of non-traditional formats, e.g. group, peer' (4.72) and 'providing specific instructions for trainees' (4.96). At first sight the identification of these possible elements of supervisor training as relatively unimportant is somewhat worrying. Unless a serious effort is made to ensure that lessons learned on training ventures are transferred into everyday practice, any commitment to continued professional development in health care can easily be presented as a waste of scarce resources (Davis *et al.*, 1992). Education should make a noticeable difference. However, an alternative interpretation of these results is that the panel members have a keen understanding of the anxieties and priorities of novice supervisors. They have articulated a 'hierarchy of need' (Maslow, 1943) in which safe practice and professional survival assume immediate prominence. Perhaps new supervisors will not be ready to seek out external feedback or experiment with a range of supervisory approaches until they have established a necessary level of role security. It is not therefore a question of irrelevance as much as one of timing – an argument made in a number of qualitative comments suggesting that some educational initiatives would be more appropriate for experienced rather than novice supervisors. We shall return later to the theme of the continued training needs of experienced clinical supervisors.

Evaluating supervisor training modules

If the promise suggested by our Delphi survey were to be translated into a more standardized set of guidelines for those organizing basic supervisor training modules, this would not, of itself, guarantee any improvement in the manner in which novice supervisors go about their task. Continued professional development is not an act of faith. The outcomes of CPD programmes need to be carefully monitored. As indicated in the introductory literature review, it will be beyond the capacity of module organizers to trace the impact of their efforts right through to possible symptomatic improvements in clients seen by the supervisees of those attending supervisor training workshops. How far can we reasonably expect responsible educators to travel along this causal chain (Holloway, 1984)?

Most current courses probably elicit 'how was it for you?' consumer satisfaction feedback from module attenders. This approach has its merits because introductory training courses for clinical supervisors are likely to be repeated at regular intervals and their character can be shaped by user preferences (for example employing more small group discussion rather than a formal lecture format). Be warned, however, that the road to hell is paved with clinical psychology training programme organizers desperately trying to placate last year's students! A more serious concern about relying on consumer satisfaction measures to evaluate the effectiveness of these CPD modules is their failure to investigate what supervisors have learned from their study and whether any new learning will find ready application in their day-to-day working lives. It is these kinds of questions that the systematic evaluation of 'learning outcomes' tries to answer (Shillitoe *et al.*, 2002).

What sort of a difference should effective supervisor training make? Certainly we would anticipate some changes in attitude – for example, novice supervisors should feel a little more confident in their new role. They should probably have acquired some fresh factual knowledge such as an understanding of the protocol for mid-placement visits. Finally we would hope that they might actually behave differently – for example, by putting into practice their good intentions to safeguard supervision slots against competing clinical priorities. Evaluation strategies can be developed to monitor each of these categories of learning outcome.

Psychologists have traditionally used a simple scaling technique termed the 'semantic differential' (Osgood *et al.*, 1957) to track shifts in their patients' attitudes. Why not use similar methods on each other? For example, the following statement could be rated on a seven-point scale from totally disagree (1) to totally agree (7):

> It is imperative that supervisors complete all course paperwork thoroughly and on time

This measure could be taken at the beginning and end of a training module for supervisors, and would test whether opinions had shifted on this issue during the course of the workshop.

The brief review of the extant research literature in the field of clinical supervision might suggest that there may not be much strictly factual knowledge to convey to would-be supervisors. However, there are some aspects of the supervisor's role for which accurate information is crucial; for example, regarding the legal responsibilities of the supervisor. Multiple choice questionnaires (MCQs) can be a useful way to check factual knowledge, especially if questions developed for one cohort of learners can be repeated with subsequent classes (Lowe, 1991). Formats vary and the approach lends itself easily to computer marking and feedback where appropriate. An example of a multiple-choice question that might grab the attention of our fellow psychologists is:

The proportion of US graduate students in psychology who have had some form of sexual relationship with one of their professional educators has been estimated as:

(a) <5 per cent
(b) between 5 per cent and 10 per cent
(c) between 10 per cent and 15 per cent
(d) between 15 per cent and 20 per cent
(e) >20 per cent

According to Glaser and Thorpe (1986) the figure is 17 per cent so (d) is the correct answer. In fact, earlier US research (Pope *et al.*, 1979) reported that 1 in 4 women who received their doctoral degree in psychology had had past sexual contact with a supervisor.

The ultimate effectiveness of supervisor training modules depends on the lessons learned in the rarified atmosphere of a specialist workshop being transferred to the much messier and demanding setting of 'NHS world'. Although the Delphi survey suggested new supervisors might not be enthusiastic about having their practice closely scrutinized, some can be persuaded to opt into a voluntary scheme that monitors their performance during placements (Green, 1997). This arrangement suits the use of goal-attainment scaling (GAS) as a means of checking whether supervisors can meet their own individually determined expectations. GAS has been employed in a range of therapeutic settings (Kiresuk *et al.*, 1994), but has also worked well in an educational context in general and the field of clinical supervision in particular (Green and Sherrard, 1999). The approach asks the individual to specify broadly what she wishes to achieve and then decide for herself what would constitute a reasonable outcome of her efforts. Once this performance indicator has been operationally defined, she must determine what would constitute both 'better than' and 'worse than' expected outcomes. So, for example, a novice supervisor might construct the goal-attainment scale indicated in Table 6.1 to map her intentions of establishing a negotiated placement contract with the trainee clinical psychologist whom she will be supervising on a forthcoming placement.

Table 6.1 Goals to be achieved within two weeks of start of placement

+2	much better than expected outcome	Full written contract negotiated with trainee meeting all placement guidelines and trainee preferences
+1	better than expected outcome	Full written contract that incorporates some of the trainee's preferences
0	expected outcome	Placement contract agreed and written up in note form; meets most placement guidelines
−1	worse than expected outcome	Verbal contract only; trainee knows what to expect from this placement
−2	much worse than expected outcome	Haven't got round to any sort of contractual discussions

The experienced supervisor

In 2000 81 per cent of trainees entering training in clinical psychology within the UK were less than 29 years old. With luck, therefore, the average qualified practitioner will be able to offer some 30 years of service to the Health Service. Our discussion thus far has centred on the training needs of new supervisors, the bulk of whom will probably have been working as autonomous professionals for only a couple of years. Even if the introductory module that we have envisaged becomes increasingly well standardized and evaluated in the future, it is doubtful whether an improved initial programme of supervisor training could serve as an effective 'once and forever' preparation (like the UK driving test). Part of the argument for regular updating of senior clinical supervisors (DCP, 2001a) relates to the inevitable organizational changes that structures of professional education undergo from time to time at both a local and national level. However, a more fundamental training concern is how best to make the expertise of experienced clinicians available to their supervisees. This is not primarily a question of keeping senior supervisors 'on the books' as it were, but more the familiar challenge of facilitating communication across generations.

The natural history of professional expertise

Researchers into expert performance across a range of professions have indicated that the more established an individual becomes in their own career the more they tend to rely on implicit understandings of their craft that have evolved as a result of accumulated experience rather than book-based knowledge (Eraut, 1994). This often makes for swift and skilful performance when the professional is able to respond intuitively to the immediate demands of any particular situation (for example, the moment-to-moment interpersonal dynamics of a psychotherapy consultation). However, there is a downside to this almost automatic application of tacit knowledge. At a time when the Health Service is heavily investing in evidence-based medicine

Unconsciously incompetent	Consciously incompetent
Unconsciously competent	Consciously competent

Figure 6.1 Sequence of skill acquisition

and consumers of clinical psychology are themselves becoming increasingly well-informed, it is something of a liability if senior practitioners cannot give an articulate account of why they do what they do. As many a golfer will attest, the charm of not knowing quite how you hit the ball down the pro-verbial middle palls considerably when you are trying to correct a virulent hook that is wrecking your scorecard. It can be very difficult to correct performance that is under the control of implicit learning (Tomlinson, 1999). Furthermore, if experienced supervisors are unable to find a way to convey their understanding to trainees and share the lessons they have learned over years of practice, their wisdom may well end up being wastefully underused and, worse still, carelessly undervalued.

It has been suggested that as we acquire skills we characteristically move through a series of levels from an initial reliance on rules and external direction, on to a more flexible and responsive style, to a final intuitive grasp of situations that is founded on a deep tacit understanding (Dreyfus and Dreyfus, 1986). This sequence is simply summarized in Figure 6.1.

The notional journey that the learner undertakes passes from a blissful ignorance about the complexity of the job at hand through an uncomfort-able recognition of his relative incompetence via a deliberate attempt to 'do it right', then on to the apparently effortless enactment that is the hallmark of truly skilled performance (Clarkson and Gilbert, 1991). Many of the conversations that occur between experienced supervisors and trainees on clinical psychology training courses can be typified as attempts made by the consciously incompetent to learn from the unconsciously competent. We should not therefore be surprised if these discussions sometimes turn out to be rather frustrating for the two participants! Equally, we should not underestimate their educational potential for both parties.

Knowing more than we can easily say . . .

The professional training of clinical psychologists is heavily loaded towards the acquisition of 'codified knowledge' (Eraut, 2000) – that is to say, know-ledge that is public, explicit and therefore examinable. The smart trainee knows this and prioritizes her learning accordingly (i.e. 'if it's not coming up in the exam I'm not interested'). The effective practice of clinical psychology, however, relies much more heavily on accumulated 'personal knowledge' of individuals, contexts and indeed the psychologist herself. Personal knowledge takes time to acquire and has a strong tacit dimension. Successful theory–practice integration requires the creative synthesis of codified and personal knowledge. Our students are not always convinced that the current structure of clinical psychology training courses best promotes this combined model of learning. Could developments in supervisor training do something to correct this perceived imbalance?

It should not be easy to produce an explanation for behaviour that relies on implicit learning. Indeed one school of thought argues that the defining characteristic of tacit knowledge is its very inaccessibility. If you can talk about it, it's not tacit (Polanyi, 1967). An alternative reading of the literature (Eraut, 2000) encourages us to view all professional knowledge as lying on an implicit – explicit continuum, and suggests that conscious deliberation can allow individuals to work out for themselves the reasoning behind some of their seemingly intuitive therapeutic work. If we wish to exhort our more experienced supervisors to 'account for themselves' in this exploratory fashion, we need to establish a safe climate for experiment. Otherwise the likely outcome will be the shallow explanations and expedient self-justifications that are our defensive stock-in-trade (Wilson and Keil, 2000). Envisage a workshop where certainty is banned and doubt admired, in which supervisors give 'thick' descriptive accounts (Pidgeon *et al.*, 1991) of a piece of therapeutic work in which they had impressed themselves but weren't sure why. As each detailed story develops more contextual information is supplied – the setting; the bodily feelings of the therapist; previous exchanges with this client, etc. Fellow supervisors are encouraged to use their own professional curiosity to support the speaker's sense of inquiry, not by offering 'ready-made' theoretical interpretations (a cardinal weakness of clinical psychologists) but by asking intriguing questions (Ravenette, 1997). 'How come you chose to make that comment when you did and not earlier?' 'Do you recall ever feeling like this before?' And so on. I've tried just this sort of experiment on several occasions and the results have always been interesting. Some conversations 'took off' more than others and it would be naive to think that this spot of relexive psychology allowed participants to unearth all the mysteries of their implicit decision-making processes (Nisbet and Wilson, 1977). However, the exercise prompted truly constructive discussions as small groups of psychologists struggled to make sense of incidents that would not usually be subjected to such a level of sensitive scrutiny. Feedback from supervisors suggested that these 'learning conversations' (Thomas and Harri-Augstein, 1985) can provide an educational pay-off for both the 'teller' and the 'enquirer'. The enquirer gets a privileged access to the thinking processes that inform apparently automatic professional competence. The teller is helped to reflect on a noteworthy clinical episode and systematically think it through so as to complete the experiential learning cycle (Kolb, 1984). In each case there is movement along the continuum from implicit to explicit understanding. All we need now is to get the supervisees involved.

Before ending discussion of the training needs of experienced supervisors a particularly painful nettle needs to be grasped. While attendance at supervisor workshops is ever an occasional venture accidentally triggered by the passing interest of individual practitioners, those whom we might consider most in need of developing their supervisory skills may well prove to be the least likely to take up the learning opportunities at hand. This is probably not a consequence of wilful neglect of a key professional responsibility. One of the saddest handicaps of incompetence is that a lot of the time we just do not realize quite how poorly we are performing (Kruger and Dunning, 1999). Nearly everybody reckons they are a better-than-average car driver, and this 'above average' effect seems to occur across a range of skills and populations (Alicke *et al.*, 1995). Furthermore, the tendency to inflate our appraisal of our own capability seems to be strongest when our performance is, relatively speaking, at its weakest. There is also some suggestion that this mismatch between confidence (how well we subjectively think we're doing) and competence (how well we actually perform according to objective criteria) tends to be more marked in experienced as opposed to novice health professionals (Marteau *et al.*, 1989). On a more positive note it appears that even these most self-serving of attributions may be open to revision if people engage seriously in skill development through training. Basically once we realize what competent performance in any particular domain entails, we can acknowledge (and therefore remedy) our past limitations.

These findings have implications for supervisor training. There is no reason to assume that clinical supervisors will be uniformly competent in their role. Those who are least well regarded may well consider their own performance perfectly adequate. Training experiences can prove an effective counter to unrealistically positive self-appraisal. The message seems clear. Develop 'advanced' training modules that all senior supervisors must attend on a regular basis. The practicalities of pursuing this policy will undoubtedly prove complex but the logic of the proposal remains compelling.

Why not have supervisee training as well?

The emphasis thus far in this chapter has been exclusively on supervisor training. The unwary reader might therefore assume that supervision is something that the supervisor does to the supervisee rather in the manner that a cook might fry an egg. The quality of your breakfast depends on the skilfulness of the chef (though it is acknowledged in culinary circles that some eggs are more co-operative than others). In fact, as the expanding research literature on the importance of the supervisory alliance demonstrates (Beinart, 2002), successful supervision is a collaborative process in which both parties must master their reciprocal roles. Why put all our efforts into training up one half of a dancing partnership?

In the UK nurses have been slower to embrace the culture of clinical supervision than their colleagues in the mental health professions such as counselling and psychotherapy. Since nursing is the largest subgroup of employees within the NHS, the task of establishing a profession-wide commitment to maintaining competence through supervision is considerable. While the intellectual arguments to support this shift in culture can be made quite persuasively (Bond and Holland, 1998), any rapid expansion in numbers of skilled supervisors presents severe practical problems. The generation of senior practitioners who are the natural resource to tap for this new role have themselves had little prior experience of the benefits of clinical supervision on which to draw. Furthermore, nursing, much like clinical psychology, has yet to establish a standardized structure for preparing clinical supervisors for their extra responsibilities. Add the suspicion that many qualified nurses may remain unenthusiastic about embracing the culture of clinical supervision (Bishop, 1994) and the challenge facing advocates of change starts to look increasingly formidable.

Cutcliffe (2001) has therefore advocated the novel strategy of committing resources to supervisee rather than supervisor training. He suggests that this initiative can have a number of both short- and long-term benefits. In the immediate future nursing students will enter placements with a more sophisticated awareness of the part they can play in making the supervisory relationship work. At a later date when these students themselves begin to take on supervisory responsibilities (in the first year after qualification in some nursing specialities) they would already be committed to the supervisory cause and so enter the new role with confidence and enthusiasm. Ultimately Cutcliffe hopes to change the professional culture of nursing in the UK by this 'bottom-up' revolution.

Within clinical psychology in Britain we do not need to be so pessimistic about the effectiveness of supervisor training, We are a smaller trade than nursing with an established commitment to supervision at both pre- and post-qualification levels. Nonetheless there is a sound case to be made for introducing teaching on supervision into the professional issues curriculum of our doctoral training programmes. For example, trainees can be inducted into the difficult art of providing a frank and thorough report of a therapeutic session, or set an essay to review the research literature on cultural factors in clinical supervision (Lopez, 1997). It is interesting, too, that our experience in Leeds of successfully running supervision workshops attended by both supervisors and final-year trainees has been repeated elsewhere (Hitchen et al., 1997). Supervisee training could yet be the 'coming thing' in clinical psychology as well as nursing.

Final thoughts

The focus of this chapter has been on the nature of clinical supervision provided for trainee clinical psychologists as a core component of their professional training. Clinical psychologists in the UK are now required to organize continued supervision of their practice throughout their careers (DCP, 2001a). While there are probably fundamental supervisory skills that apply across all supervision relationships, there is also a credible argument that supervisory style should be consciously matched with the developmental stage of the supervisee (Stoltenberg *et al.*, 1998). For example, an as yet unqualified assistant psychologist will need a level of direction that would be inappropriate for an established autonomous senior clinician. To date, the empirical evidence on which specialist developmentally sensitive supervisor training can be founded is sparse (Skovholt and Ronnestad, 1995). In particular the longitudinal studies that are necessary properly to test the theory that therapists progress through predictable developmental stages in the course of their careers have not yet been conducted (Watkins, 1995). It is a moot question whether the pressures to offer support to supervisors asked to expand their training repertoires will await the completion of lengthy prospective research programmes.

Although there have been several references in the chapter thus far to the study of clinical supervision in other professions such as nursing and counselling, the provision of supervisor training for clinical psychologists in the UK is predominantly unidisciplinary. Members of fellow mental health professions both provide supervision for some clinical psychologists and receive supervision from them. Why therefore have we so infrequently organized supervisor training on a multidisciplinary basis? The ideology of 'shared learning' raises some educators' hackles at the pre-qualification stage (Forman and Nyatanga, 1999), but surely established supervisors are secure enough in their professional identities to gain from the melting pot of inter-disciplinary training. There is an irresistible logic in the argument that the best way to prepare psychologists for inter-professional supervision is to run interdisciplinary training workshops (Leathard, 1994).

Conclusion

The prevailing *Zeitgeist* within both clinical psychology in the UK and the National Health Service supports investment in developing supervision skills as an important quality assurance measure. This sense that the time is right compensates somewhat for the tangible lack of a firm evidence base on which our training efforts can be founded. We are, however, far from clueless and can do better than sit on our hands waiting for the ultimate study in supervisor training to be published. There is probably enough professional consensus and research expertise within the clinical psychology training community in the UK to mount larger-scale and more formally evaluated programmes than have as yet been reported. This quite achievable goal would add significantly to the pool of practical and intellectual knowledge on which fellow trainers in our own and other professions can draw in the future.

Chapter 7

Difference and power in supervision

The case of culture and racism

Nimisha Patel

Introduction

The centrality of power relations in the supervisory process is the main theme within this chapter. A specific focus on the case of culture and racism is intended to provide an example of how power relations can manifest and how they can be constructively addressed to enhance the effectiveness of supervision and psychological practice.

This chapter attempts to address three main questions:

1   Why address power and difference in supervision, specifically in relation to ethnicity, racism and culture?
2   What are the key issues with regards to culture and racism and how might they become salient in the different aspects of supervision and supervisory tasks?
3   How could supervisors in particular, and supervisees, enhance the quality and effectiveness of supervision by incorporating understanding of power relations and the issues of culture and racism?

Some of the implications for supervisors, supervisees, the profession of clinical psychology, and psychological services are also considered.

Power and supervision

Supervision can be described as a process characterized by a collaboration between the supervisor and the supervisee, with the explicit task of ensuring ethical and professional therapeutic practice aimed at improving the client's psychological and social quality of life. Taylor (1994) identifies three purposes in terms of the 'overseeing therapy' aspect of supervision: transmitting the values and ethics of the profession, controlling and protecting services provided by the supervisee, and helping the supervisee to develop a conceptual framework. These purposes highlight the role of the supervisor as the educator, endowed with the responsibility towards the supervisee of both imparting knowledge and facilitating intellectual and practical skills. The role of the supervisor as an evaluator, assessor, gatekeeper and transmitter of values for the profession points to their responsibilities to the profession, whilst the role of the supervisor in controlling and protecting services provided emphasizes the responsibility of the supervisor towards the client.

The responsibilities of the supervisor, as mentioned above, thus illustrate the centrality of power relations in the supervisory process, yet the infrequent mention of power relations in literature in this field exposes one of the many 'givens' in our professional practice. The tacit acceptance and therefore the invisibility of the role of power in supervision can inadvertently lead to a misuse of power relations and often give rise to a supervisory process characterized not by collaboration but by coercion, however subtle and unintentional. In this regard, collaboration is then seen as a key principle in developing a supervisory relationship where both the supervisor and the supervisee are engaged in a learning process and where responsibility and accountability are more equally shared (Orlans and Edwards, 2001).

The notion of collaboration necessitates some exploration of common interpretations and manifestations of power in the supervisory context. Power has been described and theorized about in many ways, but in relation to supervision few meanings have been offered in the literature. Taylor (1994) suggests that a feminist emphasis in both counselling and supervision involves the sharing of power in an effort to establish a mutual, reciprocal and non-authoritarian relationship to facilitate optimal therapeutic outcomes. In this context, she focuses on the social history, the socialization and the relatively powerless structural position women face, and what she refers to as the general lack of 'real' power. Here, power is used to refer to the unequal distribution and access to resources and privileges which impact differentially on the life experiences of women, often in disadvantageous ways. In relation to supervision, Taylor (1994) thus argues that power and gender feature strongly in any therapeutic and supervisory relationship, particularly where clients seeking help themselves feel powerless in many ways, and that supervision has a responsibility to challenge inequalities in power (e.g. gender bias) implicit in our culture. The concept of social power (Cooke and Kipnis, 1986) has also been used in a similar way in relation to supervisory interactions to describe the differential distribution of and claim on power men and women have and assume in their interactions. Miller (1991) has argued that traditional constructions of power can inhibit women to assume greater power in interactions for fear of losing or jeopardizing the relationship with their interactional partner. She further proposes a model of shared power where individuals can be empowered within a connected relationship – what has also been described as relational power (Surrey, 1991). Based on this concept of relational power, Nelson (1997) posits that the supervisor (through the use of their expert power) can enable a supervisee in assuming greater power over time, and expressing their personal power within their interactions. Thus, power is conceptualized not simply as a commodity that one has and the other does not, but a feature reflecting a social reality which becomes manifest in the interactions within a relationship such as a supervisory or therapeutic relationship.

Others have conceptualized power in relation to ethnicity in similar ways; for example, describing power as 'the crucial variable in minority–majority relations and [which] affects the ability of individuals or groups to realise their goals and interests, even in the face of resistance to the power' (Kavanaugh and Kennedy, 1992: 17). In addressing the complex power relations present in cross-cultural supervision, Ryde (2000) introduces the concept of role power, which she asserts points to the power inherent in the role of the supervisor, cultural power, which refers to the power of the dominant ethnic grouping, and individual power, which points to the particular power of the individual's personality. Ryde's contributions enable a more sophisticated analysis of the many ways in which power relations become manifest, and the ways in which they may change depending on who the supervisor is, who the supervisee is and who the client is. For example, a supervisor may be white, male and from a working-class background, a client may be white, female, working class and able-bodied, and the supervisee may be black, male, middle class and gay.

Social inequalities are therefore complex and multilayered with any person in the supervisory triad, the supervisor, supervisee or the client, reflecting differing power relations, differing social positions and experiences of both privilege and disadvantage, simultaneously but on different axes. In supervision, power then becomes a complex reality requiring a sustained, committed and sophisticated social, political and psychological analysis rather than a one-off acknowledgement as a token gesture in the supervisory process. The recognition of power relations and the social and political inequalities experienced by clients, supervisees and supervisors in itself is inadequate. Here it is argued that it is both the supervisor's and the supervisee's ethical responsibility to ensure that the supervisory process attends to social inequalities and their impact on all those in the supervisory triad and, most importantly, on the client.

However, integrating this perspective into training in clinical psychology and into the training and the practice of supervisors within the profession remains a matter of choice in Britain, rather than an ethical and professional obligation. In considering how inequalities and difference in relation to 'race', culture and ethnicity can be integrated into training, supervision and continuing professional development, some attempts have been made in Britain in clinical psychology (for example, Dennis, 2001; Patel et al., 2000) and in counselling (Lago and Thompson, 1997). In the United States there is far more literature in this field and one predominant theme is the focus on describing 'multicultural supervision' and 'cross-cultural supervision'. Leong and Wagner (1994) suggest that multicultural supervision refers to those supervisory and (or counselling) situations which are affected by multiple cultural factors – for example, in relation to the client, supervisee and super-visor. Cross-cultural supervision is defined as a supervisory relationship in which the supervisor and the supervisee are from different cultural groups. Both terms have been used to refer to supervision which considers issues of culture and ethnicity, such as differing life experiences, values, beliefs, word views and ethnic identity development in relation to counselling and psy-chotherapy assessment, intervention, knowledge base and the supervisory and the therapeutic relationships (for example, D'Andrea and Daniels, 1997; Constantine, 1997; Priest, 1994; Brown and Landrum-Brown, 1995; Gopaul-Nicol and Brice-Baker, 1998). In addition, there have been some studies examining cultural and racial issues in supervision (for a brief review see Helms and Cook, 1999).

However, both in Britain and in the United States, there is a paucity of related literature focusing particularly on clinical psychology supervision and, more poignantly, there is little in the way of guidance on how to incorporate current understandings of power relations, social inequalities and issues of cultural difference and of racism into the supervision of clinical psychologists. In addition, as described in Chapter 3, current supervision models are based on specific psychological or psychotherapy theories or developed specifically for supervision, commonly referred to as developmental models.

Indeed, Banks (2001) argues that the use of supervision models based on specific theories or therapeutic models must be questioned, given that the cultural biases within those theories are inevitably reflected in supervision. Developmental models of supervision also need to be questioned as they are often presented as being universally applicable and devoid of any biases.

Before proceeding to address the second and third questions stated in the introduction, I shall return briefly to the notion of power and empowerment and the implications for integrating this into supervision.

Foucault's understanding of power (see Foucault, 1977, 1988) has been influential in the development of various theoretical, therapeutic and research practices, and perhaps it is of some relevance to the subject of supervision. Foucault's conceptualization of power pointed to the interactional nature and the constitutive force of power whereby power manifests and shares itself through everyday interactions, language, discourses, social practices, know-ledges and the ways in which we come to know of and understand personhood. The notion of resistance is an important ingredient in his theorizing of power relations, the idea that resistance can manifest itself within interactions, discourses and in people's attempts to challenge particular definitions of subjectivity, and, as such, power is neither seen as lineal nor static but as relational and as being culturally, socially and historically situated. Thus, Foucauldian analysis of power can enable us to study everyday interactions and institutional practices which can sustain regulatory systems of control.

Given that supervision is one of the main sites in which particular know-ledge is transmitted and perpetrated at the expense of other knowledge, where certain skills are fostered as institutionalized social practices (e.g. note keeping, research activities, therapeutic interventions) and where power relations permeate every aspect of the supervisory relationship and process, it is perhaps an appropriate place to focus on how issues of difference, inequality and oppression become manifest and how supervision can facilitate and nurture resistance in the struggle against oppression. However, one of the main criticisms of Foucault's analysis and theory of power is that he offered little in the way of encouragement or direction in challenging oppression and illustrating how resistance could be fostered (for example, Taylor, 1984). Furthermore, Foucauldian understandings of power neglect the material reality of power relations and their impact on people's lives, and their resistance to change. To focus only on power as it operates in everyday interactions, discourses and in regulatory systems actually serves to disguise the reality of actual material inequalities, thereby leaving the social order, and power, relatively unchanged.

Practice implications of an approach to supervision which attempts to address both interpretations of power include first, the necessity of including a social, cultural, historical and political analysis into every aspect of supervision; second, the importance of developing an awareness of how the client, the supervisee and the supervisor have been both privileged and oppressed and the impact on their lives and the significance of this in therapy and in supervision; and third, active exploration of the different levels and ways in which a clinical psychologist could intervene in negotiation with the client to create maximum change for the client in a way that would enhance their emotional, social and political well-being. These practices can be seen as opportunities for resistance in the Foucauldian sense, and, hopefully, for change in the political and personal sense. The underlying assumption is that the ultimate and desirable goal of supervision is to empower the client through the process of empowering supervision.

The following sections focus on four main aspects of supervision. For each of these, some of the key issues with regards to culture, racism and ethnicity are identified and, also, some guidance is provided on how supervision can integrate and facilitate an understanding of power relations and of issues of culture, ethnicity and racism in empowering practice. The four main aspects of supervision to be addressed are (1) the process of supervision, (2) developing knowledge, (3) developing skills, and (4) personal–professional development. In order to develop confidence and competence in addressing these issues in supervision both supervisors and supervisees would need to accept that learning to think and to question in a particular way are vital prerequisites to learning how to practise.

The process of supervision

As discussed earlier, the roles of the supervisor as educators, mentors, evaluators and trainers all accentuate the power imbalance between the supervisor and the supervisee. A supervisee from a black and minority ethnic background being supervised by say, a white majority ethnic supervisor inevitably amplifies this power imbalance by virtue of the differing histories, experiences, privileges and oppression experienced by both parties. Of course, even where both supervisee and supervisor share the same ethnic or cultural background, other variables, such as gender, age, and class will determine the nature of power relations in the process of supervision. Likewise, where both supervisee and supervisor share similar ethnicities, say white majority ethnic backgrounds, but where the client being discussed is from a minority ethnic background, power relations remain an issue for analysis and discussion.

Due to limitations on space, the focus in this chapter will be mainly on the experiences of black and minority ethnic supervisees being supervised by white majority ethnic supervisors, where clients may be from any majority or minority ethnic backgrounds. Numerous barriers exist in supervision to prevent an analysis and an exploration of the significance and effects of power relations and difference in terms of culture, ethnicity and racism. These barriers are important to understand if we are to begin changing supervisory practice to become more empowering for supervisees and for clients. Some of the common barriers include:

Colour blindness

Statements such as 'I treat all trainees in the same way, regardless of their ethnicity or colour' exemplify the commonest barrier to discussing power relations and their effects on the supervisee and the client. It is as if all supervisees are seen as colourless, culture-less and denuded of social and political contexts, as if the fact of racism and the reality of its impact on people's lives is not worthy of acknowledgement, let alone of discussion, in supervision. Ridley (1995) suggests that colour blindness can result from counsellors' (or supervisors' in this context) need to appear impartial, or from fears that they may actually be, or be thought of as, racist, or from fear of appearing ignorant or incompetent.

Colour consciousness

Ridley (1995) defines colour consciousness as the opposite of colour blindness, based on the belief that perhaps all of the client's (and the supervisee's) difficulties stem from their being a minority ethnic person. He suggests that 'white guilt' is a common cause. In supervision this can manifest itself in attributing all difficulties to being black with an implicit message that a detailed exploration of relevant issues in the supervisory relationship or the supervisory process cannot take place. Thus, the responsibility for change, if any is thought possible or desirable, rests with the supervisee, not the supervisor. Supervisees may themselves avoid raising issues of culture or oppression for fear of being themselves positioned as being overly preoccupied with such issues and with their own personal difficulties in relation to their ethnic identity or experiences of racism.

Pathologizing the supervisee or the client

Similarly to colour consciousness, supervisees often describe the process in supervision whereby they come to be held responsible for any difficulties in the client–supervisee or supervisee–supervisor difficulties, or where a supervisee fails to meet the expectations or standards set by the supervisor. Little space is allowed for a discussion of, say, the cultural biases inherent in the expectations or standards set by the supervisor, or of the cultural norms against which the supervisor may be judging the supervisee's competencies, knowledge and learning styles, or of the biases and oppressive functions of certain therapeutic models and interventions espoused by the supervisor. Supervisees, including trainees, thus can easily be labelled as perhaps 'lacking in an adequate level of competence', as 'being defensive and inflexible', as being 'resistant to feedback or reflexivity', or as 'requiring a greater level of instruction, guidance, monitoring or supervision'.

Discussion of power relations, cultural and racial oppression, the Euro-centricity of values in supervision or in the models or styles of interviewing remain absent, the supervisee carries both the blame as the perceived site of the problem and the responsibility for change.

Denying the importance of discussing power, culture and racism

Supervisors may never mention or invite or encourage any discussion at all about power relations or cultural differences. They may, if challenged or asked tentatively by a supervisee, respond that 'it's not an issue here, most, if not all our clients here are white', or 'we never see any black or minority ethnic people in this particular service/area'. The message to the supervisee is that culture, ethnicity and racism are not worthy of mention, discussion or understanding, regardless of the possible differences and inherent power relation between supervisee and supervisor. Exploration of the social, historical and political factors in why services are geared towards a relatively majority ethnic, homogeneous client population, and the implications of this for the minority ethnic population, or for the planning, design and delivery of psychological services, or for the minority ethnic supervisee working with an entirely majority ethnic client caseload, is absent.

Fukuyama's (1994) analysis of critical incidents also suggests that supervisors may tend to minimize supervisee's efforts to attend to their client's racial concerns. Helms and Cook (1999) give examples of 'supervisor minimisation strategies', including insisting that such matters are superficial and not (germane) in the client's 'real' problem; or refusing to discuss such issues, or devaluing the supervisee's competence if they choose to include such factors in their therapeutic endeavours. They suggest that in response to such strategies, supervisees may feel discouraged and reluctant to explore issues of culture or racism for fear of being negatively evaluated by the supervisor. Others have pointed out that the real fear of being scapegoated, marginalized (for example, amongst peers) and of being failed, if a trainee, can act as a major deterrent to voicing issues of discrimination even amongst peers (Patel *et al.*, 2000).

Expressing dissatisfaction with demands to integrate 'new material' into clinical and supervisory practice

Supervisors may often feel dissatisfied, pressured, misunderstood, undervalued and burdened with the increasing demands placed on them to provide a range of experience, to facilitate the development of a range of competencies and to ensure a scholarly and critical approach to the development of knowledge within supervision. Reactions include anger, irritation and outright dismissal of any suggestions or requests that supervision should include discussion and exploration of issues of culture, racism and power relations, perhaps because it is experienced as a demand, and one which arises out of an explicit criticism of the profession and clinical psychology practice (Patel *et al.*, 2000). Unfortunately, supervisees often bear the brunt and may be left feeling that they are making unreasonable demands, that they themselves or their training needs are an excessive and an unreasonable burden to the supervisor or that these issues are simply unimportant or unworthy of acknowledgement within the profession and supervision.

Not surprisingly, the supervisory relationship is fraught with complexities, anxieties, differences in expectations and perhaps mutual mistrust or suspiciousness when the supervisee and the supervisor are from different ethnic backgrounds, bringing differing histories, experiences, values, beliefs and hopes to the supervisory process. The majority ethnic supervisor's anxieties about their level of expertise or competence in understanding and addressing issues of power, culture, ethnicity and racism may be compounded by the minority ethnic supervisee's anxieties about how they will be judged, negatively evaluated and misunderstood or not understood at all by the supervisor because of their minority ethnic status. Gopaul-Nicol and Brice-Baker (1998) argue that such levels of anxiety in some minority ethnic supervisees might inhibit them from revealing difficulties in their work or weaknesses, and manifest in their reluctance to play videotapes or audiotapes, or discuss problematic aspects of a therapy session.

Crucial to any effective supervision is unquestionably the quality of the supervisory relationship. In relation to addressing power relations and their effects on the supervisor, supervisee and the client, the supervisory relationship must be prioritized as the primary area to be nurtured and developed. Martinez and Holloway (1997) suggest that both power and involvement are crucial to the development of trust and mutuality in the 'multicultural supervisory relationship'. Power is seen as a vehicle in constructing a mutually empowering relationship, and involvement is seen as referring to intimacy that includes 'attachments'; that is, the degree to which each person uses the other as a source of self-confirmation (Miller and Rogers, 1976). According to Holloway (1995) the supervisory relationship is the container of the process in which supervisee and supervisor negotiate a personal way of utilizing a structure of power and involvement that facilitates learning. But for both supervisor and supervisee to learn from one another through the process of supervision, both need to feel safe. Gatmon *et al.*'s (2001) study also highlights the importance of providing an atmosphere of safety, combined with a depth of dialogue and frequent opportunities to discuss cultural variables in the supervisory relationship, all of which were found to significantly contribute to building supervisory alliances and increasing supervisee satisfaction.

Improving supervisory practice

The question addressed in this section is how can supervisory practice be improved to facilitate the process of empowering supervision?

1   Safety and trust have been previously identified as key factors in supervision and their establishment and nurturance is arguably the most crucial goals within the supervisory relationship. The issue of feeling safe raises further questions such as: What does it mean to feel safe? Does it hold different meanings for supervisees and supervisors? How can safety and trust be achieved? Whose responsibility is it to make the supervisory relationship and process safe?

Feeling safe can mean essentially the same for both supervisee and supervisor: being able to be open, honest and reflective; being able to take risks in sharing one's concerns and doubts and being able to take risks in revealing one's own limitations in terms of knowledge and skills in relation to addressing issues of power, culture, ethnicity and racism. Feeling safe can mean being able to do the above within a trusting, honest, mutually respectful supervisory relationship where both parties are also explicit about their differing roles and tasks and the implicit power relations embedded in the relationship. Thus, feeling safe does not mean giving false reassurances that the supervisee (who may be a trainee) is not being evaluated; or that the supervisor will not be challenged if they make biased assumptions, racist comments or advocate a Eurocentric perspective. For the supervisor the challenge is learning how to model openness and learning about potentially deeply sensitive, often controversial and complex issues of cultural difference and racial oppression spanning the personal, professional and theoretical realms. For the supervisee the challenge is learning to take considered risks in being open, thoughtful, reflexive and challenging within the process of supervision.

Ultimately, and primarily, it is the supervisor's responsibility and obligation to create an atmosphere of safety and to develop a trusting relationship with the supervisee. To simply expect that the supervisee should feel safe and trust the supervisor is not enough, trust needs to be earned, safety needs to be demonstrated and the process of building a relationship conducive to mutual learning can thus be facilitated.

2 Developing a language to talk about power relations, culture, ethnicity, 'race', racism and oppression in supervision is a crucial step towards enhancing the supervisory relationship and process. Learning to talk about power and racism, for example, is often extremely difficult and anxiety-provoking. Supervisors can give permission to discuss such emotive, sensitive and complex issues and demonstrate a willingness to talk about them without being dismissive or attacking, to perhaps expose their uncertainties about the language to use or their limitations in knowledge about these concepts and issues, and to grapple with the implications for their own practice, for the services within which they work and for the profession.

3 Reflexivity on part of both the supervisor and the supervisee is a key ingredient in minimizing anxiety and in developing a supervisory relationship and a process conducive to mutual learning. Reflexivity in this context can mean the supervisor examining and reflecting on (a) their own ethnicity and culture and their ethnic identity, (b) their own experiences of power and powerlessness in their personal and professional lives and in their own supervision, (c) their theoretical models and clinical practice and inherent biases within them, (d) their assumptions, beliefs, values, biases and racism which inevitably influence their practice, their supervision and their relationship with the supervisee, (e) their stage in development as a supervisor and the related anxieties, expectations or attitudes to supervisees or to supervision, or to the demand to include newer and challenging approaches into their supervision, and (f) their own anxieties, fears, doubts, limitations, abilities and strengths in thinking about and addressing issues of power, culture and racism. The implications for how and where supervisors might do this will be addressed later in this chapter.

Reflexivity extends to the actual supervisory relationship too. Supervisors can ensure that reflection and discussion about the supervisory relationship itself is permissible, welcomed and a necessary part of the process of learning. This can include exploring cultural differences between supervisor and supervisee and their effects on each person's interactions, thinking and practice in supervision and in clinical work.

4 Establishing the parameters of who can raise the aforementioned issues, and how and when or what action might follow if such issues are raised, is essential to discuss and to negotiate in the supervisory relationship. The contracting process may begin at the point of establishing the supervisory relationship, but it is an ongoing process where the initial agreement is reviewed regularly (Scaife, 2001b). Supervisees should be given ongoing opportunities and also be actively facilitated in contributing to the contracting process and its ongoing review. The temptation for both parties may be

to avoid discussion of issues which understandably cause anxiety, discomfort and sometimes which can be very painful to acknowledge and explore. Both may collude to deny the significance of these issues and to avoid exploration of the implications, until maybe a crisis or problem arises, by which time there is already an impasse in the supervisory relationship and possibly in the clinical work. Crises in these situations typically escalate, reflexivity, discussion and analysis cease, the supervisory relationship deteriorates and is characterized by distance, misunderstandings, mistrust, fear and a lack of respect and, not surprisingly, learning comes to a halt for both supervisor and supervisee with inevitable implications for clinical work and clients.

Ideally, developing a supervisory contract which encompasses all the issues raised above, and which is conducted in an open, honest and collaborative way, will facilitate the development of a quality supervisory relationship where mutual learning can flourish.

Developing knowledge

An important function of supervision in clinical psychology is to facilitate awareness, understanding and skills in the application of a knowledge base which draws on psychological theories, research and practice-based evidence. The development of competence in this area within supervision is tradition-ally thought of only in relation to the supervisee's learning. Questions which arise include:

- who has the responsibility to impart knowledge to whom?
- whose knowledge is being imparted?
- what is the basis of that knowledge and how has it come to be produced?
- which knowledge is being privileged?
- which knowledge is absent or suppressed?

In clinical psychology training, supervision and practice the belief that all psychological theories are universally applicable, politically neutral and poten-tially beneficial, as opposed to being potentially toxic and oppressive, remains largely uncontested. Psychology's approach to 'race', racism and cultural difference in its knowledge base has historically been to either render the subject and reality totally invisible, or to focus on 'race' in an exploitative and abusive way (e.g. in examining 'race' and IQ), or to depoliticize it and to strip it of its social historical and political context (e.g. in discussing cultural difference as if it constituted nuances and idiosyncrasies which are located in the 'other'). However, some developments in psychology have contributed to a better understanding of power and racism in psychology's knowledge-production (see Henwood and Phoenix, 1999, for a summary), although this seems to have had little effect as yet on academic teaching in clinical psycho-logy or on the content and process of supervision in clinical psychology.

The Eurocentric nature of psychology's knowledge base points to the inherent limitations of this knowledge and to the potential for perpetrating oppression in theory production, and in supervisory and clinical practice. The blanket use of and the unquestioning approach to applying such knowledge to black and minority ethnic clients can be seen as amateurish at best or as abusive, or as 'secondary colonisation' at worst (Patel and Fatimilehin, 1999). In discussing the nature of unintentional racism in the use of psychological theories, Ridley (1995) describes four prominent categories of models of mental health – the deficit, medical, conformity and biopsychosocial models – in an effort to expose their limitations and their potential to perpetrate racism. If supervision is to be able to address the nature and function of power relations in psychology then it is incumbent upon supervisors to integrate an analysis and a critique of psychological knowledge, particularly in relation to their own field or speciality.

Improving supervisory practice

Supervisors can address issues of power, ideology, culture, racism and oppression in facilitating the supervisee's general competence in the understanding and application of psychological knowledge. The following includes suggestions that might aid this process:

1   Supervisors need to be committed to examining and critiquing their own knowledge base and their own previous trainings from a historical, cultural and political analysis in relation to identifying cultural biases, racist assumptions and oppressive functions of this knowledge. This can be done in private, in their own supervision, with colleagues or in their own training and services.
2   Supervisors need actively to engage in and facilitate ongoing reflection and critical discussions in supervision about commonly used theories and concepts in their field in relation to cultural biases and racism. (For guidance and suggestions for particular clinical specialities see Patel *et al.*, 2000.)
3   Supervisors can encourage discussions in supervision on identifying the merits and the potential benefits of certain theories and philosophical approaches, as well as the limitations in their application to black and minority ethnic people, or in enabling a sophisticated understanding of power relations, oppression and empowerment.
4   Supervisors can encourage exploration and discussion in supervision of alternative useful models and theories not necessarily based on psychological models founded on Western philosophies, values and understandings. For example, contributions from the fields of black psychology, Chinese medicine, Ayurveda, yoga, Buddhism, sociology, etc.
5   Supervisors can guide supervisees in developing critical thinking skills in relation to knowledge development by modelling a reflective, questioning

approach. They can pose challenging questions that invite reflection on the origins and production of psychological theories, on the role, uses and misuses of research in perpetuating biased and racist theories, on the benefits and limitations of research-based and practice-based evidence in clinical psychology, on the application of biased and racist concepts and theories in clinical practice and in service design and delivery.

Developing skills

The current focus in clinical psychology training is on developing a range of competencies with a range of clients and across a range of settings. The development of specific skills is seen as an indicator of the level of attainment of essential competencies in relation to psychological assessment, formulation, intervention, evaluation, research, service delivery, teaching and professional practice. The role of supervision both pre- and post-qualification is central in facilitating the development of such skills and competencies. However, essential ingredients in the development of competencies are the capacity, ability and commitment to developing thinking skills. As such, for supervision to facilitate an understanding and competence in addressing power relations and oppression in clients' lives, in therapeutic encounters, in research practice, in psychological services or in the supervisory relationship supervisees and supervisors have to strive to establish an essential foundation in the development of skills in critical thinking.

In relation to multicultural counselling competence, Helms and Richardson (1997) believe that it is not a unique set of skills *per se* that is required, but a particular type of philosophical orientation characterized by a responsivity to the relevant socio-political dynamics of 'race' and to principles of cultural socialization in all interactions with clients. Of course, such responsivity and a philosophical orientation have to go beyond simply an 'awareness' of and a 'sensitivity to' relevant issues. To develop and to demonstrate competence in empowerment clinical psychologists need to be able to operationalize a social and political analysis of cultural and racial oppression in their psychological thinking skills, as well as in their assessment, intervention, training and research skills. It is argued here that clinical psychology supervision is one of the most important sites where learning how to translate that philosophical understanding and commitment into clinical practice, or perhaps, more appropriately, into both resistance and into social action, can be fostered.

Improving supervisory practice

The following provides some suggestions regarding what supervisors can do to encourage reflection, discussion, debate and skills development within supervision. The main areas considered are assessment, formulation, intervention and organizational skills. For guidance related to particular clinical specialities see Patel *et al.* (2000).

Assessment

Critical to the development of appropriate assessment skills is, firstly, the ability to evaluate the validity and the appropriateness of the theoretical basis of assessment methods used; secondly, the ability to critically analyse how difference has been constructed within that theoretical approach and within the entire process by which a client has come to be referred to a clinical psychologist; thirdly, the ability to evaluate the role and function of power within the entire process of referring, assessment and the process of establishing theory–practice links during the assessment. Box 7.1 highlights a few questions which may be useful in supervision.

Box 7.1   The referral process and assessment

1   What aspects of your 'self' (culture, ethnicity, heritage, gender, age, class, etc.) could be influencing your understanding of the client referred, of the referral request and of the assessment process?

2   Who is the referrer? What might be their personal and professional understanding of the client referred to you? Could their ethnicity (or gender etc.) or their professional context have influenced how they have described the client in the referral letter, or how they construct the client's present difficulties, or possible solutions? Which theoretical constructs are used in the referral letter (e.g. 'separation problems' or 'somatization')? To what extent are those constructs Eurocentric? What are the implications?

3   In the referral process who else or which other services influenced the referral being made to you in particular (or to clinical psychology)? Which assumptions, values, stereotypes and personal/ professional beliefs might have influenced the referral route? Have these influences been made explicit to the client? If so, who explained this to the client, and how? What might be the client's fears, suspicions, expectations or understanding of what a clinical psychologist does, how and why?

4   What might be some of the implications of the way in which a referral letter constructs, say, culture (for example, culture as the only central construct, or as invisible and unimportant; that is, with the dominant professional understanding which promotes assumptions of universality in psychological responses)? What are the implications for the client and for the type of service or interventions offered to the client (or withheld from them)?

5   Who might you need to consult to enable you to conduct an appropriate assessment (e.g. which family members, which colleagues or community organizations or religious practitioners, etc.)?

6   Which language is the most appropriate for conducting the assessment? Do you need to find a bilingual therapist or co-worker, or an interpreter? What do you need to know in order to decide or to find an appropriate interpreter (e.g. language or dialect spoken or preferred by the client, gender of interpreter, etc.)?

7   What are you and the client bringing to the assessment in terms of your own cultural understandings, your values, stereotypes, histories and experiences of privilege and oppression and your expectations? How might this influence the client's experience of the assessment process? How might this influence the process of trying to establish a therapeutic alliance? How can this be addressed within the context of an empowering assessment?

8   Have you made transparent and explicit to the client how and why they have been referred to you? Have you explained the 'professional' and the 'organizational/service' rationale for the referral? Have you sought their understanding of the referral process and its implications? Have you discussed the possible limitations or inherent biases in the process of psychological assessment and in the therapy you might be offering to them? Examples include: have you explained and discussed with the client how psychological therapies used have commonly been developed in the West and rest on the assumption that 'talking' helps? Or have you explained and discussed the construct of confidentiality as it is meant in the Western professional context or in other cultural contexts?

9   If you have chosen to use formal assessment tools (standardized tests, or measures) can you justify their use and their validity for the client in question? What might be the inherent biases (e.g. cultural), limitations and the potential for abuse in these assessment tools? What are the ethical implications of using assessment methods and tools which are not reliable or valid for the client in question?

10 What is the significance of power in the assessment process? For example, as a white, male, trainee clinical psychologist how is your ethnicity, gender and position as a trainee professional significant in relation to a black, male, older client referred to you for a cognitive assessment whilst under section? What are the implications for the process of assessment or of the possible outcomes of the assessment?

11 What are the contexts central to talking with and understanding the client and their presenting difficulties? For example, what is the economic context, their familial context or the reality and the impact of poverty and racism in their lives? How can an awareness of these contexts be translated into an assessment that seeks to understand the client's difficulties, the obstacles and oppressions they may experience and possible opportunities available to them? In seeking to understand these issues, how can an assessment be conducted in a way that does not unquestioningly mirror and reinforce power relations experienced by the client in their own lives?

Formulations

The development of formulation skills is often a focus in clinical supervision. However, almost all forms of psychological formulation are derived from particular theoretical approaches, models which themselves are invariably Eurocentric and often decontextualized, depoliticized and sanitized of under-standings of power. As such, psychological formulations rarely encompass more than a cursory glance at power relations and their impact on people's lives and not surprisingly suggest little in the way of direction in terms of empowerment or social action. However, useful contributions in clinical psychology can be found in the work of Hagan and Smail (1997), who advocate power-mapping as a methodology, and Holland (1990, 1992b), who illustrates the use of a material understanding of power and its impact in her model of social action psychotherapy.

The processes of assessment and formulating inevitably develop simul-taneously, and the skills in effectively and meaningfully integrating the understanding of cultural difference, cultural socialization, racial oppression and racism in this process can be facilitated in supervision. The wheel of assessment and formulation (Figure 7.1) brings into focus the ongoing and

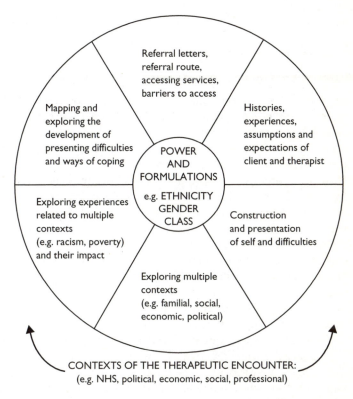

Figure 7.1 Assessments and formulations: integrating issues of difference and power

cyclical nature of this process and the different arenas in which the practitioner can integrate understandings of culture and racism. The suggested questions in Box 7.2 correspond to the different segments in the wheel and may facilitate supervision.

Interventions

The ability to continually explain and to negotiate and renegotiate with the client an appropriate and relevant approach to intervention, based on the evolving formulation, encompasses many skills. Supervision can be a forum where such skills can be formulated, articulated, rehearsed and debated in the context of mutual learning for both supervisee and supervisor. Perhaps the most challenging aspect of actually facilitating this process in supervision is how both supervisor and supervisee can demonstrate reflexivity, critical thinking, and the capacity to re-evaluate the potential for abuse and oppression in using existing theoretical models and interventions and, perhaps most importantly, the willingness and commitment to re-visioning therapeutic philosophies and interventions and reconfiguring professional roles and responsibilities in order to practise a just psychology.

Box 7.2   The process of assessment and formulation

1   How are referral letters written and by whom? What has the referral route been for the client and what assumptions on the part of the referrer have influenced the referrer? Which services are made available and accessible to the client by the referral and which have been excluded or withheld? What might be culturally biased assumptions, stereotypes or values which have operated in this process? How transparent are these in the referral or to the client? What are the implications for the client (e.g. in terms of informed consent, informed choice versus coercion in the referral process)? Would the client be able to request a particular therapeutic approach or a therapist from a black or minority ethnic background? Would the client have been given an opportunity to discuss their preferences in terms of health care approaches (e.g. traditional to the client rather than traditional Western approaches offered within the NHS)?

2   What are the histories (personal and political) that clients and practitioners bring to the assessment? How might we explore and understand the client's expectations and assumptions of who the practitioner is, what they will do, what will their position be on the client's situation and presenting difficulties (e.g. black and minority ethnic clients may have many assumptions about a white

practitioner and they may utilize effective survival strategies of adopting a distant, questioning and mistrusting stance towards them)? Similarly, what are the assumptions, stereotypes, values, biases and expectations of the practitioner in relation to the client? How might these assumptions, biases and expectations be converging to impact on the process of the assessment and formulation, and what are the implications for the validity and utility of the emerging formulation? How might such formulations influence the interventions (and their related models) chosen, offered or imposed on the client? What is likely to be the enabling or disabling and oppressive outcome of this for the client?

3   How does the client talk about and construct their sense of self? To what extent does the assessment and formulation explore the significance of the points of convergence or of divergence in the client's and the practitioner's understanding of the 'self'? Does the client talk of their self-identity as a racialized, gendered identity, or in terms of an individual, autonomous identity or a collective identity (e.g. in relation to their family, or in terms of 'the black community')? What is your understanding of the 'self'? To what extent is that influenced by your own personal, cultural history, or perhaps by your professional and academic training in psychology (e.g. the dominance of the dualist notion of self in psychological theorizing)? What are the implications for the choice of interventions or of psychological models for interventions? How can that be discussed with and negotiated with the client?

4   How does the client talk about and explain their difficulties? Which meaning-making systems (e.g. religious, political, cultural) do they employ? To what extent are these ways of understanding their distress respected, explored and privileged or superficially acknowledged or integrated into the psychological meaning-making systems (e.g. psychological models) that you might be using in the assessment and formulation?

5   How does the client present themselves and their difficulties to you? How do these ways of presenting make sense to the client in terms of their own cultural etiquette (e.g. how to respond to elders, to men or to professionals) or in terms of their own histories of oppression (e.g. how to talk or protect yourself with those in authority, or with white people in 'white institutions')? Clients present themselves and their difficulties often in ways that make sense to them; which feel safe for them; and which may determine what they are offered. How can a formulation take these factors into account?

6   What are the multiple contexts influencing the client and their difficulties? How might these influences be crucial in understanding

which resources and opportunities clients have for change, and what are the impasses to change? For example, what is the significance and the impact of the marital or familial context for the client and the related cultural factors? What are the influences and immovable forces of power in the client's economic and political context and how might that be linked to the history of racism for black and minority ethnic people in Britain, and specifically for the client? For example, is there likely to be an opportunity and any choice for a client to be able to move out of accommodation where they and their children have experienced racism from neighbours and in the area despite the impact on their well-being? To what extent might the reality of poverty and institutional racism be factors for consideration, engagement or neglect within an assessment and formulation? Does feeling powerless as a practitioner to do something about such disadvantage and oppression justify not addressing these issues in a formulation? What might be the ethical and practical implications for intervention and for the evaluation of such interventions or for the absence of any interventions addressing these material realities?

7   What are the client's experiences in relation to the multiple contexts identified in the assessment? For example, which opportunities in life have they been afforded, or denied, because of who they are as, say, a white, middle-class male, or a young, black, gay male? Which negative experiences have they had (e.g. racism at work, racist attacks, or racist, verbal abuse on the streets, or homophobia within their own family and religious community as well as within the majority white gay community)? What might be the impact and influences of these experiences on the client, their life, their relationships, their view of the world or their interactions with you? What are the implications for the models that you employ, the interventions that are planned, the appropriateness of the practitioner themselves or for the configuration, or re-configuration, of the roles of a clinical psychologist?

8   The process of mapping and exploring the development of presenting difficulties and ways of coping is one which forms the backbone of traditional psychological approaches to assessment and formulation. How does the experience of racism in the client's life, in education, employment, in the lack of opportunities, etc. manifest in and account for the presenting difficulties or for the way in which the client (or their family) attempted to manage/cope to date? How can a formulation effectively address the aforementioned questions and suggest an ethical and just approach to interventions?

It is precisely the contention here that no single Western psychological approach currently exists which can adequately address the reality of both material and relational power and powerlessness and the impact on people's lives and distress. However, contributions from narrative approaches to therapy (White and Epston, 1991) and social action approaches to therapy (e.g. Holland, 1990, 1992b) provide both hope and indication that perhaps psychological approaches can contribute to social change in differing degrees and address the issues and reality of power. However, the paramount question remains: is psychology and psychological interventions as currently configured in the West the only, or indeed the most effective, way to address social inequalities and their impact on people's well-being?

Box 7.3 highlights questions which might stimulate relevant discussion and facilitate the development of intervention skills within supervision.

Understanding organizational contexts

Another important area of competency in clinical psychology is the ability to understand the organizational contexts which encapsulate and shape service design and delivery and the ability to develop ethical, professional and just psychological practice within those contexts. Central to this competency is the unequivocal commitment to developing services which best serve clients from all sections of the population.

Supervision can provide a space to reflect on the way power operates within the organizational context, including within the legislative context as it relates to health care; within the profession, its espoused ethics, code of conduct and practice guidelines; within the particular NHS trust; within the psychological services or within the local, team context. Part of understanding the operation, functions and outcomes of power within these contexts is the opportunity to examine the role of clinical psychologists in challenging discriminatory and oppressive structures and practices which exclude and

---

Box 7.3   Interventions

1   Given your formulation, which psychological models or specific interventions might most effectively address the varying layers of experience and meaning contributing to the client's distress? For example, is there a particular approach that might be appropriate for the client in question and their difficulties, which may be a product of racism, marginalization and oppression? How might your planned intervention address the reality of, say, racism and poverty in a client's life? How would you carry out this intervention, with whom, when, and who else would you need to consult

other than the client? How will this be explained and negotiated with the client?

For example, if a client who did not speak English was assessed by a colleague without an interpreter and subsequently denied a service which you believed would be crucial or preferred by the client, how would you proceed? Would you simply organize a referral or access to the denied service in question? Would you also challenge the colleague who conducted the initial assessment, or would you alert the client to their rights and enable them to lodge a complaint or make a formal complaint yourself? How far would you be prepared to proceed, for whom, with whom and why?

2 What are the possible assumptions, values and cultural biases inherent in the interventions you have planned and in the models from which they are derived? What might be the implications of using such interventions with the client?

3 How will you explain to the client the rationale for the type of model and interventions you plan to implement? How will you facilitate the ability and create genuine opportunities for the client to question the utility, validity or appropriateness of your planned interventions? For example, how would you respond to a client who says 'How will talking help . . . we don't/I don't believe that just talking will change anything in my life?' How might you explain the culturally bound belief that talking is helpful in Western therapeutic practice and how might you facilitate the client in making an informed choice about whether to consent to whatever you are offering or to request alternatives?

4 What might be possible parallel processes in the therapeutic process and relationship which mirror, replicate and perpetrate experiences of discrimination that the client has had in their life? How can these processes be identified, and both acknowledged and explored with the client?

5 How might you reflect on and challenge your own prejudices and racism, however unintentional, in the therapeutic process? How would you know when your interventions were oppressive or racist in their outcome? How would you know when you or your therapeutic style or approach was experienced by the client as blaming or as being totally blind to or dismissive of the client's cultural beliefs, ways of living or practices? How would you enable and facilitate an exploration of these issues during therapy? Where and with whom might you want to reflect on these issues in safety?

6 To what extent do your interventions focus on the problems, weaknesses and vulnerability of the client in a way that might be experienced as pathologizing or blaming the client – for example, for their experiences of racist abuse in their workplace? Could

strategies for helping the client to be 'more assertive', or to re-evaluate their perception that 'everyone is out to get me at work ... they're constantly watching and waiting to pick on me', or to explore the reasons why they perhaps repeatedly find themselves in situations or relationships, both personally and at work, where they are victimized, be experienced as and function as being oppressive and racist in themselves?

7 How could you assess the impact of racism on a client's life and formulate effective intervention strategies? How could your interventions challenge racism in the client's life, as well as in the therapeutic relationship, in the therapeutic work and in the related professional network/team? Which personal and professional resources would enable you to challenge such racism effectively? What would 'challenging racism' look like in practice?

8 To what extent are your interventions or your therapeutic approach designed, adapted or chosen specifically for the client in question, or to what extent is the client expected to fit into and respond to your own preferred approach, or into the dominant model within your service, regardless of the client's cultural background, or specific experiences and issues around oppression? What are the implications of this for the client? What is the implication of this in terms of power and its abuses within the model used, within the service, within the profession and within your own clinical practice?

9 To what extent do your interventions assume that all of the client's presenting difficulties can be attributed to their culture, or to experiences of racism, or, conversely, that culture and racism are irrelevant factors? What are the implications of this for the client?

10 When might you choose to and how might you work with a bilingual co-worker or an interpreter in therapeutic practice? What are your beliefs about the value of working with such colleagues in therapeutic practice? To what extent do your own anxieties or possible lack of experience and skills in working with interpreters influence your choice to either deny some clients psychological therapy, or deny them a right to a professional interpreter? What might this illuminate about power relations and unintentional racism? What might be the implications for clients or 'potential' clients (those who cannot access our services)?

11 What are the range of ways in which your therapeutic interventions could be evaluated, particularly with regard to their validity and their effectiveness in addressing issues of culture and/or racism significant to the client? What role might the client themselves be entitled to and be allowed to use in enabling an honest and just evaluation to take place?

abuse, amongst others, black and minority ethnic people. The role of psychologists as potential change agents in developing more equitable and appropriate services for black and minority ethnic people is advocated by Nadirshaw (2000) and by the Division of Clinical Psychology in their Briefing paper on services to black and minority ethnic people (DCP, 1998).

Questions which could contribute to relevant discussions and to the development of organizational skills within supervision can be found in Box 7.4.

Box 7.4   Understanding organizational contexts

1   What were the historical, social, legal and cultural contexts within which the service you work in was first conceived and developed? How did these contexts and related motives operate in a way that some sections of the population were excluded, marginalized or ill-served?

2   What is the composition of the local population which your organization serves? What are the numbers of black and minority ethnic people in your area; what are their backgrounds, histories and differing needs? Are they aware of the availability (or not) of local psychological services, statutory and voluntary? What is the range of perceptions, assumptions, fears and expectations of these services or those that work within them? What evidence exists to reveal their use of, or avoidance of, or exclusion by these services? In the absence of such evidence what would we need to do to find out and to develop more appropriate services?

3   What is the composition of the client population referred to and seen by clinical psychologists? How does this compare with the composition of the local population? How is this monitored within your service, or your team, or by yourself in your own caseload? How does such monitoring impact on the design and ongoing development of services and clinical practice? If service design and delivery is changed in response to monitoring exercises then how is this change evaluated, and by whom?

4   What might be some of the reasons for an absence of or relatively very low numbers of black and minority ethnic people within your service? What are the issues of accessibility of psychological services? Or, conversely, what might be some of the reasons for an over-representation or disproportionately high number of black and minority ethnic people in certain parts of the service, such as in acute mental health wards or in forensic settings? What are the implications of this for clients, or for the local black and minority ethnic populations, or for the service? What are the roles and the ethical responsibilities of clinical psychologists in addressing these

factors? What would it mean for psychologists to remain curious bystanders or to remain disinterested or comfortably blind to the contributory processes and functions of power, and to exclusion and oppression?

5　How might clients who do not speak English be able to access and to utilize psychological services? Which services are made available to them or denied them, and on what grounds? For example, particular psychological services may be denied to people who do not speak English because of practitioners' beliefs that psychological therapy is compromised, impossible or rendered ineffective with the use of interpreters or bilingual co-workers. Such practitioners may deny their own lack of competence and experience in working with interpreters or attempt to obscure their lack of commitment to providing appropriate services equitably to all those in their local population. What are the implications for would-be clients of such practices and defences offered? What might be some of the ethical, professional and legal obligations of clinical psychologists to address these issues effectively? Which policies might need to be implemented within the organization? Which resources would be needed and how could psychological services be developed to be able to serve all those in the local population?

6　Which policies exist within the organization and within psychological services to ensure equal opportunity to access health care services? How are such policies operationalized within your own service or team? How are these measures monitored and evaluated? What is the role of clinical psychologists in this process? What steps are taken when such policies are breached? What might be your own professional and legal obligations in such situations?

7　What is the make-up of the profession, the British Psychological Society and clinical psychology training courses in terms of the proportion of black and minority ethnic people? To what extent does this reflect the composition of the national population? What might be some of the reasons for the overall under-representation of black and minority ethnic clinical psychologists in the profession and the particularly low numbers of those from specific ethnic backgrounds, and the under-representation of black and minority ethnic clinical psychologists in academia and in senior positions within the profession and in the NHS? What might be the implications of this for the profession, for psychological services and for clients?

8　How might we effectively translate our awareness and understanding of the aforementioned issues into the development of the profession and into the design and delivery of appropriate and just psychological services?

Personal and professional development

In learning how to understand and manage the dynamics related to culture and 'race' Helms and Cook (1999) argue that supervision is indeed the most logical and primary vehicle for influencing personal and professional growth and development for both supervisee and supervisor. Scaife and Walsh (2001) describe personal and professional development as an ongoing learning process about aspects of the self in relation to others. They identify three categories of aspects of self: acknowledging the personal impact of client work; the influence of events outside work on relationships at work; and the influence of personal life history, values, beliefs and personal characteristics on relationships at work. The primary and most crucial aim is to focus on professional practice that is of benefit to the client. It is also important to acknowledge that if supervision is to facilitate personal and professional development effectively then it is an obligation for both supervisees and supervisors to learn about aspects of self as it applies to the supervisory relationship and to the process of supervision itself.

Who we are, how we experience and see the world, how we relate to one another, how we practise in a professional context and the baggage and resources we bring to supervision and to our overall work are all areas for concern in personal and professional development. Learning to be a clinical psychologist is thus more that just learning about clinical psychology, it is about learning how to integrate our personal and professional identities in their totality; that is, as constituting our identities in terms of our gender, ethnicity, age, sexuality, class, etc. In supervision that can mean, for example, a supervisee being encouraged and facilitated in learning what it means to be a black, female clinical psychologist; learning how it impacts on both her professional relationships and on her clinical work; how to make oneself safe as a black professional at work where subtle and perhaps unintentional institutional discrimination is pervasive; or how to recognize, challenge and manage racism when encountered within a clinical session, within clinical supervision or within management supervision.

D'Andrea and Daniels (1997) emphasize that both ethnic and racial identity development – that is, 'the way individuals view themselves as cultural/ethnic/racial beings' – represent important considerations requiring discussion in supervision. They describe the range of ethnic identity development models which currently exist, such as Cross's (1971, 1995) model of black racial identity development, the minority identity development model (MID) (Atkinson *et al.*, 1993), white identity development models (Helms, 1995; Ponterotto and Pedersen, 1993), and assert that assessing at which stage(s) of ethnic-racial identity development supervisors and supervisees are likely to be functioning is of critical importance in understanding the process of what they call multicultural supervision. Thus, the essence of supervision which addresses personal and professional development is the ability and willingness for both supervisee and supervisor to reflect on their own, and perhaps each other's, ethnic-identity development stages in relation to clinical practice.

Improving supervisory practice

Supervision that values and actively facilitates personal and professional development is one where safety is fostered, reflection is encouraged and modelled, permission is given to explore the personal–professional interface, and where related uncertainty, confusion, anxiety, fears and ambivalence are normalized, accepted and not judged. Such supervision also requires that both the supervisor and the supervisee are committed to ongoing learning and to their own ongoing personal and professional development. The suggestions below identify some ways in which personal and professional development in relation to considering issues of culture, racism and power can be pursued:

1   Supervisors and supervisees can examine their own values and beliefs as they manifest in the supervisory relationship and in the supervisory process itself. Scaife and Walsh (2001) provide excellent examples of how supervision can be used in this way – for example, by audiotaping a supervision session with a view to reviewing it specifically to identify the values and beliefs of both supervisor and supervisee.
2   Supervisors and supervisees can reflect privately or with colleagues and perhaps discuss models of ethnic and racial identity development and how they may apply to their own supervisory relationship and to the supervision of clinical work.
3   Supervisors might seek further training in the form of seminars, workshops, conferences and courses to develop their knowledge, understanding and skills related to working with black and minority ethnic clients, and to providing supervision to supervisees from a range of minority ethnic (or majority ethnic) backgrounds.
4   Supervisors and supervisees could seek out and consult black user groups, minority ethnic community groups and black and minority ethnic colleagues to enhance their own knowledge and understanding of issues related to culture and to individual and institutional racism, etc.
5   Supervisors and supervisees could identify and reflect on their own experiences of inequality, racism, disadvantage and privilege and of being marginalized in their personal and professional lives. They could consider how this might influence their identities, values and expectations; their relationships at work; their professional activities – especially their work with clients. This might be an ongoing theme for discussion during supervision sessions.

6   Supervisors and supervisees may need to identify and use existing or potential sources of support for themselves, particularly sources which would facilitate their confidence and competence in addressing issues of culture, racism and power in all areas of their professional practice. Sources of support could include professional relationships, personal relationships (such as friends, partners and family), professional networks and user networks.

In conclusion, this chapter has attempted to explore key issues and some of the ways of improving supervisory practice in clinical psychology to enable us to develop greater understanding, confidence and competence in addressing power, cultural differences and racism. Whilst some implications for supervisors and supervisees have been outlined, the overall implications for the profession also require attention, although these will be mentioned only briefly here. Key implications include the responsibilities for our professional body in examining its own structure, policies and procedures, and its own organizational processes which reinforce a Eurocentric bias in every aspect of clinical psychology. Clinical psychology training courses also need to re-vision the content and methods of training, to examine their own biases and institutional racism and to pay particular attention to the benefits and the abuses within supervision (clinical, academic and research supervision) in relation to cultural and racial oppression. Finally and inevitably, the content and nature of training for supervisors and the monitoring of supervisors and supervision have to be important challenges for the profession to embrace.

Chapter 8

Incorporating gender issues in clinical supervision

Maxine Dennis and Gill Aitken[1]

> In line with the Society's Equal Opportunities Statement and Policy all clinical psychologists should ensure that they maintain an up-to-date knowledge of issues regarding race and culture, gender and class and how such issues can impact on their day to day work as a member of the profession.
>
> (DCP, 1999: Section 2, Principle 9)

> Given the traditional and contemporary psychological ideologies about women and/or the patriarchal nature of the institutions in which they are practised, in what way should women relate to either the ideologies or the institutions? . . . Can female therapists 'help' female patients different from male therapists?
>
> (Chesler, 1972: 105)

Introduction

Throughout this book, there is implicit, if not always explicit, acknowledgement of differences in structural relations of privilege and power along the supervisor–supervisee dimension. In clinical psychology, as in other mental health and therapy trainings, the supervision process aims to enable supervisees to learn to bring together theory, techniques and interpersonal interventions:

> Supervisors are vested with the power and responsibility, by their institutions and training programmes to evaluate, influence and judge trainees. They are also supposed to provide to the less skilled inexperienced and less knowledgeable student therapist the skill, knowledge, and personal awareness, to help the client in a professional and ethical manner.
>
> (Carter, 1995: 237–238)

In the context of the current chapter, we might want to consider how clinical supervision creates opportunities for a space and means of opening up different perspectives and dialogues which allow issues of diversity and power to be considered (McQueen, 2000). In our experience, training within clinical psychology is slowly moving towards providing awareness of how we develop and relate to one another from the (ad)vantage point of both our personal and various referent group memberships or identifications – as (trainee) clinical psychologists who are variously gendered, sexualized, racialized, and classed. The question of how we embody such (non)awareness of these identifications in our practice also requires us to be able to understand how this both reflects and informs the operation of power. However, the recognition or realization of how power relations are played out, and their differential effects, may be understood as too painful or too threatening to voice so that 'that which is unspeakable cannot be challenged', with the effect that dominant–subordinate relations are reproduced (Font *et al.*, 1998; Miller, 1986).

Within clinical psychology, it is mainly from the mid-1990s that training programmes have systematically started to offer often limited 'specialist' one- or half-day modules or workshops in relation to diversity, whether that be gender, 'race' and/or sexuality. When explicitly incorporated into the curriculum, in our (and other trainers' experiences) common questions raised by trainees revolve around the relevance of such an approach: 'we now live in a more equal society', or that 'to notice gender, disability, or "race" is in itself discriminatory', or that issues of inequality are not relevant to clinical psychology as 'we treat everyone as an individual' or 'we work collaboratively'. At other times, trainees and supervisors want to know 'how do we *do* gender in supervision?' or 'what set of skills/techniques do we need to learn?' In part, we understand such responses in the context of how paralysing, or overwhelming it can be to us as individuals as we begin to personally and professionally become aware of the privileges and access to power resources we have. In part, we might understand responses to reflect the gender and culturally neutral approach of the dominant scientist-practitioner model of clinical psychology training in which the practitioner is positioned as a neutral, objective yet 'expert' participant whether in therapy or supervision encounters (Sayal-Bennett, 1991; Nadirshaw, 2000; Aitken, 2000b). Such observations are not specific to clinical psychology training (see e.g. Carter *et al.*, 1992).

Indeed, when we look at key texts cited in course documents outside of 'specialist' gender and diversity modules, or in the wider clinical psychology literature, there is little reference to gendered and racialized identifications unless as a demographic variable. Noticeably visible in their absence are gender-related issues in both therapy and clinical supervision in the UK clinical psychology literature. When preparing for this chapter, we found four texts which featured a collection of articles or chapters which explicitly explored and debated the gendered and power implications of clinical psychology as a profession or clinical psychologists as professionals: one book and three special journal features/editions. Three at the beginning of the 1990s and one in 2000: an Open Forum in *Feminism & Psychology* entitled: 'Clinical Psychology Training: Training in Oppression' (Williams and Watson, 1991), *Gender Issues in Clinical Psychology* (Ussher and Nicolson, 1992), 'The Gender Issue' in *Clinical Psychology Forum* (Vetere and Gelsthorpe, 1994) and 'Women and Power' in *Changes* (McQueen, 2000).[2]

Here we aim to contribute in positive ways to the debates around why clinical psychology should be concerned with gender issues, and how gender issues can be thought about in supervision. We do not propose the use of a prescriptive model, or a 'recipe cook book' of techniques or strategies; rather, we draw on a range of resources to facilitate ways of thinking about and relating to these issues. Given the relative dearth of publications from within clinical psychology in the United Kingdom, we also draw on the work of wider feminist and anti-oppressive practitioners and therapists both from within and outside the UK to inform the development of thinking about gender issues within our own profession and to open up possibilities for conversations among and between ourselves.

The rest of this chapter is divided into eight main sections. In the first section, we briefly introduce ourselves (the authors) to provide the readers with some context of why we are interested in the topic of gender and power. In section two, we review some terms and definitions (around gender, power and empowerment) which are often used in working with diversity issues. This is to make more clear what we understand by these and to think about how we might need to support ourselves in preparing to reflect on and explore these issues. In the third and fourth sections, we outline a 'process' model of supervision as a framework to illustrate the complex web of relationships and contexts, which enter the supervisor–supervisee relationship, and provide some of the research evidence on the impact of wider social political contexts (section four), including clinical psychology developments (section five). We then focus on possible gender influences and effects on the process of supervision, including the supervisee–client and supervisee–supervisor relationships (section six). In section seven, we take this back out to implications for working with a client (as gendered). In the final section we discuss a case to work through, and questions we might ask ourselves.

About ourselves

Many feminists and anti-oppressive writers and practitioners argue that it is important to make more visible and transparent one's own commitments and positionings as ways to think about the power implications of what we practise (e.g. Hewson, 1999)

Gill

I have been working as a white-identified woman (trainee and qualified) clinical psychologist since 1993. In 2000, I negotiated a post explicitly as a clinical psychologist in women's services.

My interest and commitment to exploring issues of social inequalities reflect my understandings of my own gendered experiences in childhood (e.g. within a bi-European family, at school) and adulthood (e.g. first gaining work in clerical and secretarial fields). This developed through talking with others, and seeking out feminist and anti-oppressive writings. I initially entered higher education as a mature student to 'find a voice' and as a way to 'empower' myself. Entering clinical psychology training in the 1990s, I was also struck by the absence of reference to the social context of people's lives in descriptions and understandings of their presenting distress, or in the routes into clinical psychology services. Relatedly, there was little discussion about the possible differential gendered meanings and feelings of being referred to a particular service, with particular diagnoses, and in working with me as a woman psychologist and/or my possible feelings and attitudes about working with different women and men.

I understand a central aim of feminism to be to work towards social justice, but over the years I became aware that white (middle-class) feminists did not necessarily reflect or relate to the experiences of all women (hooks, 1981; Wilkinson and Kitzinger, 1996). I understand that 'white feminists must actively struggle to eliminate the structural racism from which we benefit' (Harding, 1986). Attempts to question the status quo always risk being constructed as 'too extreme' or as 'too emotive', and a person raising such issues risks problematization and marginalization or 'burn-out' (Holland, 1995; Sayal-Bennett, 1991). Resistance to changing the status quo often takes the focus away from the issues being raised (inequality, social injustice) to minimizing or trivializing the issues, or through forms of personal attack against the individual(s) (Aitken, 1996).

As I have continued to engage in reflective practice, I have moved from only focusing on the power of others (whom I constructed as dominant groups). I have become more aware of my own power resources, and power as relational. These include in my role as a supervisor (in relation to supervisees); as trainer (in relation to trainees); as clinician (in relation to client/patient), and as a white, woman professional who now has access to a range of economic resources (in relation to peers/clients). Rather than denying or necessarily experiencing my structural power as negative, I attempt to develop productive social power in relation with and in conjunction with another. In relation to both supervision (Hewson, 1999) and therapy (Aitken, 2000a), possible strategies include making more explicit power relations in encounters, identifying and negotiating how external constraints might need to be met, and maximizing choice in the context of such constraints.

Maxine

The question of how clinical teaching and supervisory practice address culture, racism and oppression have been of long-standing interest. Further, I am concerned about the provision of culturally appropriate clinical psychology and psychotherapy services.

As a manager of a primary care service, accessibility, quality and the provision of a service that adequately meets the needs of patients are central. Therefore, directly tackling issues of gender bias and factors that may hinder various communities, uptake of the service requires ongoing interrogation.

Much of my writing has focused on the impact of racism and oppression in therapy (Bennett and Dennis, 2000) and how these issues are addressed within supervision (Dennis, 1998). If we examine the literature it suggests that many black people do see the impact of racism as a more significant oppressive force than sexism (McKay, 1992). Equally the various strands of the white feminist liberation movement have been charged with being narrow and irrelevant to black women's lives. However, to separate being black from being a woman (man) does an injustice to a whole area of black people's existence and experience. The work of many theorists, for example Lorde (1984), Morrison (1992), hooks (1990, 1993), Collins (1990) amongst others, has had a great impact on my thinking and understanding.

Temperley (1984), for example, points to the ambivalence all of us feel towards the complementarity of the sexes. She states that it is easy to blame one sex or adopt an adversarial/rivalrous position which may eclipse the importance of sexual interdependence, union and creativity.

In my clinical work the aim is towards an openness and readiness to work with what the patient/client brings, in order to provide a container (Bion, 1959, 1962, 1970) which promotes some growth and understanding. An awareness of the socio-economic and political inequalities, together with the clients'/patients' connection with their community, is integral to my work. However, I continue to reflect on my practice and in so doing allow space for it to continue to evolve.

It is perhaps no surprise that Gill and myself chose to write this chapter together, for as McLean-Taylor *et al.* poignantly observe:

> The persistence of racism, like the persistence of patriarchy, is a sobering historical and psychological reality. Patriarchy, as Gerda Lerner (1986) observes, has been another name for civilization. The 'race', class, and gender hierarchy, when re-imposed generation after generation, guarantees the continuation of this equation. As women of colour remind white women of their complicity and their privilege, so white women remind women of color that they have a common interest in breaking this cycle.
> (McLean-Taylor *et al.*, 1994: 212)

We hope that this joint chapter helps take us in some small way towards a greater understanding and appreciation of these interrelated issues within the practice of supervision.

Definition and concepts

Already in this chapter we have introduced terms and concepts of gender, power, and empowerment. Here we briefly consider some of the definitions available and consider what this means for our work as clinical psychologists. What we argue is that the particular definition(s) that we might draw on will both reflect and construct our practice in relation to therapy and supervisory encounters.

Gender

Often in the literature, 'gender' is used interchangeably with 'sex'. However, gender cannot be reduced to a single dimension such as genetic, genital, gonadal or hormonal sex. For some, the concept 'sex' is differentiated from 'gender', with the former being located in biological differences whereas the latter is as a social construct – whilst others contest that both sex and gender are social constructs rooted in social judgements and expectations. Gender has been variously and interrelatedly defined as

- the social characteristics of sex;
- a dynamic structural relation between women and men;
- a process through which social life is organized at the level of the individual, the family and society;
- the central feature is power.

A general assumption underpinning such definitions is of sets of dichotomized behaviours associated with femininity and masculinity (i.e. gendered differences or polarity around the categories of women and men). Some have argued that femininity is constructed to absorb everything defined as not masculine, and always to acquiesce in domination by the masculine; and gender is often considered a property of individuals and their behaviours, rather than also social structures and conceptual systems (Harding, 1986: 34). Some authors prefer to talk about the politics of gender to highlight how power affects how women and men relate to each other and one another, and how gender is an integral dynamic of social orders (Lorber and Farrell, 1991). For example, it is argued that as we grow up socialization processes differentially affect boys and girls. That is, boys psychologically 'expand' and have increased cultural expectation about the development of an autonomous self and identity. By contrast, girls 'psychologically contract', with a sense of self developed in relation to the needs and desires of others (Larkin and Popaleni, 1994). This has been associated with men taking more instrumental roles (in external or public spheres) and women being socialized into taking more expressive roles (in internal or domestic spheres). Whilst we question this separation of public/private spheres, it can be a starting point to explore gendered aspects of everyday life.

R. J. Green (1998) highlights ten traditional norms of masculinity, which are variously affected by age, 'race', ethnicity, and education, family and peers' ideas of gender. These norms include the suppression of emotional vulnerability, avoiding feminine behaviours and activities traditionally associated with the woman's role, primacy of the work role for power status and self-esteem, independence (thus avoiding or denying dependency on others), aggression to control others or means of conflict resolution, toughness/air of confidence in the face of adversity, pain or danger; striving for dominance, provider/protector for others in family, treating sexual partners as objects, homophobia (irrational fear or anger at gay men and lesbians, avoidance of emotional closeness and affection with other males):

> a first step in creating change lies in an evolving consciousness of the straightjacket that gender norms and heterosexism impose ... In this sense therapy becomes one vehicle for the construction of male identity. It challenges roles, it positions itself as commentator on structural aspects of class and culture that intersects with gender to create oppression. Our therapy must be culturally conscious and it must promote values in keeping with changing, positive values in keeping with changing, positive definitions for both men and women. These values would include a mandate for collaboration, partnership, and equality.
>
> (Bepko *et al.*, 1998: 79)

Font *et al.* (1998), in a therapy of liberation article, provide an expanded male and female role, which one might use in supervision to help both female and male clients think about masculinity and femininity. We explore this further in the clinical example presented on pp. 155–159.

A central question for us is what might be the possible implications for us as (trainee) clinical psychologists if we internalize or reject various gender-role stereotypes or attitudes, either in relation to self or to other women or men. Awareness of such gendered assumptions or premises may enable us as therapists/practitioners, or supervisors/supervisees, to attend to these issues in our constructions of self and others, and be alert to possible constructions by others and their possible impact or relevance to therapy and supervision encounters.

Power

Power as a concept has also been variously defined and has generated numerous typologies. The definitions that we are focusing on here include:

- Power is the ability to control ourselves and others (Leigh, 1984, cited in Ridley, 1995).
- Power (can be) an awareness, an understanding, a realization that you already have power, albeit power that the culture does not recognize (Kitzinger, 1991: 120).
- Power as positive, as the capacity to produce change (Mitchell, 1974; Taylor, 1994).

As defined above, power can be, and is often, located in the individual and as possessed by the individual. However, such a perspective ignores the relational aspects of power. Power enters our everyday discourses, often signifying the value of male behaviour and the devaluing of female behaviour. Organizationally, power has meant individual progress alongside the ability to limit, control and sometimes to destroy others' power (Miller, 1986). Whilst stereotypically women's power base is relational (Gilligan, 1982), including notions of taking care, being both supportive and facilitative of others, this form of power may be less readily seen or readily defined or legitimized within organizations. 'Relational power is not only about exercising power over others more effectively, but also about facilitating power in others' (Cassell and Walsh, 1993: 113). This notion of relational power (both potentially oppressive and enabling) is the province of the chapter.

In considering the exercise of power in a supervisory context, the supervisor typically defines the relationship and is assumed to have a greater knowledge base, objectivity and status than the trainee, and as such can maximize or minimize the trainee's sense of powerlessness, which is present in the relationship. These feelings may be more evident at the beginning of training. The quality of the supervisory relationship can affect a client's feelings of powerlessness, which can be maximized or minimized depending on the power relationship set up by the therapeutic relationship. Clearly, this is not the full picture, as in being aware of the matrix of relationships which enter any interpersonal encounter we can start to be aware of how both the supervisee and the client may also have a powerful impact on the supervisory and therapeutic relationship respectively (see Figure 8.1).

In exploring power relations in supervisory encounters, Pinderhughes argues that a 'supervisor may use the helping role to reinforce . . . (his or her) own sense of competence by keeping subordinates in a one-down position' (1989: 111). In this context, trainees are vulnerable to replicating aspects of harmful, or at the very least unhelpful, interactions with supervisors in a parallel process with clients, thereby extending the influence of an unhelpful supervisor onto clients.

In any hierarchical situation, the people in power typically define reality. Men have done this for women, parents for children, majority white people for black and minority ethnic people, mental health professionals (including psychologists) for clients/patients, and supervisors for trainees (Fernando, 1995; Nadirshaw, 1999; Pinderhughes, 1989; Ussher and Nicolson, 1992). As (institutionally accredited) experts, power advantage includes enhanced credibility. The status of the supervisor means that it is often their word that is listened to rather than the trainee's, even in clear-cut differences of opinion, such as that concerning the lack of time available for supervision. If gender issues are not acknowledged as valid or legitimate areas of exploration by a supervisor, then how power relations are played out will have differential effects, possibly with a greater bearing within the supervisory relationship when the supervisee is training, and once qualified if the supervisor also has a managerial role to play.[3]

Empowerment

The concept of empowering ways of working has been particularly utilized by feminist researchers and practitioners in relation to women, and by professionals in relation to socially disadvantaged groups, including people diagnosed with severe mental health needs and learning disabilities. Three different definitions of empowerment are as follows:

* A person experiences herself as having a legitimate right to claim her voice and having expertise and a referent framework from which to act (Hewson, 1999).
* Empowerment can be felt momentarily or can be transformative when it is linked to a permanent shift in the distribution of social power (Yuval Davis, 1994).
* Empowerment involves rejecting the dimensions of knowledge, whether personal, cultural or institutional, that perpetuate objectification and dehumunization (Hill Collins, 1990).

Work around empowerment and empowering strategies typically reflects individualized approaches, which 'rely on developing in women this sense of personal agency . . . create in women a certain state of mind (feeling powerful, competent, worthy of esteem, able to make free choices and influence their world)' (Kitzinger, 1991: 122). However, the lived reality of being able to make free choices and significantly influence the world may be more restrictive than we would like to think. As Kitzinger and others caution, this risks leaving the structural conditions unchanged and ignores the structural and social realities and conditions of many women's and members of minority groups' lives (see also Bell, 1995). From such positions (or based on such arguments), teaching the historic 'disempowered' to think positively, learn how to speak up and out, or how to be assertive are unlikely to change people's experience associated with being a member of socially disadvantaged groups.

Preparing ourselves for thinking about these issues

> In western culture many men are trained to have a confident, self-advertising presentation, which can earn expert power even when they do not have relevant expertise. On the other hand, women are often trained to have a collaborative, self-effacing presentation which does not tend to earn expert power even when they have the expertise.
>
> (Hewson, 1999: 407)

Supervision is an opportunity to attend to pre-existing beliefs, stereotypes and perceptions which may impact on the ways we relate with and behave towards ourselves and others, as well as attending to more subtle aspects of gender in the (counter)transference. Killian (2001) posed a number of questions for supervisees and supervisors to ask themselves as a way to facilitate integrating gender and culture issues in supervision, which we have variously adapted. They are as follows:

Supervisee

1   How does your cultural self ('race', class, ethnicity, gender, professional identification, etc.) play out in the therapy room, in supervision?

2   How do you think your educational experiences affect your expectations of supervision in this training?

3   In which cultural context do you feel you have been practising your skills as a therapist? Which types of knowledge, skills are privileged?

4   How useful or effective would therapy be in general, or in this particular intervention, if sharing cultural similarities (e.g. gender, 'race', sexuality, class) with your client or your supervisor? What assumptions are underpinning notions of similarity?

5   How do assumed 'differences' in cultural context inform how you would set up therapy and supervisory encounters?

Supervisor

1   What is your knowledge of the ecosystems of culture, ethnicity, 'race', class, and gender, how do they relate to one's cultural self and affect perceptions of the world? When and how is this made explicit with supervisees?

2 What is your understanding of past and present relationships between your own culture and that of others? How is this communicated in supervisory encounters?

3 What is your understanding of how indirect and direct, covert and overt discriminatory practices may operate to marginalize and oppress members of particular social groups? Do you think such issues are relevant to clinical psychology?

4 What might facilitate or be a barrier to understand self and trainees as cultural and 'racial' beings?

To facilitate preparing ourselves to be able to 'speak about' these issues, supervisors and clinicians need to be familiar with some of the debates and research and publications (which may appear outside of mainstream texts and publications) on gender. These may include possible impact on clinical judgements of mental health, which are played out in the interaction of gender with 'race', class and age.

We would argue that it is the (ultimate) responsibility of supervisors to create the conditions for trainees actively to explore values and beliefs. This would include explicitly naming that as supervisors we welcome challenge to our own ideas, and that exploration of different viewpoints is a part of the learning and growth process for all (including a supervisor). As Killian's (2001) work highlights a holistic view of supervision, which incorporates cultural (and we would argue socio-political) contexts of any encounter, it is central to relate and connect supervisory with therapy processes, including power relations and interpretations.

One approach is for supervisor and trainee to name and discuss power imbalances during the initial placement contract. Clear boundaries, awareness of respective roles and responsibilities open up possibilities for a basis for a range of issues to be explored in non-condemnatory ways. This includes both 'visible' differences of 'race' and gender etc., which trainee and supervisor feel they have little choice about bringing to the encounter, and the potential more 'invisible' differences of sexuality and class, etc., which the individual may feel more able to choose. Any opportunity for self-reflection requires dialogue and the recognition that our learning is an ongoing process.

The supervisee's feeling towards and about the supervisor, how they are treated, whether conflict is addressed between them, and the encouragement to discuss things, can provide a parallel frame in deepening our understanding of our direct clinical work with clients. The enabling and containing aspect of the supervisory relationship is crucial. It may be that as supervisors we need to look at flexible formats for supervision in order to provide 'safe' spaces for supervision across gender (Milne and Oliver, 2000).

For example, in taking account of the 'female' relationship between work and power (indirect) and the male relationship (direct) within the psychology profession (a caring role) about equality and collaboration relations, there may be perceived tensions between power and 'perceived' position. Patel (1998), in relation to 'race' and professionalism in 'black' (professional)–white (client) therapy encounters, highlighted the complexity of such issues. She noted that when occupying contradictory positions of 'perceived' subordinate (black-identified) group membership and 'dominant' (e.g. clinical psychologist), practitioners may find themselves drawing on strategies and tactics to reflect increased professional power to enhance credibility with a client expecting a dominant 'valued' ([*sic*]: white, identified therapist) (see also Aitken, 1998; Leary, 1997). This will have implications for supervision and issues that need to be addressed throughout placement and supervision experiences (see also McQueen, 2000).

Process model of supervision

We draw on a process model of supervision (Hawkins and Shohet, 1989) as a framework to visualize the richness and complexity of any supervision or therapy encounter. As indicated in Figure 8.1, we can identify a number of elements: client, trainee and supervisor, both as individuals and in various

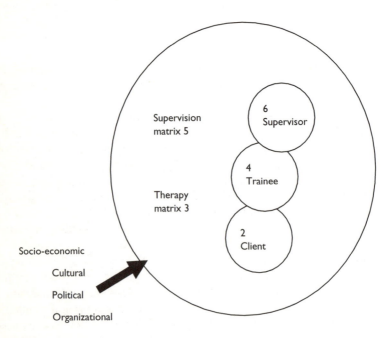

Figure 8.1 Process model of supervision
Source: Hawkins and Shohet (1989)

relations to one another (e.g. therapy matrix and supervision matrix). Such a model further makes explicit how any individual or encounter is necessarily embedded within and affected by (particular) socio-economic, political, cultural and organizational contexts. *How* we understand the effects of the wider (social, organizational, professional) contexts on supervision and therapy will in part be dependent on our 'conscious' awareness of such issues.

As an example, we first consider the wider social context (as represented outside the circles). If as practitioners we adopt a consensus view of society (i.e. there is no conflict in wider society) then undertaking a gender-neutral approach to therapy will not be experienced as problematic or limited. That is, psychological distress is understood as reflective of individualized 'break down' which can be 'fixed' through individualized solutions, including psycho-educative solutions. This may involve the sharing of individualized techniques such as the learning of more adaptive cognitions, or behaviours, but which risk leaving the person as still unknowing about herself and her personal histories, connections and commonalities with others but which will inherently leave structural conditions unchanged. We might argue that such a societal view is the one into which we are socialized through clinical psychology training.

This is contrasted when holding a conflictual view of society, as one which is structured by social inequalities through which different individuals share commonalities (of exclusions and strengths) with others along dimensions of gender, 'race', class and the intersections of these. Such an approach necessitates the clinician and supervisor being aware of social inequalities and how such factors organize our existence *internally and externally*. That is, to hold a framework in which a person is understood as a social being and being aware of the ways in which institutionalized structures and systems of gender, ascribed 'race' and class are differently oppressive and constraining, both in the therapy encounter as well as any supervisory encounter.

In addressing issues within any therapy encounter, Sue Holland argues for a four-stepped 'social action' model. In this model the clinician is responsible for creating the conditions which go beyond an individualized 'fix' or curative approach. For example, for a woman being referred for depression, this would involve moving (but not imposing) the woman from patient (to be passively cured) to relating with another person (therapy) to explore meanings and how we relate to self and others. This can be developed by exploring options for the woman to link with others (e.g. group work) as a space to discover common histories to possibilities of a collective voice to work for change in our communities (i.e. social action) (Holland, 1992a: 73).

Within a process model framework we need to be aware that whether self-identifying as woman or man, transgendered, lesbian, gay, bisexual or asexual, or as of black, white or mixed parentage, that growing up in Western society we have likely internalized powerful gendered and cultural messages about what is (un)acceptable and (de)valued just as have our women/men clients.

We might ask ourselves to what extent do we make explicit to ourselves, or to our clients or in the supervisory context, our attitudes towards women and men, or what we consider as the normative limits of masculinity or femininity (see R. J. Green, 1998), and how comfortable does this fit with our ideas of ourselves as professionals. Within supervision, it may feel that to raise such issues from a structurally less powerful position (supervisee) risks positioning ourselves in relation to the supervisor or to a psychologist as 'less than professional'.

As 'professional' men or women practitioners how do we experience sitting with a crying or angry man or woman client? How does it differ, if at all, if the client identifies as the same or other gender to us? What would be different if we, or they, also identified as gay or lesbian or heterosexual? Exploring within supervision should enable the beginning of the super-visee's own capacity for self-reflection, which Casement (1988) calls the internal supervisor, which is supported by the external supervisor pre- and post-qualification. At post-qualification one would expect a move towards more autonomous functioning.

Impact of wider social political context

In this section we present some background research findings, which have implications for supervision in connecting the external world (of out there) with the internal world (of psychology, of a supervisory relationship and of the individuals who come together). The specific knowledge base that we draw on will influence what is understood as significant and what is then validated.

The (everyday) material, social, psychological and political effects of the differential positions of men and women in UK society have been widely debated for decades. Research provides consistent evidence of differential effects, which seem to cut across cultural and class identifications. For example, in Bostock's (1997) review, differences are summarized under three broad headings.

Status and role expectations

Relative to men, women are accorded lower social status and more restrictive role expectations than men. This has been evidenced in the representation in structural positions of power in wider society, from the political sphere to the private and public sectors. For example, women are over-represented in heading up lone-parent families, looking after children, adults, older adults; as well as working at grass-roots level in the identified 'caring professions'.

Relating this to supervision, as practitioners, if discussing the needs of a male primary carer of children, we may be prone to idealize his role and work harder to offer greater practical support to him than we would a woman carer. Women who have harmed their children are more readily demonized, as they have transgressed both their mothering and caring roles.

Abuse and neglect experiences

Women are likely to have greater exposure to adverse emotional, physical and sexual abuse and neglect from childhood continuing into adulthood, with increased risk of social isolation.

Not only might this be reflected in the experiences of the women and men with whom we work, but also (as we are gendered) with our own experiences. How do we as men or women identify or un-identify with our clients, and with abuser/perpetrators and the abused/survivors? Do we even explore these issues within therapy encounters? What are the boundaries? If we hear about grooming and silencing strategies of male perpetrators, do we link this with our attempts to socialize our clients into our particular therapy approaches? What happens if we feel attracted to or feel hate towards our client? What happens if we become overt perpetrators, or we suspect a colleague or supervisor?

A salient reminder that as professionals we are not immune to reproducing such gendered inequalities can be found in the work of the Prevention of Professional Abuse Network (POPAN) (1994) and Garrett (1998, 1999). In a study of 171 cases studies of reported abuse by professionals in the National Health Service, men comprised 78 per cent of the perpetrators, of which 22 per cent and 51 per cent were known or suspected serial abusers. Of the survivors, 89 per cent were women and 15 per cent were trainees/workers in health care. In the reported cases, 12 per cent were psychologists (POPAN, 1994). In a 1988 survey of clinical psychologists (4–8 per cent) reported sexual contact with clients, with 35 per cent knowing of sexual contact between psychologists and clients (Garrett, 1998). This has clear relevance for supervisory encounters.

Access to societal resources

Women will have more limited access to economic, material and social resources. This is evidenced by figures which show that women are paid less than men, and that they form the majority living below the poverty line, being dependent on benefits, with implications for housing and contact with statutory agencies.

Failure of clients to attend for therapy is one example. As trainees, and supervisors, we are governed by narrow rules with pressures of waiting list times where failures to attend are often assumed to reflect a client's lack of motivation. What understanding do we have, and how do we support women with childcare issues who also have a restricted social support network and where our service may be one statutory appointment among many (social services, housing, general practitioners, etc.)? In supervision, do we discuss such issues? Do we consider such practical issues to be the province of clinical psychology? In supervision we have explored with trainees, how we can try to engage with a woman to explore possible conflicting needs. Given our earlier arguments about women's possible socialization to meet the needs of others, then it is important to explore how being available to her children may be experienced as in opposition to a woman having a space to explore her (internal) needs. This can be done without the therapist taking up the position of a persecutory figure. Often client attrition can (privately) become a way to manage a waiting list, but without publicly rejecting a client.

Again, there are also gendered differences in access to societal resources within psychology as a profession. For example, in a review of grades in clinical psychology in 1988 men outnumbered women by 3:1 in the top grades (Ussher and Nicolson, 1992). Further, Ussher and Nicolson noted that women achieving success are often the fiercest advocates of gender neutrality (1992: 14). This, they argue, may reflect the pervasiveness of gendered inequalities and the internalization of gendered assumptions. Within supervision we are mindful of the pressures on trainees (and supervisors) to take a gender-neutral perspective to meet the demands of the profession when 'core' competencies and the evaluation of trainee placements do not explicitly identify inequality or gender as an evaluation measure.

Drawing these threads together, the content and process of case formulation in supervision would need to be aware of the different frameworks in thinking about the ways men and women present distress. From a social inequalities perspective, women and men are differently socialized into subordinated and dominant positions respectively, and as part of the psychology of subordination it is argued that, for example, women are at risk of developing 'emotional/psychiatric disorder' or finding ways to exert control in indirect ways (e.g. use of alcohol, difficulties with eating and self-injury) to alleviate internal distress.

At one level we might argue that this is an extreme position to take, yet we see women over-represented in categories of affective related disorders (e.g. depression, anxiety, borderline personality disorder, affective psychoses), whereas men appear more often in the figures for substance misuse and personality disorders.

Debates have centred on whether or not men and women experience the same levels of distress, but that differences arise because of

- gender bias in assessment/referral/forms of interventions (under/over-representation *re* forms of mental health needs), and because
- women express distress differently.

Or whether men and women are predisposed to experiencing different levels/patterns of distress and that differences arise because of:

- social inequalities – internalization of negative stereotypes, for example; low self-esteem;
- social roles – marriage/forms of employment/carers/multiple roles;
- biological factors – hormonal, genetic;
- unconscious conflicts/internal object relations.

Our particular understanding of presenting distress, will impact on the way we talk about and open up therapeutic possibilities. The acknowledgement of inequalities is indicated in changes in legislation over the years. For example, although women comprise about 50 per cent of the total population numerically, women as a category can be considered a psychologically and economically oppressed or dominated group in that they have been routinely and legally discriminated against in society (e.g. Miller, 1976/1986; Ussher and Nicolson, 1992). Attempts to legislate out such discriminations in the UK are evident in the Equal Pay Acts of 1975, 1984, for example; in the Sex Discrimination Acts of 1975, 1986; in the Employment Protection Act, 1975; in the Race Relations Act, 1976; in the Race Relations (amendment) 2000; and in the Disability Act, as well as in BPS Guidelines such as the 'Equal Opportunities Statement' of 1994.

Clinical psychology developments

How aware are we as supervisors or trainees of the critiques of our profession. In our approaches to supervision we attempt to engage trainees with such literature and debates in ways which manage the tension between the trainee getting through the programme's requirements and the enabling of (de)stabilizing critical thinking rather than a passive acceptance of the mainstream status quo. This means that the supervisor has to move out of the position of ascribed expert and alongside the supervisee into a position of potential conflict when he or she may desire certainty.[4]

Over recent years, both in the United States and in the UK, the profession has been critiqued as a cultural mechanism which sustains the interests of those in power and which rarely challenges prevailing beliefs and stereotypes which affect thinking, diagnosis and selection for psychological work. Yet clinical psychology positions itself to 'achieve the alleviation of psychological distress and dysfunction and the promotion of psychological health and well being' (BPS, 1998a). Psychological theories, models and the research on which they are predicated have been critiqued for being partial, specifically reflecting white, middle-class, male and heterosexist assumptions and norms about what is normative and acceptable and for focusing on the individual as the site of both the problem and the solution. Such criticisms have emerged both from those outside the profession as well as within (Aitken, 1996; Fernando, 1995; Patel *et al.*, 2000; Nadirshaw, 2000; Prilletensky, 1989; Ussher, 1991; Ussher and Nicolson, 1992), and usually from those identifying with subordinated groups. Such theories and practices have been identified as excluding particular groups from accessing psychological services or for problematizing the individual as being 'deficient' when in services.

Yet given what we have argued about the gendered socialization of women and men in our society, there are a number of apparent paradoxes at work. According to available Division of Clinical Psychology figures, clinical psychology is now a predominantly female occupation. In 2001 women comprised 64 per cent of the registered DCP members, compared with 57 per cent in 1989. This increased 'feminization' of clinical psychology looks to continue, since entry into the profession is predominantly by women who have consistently comprised 78–81 per cent of all successful applicants since 1995. In 2001, 367 of the 1,198 women applying gained acceptance to the 454 places available (compared with 87 of the 288 men applying). The interrelationship between gender and 'race' was not analysed – although from 1995 to 2001 8–9 per cent of all applicants have identified as (visible) minority ethnic categories. In 2001 the people of minority ethnic heritages comprised 7 per cent of all successful applicants.

We might expect that if women comprise the majority of workers, arguments about the adverse effects of gender bias operating within psychology will be countered. Further, given that women comprise the majority of clients as well as the majority of workers (both supervisors and supervisees) those structural inequalities would be mitigated. One explanation for the reproduction of inequalities is that women as a group, and men as a group, are not homogeneous, but inequalities intersect with class, 'race', sexuality, and professional dimensions. Further is the finding that few women (whether achieving ascribed professional status or in traditional roles) perceive or experience themselves as members of an oppressed group (Ussher and Nicolson, 1992). In part, this is understood as a possible reflection of internalization as an subordinated group – i.e. socialized into the normalcy of society, socialized into the dominant models of clinical psychology, engaged in denial of oppression, or identifying with the dominant group (psychology and male norms). Thus women and men reproduce the status quo, rather than bring about change to it. There is a parallel process and these issues are then seen as unimportant, split off and located in a few to examine or push for change. There is a need for changes to the structure of the profession (Nadirshaw, 2000). In supervision, a change in emphasis about what are considered valid topics for exploration may be a necessary step.

Gender in the supervisory relationship

A social movement that is transformative must break the isomorphism of power that it critiques.

(Almeida, 1998: 2)

Returning to the process model of supervision, Hawkins and Shohet (1989) suggest that there are two main supervisory styles: (1) supervisors who attend to the therapy matrix via reports, written notes and tapes, and (2) those who attend via the 'here and now' of the supervisory process. In thinking through gender issues and the possible ramifications for supervision, in order for the second supervisory style (the here and now relationship), it would be necessary to explore and discuss gender issues early in the supervisory relationship in order to be clear about what might belong to the client, supervisee, and the supervisor.

These approaches to managing supervision are further divided into six modes of supervising. In brief:

- Reflection on the content of the session. The supervisee is helped to become more aware of what they are doing in the session with the client.
- Focusing on strategies and interventions. What interventions are made and why, reasons behind them, how they were made and the next step with the client (Davies, 1987).
- Focusing on the therapy process as a system that the two parties create together. This will include the conscious and unconscious interaction between the therapist and client (i.e. client's transference).
- Supervisee's counter-transference. What does the client stir up? Influences on the way a therapist views the client through their own belief and value system may include conscious prejudice, racism, sexism and other assumptions that colour the way we miss-see, miss-hear or miss-relate to the client (Kelvin, 1987).
- Supervisory relationship (the importance of this is addressed in earlier chapters of this volume).
- The supervisor's counter-transference. Here sudden changes and eruptions are used to examine the fantasy relationship between supervisor and client.

According to this model, good supervision must integrate all aspects and have some awareness of the developmental stage of the supervisee. At the beginning, the focus may be on the first two aspects, to facilitate holding an overview as they begin to look at what is actually happening rather that acting prematurely and speculating. The latter aspects become central as the supervisee becomes more sophisticated. Additionally, there are a number of tasks that need to be addressed. These include the nature of the work of the supervisee, style of their work, personality of supervisee, openness and trust established in the relationship; the personal exploration (e.g. therapy) is also important.[5] From what we have argued throughout this chapter, gender issues can be integrated into all aspects of this work.

Linking back to the client

We wish to make a few points here – notably, that therapy is never a neutral space. A task is to make more visible or explicit how we negotiate power relations and develop trust, through shared understandings, transparency, collaboration and honesty. Tensions or 'ruptures' to a seemingly 'collaborative' alliance can be used as important resources and as a space to renegotiate power relations. If, at the minimum, visible or structural differences (e.g. 'race' and gender, professional–client, supervisor–supervisee) are acknowledged explicitly early in the relationship, this may enable the client to come back in an in-depth way later when they feel more secure within the relationship.

The contexts of therapy (and supervision) of how the client accesses care and appropriate therapy, and whether the psychologist is seen as the 'acceptable' face of oppression, are going to be salient to issues around engagement and continued contact with the client. Clearly, social norms and cultural discourse impact on assessments (Harris et al., 2001) and the social constructions of gender and power. These are significantly influenced by cultural ideologies, but are receptive to training (Leslie and Clossick, 1996).

In therapy, a good experience is important through us being committed and supportive to women/men with mental health needs; but commitment is not enough. We need to recognize the importance of early childhood and the socialization of women's and men's emotional development, and, for example, ongoing experiences of oppression and injustice. Individuals who are bound up in a struggle for survival may feel vulnerable to threats from within the external as well as their internal world and often do not have the emotional reserves/energy to bring about change. These may include resources from the outside in the form of care and other nurturing experiences so that energy can become self-generating.

If we relate this to supervision, containment of this complex matrix can be compounded without clear boundaries that allow for the emergence of trust and which can withstand, contain or work through tensions. A clear contract about the parameters of the supervision may enable a discussion about the supervisory relationship, something that needs to be on the agenda throughout the supervision.

The supervisor needs to be committed and will need to be cognizant of the effect interruptions (telephone calls) or cancelled supervision sessions due to planned or unplanned absences (crises) can have on establishing and maintaining a good working alliance. In order to provide a space that integrates new ways of working a supervisor may use their power to empower the trainee via sharing their knowledge (Wheeler et al., 1986). The encouragement of respect by identifying the supervisee's competencies, affirming improvements and supporting individuality may enable progress and also form a basis from upon which constructive criticism can be heard. Tools for thinking about how to enable differences to be explored (not just visible differences) are presented in Figures 8.2 and 8.3: cycles of mistrust and trust, respectively.

We might ask of ourselves in clinical supervision whether the conditions are created that can enable the development of a creative cycle that can address difference and conflict.

Case study

The following scenario is an attempt to demonstrate how thinking about gender issues can enter therapy and supervisory contexts. In this example, we position an older male supervisor with a young female trainee; the male client is a similar age to the trainee.

A client is referred for panic attacks[6] and upon allocation was seen as a 'straightforward CBT referral'. During the initial assessment, the trainee (privately) felt she could have been friends with the client if they had met outside of therapy. The client was able to use the therapy to good effect, as seen by his self-reported reduction in the Beck's Anxiety Inventory (Beck *et al.*, 1988) scores and the trainee's observations.

The trainee looked forward to the sessions as she felt there was good rapport and the client appeared to make use of the therapy. Mid-point during therapy the client starts to wear excessive amounts of aftershave, paying the trainee a lot of compliments and requests self-disclosures regarding her social life. The trainee attempts to play down or ignores the comments about her clothing and attractiveness. Increasingly she becomes aware of how she is dressed over the course of the therapy sessions and of the different degrees of exposure of her body.

She attempts to bring this to supervision, by wondering whether the collaborative client–therapist relationship is breaking down. She explicitly names 'friendliness' as interfering with the homework and tasks within her clinical sessions. The supervisor focuses on providing strategies and techniques to orient the client back to the tasks of therapy. There is no explicit discussion around gendered issues, power or acknowledgement of the threat (awkwardness) the trainee is experiencing. The trainee does not feel able to bring these concerns to session again, and the supervisor does not raise the issue.

Nearing the end of therapy, the client says 'he has got something for her and he will give it to her in the last session'. She becomes increasingly worried regarding what the 'something' is. In fact he doesn't turn up for the last session. She is left with feelings of unease, but also relief. At the penultimate session, the client's symptoms have objectively improved.

The supervisor validates the fact that the client attended most of his sessions and that his BAI scores had been reduced. Referring to the vicious cycle of difference model in Figure 8.2, the supervision example has followed a cycle of mistrust (Figure 8.2) rather than trust (Figure 8.3).

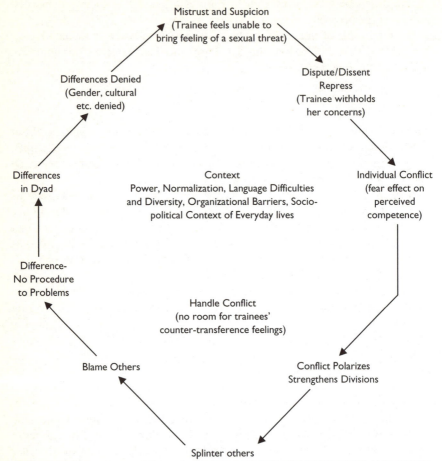

Off/fragment (trainee is unavailable to client) TOOLS TO EXPLORE DIFFERENCES AND POWER

Figure 8.2 Cycle of mistrust
Source: Nadirshaw, Z. (in press) *Transcultural Clinical Supervision in Healthcare Practice*, London: Department of Health/University of Bradford.

A man presenting with anxiety can set up the dynamic in a mixed-gender therapy for the woman trainee wishing to rescue a vulnerable male (see also Walker and Goldner, 1995). In our experience, this is often (but not always) different for a woman working with a woman referred for anger issues. In part, we understand that this is because such a referral would reflect a non-normative expectation about acceptable women's behaviours, but it also challenges a woman practitioner's awareness and acceptance of anger within herself which might be different to a male practitioner's awareness.

The attempt to bring the (erotic) transference to supervision was named by the trainee wondering whether their collaborative relationship was breaking down. She explicitly named 'friendliness' as interfering with the homework

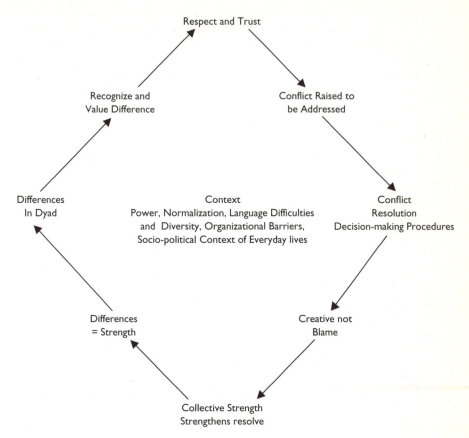

Figure 8.3 Cycle of trust
Source: Nadirshaw, Z. (in press) *Transcultural Clinical Supervision in Healthcare Practice*, London: Department of Health/University of Bradford.

and tasks within sessions. However, she privately experiences discomfort with the client, but in public is not able to frame this as she fears it would undermine her competency as a woman trainee. The supervisor's focus on technique and with no explicit discussion around gendered issues, power or acknowledging threat (awkwardness) to trainee experience, left the trainee feeling unable to bring this concern to session again. Without the space in supervision to explore these issues, the trainee attempts to play down or ignore her awkward feelings. However, these feelings direct her dress code, which she becomes increasingly aware of (a gendered response, being the object of desire and aware of how different clothing is relational to body exposure). Over time she starts to wear trousers: a concrete solution to a tricky therapeutic encounter. She also has some feelings of guilt as she recalls when first meeting the client that if they had met outside of therapy they could have been friends.

Our approach would be to explore from the outset possible identifications and playing out of power relations with the client around age-related issues, sexualized attraction, as well as a wish to succeed as an effective practitioner. As supervisors we pay special attention to the language that the trainee brings to our encounter. Words, such as 'friendliness' would be explored in ways which would recognize possible sexualized presentation as a valid topic for supervision. This might be done through referring to male–female relations in general, literature that refers to erotic transference (Bollas, 1994) and counter-transference in same or mixed-gender therapy. From the scenario, the trainee experienced a blurring of boundaries that caused her to worry that her dress code/appearance was provocative (women as causal of male desire) – but the supervisor, in not creating the opportunities, effectively silenced the trainee. On exploring the meaning and impact of requests for disclosures about personal information we are aware that some women trainees have experienced such requests by males as intrusive (violation of boundaries) and disabling whatever the stage of training, and more often experience such requests as attempts at connection when requested by women patients.

By making more explicit possible identificatory and power relations issues, this would enable an understanding of gendered perspectives as to why a client may be making comments in the context of gendered positions in wider society, which therapy encounters are not immune to. We aim to enable the trainee to be aware of how to speak with the client to pick up on his anxieties so that she can contain his vulnerability rather than it being reversed – that is, the client's vulnerability has become turned around, and the trainee's need to be looked after undermines her professional position and sense of competency as she feels her need is not legitimate and has not been validated in supervision.

When taking a gendered perspective, this should not be to the exclusion of wider diversity and similarity issues. In Figure 8.2 we have added other examples of points of mistrust, and readers might want to think what could have been different at different points to create a cycle of trust.

We might ask that if the supervisor and supervisee were both women, would the trainee feel more able to bring this to the supervisor, or if all three participants were women would the comments on the part of the client engender different feelings or interpretations? How would this differ, if at all, if the trainee (or supervisor) was a self-identified 'lesbian' or 'bisexual'? It is important not to portray a scenario of an 'all-knowing' supervisor without recognition of the supervisee within this relationship. What the supervisee brings to this relationship and how this affects her understanding and expression of the therapeutic encounter, as well as her readiness and willingness to use her supervision, has to be considered as an important part of the equation. In summary, both supervisor and supervisee are active participants in the supervisory relationship.

Trainees (later to become supervisors) will enter supervisory encounters with their own motivations for becoming a therapist or clinical psychologist. Just like the supervisor, the trainee may or may not have the privilege of a theoretical or experiential framework, which values the need to consider the impact of wider cultural context on therapeutic and supervisory encounters. We need to think through how to support and facilitate a learning environment in which the cultural context (of which we are all part) can be reflected upon. We suggest some examples of learning outcomes which may be usefully agreed at the beginning of a supervisee's placement (see Appendix).

Clearly, learning within supervision is not a static process for the supervisee or the supervisor. Specific training for supervisors and ongoing training need to be integral parts of continued professional development.

We have used a CBT case, but note that therapy approaches which attend more to the process (e.g. exploratory therapy) may more readily lend themselves to attending to the issues raised as part of therapy. In saying that, whichever therapeutic approach is used it is possible to come up against conceptual vacuums which need to be explored within supervision. Supervision can help the supervisee to become aware and to address difficult issues in order that the patient/clients may make sense of the issues being addressed or confront issues within the therapy. This is in addition to the phases of the beginning, middle and ending of the therapeutic relationship, when focus may be placed on obvious differences as a distraction from the more general anxieties about therapeutic engagement, feelings of dependency, and concerns about separation and loss respectively.

Conclusion

To move away from the limiting idea of clinical psychology as a non-reflexive 'scientific' and 'objective' discipline and profession we must be seen proactively to encourage challenges to our established assumptions and practices, and to be prepared to question our assumed expertise in knowing what is necessarily 'best' for the client and/or researched. It is not simply a case of incorporating additive gender, 'race' or culture packages into our training programmes or clinical practice; rather, it demands a transformative process. Qualitative, feminist and/or anti-racist research approaches can play a vital role in enabling and empowering clinical psychology as a profession and a discipline to become aware of its own heritage and its relation to those groups it considers can benefit from clinical psychology theory and practice. We must remember that constructions of 'difference' may have specific and general effects for women and men, both within and outside of the therapy and supervisory encounters. A professional may attempt to minimize differences around structural relations of, for example, therapist and client. However, these can still (implicitly or explicitly) figure centrally in a therapy encounter, coexisting with (as well as independent of) other 'differences' in which gender, 'race' and/or class may figure. The socio-politico-historical context of clinical psychology and the cultural heritages of those training (in terms of 'race', gender, and/or class as exemplifiers of differences) need to be made explicit. Unless therapists and trainees are provided with the conditions in which to feel safe themselves (this does not mean unchallenged) to explore uncertainties, and the powerful feelings which emerge when dealing with issues relating to structural differences, how can we expect to be able to provide the conditions for a client to raise such issues without feeling vulnerable to further problematization, pathologization and/or exclusion by a professional. It may be that clinical psychology has to consider crossing disciplinary and/or professional boundaries in order to inform itself of alternative forms of analysis (see also Holland, 1995).

The capacity to tolerate self-reflection on our own personal and professional cultural heritages, and our role in perpetuating assumptions and practices which effectively disadvantage 'others', is central to changing dominant power relations as structured around 'race', gender and professionalism.

Appendix: learning outcomes

1   To be able to identify a range of issues about why psychologists should be concerned with gender, 'race', and culture and diversity.
2   Increased awareness and knowledge about how the unquestioning application of psychological theory and practice may mitigate against the provision of just and equitable services.
3   Increased awareness of how power relations are played out along dimensions of culture, professional, mental health and specific interactional contexts.
4   Increased recognition of the importance of our own personal, professional and institutional cultural heritages which necessarily enter all therapy and supervisory encounters.
5   Awareness of supervisors' and trainees' positions as being part of different systems in relation to client (acknowledging power relations), issues of client's interests and limited confidentiality. To what extent are the foregoing made explicit with the client?

Notes

1 We would like to thank the clients, trainees and colleagues we have worked with over the years, who inform our thinking and practice. The views expressed here are personal and do not necessarily reflect those of our employing institutions.
2 In addition to such collections of articles, there are some published individual articles by British clinical psychologists – although we could find none relating specifically to clinical supervision.

3 For further reading around issues of power across different dimensions and contexts relevant to clinical psychology (professional, class, in therapy) see also Beckwith (1999), McQueen (2000) and Proctor (2001).

4 As supervisors we accept our authority, responsibility and accountability in relation to trainees, but we aim to challenge the view that we are sole bearers of expertise in particular areas. To accept the expert position prevents others from recognizing the necessary struggle which is part of the process of development.

5 Carroll (1996) uses a social role model to differentiate among the tasks of supervision. These include the learning relationship, pedagological features, evaluation, monitoring of professional ethical issues, advisory role, consultancy role and to monitor administrative aspects.

6 A male patient diagnosed with panic attacks is a reversal of the usual picture where 70–95 per cent of anxiety-related disorders are diagnosed in women.

Chapter 9

Trainees' and supervisors' perceptions of supervision

Delia Cushway and Jacky Knibbs

Introduction

This chapter is concerned with perceptions about helpful and unhelpful aspects of supervision during clinical training, as seen through the eyes of both trainees and supervisors.

One author (Jacky) has been a supervisor for many years and has supervised more than a hundred trainees. The other author (Delia) has been involved in clinical psychology training and clinical supervision training, also for many years. But both of us can vividly remember being trainees and what our supervisors did or didn't do and how crucial that experience was to our future as psychological therapists.

Early research about trainee stress (Cushway, 1992) suggested that supervision was unique in that it ranked among the top five stressors, but it also ranked among the top five coping strategies. This seemed to indicate the power of supervision both to punish and to reward. Thus, when supervision goes wrong it can be a very negative experience for both supervisor and trainee alike. However, when supervision goes well it is experienced as a very powerful learning and sustaining experience.

It is important to remember that, while many trainees regard supervision as mainly for their benefit, its primary purpose is actually to safeguard the client. It therefore behoves us to explore how we can get the best out of supervision for the benefit of trainees and supervisors, but most of all for the clients we serve.

In the first part of this chapter we will explore what the literature tells us about helpful and unhelpful aspects of supervision. In the second part, we will report the results of recent studies we have carried out in which we compared supervisors' and trainees' perceptions of helpful and unhelpful aspects of supervision. Finally, we will explore the implications of these findings for the roles and responsibilities of trainees in the supervisory relationship.

Literature review

What is supervision?

There have been many definitions of supervision, as outlined by Scaife (2001a). Currently the most popular definition, and that adopted by Watkins (1997b) in his comprehensive handbook, is that of Bernard and Goodyear (1998) who define supervision as:

> an intervention that is provided by a senior member of a profession to a junior member or members of that same profession. This relationship is evaluative, extends over time, and has the simultaneous purposes of enhancing the professional functioning of the junior member(s), monitoring the quality of professional services to the clients that she, he or they see(s), and serving as a gatekeeper for those who are to enter the particular profession.
>
> (Bernard and Goodyear, 1998: 6)

Milne and James (1999) remind us that, while recognition of the importance of supervision has increased recently for all NHS professions, supervision in clinical psychology generally, as well as in training, has reached a watershed because of demand outstripping supply. For these reasons alone, we need to be optimizing the quality and efficiency of the supervision we provide.

Even a cursory look at the literature shows us that most of the research on supervision has been carried out in the USA. Some notable British exceptions are the writing of Carroll (1996) and Wheeler and King (2001), both of whom are writing from a counselling perspective. A welcome recent addition to this literature has been Scaife's (2001a) book for mental health practitioners. Thus, most of the literature reviewed below is not directly written for, or about, British clinical psychologists. Nevertheless, we consider that many of the process issues in clinical supervision are relevant across therapy professions.

In this chapter we wish to consider helpful and unhelpful aspects of supervision as seen through the eyes of trainees and supervisors. So what does the literature tell us?

An early review by Carifio and Hess (1987), entitled 'Who Is the Ideal Supervisor?', summarized their attempt to answer this question in the following way:

> Published literature suggests that high-functioning supervisors perform with high levels of empathy, respect, genuineness, flexibility, concern, investment, and openness. Good supervisors also appear to be knowledgeable, experienced, and concrete in their presentation. They use appropriate teaching, goal-setting, and feedback techniques during their

supervisory interactions. Last, good supervisors appear to be supportive and non-critical individuals who respect their supervisees and do not
attempt to turn the supervisory experience into psychotherapy.

(Carifio and Hess, 1987: 244)

While it does seem that these are all laudable qualities, this review doesn't
highlight one important problem with perceptions of helpful aspects. This is
that, even were all the reviewed studies to be methodologically sound, there is
no demonstrated relationship between supervisee perceptions and outcome.
Thus we do not know how any of these attributes or behaviours relate to
performance as supervisee, let alone performance as therapist or client change.
Nevertheless, there is much of importance to be gleaned from exploring supervisee and supervisor perceptions providing that we are realistic about what
these actually tell us.

Qualities/characteristics of supervisors

Gender differences

Some studies (e.g. Allen *et al.*, 1986) have found no gender differences in the
rated quality of supervision, but there is some evidence that male and female
supervisors behave differently. Female supervisors have been perceived to
be more effective (Putney *et al.*, 1992), less likely to structure the supervision
session (Lichtenberg and Goodyear, 1996), and more likely to use minimal
encouragers, whereas men used more self-enhancing and critical messages
(Nelson *et al.*, 1996). Long *et al.* (1996) found that female supervisees perceive
their supervisors to be more self-disclosing than do male supervisees.

Age and experience

There is some limited evidence that supervisors with more experience are
rated more highly than inexperienced ones (e.g. Marikis *et al.*, 1985). In this
study, experienced supervisors were more prepared to self-disclose and to
give direct instructions than supervisors with no experience. Worthington
(1984) found that more-experienced supervisors used humour more often
than less-experienced supervisors. Neufeldt *et al.* (1997) comment that this
is consistent with a finding that therapists lose their sense of humour during
training but regain it after qualifying as they acquire experience (Skovholt
and Ronnestad, 1992). It seems fortunate that it appears that one's sense of
humour can return after training!

A study by Reeves *et al.* (1997) utilized the Supervisory Styles Index,
which was devised by Long *et al.* (1996). This measure was developed to
examine affiliative, non-directive, and self-disclosing supervisory styles within
the supervisory relationship. Reeves *et al.* found that younger supervisors

were less likely than older supervisors to decide what to discuss in supervision, or to insist on supervisees' strict adherence to supervisor directives. In contrast with the Marikis findings, younger supervisors in this study felt more comfortable sharing personal experiences as a therapist with supervisees. Supervisors who were 50 and over were less likely to consider 'joining', an important part of the supervision process.

Trainee perceptions of supervisor competence

The Supervisor Rating Form (Heppner and Handley, 1981) was an early instrument designed to measure trainee perceptions of supervisors along the dimensions of expertness, trustworthiness, and attractiveness; the latter is defined as likeability by and compatibility with the supervisee. These authors, and others, found that these three variables were highly correlated with supervisee satisfaction, evaluations of supervisors, and supervisees' performance as rated by supervisors (Allen *et al.*, 1986; Dodenhoff, 1981; Carey *et al.*, 1988). The fact that when supervisees and supervisors like each other they rate each other favourably is hardly surprising. However, in their exhaustive review, Neufeldt *et al.* (1997) comment that in the Heppner and Handley (1981) study the supervisees' ratings of supervisors on the variables of attractiveness and trustworthiness were related to supervisors' ratings of supervisee performance and their willingness to supervise them again. Neufeldt *et al.* (1997) suggest that this calls into question the evaluations given by supervisors to trainees as legitimate outcome variables, particularly as Najavits and Strupp (1994) found that supervisors' evaluations of therapists were not correlated with those of outside observers or clients. Nevertheless, Heppner and Handley (1982) found that supervisors were also rated as more expert, trustworthy and attractive when they were perceived to be evaluating their supervisees.

Supervisor perceptions of trainee competence

One of the few British studies explored supervisors' ratings of clinical trainees' competence (Fordham *et al.*, 1990). Factor analysis revealed that the supervisors' judgements fell across two dimensions: one dimension relating to interpersonal skills, which accounted for most of the variance, and the other relating to organizational ability. The authors caution that it is not obvious that these judgements directly reflect the trainees' clinical performance. They suggest that the interpersonal skills dimension could be either an indication of the assumptions supervisors make about trainees judged good or bad on other criteria, or simply a reflection of supervisors' personal judgements of the trainees rather than a reflection of trainees' therapeutic ability at all. Clearly then, it appears that the issue of how well trainees and supervisors get on together may contaminate perceptions of the other's ability.

Summary of supervisor qualities/characteristics:

• There are limited findings in relation to gender and experience.
• Supervisors and supervisees who like each other rate the other favourably, but this may not be an accurate reflection of the other's ability

The supervisory working alliance

Some studies have focused on the importance of the relationship between the supervisor and supervisee. These suggest that the quality of the supervisory relationship will be an indicator of outcome in the same way that the working alliance in therapy has been shown to be a good predictor of psychotherapy outcome. Lambert (1980) reported that most authors agreed that appropriate levels of empathy, respect, genuineness, and concreteness, often called 'facilitative conditions' after Rogers (1961), are required in supervisor–supervisee interactions. Bordin (1983) extended the concept of the working alliance to supervision. A US study of graduates of clinical and counselling psychology doctorates found that supervisors who were rated high on providing the facilitative conditions were also those who were rated as contributing most to the graduates' therapeutic effectiveness.

In a more recent qualitative study, McNeill and Worthen (1996) explored good supervisory events and emphasized the importance of the supervisory relationship, which they considered was characterized by empathic attitude, a non-judgemental stance, a sense of being validated and affirmed, with encouragement given to explore and experiment. In a similarly conceived qualitative study of experienced supervisees, Weaks (2002), in a rare British study, confirmed that, without exception, all her participants judged the supervisory relationship to be of paramount importance. Weaks describes three 'core conditions' of the supervisory relationship as safety, equality and challenge.

The Supervisor Working Alliance Inventory (SWAI) developed by Efstation *et al.* (1990) has a supervisor version with three factors: client focus, rapport and identification, and a trainee version which has two factors: client focus and rapport. Webb and Wheeler (1998), in a recent British study, used the SWAI in a survey of 96 counsellors and found that there was a positive correlation between the quality of the supervisory working alliance, as measured by the perceived level of rapport experienced by the counsellor, and the extent of his or her disclosure in supervision. In this study, trainee counsellors were found to be significantly less able to disclose sensitive issues in supervision. The authors suggest that, in view of this finding, if a supervisee does not enjoy good rapport with their supervisor this may have significant implications for their clinical practice. This is particularly true for trainees, where an ability to disclose and discuss difficult issues with their supervisors is imperative for safe and ethical practice.

Summary of working alliance findings:

- There are suggestions that the quality of the supervisory relationship will be an indicator of supervisory outcome. (For further discussion see Chapters 2 and 3 of this volume.)
- The importance of the supervisory relationship has been confirmed by recent qualitative findings.
- Poor rapport in the supervisory relationship has implications for trainee disclosure and therefore clinical practice.

Supervisory style/behaviours

Helpful aspects of supervision

SURVEY FINDINGS

When supervisees are asked in surveys what they value in their supervisors, they generally want a positive supportive relationship with their supervisor alongside teaching and feedback that allows them to increase their competence. In an early study, Nelson (1978) found that a mixed group of trainees, including clinical psychology trainees, wanted supervisors to be competent practitioners who were willing to model therapeutic skills as well as to observe supervisees directly. While valuing supervisor activity, trainees also wanted their supervisors to be flexible, self-disclosing and congenial. This finding was supported in a study by Worthington and Roehlke (1979), who also found that trainees wanted structure and teaching in the context of a supportive relationship. Specifically, beginning trainees also wanted their supervisors to give didactic instruction as well as provide relevant literature. Although beginning therapists particularly request instruction, studies have been unable to detect differences in supervisor style according to level of supervisee development (Worthington, 1987; Krause and Allen, 1988). Neufeldt *et al.* (1997) suggest that in the more recent studies trainees express less of a desire for instruction and more of an emphasis on trainee personal development and self-understanding.

In Worthington and Roehlke's (1979) study of supervisee and supervisor ratings of helpful aspects, the authors point out that the behaviours that the supervisors believed to be important to good supervision were not always the same as those rated by supervisees. Specifically, supervisors seemed to perceive good supervision to be predominantly based on feedback, whereas beginning trainees valued direct teaching within the context of a supportive relationship, as outlined above, followed by encouragement to try out new skills. These authors comment that, although trainees often request positive and negative feedback, they can be threatened by evaluative feedback, particularly if negative. They suggest that trainees want to become self-confident by having supervisors disclose their own experiences, provide relevant literature and give feedback about strengths but not necessarily weaknesses. Nevertheless, two recent qualitative studies have suggested that supervisees do want to be challenged. McNeill and Worthen (1996) and Weaks (2002) suggest that good supervision involves challenge in order to raise the supervisee's ability to perceive greater depth and complexity. As a consequence of effective challenge supervisees felt more confident to experiment with new ways of handling difficult situations. However, the latter study was carried out with experienced supervisees rather than trainees, who may feel less confident with challenge. These findings reinforce the importance of Kolb's (1984) model of experiential learning, aspects of which involve the setting of challenging tasks, self-assessment and facilitating awareness.

In the context of the perceived importance of the supervisory working alliance and the finding about trainees liking supervisors to disclose aspects of their own experience, Ladany and Lehrman-Waterman (1999) explored supervisor self-disclosure and its relationship to the supervisory working alliance using the SWAI. They found that the more supervisors made self-disclosures, the stronger emotional bond trainees felt with their supervisors. Specifically, trainees perceived a stronger emotional bond with those supervisors who revealed counselling struggles, as opposed to neutral or personal counselling disclosures. McNeill and Worthen (1996) confirmed the helpfulness of supervisor self-disclosure, which they reported enabled tacit relabelling of mistakes as learning experiences and so reduced the need for supervisees to feel self-protective.

STUDIES BASED ON DIRECT OBSERVATION

A few studies have based their exploration of helpful aspects of supervision on direct observation rather than surveys. Friedlander and Ward (1984) developed the Supervisory Styles Inventory. In this study trainees used the trainee version to observe well-known supervisors with different orientations. They were able to distinguish between a highly task-oriented style of supervision that was endorsed by cognitive-behavioural supervisors and a highly interpersonal style that was more likely to be adopted by psychodynamic and humanistic supervisors. These authors also found that supervisory styles were related to trainees' level of experience in that supervisors were more task-oriented with beginning therapists and more 'interpersonally sensitive' with more experienced therapists.

Two studies by Shanfield et al. (1992, 1993) utilized the Psychotherapy Supervision Inventory devised by these authors to rate the styles of 34 supervisors in videotaped supervision sessions. In the first of these studies they found that raters reliably rated 'excellent supervisors' and that 72 per cent of the variance in rater-perceived excellence was accounted for by 'empathy', with 'focus on the therapist' accounting for an additional 5 per cent. In the later study Shanfield *et al.* found that supervisors with high ratings allowed the supervisee's story about the encounter with the client to develop. They consistently tracked the most immediate aspects of the supervisee's emotionally laden concerns. Further, most of the comments were directed towards helping the supervisee further understand the client and remained specific to the material presented in the session. These authors conclude that 'the ability to track residents' concerns is at the center of supervisory activities rated as excellent. The resident provides data about what occurred and new knowledge is constructed in the supervisory interaction' (1993: 1081).

QUALITATIVE STUDIES

Weaks (2002), in her qualitative study of experienced supervisees, reports individual difference in what supervisees are looking for in supervision. She identified four supervisee styles, which she named as affirmation seeking (seeking a warm and welcoming supervisory experience); perfect practice seeking (supervisees wanting confirmation that they were operating skilfully and ethically); knowledge seeking (supervisees continually searching for increased knowledge of themselves and their clients); and satisfaction seeking (dissatisfied supervisees who fantasized about the ideal supervisor).

Unhelpful aspects of supervision

There have been very few studies looking at what trainees find unhelpful about supervision. However, Rosenblatt and Mayer (1975) explored the complaints of social work students. Neufeldt *et al.* (1997) summarized the latter authors' findings in the following way:

> What did they find objectionable in their supervisors? Supervisors who limited supervisees' autonomy; failed to provide adequate direction and clarity; or were cold, aloof, and/or hostile, contributed to students' stress. Trainees also objected to supervisors who acted as therapists and explored trainees' personal issues.
>
> (Neufeldt *et al.*, 1997: 515)

Watkins (1997b) has identified what he considers to be ineffective supervisor behaviours and suggested that they are lack of empathy, intolerance, being discouraging, defensiveness and lack of interest in supervisor training. A recent qualitative study by Magnuson *et al.* (2000a) used data from interviews with experienced supervisees to explore ineffective supervision practices. While this study examines views of post-qualified counsellors, we think that the general principles may still be relevant for clinical psychology trainees.

The data yielded six overarching principles of bad supervision, which encapsulated the behaviours described. The principles were:

1   Unbalanced, i.e. too much or too little of all elements of the supervision experience.
2   Developmentally inappropriate, i.e. non-responsive to changing developmental needs of supervisees.
3   Intolerant of differences, i.e. failing or unwilling to be flexible.
4   Poor model of professional/personal attributes, i.e. models what not to do as a supervisee or models unethical behaviour.
5   Untrained, i.e. unprepared to manage boundaries, difficult issues, or other interpersonal exchanges.
6   Professionally apathetic, i.e. lack of commitment or initiative for the profession, supervisee, and client.

Moreover, Magnuson *et al.* suggest that these overarching principles are found in three general spheres of activity. These are in the organizational/administrative arena; in technical skills and in the relational sphere.

Summary of helpful and unhelpful aspects of supervision:

•   Supervisees want a positive and supportive supervisory relationship.
•   Beginners want specific didactic instruction, as well as feedback.
•   Supervisors place less emphasis than trainees on instruction and more on feedback.
•   Recent findings suggest that trainees do value challenge if it is offered sensitively.
•   Trainees perceive supervisor self-disclosure as helpful.
•   Supervisors are more task-oriented with beginning therapists and more relationship-focused with experienced supervisees.
•   Supervisors were rated as 'excellent' if they stayed with the trainees' concerns in supervision.
•   Preliminary evidence is emerging of different supervisee styles.
•   So far there have been few studies on unhelpful aspects of supervision.

Research issues

Some problems have been highlighted with the research so far. The most important issue is that highlighted earlier in the chapter, which is that supervisory behaviours have generally not been assessed in terms of their impact on supervisee competence. We do not even have much information about the role that supervision plays in developing good therapy skills. Wampold and Holloway (1997) suggest that in the general causal model, outcomes of supervision are found in changes in therapist characteristics. The goal of supervision is to produce a competent therapist delivering competent psycho-therapy, which in turn will result in positive change for the client. These authors identify several classes of outcome. These range from reaction to supervision, to performance as supervisee, through therapist characteristics to performance as therapist, and finally to change in client. Clearly, most of the research so far has focused on the supervisee's reaction to supervision. While the emphasis on descriptive research can be criticized, it can be seen from the possible outcomes listed above that supervision research is a very complex process.

The main reviewers of research in this field have agreed that there has been relatively little attention to testing existing supervisory theory (Ellis and Ladany, 1997; Neufeldt *et al.*, 1997). However, they differ in their opinion about other aspects of the research. Ellis and Ladany report that much of the research is poor quality, that there have been few replication studies and that there is a dearth of viable measures specific to clinical supervision. Neufeldt *et al.* have a somewhat more optimistic viewpoint. They consider that the research has evolved from descriptions based on supervisor and supervisee report to microanalytic accounts of supervision sessions. They also suggest that reliable scales designed for supervision do differentiate among supervisors on the basis of style and behaviour. However, all the reviewers agree that supervision research has a long way to go.

Summary of research issues:

- Supervision research is largely descriptive.
- Most studies have focused on supervisees' reaction to supervision with little attention paid to outcome.
- Reviewers of supervision research suggest that it is at an early stage.

In Britain there has been even less research, as highlighted earlier. We could identify only a very few published studies that have explored what the helpful and unhelpful aspects of supervision are from the point of view of the trainee and the supervisor. We cannot assume that the research from the US will travel into this different context. Thus we decided to carry out our own research for the purposes of this chapter.

Current research

We will report research findings from two sources in this chapter. First, we will report the results of an exercise carried out at a recent Supervisors' Workshop in the West Midlands of the UK; second, we will report the results of a recent survey, also carried out in the West Midlands, in which we compared trainees' and supervisors' perceptions of helpful and unhelpful supervision.

Supervisors' workshop exercise

At a recent residential supervision workshop, 33 trained clinical psychologists were invited to reflect on their own experiences of being trainees. Each of them was asked to think of three of their most helpful supervision experiences, and three of the most difficult or unhelpful aspects of being supervised. The results were all produced independently but, as can be seen from the data, there were a number of overlapping items.

Most helpful aspects of supervision

An initial attempt was made to group the responses obtained here about the best supervisory experiences according to the 13 factors identified by Herbert *et al.* (1995). In the analysis of results obtained using the supervision questionnaire (SQ–R), these authors had investigated three dimensions of supervision – satisfaction, supervisor competence, and the contribution of supervision to the improved ability of the supervisee. The 13-factor model proved to be too cumbersome for present purposes and inadequately reflected process issues. Similarly the dimension descriptors failed to capture the depth of the personal and professional development opportunities identified by our participants. In a very recent paper, Weaks (2002) uses qualitative methods to generate a series of themes of helpful supervisory experience as described by experienced counsellors. She identifies the three 'core conditions' for establishing an effective supervisory relationship as equality, safety and challenge. These seem to have a higher face validity in relation to the results here, although the 'equality' condition is perhaps under-represented in our sample, as we were inviting practitioners to reflect on their supervision experiences whilst inexperienced in the field. The two dimensions covered in Efstation *et al.*'s (1990) Working Alliance model – rapport and client focus – are also helpful categories here. The best fit for our results has been achieved by combining the overarching supervisory relationship descriptors *'rapport and safety'*, and the more specifically client-related professional development constructs *'client focus and challenge'*. The helpful aspects of supervision responses are therefore listed under these two major themes, each with a number of sub-headings:

HELPFUL ASPECTS OF SUPERVISION

1   *Rapport and safety*
    - **Affirming and safe (27 items)**
      e.g. being respectful of differences; honesty, feeling contained to admit difficulties
    - **Emotional support (10 items)**
      e.g. help to contain emotions and panic

- **Supervisor qualities (8 items)**
  e.g. being warm, honest, with a good sense of humour
- **Supervisor's self-disclosure/normalizing (4 items)**
  e.g. sharing/disclosure by supervisor
- **Feedback (3 items)**
  e.g. spontaneous positive comments
- **Practicalities of supervision (2 items)**
  e.g. available and regular
- **Endings (1 item)**
  planning and preparation for ending the placement

2   *Client focus and challenge*
- **Challenge and direction (13 items)**
  e.g. being challenged but with evidence
- **Introducing new ideas (9 items)**
  e.g. stimulating new ideas, introducing different models
- **Reflection (7 items)**
  e.g. giving space to reflect about clients
- **Client focused (6 items)**
  e.g. talking through a case in detail
- **Therapeutic process (3 items)**
  e.g. helping to explore counter-transference
- **Direct learning (3 items)**
  e.g. being able to observe the supervisor working with clients
- **Theory–practice links (3 items)**
  e.g linking clinical work to theory and suggesting literature

TRAINING IMPLICATIONS

There are some practical implications of these findings for supervisor training. Feedback to supervisors about 'rapport and safety' needs of trainees, most specifically the perceived usefulness of supervisor self-disclosure, is explored in more detail by Ladany and Lehrman-Waterman (1999). The value for trainees of hearing about supervisors' own learning experiences may not be immediately evident to new supervisors, and could be made explicit and rehearsed in supervisor training. Similarly, normalizing trainee concerns and difficulties is a potentially useful rehearsal topic. More obvious to supervisors will be the need for positive feedback and supervision planning from supervisors, but reiteration in supervisor training may help to enhance practice. The 'client focus and challenge' requirements may be role-played in supervisor training sessions – for example, introducing different models and making links between theory and practice. The usefulness of direct learning (i.e. observing supervisors working with clients) is often evaluated at mid/end placement and supervisors' behaviour hopefully shaped up accordingly.

Most difficult/unhelpful aspects of supervision

It similarly seemed appropriate initially to map our qualitative responses in relation to unhelpful supervisory experiences, according to the six overarching principles flagged by Magnuson *et al.* (2000a). These poor supervision descriptors are, namely, 'unbalanced', 'developmentally inappropriate', 'intolerant of differences', 'poor model of personal and professional attributes', 'untrained' and 'professionally apathetic'. Most of the spontaneously generated items obtained from our group fitted quite neatly into these categories suggested by Magnuson, although it was notable that there were very few responses suggesting experiences of 'unbalanced' or 'apathetic' supervision. There were also two frequently identified groups of items which were not specifically mentioned in the Magnuson *et al.* paper, although arguably they could be seen as extensions of the categories listed by those authors. These were, firstly, problems with the practical boundaries of supervision, most notably, insufficient attention being paid to ring-fencing the supervision space. The second significant group of difficulties reflected hypercritical supervision. Again, these have been grouped for present purposes as an extension of the 'inflexible' category according to the Magnuson principles. Interestingly, this aspect of the supervisory experience, whilst clearly highly salient for our group of respondents, is not described by those authors. Thus the most difficult aspects of supervision reported by our respondents are presented below grouped according to Magnuson *et al.*'s (2000a) six overarching principles of poor supervision, with some further sub-divisions.

UNHELPFUL ASPECTS OF SUPERVISION

1   **Unbalanced** – *too much/little of all elements of supervision experience* **(2 items)**
     e.g. supervisor being too analytical
2   **Developmentally inappropriate** – *non-responsive to changing developmental needs of supervisees*
     •   **Not directive (8 items)**
          e.g. being denied help and advice when needed
     •   **Not challenged (5 items)**
          e.g. not being stretched or challenged enough
     •   **Prior experience ignored (4 items)**
          e.g. undermining supervisee's experience
     •   **Too directive (11 items)**
          e.g. always telling what to do and how to do it
3   **Intolerant of differences** – *failing or unwilling to be flexible*
     •   **Negative responses (13 items)**
          e.g. unconstructive, personal, punitive criticism
     •   **Theoretical models (2 items)**
          e.g. inflexible supervisor with regard to theoretical models

4   *Poor model of personal/professional attributes* – *models what not to do as a supervisee or models unethical behaviour*
   • **Practicalities of supervision (13 items)**
      e.g. supervisions being cancelled, unreliable or rescheduled
   • **External issues (7 items)**
      e.g. supervisor being engrossed in own issues
5   *Untrained* – *unprepared to manage boundaries, difficult issues or other interpersonal exchanges*
   • **Supervisor qualities (6 items)**
      e.g. supervisor being unable to admit to not knowing
   • **Boundaries (7 items)**
      e.g. supervisor shifting from supervision to therapy
6   *Professionally apathetic* – *lack of commitment or initiative for the profession, supervisee and client*
   • **Negative responses (4 items)**
      e.g. dismissive

SUMMARY

The data seem to show a reasonable concordance with the existing literature outlined earlier in the chapter, particularly in respect of helpful factors in supervision. Broadly these fall into person-oriented aspects and task-oriented aspects. There is much less literature exploring unhelpful factors in supervision. Specifically it would be helpful to know if the clusters of good and bad aspects are separate and distinct or whether they are simply opposite ends of the same dimension; that is, does the converse of the helpful aspects fully represent what is understood by bad supervisory experience. In an effort to answer this question, as well as to explore the views of actual trainees, we carried out the following survey.

Supervision survey of trainees and supervisors

Participants

Supervisors and trainees from the West Midlands were asked to complete an anonymous postal survey in which they were asked to rate helpful and unhelpful aspects of supervision. Approximately one-third of all clinical psychology trainees and clinical psychology supervisors completed the survey. While it was impossible to chase up non-respondents, due to the anonymous nature of the survey, the demographic characteristics collected did not suggest that the samples were particularly skewed. Ninety-seven supervisors, of whom 35 per cent were men, filled in the questionnaire. Over three-quarters of the sample reported that they did not subscribe to any particular model of supervision, while one-quarter subscribed to a named model of supervision. By far the greatest number of these latter respondents named the Hawkins

Table 9.1 Distribution of responding supervisors by placement offered and therapeutic orientation

Type of placement offered	%	Therapeutic orientation	%
Core learning disabilities	11	Eclectic and integrative	55
Core older adult	10	Cognitive-behavioural	27
Core child	20	Psychodynamic	10
Core adult	32	Other (includes systemic, Gestalt)	8
Specialist	26		

Table 9.2 Distribution of responding trainees by year of training, placement and placements completed

Year of training	%	Current placement	%	Placements completed	%
1	48	Core learning disability	17	Core learning disability	40
2	28	Core older adult	12	Core older adult	49
3	24	Core child	21	Core child	59
		Core adult	24	Core adult	78
		Specialist	17	Core specialist	24
		Parallel	9		

and Shohet (1989) process model of supervision. We think that this model is popular for several reasons. Firstly, it purports to be a process model that is neither tied to nor dependent on theoretical orientation. Secondly, supervisors in the West Midlands have been exposed to a lot of training utilizing this model, much of it actually run by Peter Hawkins!

Table 9.1 shows the distribution of placements offered and the therapeutic orientation of the responding supervisors. Fifty-eight trainees, 86 per cent women and 14 per cent men, responded to the survey. Table 9.2 shows the percentages of respondents in each year of training, the percentage of responding trainees in each type of placement and the percentage number of responding trainees who have completed the various placement types. It is noted that almost 50 per cent of the responses come from first-year trainees, while the third years had the lowest response rate. We speculated that first years are less resilient to difficult or unhelpful experiences and thus may be more motivated to fill in the questionnaires. Alternatively, it may be that second years and, more particularly, third years are both busier as well as being more jaded by persistently being asked to fill in research questionnaires.

Measures

In this study we wanted to use existing measures wherever possible but, since they were all American, we found that a few wording changes were necessary in order to adapt them to a British clinical psychology training context.

The following measures were used with both supervisors and trainees:

- Worthington's (1984) Supervision Questionnaire Revised (SQR), has been used to assess the frequency of supervisory behaviours. However, we added a scale to explore degree of perceived helpfulness of the behaviour.
- The Supervisor Working Alliance Inventory (Efstation *et al.*, 1990).
- Since there are no scales exploring unhelpful as opposed to helpful behaviours, we devised a new scale 'The Supervisory Difficulties Questionnaire' (SDQ), derived from Magnuson *et al.* (2000a). Like the Supervision Questionnaire Revised, participants were also asked to rate the frequency as well as the degree of unhelpfulness of difficult supervisory behaviours.

Additionally trainees completed:

- The Supervision Questionnaire (Ladany *et al.*, 1996), which provided a measure of trainees' views about the quality and outcomes of supervision received.

Results

WHAT DO TRAINEES AND SUPERVISORS FIND HELPFUL?

Table 9.3 shows the top ten most helpful supervisor behaviours (taken from the 46-item SQR) for both supervisors and trainees ranked by degree of helpfulness. Perhaps what is most immediately obvious from this table is the striking degree of overlap between what the trainees consider to be important and what aspects the supervisors rate highly. While possibly not surprising, this similarity is certainly an encouraging finding. As the literature previously reviewed has found, what seems to be of paramount importance is establishing a good rapport and giving positive feedback to the trainee. It may be that unless a good rapport is established, little else of value can happen, or at the very least learning is hampered. Alongside a positive supportive relationship each group values teaching and feedback that allows the trainee to increase their competence and confidence. There are slight differences between the groups. Supervisors seem to rate as important the holding and containing aspect of supervision a little more than the trainees, who value teaching and critical appraisal. Perhaps importantly and maybe not surprisingly, trainees also rate being able to observe their supervisor directly as more important than the supervisors. It should be remembered that the trainee group is skewed more towards the earlier part of training in that half the respondents were first-year trainees. Supervisor training could emphasize the importance of direct observation, particularly at earlier stages of trainee development. There may be a number of reasons, both legitimate and less appropriate, for avoiding observational experience

Table 9.3 Top ten most helpful supervisory behaviours for supervisors and trainees

Rank	Trainee ranking of degree of helpfulness of supervisory behaviours	Supervisor ranking of degree of helpfulness of supervisory behaviours
1	Establishing good rapport	Establishing good rapport
2	Giving appropriate positive feedback	Giving appropriate positive feedback
3	Giving appropriate feedback about less helpful behaviour	Supervisory session lasting at least one hour
4	Supervisory session lasting at least one hour	Helping trainee to establish self-confidence as an emerging therapist
5	Helping you to develop self-confidence as an emerging therapist	Establishing clear goals conjointly
6	Allowing you to observe, do joint work or listen to/watch tapes of supervisor working	Helping trainee to develop assessment skills
7	Providing relevant literature or references	Helping trainee to conceptualize cases and evolve a joint conceptualization
8	Suggesting alternative ways of intervening with clients	Consulting with trainee if emergencies emerge with clients
9	Helping you to experiment and discover your own unique style	Being available for consulting at times other than regular scheduled meetings
10	At least 45 minutes of each session is spent discussing clients or therapy	Giving appropriate feedback about less helpful behaviour

during placements, and these might be explored and challenged in supervisor training. Overall then, these ratings mirror the findings in the literature as well as confirming the qualitative findings from the supervisors' workshop. The groupings emerging there of 'rapport and safety' and 'client focus and challenge' could also encapsulate the ratings in Table 9.3.

Summary of most important helpful supervisory behaviours:

- Significant overlap between trainees' and supervisors' ratings of most helpful supervisory behaviours.
- Survey results here are in line with previous research and our qualitative workshop findings.
- Establishing good rapport, and giving appropriate positive feedback ranked as top two most helpful behaviours by both groups.
- Supervisors rate holding/containing aspect of supervision slightly more highly than trainees.
- Trainees rate teaching, critical appraisal and direct observation of supervisor, more highly than supervisors.

Table 9.4 Rankings for the top ten most frequent helpful supervisory behaviours

Rank	Trainee ranking of frequency of helpful supervisory behaviours	Supervisor ranking of frequency of helpful supervisory behaviours
1	Supervisory session lasting at least one hour	Supervisory session lasting at least one hour
2	Giving direct suggestions when appropriate	Giving appropriate positive feedback
3	At least 45 minutes of each session is spent discussing clients or therapy	Reviewing goals with trainee at mid-placement
4	Evaluating you at mid-placement	Evaluating trainee at mid-placement
5	Reviewing your goals at mid-placement	Discussing experiences in placement in addition to client work
6	Giving appropriate positive feedback	Establishing clear goals conjointly
7	Establishing good rapport	Being available for consulting at times other than regular scheduled meetings
8	Helping you to develop self-confidence as an emerging therapist	Helping trainee to develop self-confidence as an emerging therapist
9	The focus of most supervisory sessions is on the content of the therapy	Establishing good rapport
10	The focus of most supervision sessions is on understanding the clients' difficulties	Allowing trainee to observe, do joint work or listen to/watch tapes of supervisor working

Table 9.4 shows the trainee and supervisor rankings for the top ten most *frequent* helpful supervisory behaviours (taken from the 46-item SQR). The previous table showed the ratings for what trainees and supervisors considered to be important, whereas Table 9.4 asked both groups to rate the frequency of helpful behaviours (i.e. what actually happens). Again the similarity between the ratings of the two groups is striking. Six of the behaviours appear in both lists. Clearly the 'sanctity' of the supervisory hour and the mid-placement reviews are valued. Given the BPS accreditation criteria, it is to be expected that these behaviours would appear as occurring frequently. Encouragingly, establishing good rapport, giving positive feedback and helping the trainee to develop self-confidence also appear again in both lists. Trainees clearly value the importance of client focus in the supervision sessions and also value being given direct suggestions. Supervisors appear to think that they offer opportunities to be observed or do joint working, rather more than the trainees do. Generally it appears that supervisors want to discuss issues whereas trainees, at least in the early stages, value being told what to do. As suggested in the literature, there may be developmental differences according to level of experience. Stoltenburg *et al.* (1998) proposes four levels of trainee/professional development. Whilst developmental models of trainee progress remain to be fully evaluated, Stoltenburg's stages of development have high face validity, and link with the findings here. At level one, for example, the 'novice' is

clearly reliant on tutors' directions and may be more concerned about personal performance, rather than being more focused on the needs of the client. The predominant concern at this stage with basic techniques has implications for supervisors being more structured and direct with instructions for trainees early in their training. Experienced supervisors may forget the earlier developmental need of trainees to be given explicit direction. It is reassuring and encouraging that, for the most part, both trainees and supervisors agree on what is important in supervision, as well the frequency of helpful behaviours.

Summary of most important helpful supervisory behaviours:

*   Again, major overlap between trainees and supervisors' results (six items occurring in both 'top 10' ranks).
*   Supervisory session lasting at least an hour flagged as most frequent by both groups.
*   Other areas of overlap include mid-placement reviews, establishing good rapport, giving positive feedback and helping trainees' confidence.
*   Some possible developmental discrepancies were highlighted, with less-experienced trainees valuing frequent direct suggestions more than supervisors.

WHAT DO TRAINEES AND SUPERVISORS FIND UNHELPFUL OR DIFFICULT?

Table 9.5 shows what supervisors and trainees regard as the top ten least helpful or most difficult supervisor behaviours (taken from the 46-item SDQ) and ranked for degree of unhelpfulness or difficulty. Again there is a great deal of correspondence between the ratings of supervisors and trainees. Seven of the items appear in both lists. There is a focus on unprofessional and incompetent behaviour, as well as lack of respect for boundaries. The trainees also consider lack of time in supervision, time interruptions, lack of feedback and apparent lack of supervisor training to be particularly unhelpful; supervisors rate giving negative criticism and giving the trainee too much non-client work to do as unhelpful.

Summary of most unhelpful/difficult supervisory behaviours:

*   High level of agreement again between supervisors and trainees (seven items occur on both 'top 10' lists).
*   Focus on unprofessional and incompetent behaviour and lack of respect for boundaries.
*   Trainees emphasize unhelpfulness of lack of time in supervision, time interruptions, lack of feedback and apparent deficiencies in supervisor training.

Table 9.5 Supervisors' and trainees' ratings of the top ten least helpful supervisory behaviours

Rank	Trainee ranking of degree of unhelpfulness of supervisory behaviours	Supervisor ranking of degree of unhelpfulness of supervisory behaviours
1	I do not think that my supervisor is a competent practitioner	Unethical or illegal behaviour from supervisor
2	I don't get enough time from my supervisor for adequate supervision	Supervisor is an incompetent supervisor
3	I do not think that my supervisor is a competent supervisor	Supervisor is an incompetent practitioner
4	I think that my supervisor's behaviour in one or more situations is unethical or illegal	Supervisor doesn't care very much about the clients or the work
5	My supervisor just doesn't care very much about the clients or the work	Supervisor doesn't provide adequate time for supervision
6	I consider that my supervisor modelled unprofessional behaviour	Supervisor is personally intrusive
7	My supervisor does not respect the time and allows interruptions	Supervisor gives too much negative criticism to trainee
8	My supervisor seems untrained in supervision techniques	Supervisor models unprofessional behaviour to the trainee
9	I don't feel safe because I thought that my supervisor was personally intrusive	Supervisor is not a reliable professional resource
10	My supervisor gives me no feedback and I feel lost	Supervisor gives trainee too much other work to do

• Supervisors rate negative criticism and too much non-client work for trainees as particularly unhelpful.

Table 9.6 shows the top ten *most frequent* unhelpful supervisory behaviours reported by trainees in rank order. While the previous table attempted to explore what trainees and supervisors considered to be the most unhelpful or difficult behaviours, this table shows the *actual* unhelpful behaviours reported by trainees. Supervisors were not asked to rate this, as it was the trainee experiences that were thought to be the most pertinent.

The most frequent unhelpful aspects are somewhat different from the least helpful supervisory behaviours. This is encouraging in so far as trainees, for the most part, do not appear to be experiencing the kinds of unprofessional behaviour and incompetence listed in Table 9.5. Trainees report that they would like more opportunities both to be observed and to observe. This mirrors the findings from the helpful behaviours regarding trainees' views about the importance of observation. Trainees clearly seem to regard direct observation, both ways, as more important than supervisors. Trainees also report feeling constrained about the evaluative nature of the supervisor's

Table 9.6 Top ten most frequent unhelpful supervisory behaviours reported by trainees

Rank	Trainee ranking of frequency of unhelpful supervisory behaviours
1	I am not given enough opportunities to be observed working by my supervisor
2	The criteria for evaluating my performance are not clear
3	I don't receive enough critical appraisal from my supervisor
4	I am not given enough opportunities to see my supervisor working
5	I feel constrained during supervision by the fact that my supervisor is also my evaluator
6	I have to cope with different styles of work and supervision from my supervisor compared to other supervisors
7	My supervisor concentrates on one/some aspects of the work to the exclusion of others
8	My supervisor doesn't give me enough guidance
9	I don't feel safe to discuss my professional weaknesses because I am not sure how I will be evaluated
10	My supervisor is not punctual and doesn't keep to time

role and unclear about the criteria for the evaluation of their performance. This finding may have implications for the 'assessment of competencies' debate, in that the definition and delineation of specific clinical competencies may allow for clearer and more transparent, as well as more objective evaluation criteria. However, trainees also report wanting more critical appraisal and direct guidance from supervision. Being given appropriate feedback about less helpful behaviour was also rated highly on the helpful behaviours list. This leads us to speculate about whether supervisors feel unskilled in challenging appropriately and are therefore reticent to give critical appraisal, since it can be taken as, and indeed sometimes is, negative criticism. Given the nature of the evaluative role of the supervisor, trainees can be acutely sensitive to anything that might be construed as negative criticism.

Summary of most frequently experienced unhelpful supervisory behaviours:

- Most difficult supervisory behaviours outlined earlier are not experienced frequently by trainees.
- High levels of overlap between present survey results and workshop feedback.
- Trainees would like more opportunities to observe and be observed.
- Evaluative nature of supervisory relationship and unclear evaluation criteria are frequently experienced as unhelpful by trainees.

There is considerable correspondence between these survey findings and the qualitative findings regarding unhelpful supervisory behaviours gathered from the supervisors' workshop. The top ten most unhelpful behaviours, shown in Table 9.5, straddle Magnuson's (2000a) overarching themes. Most could be subsumed under the themes of 'poor model of personal and professional attributes', 'untrained', 'intolerant of differences' and 'developmentally inappropriate'. A few items could also be categorized as 'professionally apathetic' or 'unbalanced'. When considering the top ten most frequent unhelpful supervisory behaviours reported by trainees and shown in Table 9.6, there is less correspondence with Magnuson's categories. Some of the items could be subsumed under the 'unbalanced' or 'developmentally inappropriate' category, and one item, relating to not keeping to time, would fit best under the 'poor model of personal/professional attributes'. However, several items relating to the difficulties of being supervised and evaluated by the same person do not fit easily into any category. It may be that this problem takes on added significance in clinical psychology training, where the consequences of failing a clinical placement are so serious.

SUPERVISION FACTORS

A preliminary factor analysis of the two trainee questionnaires asking about unhelpful and helpful supervisory behaviours suggested four factors. These are listed below with descriptive titles and some illustrative behaviours that load highly on each factor.

Factor 1: Supervisor disinterested and/or remote. Poor therapeutic focus on trainees and clients.
1   My supervisor just doesn't seem to care very much about the clients or the work.
2   My supervisor only seems concerned about service issues and seems insensitive to my professional and developmental needs.
3   My supervisor is inadequately prepared for supervision.
4   My supervisor gives me no feedback and I feel lost.

Factor 2: Supervisor incompetent and unprofessional.
1   I think that my supervisor's behaviour in one or more situations is unethical or illegal.
2   I think that my supervisor is not a competent practitioner.
3   I consider that my supervisor modelled unprofessional behaviour.
4   My supervisor imposes a personal agenda on our supervision sessions and only wants to talk about his/her issues.

Factor 3: Supervisor skilled and gives facilitative feedback.
1   My supervisor helps me to assess my own weaknesses.
2   My supervisor confronts me when appropriate.
3   My supervisor helps me to assess my own strengths.
4   My supervisor labels my behaviour as effective or ineffective rather than right or wrong.

Figure 9.1 Proposed dimensions of supervisory behaviours

Factor 4: Supervisor establishes good rapport and is approachable.
1   My supervisor establishes good rapport with me.
2   My supervisor uses humour in supervision sessions.
3   My supervisor makes it easy for me to give feedback about the supervisory process.
4   My supervisor is not too formal with me.

These factors are similar to the themes identified earlier from the workshop findings and we suggest that there might be two dimensions: a relationship construct and a professional competence dimension (see Figure 9.1).

Most of the supervision literature and the findings above emphasize the role of the supervisor and/or supervisory relationship, whilst there is relatively little emphasis on trainee responsibility for this process. Our final comments highlight the trainee's role.

Roles and responsibilities of trainees

Clearly within a developmental–relational model (Evans, 1998), the trainees' position will be an evolving and reciprocal one, but there are some useful indicators to trainees for maximizing their supervisory experiences. Inskipp and Proctor (1993) have produced a text on 'making the most of supervision' which is aimed at both supervisor and supervisee. It includes suggestions for the trainee to bring and share work 'readily and accessibly' with their supervisor, and to be both open to feedback and to provide feedback within supervision. Milne and Gracie (2001) have specifically addressed the role of the supervisee in a recent survey of supervision methods and trainee contributions. Collaborating in the supervision process was identified as the most significant theme. The authors indicate the importance of participating actively, sharing responsibility and operating as equals within the supervisory relationship. The results from our recent survey clearly highlight trainees' keenness for observational feedback (and supervisors' relative reluctance to prioritize this). Themes emerging from Milne and Gracie's work include an emphasis on the trainee taking responsibility for prompting supervisory activities such as observation, as well as preparing for supervision, feeding back to the supervisor and organizing (e.g. alternative supervision experiences). Together these are seen to constitute 'a healthy acceptance of an adult learner's responsibilities within a professional training programme'.

To summarize, trainees' responsibilities within supervision include:

*   working on establishing a collaborative relationship
*   presenting as an adult learner
*   sharing responsibility for supervision
*   being an active participant; maximizing the available supervision time
*   clarifying needs within supervision
*   being forthcoming in bringing work to supervision
*   preparing; presenting work in an accessible way in supervision
*   prompting supervisory activities (e.g. observation)
*   being open to feedback from supervisor; self-monitoring and applying suggestions as appropriate
*   offering feedback to supervisor
*   arranging supplementary supervision experiences where required

Conclusions

The predominantly US literature we reviewed highlights the importance of the quality of the supervisory relationship and suggests that there may be developmental differences in the needs of trainees. Most of the research is descriptive and focuses on supervisees' reactions to supervision, with little attention paid to outcome. We found few studies on unhelpful aspects of supervision. We concur with the reviewers who suggest that supervision research is at an early stage. Our research findings identify high levels of agreement between trainees' and supervisors' views of helpful and unhelpful aspects of supervision, with good concordance between qualitative and quantitative results. These give some useful pointers for supervisor training, particularly about the developmental needs of trainees and the importance of observational learning. The role of trainees in making their needs explicit to supervisors has been indicated.

There has been a recent burgeoning of supervision research studies and literature in Britain and evidence-based courses for supervisors are becoming established. Supervision needs in clinical psychology are now being comprehensively addressed with clear benefits for trainees as well as for the profession and the clients it serves.

Chapter 10

Therapy models and supervision in clinical psychology

Shane Matthews and Andy Treacher

Introduction

Our motivation in writing this chapter was clear to us from the start – we wanted to write a practical, yet well-grounded chapter which would hopefully be of value to most clinical psychology supervisors. The chapter can't be as practical as some manual-based supervision texts (e.g. Morrison, 1993), but we hope its pragmatism will be valuable to readers. In order to decide what to include and what to exclude we have been guided by two different considerations. Firstly, by the orientations readers of this chapter are likely to have. Secondly, by what we have found valuable ourselves in our attempts to develop a model of supervision.

Working to the first consideration is hazardous because of the lack of research. We therefore have to rely too heavily on the results of somewhat dated survey of clinical psychologists' therapeutic orientations by Norcross *et al.* (1992). We assume on the basis of this survey that the majority of clinical psychologists are likely to espouse one of four models – cognitive-behavioural, systemic, integrative/eclectic or psychodynamic/psychoanalytic. Readers may be interested to compare this typology with that described in Chapter 2. Basing ourselves on the popularity of these four models we have elected to choose four supervision models which are hopefully congruent with the ideas that these approaches contain.

Having clarified which models we want to explore it is important to describe how we will do so – and point out the hazards of our approach too. Rather than reviewing all four models in depth we will adopt a more idiosyncratic approach. We will initially explore three models – psychodynamic, systemic and cognitive-behavioural therapy – but our exploration will be focused by the question of what we wish to take from these three models to create an integrated supervision approach that fits with our experience. From a scientist-practitioner point of view our strategy is clearly very problematic because we need to abandon any pretence that our approach is guided by research findings.

In an ideal world each of the models of therapy we've chosen would be paired with its respective model of supervision, and there would be a body of research supporting the links between each of the pairings so that practitioners could feel secure that they were basing their supervisory practice on sound foundations.

Researchers have paid more attention to this issue recently. They have tended to use the notion of an educational pyramid to focus on the levels that need to be examined in order to link supervision to therapeutic outcome. Normally the pyramid is assumed to have three tiers – the supervisor at the top, the supervisee in the middle and the client at the bottom. According to a recent review by Milne and James (2000), studies focusing on the pyramid are quite numerous but they lack 'empirical rigour'.

In order to emphasize this point they cite Binder (1993: 304), who sums up the field as follows: 'scientific investigations of the procedures used by psychotherapy supervisors and their efficacy are practically non-existent . . . studies that have attempted to assess the impact of supervision on trainee performance in actual therapy settings have had discouraging results'. According to Milne and James (2000) the Achilles' heel of these studies is that there is insufficient focus on therapeutic efficacy.

It's very creditable that Milne and James's own paper has attempted to correct this weakness in the literature. Drawing on the important methodological advice of Ellis *et al.* (1996) they undertake a review which collates papers that address a more sophisticated educational pyramid – in addition to the three tiers we have already mentioned, a fourth tier is added in order to encompass an extra process which involves a consultant providing consultancy to the supervisor. Milne and James collate 28 papers relevant to this pyramid and are able to conclude that cognitive-behavioural supervision can be demonstrated to be effective.

Milne and James are cautious in interpreting the generalizability of the results of their study because the majority of the papers they reviewed described relatively straightforward skill-teaching interventions. Clinicians working with clients where the nature of the therapeutic work is more complex may well be highly sceptical of these findings, but nevertheless Milne and James have thrown down the gauntlet to all of us to validate our work in a similar way.

We would suggest that this highly rigorous approach may not be easily welcomed by us as clinical psychologists. As a profession we have learnt to espouse a scientist-practitioner model, but it is not at all clear that we actually adhere to the model. We may, perhaps, be able to claim that our work is more research-oriented than other health care professionals, but that does not mean we directly base our day-to-day practice on research findings (see Pilgrim and Treacher, 1992, chapter 3 for further discussion of this issue). To illustrate this point it is important to record how we ourselves came to supervise in the way we do.

One of us (AT) became a clinical psychologist through the now extinct British Psychology Society Diploma in Clinical Psychology route – supervision was undertaken by three different supervisors: two clinical psychologists and a family therapist who had social work training. Each supervisor had a different style of supervision, but there was never any discussion of the model of supervision adopted, its theoretical underpinnings or its possible research base. The other of us (SM) trained in clinical psychology at Plymouth. Supervision was received from five supervisors, but the experience was essentially the same. Later on both of us became clinical tutors and it was only the tasks associated with the role of being tutors (e.g. helping train supervisors) that forced us to examine our own weaknesses as supervisors. We then began to read the supervisory literature, with one of us (SM) completing a diploma in supervision which examined various supervisory models and approaches. Our goal was to explore which approach to supervision made sense to us. The choice we made was not influenced by the concept of the scientist-practitioner – to be honest it was the theoretical aspects of the approach that attracted us. Employing the model in our work then gave us anecdotal confirmation of its value, but there was never any question of being able to validate the model's efficacy by undertaking research within the paradigm advocated by Milne and James.

The model that we have been experimenting with for the last ten years or so is the well-known approach developed by Hawkins and Shohet (1989, 2000). The model is firmly based in the psychodynamic tradition and therefore may be off-putting to supervisors who adopt either a CBT or systemic approach. However, we believe that the model's great strength is its flexibility. We hope to illustrate this point in the final section of our chapter, but in order to (hopefully) make our chapter user-friendly we will explore the ideas we take from our three chosen models to flesh out our fourth (integrated) model.

Psychodynamic approach to supervision

Because of its important historical contribution to the development of supervision it is important to start our discussion with an exploration of the psychodynamic tradition. However, since neither of us have been specifically trained within this tradition it is important to clarify our approach. We value many of the ideas that come from the tradition and feel it is helpful for all integrated therapists to draw upon some psychodynamic ideas. This does not mean, however, that we are capable of undertaking psychodynamic psychotherapy. If we do undertake individual therapy then both of us tend to utilize systemic and CBT approaches but, at the same time, we will use aspects of the psychodynamic approach in order to reflect on what is happening, interactionally, between the client and ourselves.

Psychodynamic models have traditionally been expert-driven models involving considerable role confusion. Freud himself began to supervise groups of his disciples once his ideas had gained a following. His role within these groups had three facets – he taught, supervised and analysed (as Binder and Strupp, 1997, have pointed out). His approach led to the establishment of the well-known 'tripartite' model of training which involved didactic course work, the supervision of the treatment of several patients and (most importantly) the undertaking of a personal analysis. The core of the training was, of course, the analysis – the theoretical assumption being that successful therapy could not be undertaken unless the would-be analyst was relatively free of neurotic conflicts. Clinical psychology as a discipline has not chosen to train its incumbents in this way, but nevertheless the profession is increasingly aware that it needs to respond to the challenge of psychodynamic ideas by trying to incorporate self-reflective ideas into training. Indeed we are aware of at least two of the doctoral training programmes (Oxford and Bristol) whose promotion of the reflective scientist-practitioner model has included support for some limited sessions of personal therapy for their trainees. Generally we feel that it would be unlikely for a trainee not to get a chance at some point in their training to begin to understand how their own personal history (and personality characteristics) influence their ability to be a clinical psychologist.

Our own approach to the psychodynamic tradition is frankly pragmatic. We are reassured that contemporary writers such as Frawley-O'Dea and Sarnat (2001) have created a model of supervision which has seriously modified the traditional approach. They have replaced the hierarchical expert supervisor with the highly self-reflective post-modern supervisor who takes co-constructionism to heart. Their model can build bridges to post-modern versions of family therapy, but it is less congruent with CBT models of supervision. We are still absorbing their ideas, which are, fortunately, highly compatible with Hawkins and Shohet's (2000); but despite their great emphasis on the relational nature of the model there is a curious lack of emphasis on alliance building. They argue that it is still the openness and self-reflectivity of the supervisor that is crucial in creating the context for successful supervision. They do pay attention to contract making (which is essential to alliance building), but much to our surprise they do not make reference to it directly.

For us the idea of the therapeutic alliance between client and therapist is a very crucial one. We have built our approach on the work of Bordin (1979) and Dryden and Hunt (1985), who have summarized Bordin's position as follows:

> the therapeutic alliance is made up of three major components . . . the *bonds* refer to the quality of the relationship between the participants, the *goals* are the ends of the therapeutic journey while their *tasks* are the means for achieving these ends. Disruption to the therapeutic journey might occur because the 'travellers' (a) do not get on or have a relationship which is not conducive to the goals or task of therapy (weak or inappropriate bonding); (b) disagree on the journey's end (non-agreement about goals); and/or (c) prefer different ways of reaching the therapeutic destination.
>
> (Dryden and Hunt, 1985: 123)

Bordin's analysis has a pragmatic appeal to us as therapists, and as super-visors we have little difficulty in applying his idea of the alliance to the process of supervision. If we experiment by replacing the word 'therapeutic' by the word 'supervisory' then we seem to have the beginnings of a working blueprint for undertaking supervision.

There are, however, one or two elements missing from the blueprint. If we compare Bordin's alliance building with Hunt's (1976) own ideas about the alliance, then we achieve a more rounded understanding of what needs to be attended to. In defining what she means by the term 'supervisory alliance', Hunt offers us the following inventory: 'openness and clarity . . . [about] . . . the methods to be used . . . and why they are used, the style of supervision, the goals of supervision, the kind of relationship it is helped to achieve and the responsibilities of each partner in the supervisory relationship' (cited by Hawkins and Shohet, 2000: 28).

Hunt's list adds two new elements – responsibility and style. These are important dimensions, but we prefer Bordin's ordering of the tasks that face us. We believe that it is essential to concentrate initially on the emotional/relationship aspects of the alliance. As supervisors if we do not succeed in building a good-enough relationship with our trainees then there is a real danger that the tasks involved in supervision will not be completed so that the goals are never achieved. The crucial practical question is how to estab-lish a working relationship. Both of us have family therapy backgrounds and are used to undertaking genograms with our trainees, albeit in a small-group situation (i.e. one trainer to two or three trainees). Sharing genograms one to one may seem intense. Nevertheless, if carefully undertaken, genograms can be very helpful to both participants, but a number of rules need to be observed. First, each genogram needs to be started as a narrative – 'this is my personal story about me and my family. By all means ask questions about what I share and make supportive comments but I reserve the right to tell you what's off limits.' Second (and in order to prevent the supervisor becoming a therapist to the supervisee), the concluding phase of the genogram needs to explore two further series of questions. The supervisor needs to discuss their own genogram and explore linking questions, such as 'what are my strengths and weaknesses when working with my clients?' They also need to initiate conversations about how they themselves have developed their own reflections about their own genograms. For example, 'these are clients I feel most at ease with; these are the clients I feel least at ease with. Thinking through my genogram I am beginning to make sense of why this is so.' If the supervisee is willing the supervisors can then invite the supervisees to think about their clients and their genograms in the same way. The final part of the approach involves the supervisor initiating a discussion of how the two genograms set up interesting hypotheses about how the supervisor and the supervisee will be able to work together. Useful questions that can be asked are as follows: 'Looking at both our genograms can we work out how we think we will get along? Are there any possible instances which will help or hinder us?'

Spending supervisory time sharing genograms is also valuable because it gives the supervisee a chance to explore a whole series of questions that she can use in undertaking a genogram with a client or with a family. One of the best books for developing this type of work is Wachtel and Wachtel's (1986) book *Family Dynamics in Individual Psychotherapy* (especially their chapter 3 – 'Asking Questions that Review the Family System'). We have also found McGoldrick and Gerson's book *Genograms in Family Assessment* (1985) very useful, both to us and supervisees, because of its copious examples of genograms (including Freud's).

In order to demonstrate the value of undertaking genograms as an essential part of a supervision package, one of us (AT) can provide a very painful illustration of how a placement nearly failed because of an overenthusiastic approach which did not take relationship building seriously. I offered placements to two supervisees whose arrival was staggered because of timetable difficulties. The first to arrive was very keen but very inexperienced. We seemed to get on well but a month later we were joined by the second supervisee who was much more experienced and, to make matters worse, I had worked with her before in a different setting. The first supervisee found the transition from the twosome to the threesome very difficult, but fortunately had the courage to confront my lack of thoughtfulness in handling the situation. By chance the trainee's family background had painful echoes of our situation. The memory of the arrival of a younger sibling was dominated by a sense of parental abandonment. Fortunately, undertaking our genograms at this point of crisis was very helpful – we were able to understand better how we fitted together as a threesome and were able to begin to understand the strengths and weaknesses we brought to the situation. Fortunately, for me my supervisees were able to accept my mistake. Obviously my lack of forethought had created the supervisory context which had exacerbated the resonances between our newly formed supervisory system and the family systems we brought to the situation.

Our stress on relationship building reflects the fact that we both draw heavily on attachment theory ideas (e.g. Byng-Hall, 1995), but we believe our attachment to attachment theory is not naive. Supervisors, as attachment figures, are potentially ambivalent – inducing figures because of their dual role. Supervision, as defined in the strict sense by Bernard and Goodyear (1992), stresses the gatekeeping role of the supervisor who must be sure to examine the performance of the supervisee rigorously. The idea that the supervisor can be an examiner of the supervisee while at the same time forming a relatively close bond with them may, at first sight, seem an impossibility. Our experience contradicts this idea. Providing we use co-constructive methods in undertaking the task of examining the supervisee the two roles become compatible. Such an approach enables the supervisee to take on a great deal of responsibility for

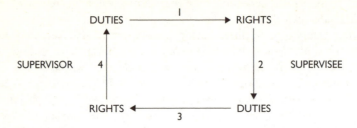

Figure 10.1 Supervisory interaction model
Source: Adapted from Scanzoni (1970)

ensuring that the learning process during the placement is effective enough to achieve a graduating performance. The first step in establishing the co-constructivist approach is to negotiate a contract with the supervisee that clearly recognizes the responsibilities of both the supervisor and the supervisee. The crucial task the supervisor faces is to create a supervisory context that is good enough to enable the supervisee to enhance his/her performance sufficiently so that they can function well enough to pass the placement.

The supervisee's crucial challenge is to be able to respond to the supervisor's input in such a way that he/she feels secure enough to be open to the process, so that the supervisor can supervise appropriately. The rights and duties of the supervisor and the supervisee can be seen to interlock in Figure 10.1, which is based on a well-established model of marital interaction proposed by Scanzoni (1970), and which in our view fits many elements of the supervisory relationship.

This apparently crude exchange theory model works in the following way. If the supervisor sets the initial conditions for supervising effectively then the supervisee feels that he/she is being both well held and intellectually stimulated by the supervisor. Internally this prompts the supervisee to reciprocate by carrying out his/her duties diligently. In turn, this behaviour satisfies the rights of the supervisor; for example, one especially important duty of the supervisee is to be non-defensive in sharing the work he/she has undertaken so that the supervisor has valid information which can be utilized as the basis of supervision. Impression management by the trainee will disrupt this process, leading to the supervisor distrusting the supervisee and vice versa. Genuine reciprocity can be built provided four conditions are met:

1   A complex enough contract has been negotiated.
2   Ongoing evaluation is utilized (especially by the supervisor) so that genuine feedback can be obtained.
3   The initial relationship built between the supervisor and supervisee has been good enough to create a sufficient level of trust for openness, rather than defensiveness, to be currency of the exchange between the two participants.

4   Both participants are emotionally mature enough to handle the feed-
     back they give each other effectively; lack of genuineness will deaden
     the feedback so that it is invalidated.

This final point takes us back to psychodynamic theorizing again. Traditionally psychodynamic supervision concentrated on exploring the transference
and counter-transference between the therapist and patient. The supervisor
remained opaque – the assumption being that the supervisor was somehow
not part of the equation because they had been purified by their own analysis.
(The ghost of Freud clearly looms here – he, as a supervisor, adopted a
hierarchical position which did not invite examination.) Frawley-O'Dea and
Sarnat's (2001) co-constructivist model offers a very different approach, as
this quotation from their book clearly illustrates:

> When supervision goes well, it is alive, vibrant and vibrating, with
> the cognitive, linguistic, affective, somatic and relational responses of
> supervisee and supervisor to the patient *and to one another*. It is through
> the mutual regulation and renegotiation of the movement of supervision
> that more becomes possible within the potential space of supervision
> and, in turn, within the analytical work of the supervisee. Even when
> there is dissonance in one or both of the dyads, more becomes imagin-
> able, sayable and playable for the supervisor, supervisee and patient
> as co-contributors to the supervisory matrix . . . There are, of course,
> potentially moments of dissonance or relational disjunction that, when
> named, processed and worked through, become precipitants to new
> understandings and/or heretofore unavailable narrative threads central
> to the supervised treatment, the supervisory relationship or both.
>
> (Frawley-O'Dea and Sarnat, 2001: 70; emphasis added)

This, we think, is a very valuable quotation for anybody interested in
supervision. For ourselves we delete the word 'analytical' (because it is not
relevant to us), but we can agree with all the other points made. Hawkins and
Shohet's model is particularly effective in offering practical ways of exploring disjunctions (as we will illustrate on pp. 200–206), but the psychodynamic
thinking of Frawley-O'Dea and Sarnat is particularly valuable in prompting us to think about all aspects of the triangular space that is involved in
therapy. Psychodynamic theorists no doubt find the concepts of transference and counter-transference useful in conceptualizing their work, but we
personally find the concepts too limiting and too linear to be of direct value
to us. As we understand it, the term 'counter-transference' is itself predicated
on the assumption that transference has been created during therapy by the
client projecting on to their therapist. Counter-transference is therefore a
secondary process triggered in the therapist by the client's active involvement
in a transference relationship. This way of punctuating the process is perfectly
valid from a theoretical point of view, but empirically we would assume that

the process can happen in reverse; that is, a client can also be the object of a transference relationship created by their therapist. Counter-transference may well then be induced in the client, who may not be able to cope with the transference input from the therapist.

Our own way of conceptualizing these recondite processes is very different. We prefer to replace the ideas of transference and counter-transference with the broader and (perhaps) less theory-laden notion of unfinished business. We assume that all the participants in the pyramid (supervisor–supervisee–client) bring their own complex experiences to the encounters they participate in. The essential trust in both the dyads involved (supervisor–supervisee, supervisee–client) is to create narratives about these encounters which free all participants to be more reflective about what is happening to them as they work together.

As always, the devil is in the detail – how precisely is this storying to be achieved? Is the triadic structure sufficient to the task or is a fourth level – consultation – required in order to cope with the difficulties a supervisor may have in creating benign conditions which enable the whole system to function? This will be discussed in the final part of our chapter when we review our revision of the Hawkins and Shohet model. One of the model's great strengths is its ability to handle these issues practically and economically.

Systemic supervision

We are sure you will have already noticed that we have not been able to keep our comments neatly corralled by the framework we have utilized. In discussing the psychodynamic approach we have already talked about the significance of genograms, and a lot of our language and thinking owes a debt to narrative approaches (e.g. White and Epston, 1991), which are so fashionable amongst contemporary family therapists. These intrusions from the systemic and narrative camps reflect the fact that we are non-purist, integrationist theorists. Faced with exploring the contribution of systemic thinking we are, however, once again in a quandary about what to include and what to exclude.

Liddle *et al.*'s (1988) definitive tome on family therapy supervision inventories so many models that the task of selection seems impossible, but such is the fashionability of family therapy that many of the models reviewed are already (we suspect) redundant. The only visible tactic that we can realistically adopt is our usual pragmatic one of cherry-picking. We are prompted to select what has helped us most from the literature and from our own experience.

Fortunately for us our ideas correlate quite well with Liddle's own approach to supervision (Liddle *et al.*, 1997). He and his co-workers stress the importance of adopting a multidimensional approach to therapy (MDFT) so supervision, of necessity, has to be multidimensional too. This stance matches our own approach quite neatly, but it is noticeable that Liddle, before introducing his own model, explores some additional facets of supervision that he believes to be specifically important within the field of family therapy.

These include the person of the therapist, which we have discussed already in the chapter, and some of the research into family therapy supervision, which unfortunately is rather insubstantial and now somewhat dated. What we will include are three further dimensions: (1) live supervision and videotape supervision, (2) thinking about family process, (3) using a lifespan framework.

Live supervision through a one-way screen (Montalvo, 1973) is a significant factor in training family therapy trainees and perhaps the most valuable form of supervision that either of us has encountered. But, of course, there can be a downside. If a supervisor is not good at relationship and trust building then live supervision can be experienced as aversive. So the use of joining techniques (e.g. sharing genograms as we have already established) is essential before exposing supervisees to the fish bowl atmosphere of the screen room with its one-way screen and video camera. It is important to stress, however, that there are user-friendly versions of these high-tech approaches, which can be used if supervisees are uncertain about the value of such methods. Former colleagues of one of us (AT), Donna Smith and Phil Kingston, pioneered an in-the-room version of supervision. This approach involves the supervisor (with or without team members) being present in the room with the supervisee and the family. There is an obvious danger of this approach becoming some form of co-therapy, but a structural rule helps prevent this from happening; that is, the supervisee invites the family members to communicate directly only with him or her and not with the supervisor who communicates directly only with the supervisee. This pattern of communication can feel strange when first used but the implementation of the structural rule means that the supervisor can maintain a so-called 'meta' position which enables her to retain an overview of what is happening. For a more detailed discussion of how live consultancy and live supervision work, see Smith and Kingston (1980) and Kingston and Smith (1983); see also Zarski *et al.* (1991) for a similar approach (which has been called the invisible mirror technique).

The use of the one-way screen for training purposes is quite a big topic in its own right, but it is important for us to point out that there is no need to use the screen in the usual hierarchical way (i.e. having the supervisor ringing the supervisee to communicate either the supervisor's ideas or the team's ideas, or both). A more supervisee-friendly approach encourages two-way communication – the supervisee can opt to ring the supervisor, asking for ideas or confirmation that the line of questioning being utilized is appropriate. The supervisor (after due negotiation with the supervisee) can also have the option of moving from the screen room to the interview room in order to offer ideas to the family and supervisee.

The reflecting team approach of Andersen (1987, 1990) is an idea that has had a huge impact in systemic work. This approach offers the family in therapy a chance to hear the reflecting team who have observed them either in the room or through a one-way screen. If a supervisee is involved initially as a member of the team then they can gradually develop their role in a clinic, without feeling over-exposed by taking on the role of therapist. The Andersen (1987) guidelines for participating in reflecting team work are very useful because they provide a structure for participation. Without this structure a supervisee (unless they had considerable prior experience) could feel out of their depth, particularly if other team members are used to working with each other.

One of us (SM) uses reflecting teams in much of his work, and I am aware that being a member of a reflecting team has enabled involvement in a supervisee's direct work with families without having to supervise the work proactively. Reflecting-team work has an in-built structure which allows supervisory ideas to come to the surface within the reflecting team. Several supervisees have found that by giving them more space and less direct supervision they have been more effective in developing their skills.

Ideally when a supervisee is working with a supervisor trained in family therapy they should get a chance to experience a variety of working methods. Each approach can undoubtedly contribute to the development of the supervisee's work, but we personally feel the use of just one method is counter-productive. It is also important to remember that clinical psychologists often have to undertake family therapy solo (perhaps even home visiting) so they need to develop self-reliance rather than team dependence.

Videotape supervision is another important area of supervision which needs careful thought. Clinical psychology trainees vary in their experience of being audiotaped or videotaped for the purposes of supervision, so the 'threat' of being videotaped needs to be carefully handled. Very often the time constraints of traditional clinical psychology supervision militate against using such supervision effectively. There is, however, one way round this constraint that can work. If a supervisee is keen and values the approach then there is obviously a strong incentive for them to review their own tapes so that they can identify sections of the tape which they feel they need feedback about. To encourage this process, the supervisor can model one or two sessions of feedback, preferably by using a tape of their own work rather than the supervisee's. By providing a narrative about what they see on their own tape and stopping to illustrate the strengths and weaknesses of their own work, the supervisor can create an invitational framework which communicates 'I can critique my own work non-defensively, owning both when I'm working well and not so well.' When the supervisor reviews the supervisee's tapes then the prime role is to be supportive and identify skilful work. When needing to give more critical feedback negativism can be avoided by inviting the supervisee to be self-reviewing. A good opening gambit is to say 'I feel you're struggling here. Can you remember what you had in mind to do? With the benefit of hindsight can you think how you could have done this differently?'

Helping supervisees to understand family process (another of Liddle's dimensions) is something we also stress. Narrative approaches have tended to neglect this aspect of the development of therapeutic skills. Our approach (and hence our language) here will cause the purist narrative therapist difficulties. We find there are merits both in Tomm and Wright's (1979) inventory of family therapy skills and in Flemons *et al.*'s (1996) post-modern inventory. Introducing supervisees to these inventories, and then exploring with them through self-evaluation which skills they feel they want to develop, can be very productive. Conceptual skills are perhaps the most difficult to develop, but this is where videotape reviewing, once again, comes into its own. It is one thing to conceptualize on the hop when you're interviewing a family; it is quite another to do it in the calm context of a video review with input from a supervisor and/or other team member. Clearly in the latter situation there is much more chance for learning to occur because the supervisee can adopt a far more observer/reflective mode which enables supervisees to take their time in trying to conceptualize what's happening.

Finally before moving on to our third model (CBT), it is worth briefly exploring the role that developmental models play in helping supervisees orientate to family therapy. We agree with Liddle that it is essential to help supervisees think within a life-span framework. Perhaps the best source of all for this approach is Carter and McGoldrick's (1999) book *The Expanded Family Life Cycle – Individual Family and Social Perspectives*. This is the third edition of a book which is something of a social document itself. Over the course of the twenty or so years since it was first published this book has been expanded and extensively rewritten in order to reflect the changing nature of American families. The impact of social and cultural changes (e.g. divorce), coupled with its very focused interest in gender, class and ethnicity, makes it essential reading for any supervisee who wants to develop systemic ideas which are contextually honed to be relevant to a caseload of families that come from diverse backgrounds. The first chapter of the book by Lerner (1999) is also particularly interesting from a supervisory point of view. He explores the interaction between the therapist's and client's life cycle stages, providing a useful checklist (see appendix at the end of this chapter) of interfacing dimensions between therapist and family. Asking a supervisee to use the checklist with at least one of their families is a realistic task to set, but the checklist is particularly valuable if a supervisee is in difficulties in working with a family and yet neither she nor her supervisor can identify why. As we will explore later on, the most comprehensive way of exploring the phenomenon involves using all the modes (or levels) of the Hawkins and Shohet model; nevertheless, using the checklist is usually productive and creates a number of points for further exploration during supervisory sessions.

Cognitive-behavioural therapy supervision

Although our basic orientation as therapists is systemic we are well aware of the value of CBT approaches and will often utilize CBT techniques in working with specific clients. Ricketts and Donohoe (2000) outline 'hallmarks of supervision within a cognitive behavioral approach', which include:

- emphasis on skills development;
- structured approach and goal orientation;
- considerable educative function;
- preference for live supervision (or use of video);
- skills practice demonstration (modelling by supervisor).

All these areas find a place within our integrative approach. We have also been interested in Padesky's (1996) ideas that there may be an 'advantage' in using CBT ideas to tackle personal difficulties before using them as a therapist, as it resonates with our espousal of a reflective approach.

While it is quite easy for us to integrate CBT work with systemic work when working with our own clients, it is not always so easy when we want to encourage supervisees to follow our lead. If we are primarily contracted by a supervisee to provide them with family therapy supervision in a family therapy clinic then it can look impossible to integrate CBT as well. However, one of us (AT) has devised the following pragmatic solution to the problem. Rather than expecting the supervisee to undertake the work I abandon my role as supervisor and become the therapist who undertakes the CBT work while the supervisee views my work from behind the screen. Normally I do CBT work with parents or partners – if the family is a lone-parent one then obviously I work just with that parent, if it's a two-parent family then I'm very keen to try and negotiate a contract to involve them both, despite the fact that one of them may (because they are exhibiting clear symptoms) appear to be in greater need of help. Involving both in the CBT work is much more productive because it keeps both involved and prevents therapy from becoming lopsided and over-focused on one individual.

Feedback from supervisees using this approach has been very positive. They are intrigued to see how an individual psychotherapy technique can be integrated into the work. In related training sessions they are introduced to CBT techniques (using the self-help book by Burns, 1980, as my main text so that they have the option of using the techniques themselves). This works well, particularly if the supervisees chose to work, for example, on performance anxieties which may be affecting their performance in the clinic. Obviously this approach has some risks of fudging the supervisor/therapist boundary, but because the work is undertaken in a group situation it is possible to maintain the boundary.

The more usual situation involving the integration of CBT ideas is when we are supervising individual trainees in our role as clinical psychology supervisors. Here the task is more straightforward because we are not confined by the structure of the training clinic. If we are going to undertake supervision of a case involving a lot of CBT work then we have modelled our approach on the structure outlined by Liese and Beck (1997) who advocate a supervisory session which has effectively seven steps to it:

1   Check-in.
2   Agenda setting.
3   Bridge from previous supervision setting.
4   Inquiry about the process and outcome of previously supervised therapy cases.
5   Review of any homework tasks set at the previous session.
6   Prioritization and discussion of agenda items.
7   Assignment of her homework.

Liese and Beck also advocate the use of (a) capsule summaries (to make sure the supervisor is not being garrulous and leaving the supervisee unfocused as a result of too many ideas explored), (b) feedback techniques (in order to evaluate the value of the supervision to the supervisee).

The rigour of Liese and Beck's approach is important to us, because as family therapy supervisors (who quite often use narrative approaches) we are aware of just how discursive our supervision can become. This may well be helpful creatively but it can leave supervisees under-focused and ill-prepared for their next session with a client. Asking for feedback *during* the supervisory session rather than (usually hurriedly) at the end of the supervision session is also salutary. The use of well-honed feedback questions enables the supervisee to evaluate the supervision there and then. Good feedback enables both sides to refine the supervision to make sure it's at least trying to deal with the most relevant areas. With a busy caseload, and perhaps only one hour to deal with a number of cases, it's essential that both partners are doing their best to ensure that the process is effective.

Liese and Beck's emphasis on agenda prioritization is also very important to us, and there is an obvious developmental aspect to this. The supervisee may well want to pay attention to all their current cases at the beginning of a placement (and the supervisor may well want to monitor progress too). By the middle of the placement there should, of course, be a maturing in the supervisee's abilities so that they will feel freed up to perhaps concentrate on one or two cases, knowing that other casework is at least proceeding on a good-enough basis. Clearly there is a possibility of a parallel process here – if the supervisor has modelled the use of feedback well in the supervisory sessions (and is encouraging her supervisee to utilize ongoing evaluation and feedback techniques when working with her clients) then the supervisee is in a good position to know which cases to bring to supervision and which can be held over.

Another strength of the Liese and Beck approach is their use of a Cognitive Therapy Adherence and Competence Scale (CTACS). This type of scale offers the possibility of being able to obtain accurate information about how a supervisee is progressing over a period of supervision. The scale has 25 items (rated 0–6) grouped under four headings: structure of the session, developing a collaborative therapeutic relationship, development and application of the core conceptualization, cognitive and behavioural techniques. The scale is (strictly) designed to be utilized by the supervisor when reviewing tape-recorded sessions. This usage is obviously very appropriate, but the scale curiously doesn't include any items about the utilization of supervision itself. Liese and Beck's work has prompted us to begin to develop a more comprehensive scale which does include items which explore supervisees' utilization of supervision.

Developing an integrative model

So far we have explored the ideas and techniques which we have absorbed from three major models of supervision. As a reader you may well be thinking that it's all very well to be eclectic, but being eclectic does not magically create an integrative approach. To create an integrative model we have had to adopt an alternative strategy. This strategy has involved looking at existing models of supervision, finding one that fits our approach reasonably well and then modifying it in order to incorporate ideas that we value but are missing from the model we have selected.

As we have already hinted, the model we chose was Hawkins and Shohet's (1989) process model. This model attracted us because its psychodynamic orientation meant that it contained many ideas that we have valued in supervision. Fortunately, because the model is process-oriented, we believe systemic and CBT ideas can be grafted on in a way that enhances the original model by giving it a new vitality. Hawkins and Shohet (2000) have themselves attempted to broaden their model by adding a seventh (contextual) model; however, we feel that their revision is not likely to be successful. In our opinion systemic, contextualizing ideas need to permeate all six modes of the approach rather than being confined to an additional mode.

As we began to utilize the original model in our own work and encourage supervisors to use the model, there was a potential problem. We were aware that the primarily psychodynamic language of the model did not fit with many of the supervisors we were working with. In response to this, a working group developed a brief document, using the broad ideas of the model and in particular the 'six modes' of supervision, but written in a less theory laden way. What became apparent was that the model, when given this more neutral framework, was attractive to supervisors and allowed them the flexibility to use ideas that were current in their practice within supervision. Typically many clinical psychology supervisors have developed their therapeutic skills either broadly in the traditions we have outlined or more specifically in areas such as cognitive analytic therapy, solution-focused approaches, dialectical behaviour therapy, etc. Also, supervisors and supervisees (of whatever primary therapeutic orientation) were able to find a way of looking at the relationship aspects of supervision and estimating the role of unfinished business in influencing the therapeutic work being undertaken.

In the next section of the chapter we will explore each of the six modes in turn. We begin with Hawkins and Shohet's original description and include the more general description of the mode we use in parentheses. We go on to explain how we have chosen to modify each mode so that we can genuinely 'own' them at a conceptual level. We hope this owning is not an idiosyncratic process – we suspect that in many ways we are typical integrative psychologists who seek to utilize CBT, systemic and psychodynamic ideas in providing useful reflections for anybody we supervise. Table 10.1 provides a summary of how we describe the modes in a less psychodynamic way and contains a list of key questions which we typically use when we are supervising using all six modes of the model.

Table 10.1 Supervision template

Mode	Possible emphases for Clin. Psych.
1 Thinking about the content	What is the client's social context?
	How do you understand the client's relationships with those around them?
	What are the issues that you are curious about in relation to your client?
2 Thinking about interventions	How was this intervention chosen?
	What are the stories around the intervention for the client(s) and therapist?
	Are there skills training issues?
3 Thinking about the client–therapist relationship	What is the meaning of the relationship between the client and the therapist?
	Has the role of the therapist and way of working been adequately explained?
	How collaborative is the work with the client?
4 Thinking about emotional reactions or resonances for the supervisee	How does the supervisee's family pattern and background input on the work?
	What are the areas that the supervisee is willing to share?
	What are the supervisee's prejudices about these kinds of situations?
5 Thinking about the similarities between supervision and the therapy	Are there similar patterns within therapy and the supervision?
	Is the supervisory approach similar to the therapy?
6 Thinking about resonances for the supervisor	What is the impact on the supervisor?
	Has the supervisor access to supervision?

Mode 1: Reflection on the content of the therapy session
(Thinking about content)

Here discussions between supervisor and supervisee concentrate on 'the actual phenomena of the therapy session; how the clients presented themselves, what they chose to share, which area of their life they wanted to explore, and how this session's content might relate to content from previous sessions'.

Helping the supervisee to think about the phenomenological aspects of their client and their session enables us to maintain a stance of curiosity about what is happening, and this process in turn helps us to encourage our supervisees' curiosity (Cecchin *et al.*, 1993). Hawkins and Shohet (1989) describe a number of Gestalt-type approaches encouraging supervisees to think about such things as client presentations, speech, posture, movement, etc. These exercises are very valuable, but we also encourage our supervisees to think about their clients contextually (e.g. how they relate to their families, their communities and their culture).

Clinical psychologists are perhaps correctly criticized for being too focused on formulating and intervening. This can mean moving out of what most clinical psychologists would understand as the assessment phase very quickly. Our supervisory experience enables us to encourage supervisees to think about the relationship clients have with those around them and their social context. This reflective process helps us stop a 'closing down' process which prevents the supervisee from thinking about their client's unique situation. Some of Carter and McGoldrick's (1999) life-cycle ideas are generally very useful in helping this reflective process (as we have already mentioned), but it is an example relevant to supervising work with learning-disabled clients that comes most readily to mind.

A local supervisor described how she encouraged a supervisee to think about how an academically and socially successful younger sibling might influence the behaviour of a learning-disabled client with severe challenging behaviour. The supervisor asked the supervisee to draw on how the supervisee saw the relationship between different family members. Ultimately these exercises influenced the next stage of therapy – they encouraged a clearer discussion with the client and her parents about 'success' and family expectations.

Mode 2: Exploration of the strategies and
interventions used by the therapist
(Thinking about interventions)

This involves discussions concerning 'the choice of intervention made by the therapist', when and why to use particular approaches and what alternatives might there be. Hawkins and Shohet (1989) emphasize that the main goal of this mode is 'to increase the therapist's choices and skill in interventions'.

This mode – the most pragmatic of all the six – is the mode which fits the scientist-practitioner approach best. If a supervisee has been successful in establishing a working alliance with their client then they will be able to garner a great deal of information about their client's predicament. Once more, this is best understood by most clinical psychologists as the assessment process. This information flow is useful to the supervisor who can begin to prompt the supervisee to begin to formulate her ideas about what is happening and to begin to think of possible interventions.

Our experience is that clinical psychology supervision often remains in this mode, and from a pragmatic point of view there is no reason to be concerned about this. If there is therapeutic movement, and ongoing evaluation reveals that change is occurring, then we would argue that good-enough therapy is taking place and there is no reason to complicate the therapy by seeking to widen our discourse about what is happening. From a training point of view it may, however, be important (as we've discussed earlier) to offer the supervisee very focused feedback (e.g. through reviewing videotapes or audiotapes). If CBT supervision is being utilized then Liese and Beck's format is particularly appropriate, but care needs to be taken to ensure that the supervisee is increasingly in the driving seat as far as formulating is concerned. If the supervisor is too expert then there is a danger of supervisor dependency being created.

If the therapy is not unfolding and 'stuckness' (Carpenter and Treacher, 1989) has been created then the Hawkins and Shohet model comes into its own (as we will illustrate as we consider the further modes), but it is important to think about other aspects of this mode of supervision. Our own therapeutic work is influenced by post-Milan ideas about interventive interviewing (e.g. Tomm, 1988). This approach assumes that the use of a whole range of questioning techniques creates different types of information flow between the therapist and family members. The questioning helps family members to think differently about what is happening to them; this process is therefore interventive because it may lead to change in behaviour as well.

This therapeutic approach is also useful in helping supervisees and supervisors to be more thoughtful about how they themselves have an impact on the clients they work with. For instance, what might be the meaning for both the client and the therapist of the kind of intervention that is being used? Has a client experienced something very similar before or something very different? Has the therapist worked in this way before?

Mode 3: Exploration of the therapy process and relationship
(Thinking about the client–therapist relationship)

The suggestion here is that supervision pays particular attention to 'what was happening consciously and unconsciously in the therapy process; how the session started and finished . . . metaphors and images that emerged . . . changes in voice and posture'. They describe the main goal being 'insight and understanding of the dynamics of the therapy relationship'.

Our approach to this mode is simply to broaden its scope by asking our supervisees to think about their relationship with their client in the broadest terms. Initially, if we link this question to the therapeutic models we have considered, the answers might be very different. For the psychodynamic therapist it might be the key to the therapeutic endeavour. A systemic therapist might be wary of a relationship developing that is investing them with too much expertise. A cognitive therapist might be more comfortable with this as long as there is a clear sense of collaboration between therapist and client.

However, as we established at the beginning of our chapter, we suspect that the majority of clinical psychologists are not working to a pure therapeutic model. We would nevertheless argue that whatever approach is used the therapist–client relationship is all-important. For example, Clarkson (1996) and others have argued that the quality of the relationship has much more impact on the client than the type of therapy being utilized. In our work with supervisors we have found that they are increasingly prepared to discuss the importance of the therapeutic relationship, but this willingness is often forgotten in supervisory situations because they feel the need to focus on the content issues that supervisees bring to sessions. Our advice is to respond to this pressure pragmatically – most supervisory time will be devoted to mode 2 issues, but a supervisor can encourage a supervisee to take an in-depth approach to at least some of their clients. This also fits with developmental notions within the supervisory relationship (Stoltenberg and Delworth, 1987), where it is suggested that this more 'process'-oriented focus comes with trainee confidence and development. We are very keen to stress that we do not feel there is a hierarchy that places more value on the *process* focus of this and the following modes as opposed to the *content*-based modes 1 and 2. In our view each has value, and a challenge for a supervisor is to consider where an emphasis at any time might be.

Hawkins and Shohet offer some very useful playful ideas about how to explore the therapeutic relationship. They use a number of questions to prompt supervisees to think more reflectively. For example, how might you name a film of the therapeutic relationship, and what actors would you get to play yourself and your client?

Another focus around the client and therapist relationship is an exploration of the pattern that might be emerging in the therapeutic work and whether that might be helpful or constraining. Useful questions in supervision might be: How might your client respond if you asked them if a session or part of a session was addressing the right issues? Might your client think there are things you avoid asking them about that may be helpful?

These kinds of questions, if used skilfully, will help the supervisee to take a much more wide-angled approach to their work. It helps them move beyond problem-solving towards a more reflective way of thinking about therapy. The clinical work emerges far more as an encounter between two human beings who both bring a great deal of prior experience to the encounter. This way of thinking opens up deeper issues, which are more explicitly explored by mode 4 supervision.

Mode 4: Focus on the therapist's counter transference (Thinking about emotional reactions or resonances for the supervisee)

In this mode the supervisor looks at 'whatever is still being carried by the therapist, both consciously and unconsciously, from the therapy session and the client'. They describe different types of transference such as the 'personal material of the therapist', and the 'tranferential role that the therapist has been altercasted into by the client'.

When supervising in this mode we ask our supervisees to think about any emotional reactions or resonances that they experience while working with the client they have in therapy. We prefer this broader framing rather than using the stricter concept of counter-transference. One reason for doing this, as we have discussed earlier, is to make the supervision model fit with as many supervisors as possible. Another is because, as some supervisors who have trained psychodynamically have reminded us, the notions of transference and counter-transference are complex and are understood and misunderstood in a variety of ways.

Our approach, of necessity, assumes that a comprehensive supervision contract has been negotiated and that the supervisee is willing to explore supervisory issues relevant to this mode. The genogram work we would have undertaken at the beginning of the placement now becomes relevant again because there is an opportunity to help the supervisee explore her own family patterns in relation to the patterns explored in the client's life. Within this mode it is also possible to explore the value system that the supervisee brings to their work. A major influence for one of us (SM), has been Cecchin *et al.*'s (1993) discussion of therapist values. He argues that since we all have prejudices and loyalty to certain ideas, a key skill (particularly for a beginning therapist) is to develop some irreverence to all beliefs about therapy, including their own and those of their supervisor. While this approach may be a little idiosyncratic for some tastes, it does focus attention on how the responses we have to situations we find ourselves in with clients are filtered by our own experiences. There is also a further important question for the supervisee that needs to be explored: To what extent should the supervisee's emotional responses be shared with the client? Different therapeutic models will answer this question very differently. Interestingly, the more recent systemic models of Hoffman (1993) and White (1995) describe the use of 'self' as a possible appropriate therapeutic strategy within the context of the development of a more collaborative approach.

Mode 5: Focus on the here-and-now process as a mirror or parallel of the there-and-then process (Thinking about similarities between supervision and therapy)

The focus here is the relationship between supervisor and supervisee and what happens in the supervision sessions 'in order to explore how it might be unconsciously playing out or paralleling the hidden dynamics of the therapy session'. The example they give is how if a client was acting in a 'passive-aggressive' manner, the same pattern may be unconsciously present in supervision.

Thinking about similarities between supervision, and therapy and in particular the notion of a parallel process between these two, has been described by Hawkins and Shohet and others. According to McNeill and Worthen (1989: 330) parallel process occurs 'when certain vestiges of the relationship between a supervisee and his or her client appear in supervision'. While doing further training in supervision, one of us (SM) was struck by the attention paid to this by therapists with a psychodynamic or humanistic background. Alongside transference there was a sense of it being at the heart of the supervision. For many clinical psychologists this does not necessarily fit their view of supervision. However, our experience of working with supervisors has taught us that this idea can be very useful, particularly when exploring 'stuck' situations. For example, the idea of a supervisee mirroring a client by blocking all ideas for change ('yes, but') rings a bell for a lot of supervisors.

A possibly more accessible notion is that patterns in therapy can be repeated in supervision and it can be helpful to consider how both might be changed. The link between this and a parallel process is very strong, but the feedback we have had is that thinking about patterns is more concrete and meaningful to therapists who do not work in a psychodynamic way. Another useful question here is whether or not the supervision offered is coherent with the therapeutic approach being offered by the supervisee. Certainly there is some research evidence (e.g. Neufeldt *et al.*, 1997) that supervisees rate supervisors more highly if there is a shared therapeutic orientation. From a systemic viewpoint, key questions that need to be asked are whether ideas about expertise and how change occurs are consistent within the two domains (therapy and supervision). For many clinical psychologists there is also the important and appropriate caveat that they would not want to seek to turn supervision sessions into therapy sessions. Again this connects with our earlier comments on boundaries and the negotiation of clear contracts.

Mode 6: Focus on the supervisor's counter-transference (Thinking about resonances for the supervisor)

The supervisor 'primarily pays attention to their own here-and-now experience in the supervision . . . and . . . uses these responses to provide reflective illumination for the therapist'. They make the point that unconscious ideas may 'emerge in the thoughts, feelings and images of the supervisor'.

We prefer to use the term 'resonances for the supervisor' rather than focusing once again on counter-transference. At a practical level it is asking a lot of a supervisor to be consistently in touch with what is happening to them while the supervision takes place. Careful note-taking during supervisory sessions can help, but ideally a supervisor needs to be working with a consultant or participating in a supportive peer supervision group.

Our systemic approach is generally helpful in supporting supervisors as they seek to clarify what is happening when they supervise. The use of genograms (as discussed earlier in the chapter) can be an essential tool for anybody who wants to keep checking how they are influenced by the complex processes that are involved in supervision. Second-order cybernetic ideas (summarized by Dallos and Draper, 2000) are also highly relevant to this mode. These ideas challenge the notion that a therapist can be entirely objective or detached. By engaging in either the therapeutic or supervisory process we become part of the process we are trying to observe. Our ideas and beliefs obviously influence the overall process but we are also influenced by the process in a reciprocal fashion.

Summary

We set out to produce something that may have practical value when considering therapeutic models and their link with supervision. In relating something of our collaborative work with our colleagues in the South West of England of modifying Hawkins and Shohet's valuable supervision model, we hope there are connections for readers both as potential supervisees and potential supervisors.

We are convinced that the model is heuristic – it has certainly influenced the way that we supervise, and the experience of sharing it with other supervisors has been rewarding. What has been attractive to us is that supervisors can be encouraged to explore these ideas and to use the aspects that connect most to their practice. As a model we have seen it used concretely and explicitly with supervisor and supervisee working through each mode sequentially, or as a background template where supervisors have more elegantly incorporated some of the modes into their supervisory sessions. While not all clinical psychologists will take to this as a model, they do seem to respond to the challenge it carries with it of being prepared to look more closely at the way they themselves supervise.

A final point needs to be made. Supervision has been neglected as a topic within clinical psychology training. A survey in the North West of England by Gabbay *et al.* (1999) suggested that a significant number of clinical psychologists (over 40 per cent of a 40 per cent response rate) felt that the supervision they received could be improved. A recent survey in the South West with over 165 supervisor replies (by SM) revealed that over 60 per cent of respondents had received no training at all in this area. However, the same survey also revealed that a majority of supervisors do want training in supervision and that receipt of training is correlated significantly with having taken on more supervisees. Our experience in working with supervisors has been extremely positive because it has reflected this desire to engage with the complexity of supervision as a topic and to raise supervisory standards.

As a profession we need to take the next steps by setting up supervision courses utilizing the type of heuristic model offered by Hawkins and Shohet and encouraging supervisors to form support groups so that their interest in supervision can be supervised. It should be that the NHS agenda of expanding training numbers and clinical governance will provide support for this as supervision increasingly becomes understood as a key component of any clinician's work.

Appendix: Adaptation of Lerner's list of the interfacing dimensions between therapist and family

---

Multigenerational history
Unresolved emotional issues with significant others
Other family patterns and legacies
Sibling position
Family life cycle
Age
Current life events
Health/disabilities*
Culture
Gender
Race
Class
Ethnicity
Sexual orientation
Religion
Politics
Community, work system, friendship circle

---

* Added by us (AT/SM)

Chapter 11

Conclusions and future perspectives

Ian Fleming and Linda Steen

This book has attempted to provide an overview of the issues directly relevant to supervision within the profession of clinical psychology. This has been achieved through contributions both by leading figures in the field of clinical psychology training in the UK and by experienced clinicians and supervisors, covering the most up-to-date practice and research.

As acknowledged in Chapter 1, the book would have been slimmer if the literature on supervision from counselling and psychotherapy had been excluded. Chapters by Sue Wheeler, Helen Beinart, and Delia Cushway and Jacky Knibbs discussed the relative paucity of research dedicated both to supervision within clinical psychology and to supervisory practice in the UK, and the questions remain: how much of the literature is transferable to clinical psychology and what are the particular issues for clinical psychology in the UK? Is it the case, as suggested by Delia Cushway and Jacky Knibbs in Chapter 9, that many of the process issues in clinical supervision have relevance across therapy professions?

Lawton and Feltham (2000), cited in Chapter 3 of this book, suggest a distinction between supervision in counselling and supervision in clinical psychology, the former being more process-focused and the latter more goal-oriented. Whilst much is still unknown about the practice of supervision within clinical psychology, this view would certainly concord with our experience, both as clinicians and as trainers; the work of clinical psychologists often involves setting goals and demonstrating outcomes.

In this chapter we will review the main themes of the book and consider the future issues for supervision within clinical psychology. The extent to which the existing literature can be generalized to supervisory practice within clinical psychology in the UK will be considered throughout.

Is there an accepted model of supervision within clinical psychology?

One suggestion within this book is that there is no clear model of supervision within clinical psychology. Indeed, as noted in Chapter 1, the BPS, DCP *Policy Guidelines on Supervision in the Practice of Clinical Psychology* explicitly state 'there is no one model or style of supervision that will apply to all clinical psychologists' (BPS, 2003: 2). In Delia Cushway and Jacky Knibbs's survey of clinical psychology supervisors and trainees described in Chapter 9, over three-quarters of the sample of supervisors reported that they did not subscribe to any particular model of supervision; the majority of those who did subscribe to a model cited Hawkins and Shohet's (1989) process model of supervision. In Chapter 10, Shane Matthews and Andy Treacher review different models and suggest that there may well be a discrepancy between chosen therapeutic models and those adopted by supervisors for supervision. If this is the case, and there is a lack of empirical evidence concerning clinical psychology supervisors, this contradicts the conclusions from the general literature that supervisors tend to rely on their therapeutic approach in supervisory practice. As Hawkins and Shohet (2000: 59) point out, 'one's style as a supervisor is affected by the style of one's practitioner work'.

Kadushin has suggested that this may be ameliorated by training: 'Lacking training in teaching but possessing clinical skills, the temptation for the clinician-turned-supervisor is to utilize the preferred clinical approach in teaching' (1992: 157).

However, if these comments are accurate, what is it about supervisory practice that training needs to modify? Furthermore, what are the particular skills that supervisor training needs to develop and emphasize?

Pre- and post-qualification supervision

A great deal of the general supervision literature considers both pre- and post-qualification supervision (referred to by Page and Wosket, 1994, as *trainee* and *practitioner* respectively). The emphasis within this book has been on the former, which reflects the relative absence of empirical descriptions of and attention to post-qualification supervision in clinical psychology to date. Thus in some books, considerable discussion is given over to the issues involved when qualified in selecting and working effectively with a supervisor. In particular the myriad interpersonal aspects are attended to, as are the service and organizational contexts in which the supervision is occurring and the potential discrepancies in therapeutic stances between supervisee and supervisor. Clearly the latter can be seen as having greater salience where both parties have equal professional status than in pre-qualification supervision where the greater experience of the supervisor is conflated with greater power (Holloway, 1995).

Fleming and Steen (Chapter 1) drew attention to the relatively short history of supervision within clinical psychology training in the UK. The parallel volume about supervision after qualification would be a very thin book indeed. As will be discussed below, as continuing professional development for clinical psychologists is becoming recognized as increasingly important and necessary, so too is the notion of post-qualification supervision.

As an empirically based profession, how does clinical psychology address issues of effectiveness and evaluation?

Clinical psychology as a profession prides itself on its abilities both to carry out research and to transform its practice through the assimilation of research. One of the commonly found core statements of the profession refers to its members as scientist-practitioners (DCP, 2001b). How does this perception measure up to the practice of supervision and supervisor training?

Although there have been masterly reviews of effectiveness (e.g. Ellis and Ladany, 1997) which have drawn rather pessimistic conclusions about the effectiveness of supervision, there are alternative conclusions that can be drawn.

From a more selective review of the literature we do know what is effective in supervision, and we have models (e.g. Kolb's experiential learning cycle) and some empirical knowledge to support it (Milne and James, 2002). We can learn from the evidence in order to develop effective practice. In addition we can learn from the staff training and management literature about the important factors for introducing and maintaining change in behaviour.

Ellis *et al.*'s (1996) review can be used to identify what good research about supervision would look like. The available knowledge could supply the content for supervision training, and it is of interest to ask, although elements feature in the programmes of training put on for supervisors (Chapter 5), why this is not in place? Similarly, with regard to evaluative tools: if elements of experiential learning skills form the content of supervisor training, then why not use the Supervisory Skills Survey (Fleming *et al.*, 1996) as an instrument to evaluate change resulting from the training (Chapter 5)?

Supervision has been more developed over a longer period of time in counselling and psychotherapy. Given that these traditions have placed a greater value on anecdotal evidence and personal experience, this may be reflected in the research. The greater scientific rigour claimed by clinical psychology may make the profession well placed to carry out research into the important factors hypothesized to play an active part in supervisory effectiveness. From descriptions of research contained in the current book, both quantitative and qualitative research methodologies would appear to be useful; Helen Beinart (Chapter 3), for example, described her research that used both quantitative methodology and grounded theory.

In view of the multitude of variables that would need to be under experimental control, it may be that seeking resulting changes in supervisee behaviour or client outcome are not legitimate goals of supervision or supervisor training. As several of the contributors have outlined (e.g. Chapters 6 and 9), there are a range of classes of outcome of both supervision and supervisor training. For supervision, for example, these include the supervisee's reaction to supervision, performance as a supervisee, therapist characteristics and change in client. In supervisor training, there is the added element of change in supervisor's behaviour, knowledge and attitude as a result of the training.

Is insisting on improvements in therapeutic outcomes a legitimate goal of supervisor training or are we seeking an unjustifiable holy grail that makes research almost impossible to carry out?

Different therapeutic models would of course consider outcomes differently. Many schools would consider inadequate any goal that did not include consideration of the client, arguing that the parallel process or mirroring requires that the client cannot but be a feature of the supervisor–supervisee dyadic relationship (see, for example, Hawkins and Shohet, 2000).

What are the future issues for supervision within clinical psychology?

Accreditation of supervision within pre-qualification training

Several of the contributors have raised the issue of accreditation of supervisors. Sue Wheeler (Chapter 2), for example, outlined the accreditation process for supervisors within the British Association for Counselling and Psychotherapy. In Chapter 4, Turpin *et al.* described a model of accreditation of training units. In the wider clinical psychology literature, too, the issue of placement accreditation has been under discussion for some time (Milne *et al.*, 2001).

The possibilities of introducing accreditation for supervisors were discussed in some detail in Chapter 5. The discussion placed accreditation within a logical context framed by demands for quality assurance and supervisor training. Although the training of supervisors, with its relevance to those supervisors' CPD, could clearly be seen as a legitimate activity of *pre-qualification* training programmes for clinical psychologists, there remains a question of its extension to an evaluative and arguably managerial activity in relation to *qualified* clinical psychologists. There might well be a concern that any extension of evaluative training from those entering the profession to those well established within it may be a crossing of the Rubicon for clinical psychology training programmes and programme staff. Clinical tutors may have legitimacy in organizing voluntary training for supervisors, but will this extend to a role of accreditation with the accompanying professional attributes and rewards?

Any hesitation about the role of the programme staff in accrediting fellow professionals might be compounded by a pragmatic concern about placement availability and supervisor numbers (Chapter 4). Hesitation about the introduction of accreditation may be linked to real concerns that the introduction of any additional 'hurdles' might (at least in the short term) exacerbate the problems caused by the shortage of training placements. Clinical psychology training programmes report that their placement planning arrangements could become critical if very small numbers of supervisors decided that they could not supervise because of new requirements for training or accreditation. It will be important in future to reconcile these issues of 'quality control' and to ensure a maximum number of supervisors who are able to offer supervision and placements on a continual basis. Interestingly, it is the authors' impression that this has become less of a concern over time: in Manchester we gain the impression that more newly 'qualified' cohorts of supervisors expect quality issues to be attended to. The culture of qualification bestowing 'independent professional practitioner' status upon one without a need for direction and governance is becoming historical.

The relationship between supervision, CPD and accreditation

The benefits to the profession of linking supervision with CPD and emphasizing it as a core activity are clear. Such a development could make it easier to introduce mandatory arrangements for receiving (and providing) supervision, thus easing the barriers to the expansion of training and the growth of the profession.

At the time of writing no clear arrangements have been organized to equate supervision activity and training with CPD requirements. To date it has been suggested that attendance at supervisor training events could constitute a second level of CPD, with supervision as a core activity. It would be relatively simple for supervisors to keep a logbook of their experience and of their training, especially if they provided training placements for more than one clinical psychology programme. This would acknowledge that currently supervisor training is not standardized and that training is not a prerequisite to supervising. As discussed in Chapter 5, more direction about the content and methods of supervisor training and linking this to standards would be helpful, if not necessary, for the introduction of an accreditation scheme, and there is no reason to suggest that this would not be welcomed by clinical psychologists in general.

Improving supervisory practice: learning from other professions

At the time of writing, there are very few detailed descriptions of the supervisory practice of clinical psychologists. Cushway and Knibbs's research (Chapter 9) highlighted the elements of supervision found to be helpful and unhelpful by trainees and supervisors and, in doing so, gave some very helpful pointers for good supervisory practice. Matthews and Treacher (Chapter 10) described their approach to supervision in some detail, thus giving the reader a flavour of their supervisory practice. More work is needed if we are to obtain an accurate view of what happens in clinical psychology supervision.

From a review of the general supervision literature, there is some consensus on what good supervision involves; two themes that emerge as being central to good supervisory practice are the establishment of a good supervisory relationship and, related to this, the negotiation of a clear supervisory contract.

Supervisory relationship

The importance and, indeed, centrality of establishing a good supervisory relationship has been highlighted in several of the chapters. In Chapter 2, for example, Sue Wheeler cited research evidence in support of this assertion and pointed to the finding that uncertainty about supervisory expectations can affect relationship dynamics (Ladany and Friedlander, 1995). She also described her own work (Webb and Wheeler, 1998) which found there to be a correlation between quality of the working alliance and the extent of supervisees' self-disclosure in supervision. This seems to be particularly pertinent to the situation in clinical psychology training, where supervisors often rely on trainees' self-reports of their work rather than direct observation (see Chapter 6).

In a survey of clinical psychology trainees and supervisors conducted specifically for the writing of their chapter, Delia Cushway and Jacky Knibbs (Chapter 9) found that 'establishing a good rapport' was rated by both parties to be the most helpful aspect of supervision.

Helen Beinart (Chapter 3) described Holloway's (1995) SAS model of supervision, which sees the supervisory relationship as 'the container of dynamic process' (p. 41). She then went on to describe her own research in which supervisees (both trainee and newly qualified clinical psychologists) were asked specifically about their experience of supervisory relationships and the factors that had contributed to their effectiveness as clinical psychologists. This led her to develop her own model of the supervisory relationship, which is described in Chapter 3.

Given the acknowledged importance of the supervisory relationship, it is relevant to consider the extent to which this is attended to in supervision within clinical psychology.

In the context of pre-qualification supervision, the BPS (1995a) *Guidelines on Clinical Supervision* acknowledge the importance of establishing a good supervisory relationship, as is evidenced in the following statement: 'the care taken in the early stages to build up a good relationship will enhance the quality of the clinical supervision' (BPS, 1995a: section 7.1). No specific guidance is given, however, on how this should be achieved.

Supervision contract

In the general supervision literature, establishing a supervision contract is seen as a way in which the parameters of the supervisory relationship can be negotiated at the outset and regularly reviewed. Several writers have highlighted this. Inskipp and Proctor (1989), for example, see the contract as being 'critical to establishing a way of being together in the supervisory relationship' (cited in Holloway,1995: 52). As well as covering the practicalities of the supervision, such as frequency of meetings, evaluative aspects, etc., the contract should enable both parties to express their expectations, hopes and fears about the supervision and the relationship. In Chapters 7 and 8 of this book, Nimisha Patel and Maxine Dennis and Gill Aitken pointed to the central role of the contracting process in addressing power imbalances. Whilst it is expected that the supervisor will initiate the contract, the supervisee will have an equal part to play in this process (for further discussion of the role of the supervisee, see Chapter 9 of this book).

In Chapter 5 it was noted that some clinical psychology programmes organize training events for supervisors on supervision contracts. Little is known, however, about the types of supervisory contract used within clinical psychology.

For pre-qualification supervision, the guidance from the BPS is as follows:

> The general aims of the placement should normally be agreed within the first two weeks of the placement and a clinical contract should be written. Attention should be paid in the clinical contract to the range of opportunities available in the placement, and to the needs, interests and previous experience of the trainee . . .
>
> (BPS, 1995a: section 4.1)

As can be seen from the above statement, whilst there is a clear recognition of the need for a contract at the start of placement, the expectation is that this will be concerned with the practical aspects of the placement rather than with the supervisory relationship.

If we are to take seriously the research findings about the crucial role that the supervisory relationship plays in determining the course of supervision, it would seem that there is a clear need for clinical psychologists to follow the lead of others, notably counsellors and psychotherapists, who advocate the explicit discussion of these issues at the start of any new supervision arrangement.

As mentioned earlier, in addition to a placement contract the Manchester clinical psychology programme recently introduced the idea of drawing up a psychological contract (Schein, 1980) with the recommendation that trainees and supervisors explicitly address their worst fears and wildest hopes, and what each expects from the other. From our discussions with colleagues on other training programmes we know that we are not alone in this practice, although the exact extent to which other clinical psychology programmes require similar contracts is not known.

As stated earlier, little is known currently about the practice of post-qualification supervision in clinical psychology, and this includes the issue of supervision contracts. In the absence of any guidelines for post-qualification supervision it is possible that this aspect of supervision could be neglected. Different models of supervision (peer group, one-to-one, managerial) will require different factors to be considered in the process of negotiating the contract (Hawkins and Shohet, 2000). For example, it might be important to consider the organization and the professional context within which the supervision is taking place; this is likely to be all the more important in inter-professional supervision.

Improving supervisor training

> One hindrance to the development of more universal training of supervisors has been that many mental health professionals apparently have believed that to be an effective therapist is the primary pre-requisite to being a good supervisor.
>
> (Bernard and Goodyear, 1998: 5)

In relation to the above statement, as discussed in Chapter 6, whilst there are some transferable skills that therapists can use in their supervisory practice – for example, the ability to establish a good working relationship and empathic listening – the goals of supervision are very different to those of psychotherapy and require different skills. It is suggested that one of the purposes of supervisor training should be to alert new supervisors to the ways in which supervision and therapy are similar and different.

In Chapters 5 and 6 of this book, research was reported upon which gave a clear picture of both current and suggested practice for supervisor training within clinical psychology. It was seen that training is currently being provided by clinical psychology training programmes on an increasingly systematic basis. Whilst this research provides a very good starting point from which to further develop supervisor training, it was acknowledged that there is much that is still unknown about both the content and the effectiveness of supervisor training. Supervisor training will be considered in more detail later in this chapter, and suggestions made for the future.

Addressing issues of diversity

Culture and 'race'

In Chapter 7, Nimisha Patel made clear and substantial points about issues of power within supervision. She proposed that supervision has a responsibility to challenge inequalities in power and identifies strategies for doing so. Holloway (1995), too, in *Clinical Supervision: A Systems Approach*, examines the interaction of power and supervision to the interpersonal identity of a supervisory relationship. Such an explicit position is not central to the ideology of British clinical psychology, however, and it is interesting to consider what may be needed to shift the professional culture so that this viewpoint can be accepted and adopted. Where within the mainstream clinical psychology literature, for example, would supervisors find legitimacy for exploring the social political and historical factors that she identifies as important? In Manchester we have experience of leading training workshops for supervisors that provide an introduction to these themes (see Chapter 5), and there appears to be a lower application rate for this workshop compared to other supervisor training events. It may be significant that until 2002 the only workshop cancelled because of inadequate interest was one around this theme. Anecdotal comments from a senior colleague in the training arena suggest that our experience is not unique.

Again, with respect to the 'legitimacy' of this area within clinical psychology, the Manchester Clin.Psy.D. programme has developed teaching about issues of political and interpersonal power for some years and implemented a requirement for social context to be demonstrated in examinable work. The experience has not been uniformly successful (Fleming and Burton, 2001) and there still appears to be a need within clinical psychology to assert the issues described by Nimisha Patel.

How does the situation in clinical psychology compare with that in related professions? As mentioned earlier in the book (Chapter 1), Carroll (1996) admonishes counselling and psychotherapy texts in the UK for their ignorance of issues of culture in supervision.

One imagines that the situation has changed in the interim period.

In the second edition of their text on supervision, for example, Hawkins and Shohet include a chapter on working with difference, 'in order to correct a major omission in the first edition, that of looking at how differences, including race, class, gender etc. inform and affect the supervisory relationship' (2000: xviii).

The importance of training in diversity for supervisors is supported by the research carried out with clinical psychology trainees in South Africa by Kleintjes and Swartz (1996). This demonstrated the difficulties faced by supervisees (trainee clinical psychologists) in discussing issues of culture and diversity if their supervisors had not done so.

Gender

Maxine Dennis and Gill Aitken (Chapter 8) addressed the issues of how gender acts upon the supervision process.

On the Manchester clinical psychology programme, training both for supervisors and trainees attends to some of the issues identified by the authors, but not in the depth or complexity suggested by the authors.

Aitken and Dennis refer to ways in which both parties to the supervisory process can begin to address power imbalances related to gender. It is our experience that the use of 'psychological contracts' (Schein, 1980) in which expectations and 'non-specific' factors involved in supervision are identified and negotiated has been helpful in drawing the attention of both parties to these issues and the ways in which they affect supervision.

The authors refer to the lack of diversity among clinical psychologists, and the profession's lack of representation of the different cultures within the general population. This is of increasing concern to those responsible for training, and the Group of Trainers in Clinical Psychology (GTiCP) directly addressed this issue at its 2002 annual conference. At the time of writing, work arising from the conference is ongoing and these issues are likely to remain at the top of the profession's agenda for the foreseeable future.

Post-qualification supervision

[S]ince post-qualification professional supervision is a woefully under-researched area, it is not easy to cite well documented examples of good practice to follow or prescribe established standards that might inform local audit procedures. It is therefore politic to incorporate some element of careful appraisal of both process and outcome when evaluating initiatives in continuing supervision for qualified clinical psychologists, both to improve the service for participants and to provide feedback for the host organisation.

(DCP, 2001a: 9)

As has been mentioned previously, it is only relatively recently that the BPS has recommended that all qualified clinical psychologists should receive supervision as an essential part of good practice and professional development. At the time of writing, we know very little about the practice of post-qualification supervision within clinical psychology. Whilst there are some data to suggest that supervision is regarded as an important, if not essential, part of post-qualification practice for many clinical psychologists (e.g. Golding, 2003; Lavender and Thompson, 2000), it is known that a substantial percentage of clinical psychologists do not receive supervision (Gabbay et al., 1999). The exact reasons for this are unclear but there is some evidence to suggest that they include both personal and organizational factors (Gabbay et al., 1999).

There are several issues that need to be addressed with regard to supervision for qualified clinical psychologists. These include a consideration of both the functions and models of post-qualification supervision and the process of choosing a supervisor.

Writing from a social work perspective, Kadushin (1992) identifies three main functions or roles of supervision, namely educative, supportive and managerial. These functions would seem to fit very well with the expectations of pre-qualification supervision and we, along with colleagues from other training programmes, often use them as a starting point for supervisor training. It is interesting to reflect on the extent to which these functions are explicitly acknowledged in post-qualification supervision, where the evaluative or managerial aspect may be less pronounced, although just as important. Here, as elsewhere, the need for an explicit supervision contract would appear to be essential.

In Chapter 1 we alluded to the fact that traditional one-to-one models of supervision may be neither appropriate nor possible in post-qualification supervision. We do not have a clear picture of current supervisory arrangements for qualified clinical psychologists, although in our experience it seems that one-to-one and peer group supervision are the most commonly used models. In a national survey of supervision practice of therapists who were accredited through the British Association for Behavioural and Cognitive Psychotherapies (BABCP), Townend *et al.* (2002) found a range of supervisory arrangements including individual supervision with the same person, group supervision with a nominated chairperson, group peer supervision, pair peer supervision, and extending to supervision via telephone and e-mail. The BABCP is a multidisciplinary organization, comprising, amongst others, nurses, clinical psychologists, counsellors, psychiatrists and social workers, and the sample was relatively small so it is not possible to draw any conclusions about the practice of clinical psychologists. Nonetheless, it is useful to consider the extent to which this range of supervision arrangements could be applied to clinical psychology supervisory practice.

As was mentioned earlier in this chapter, in much of the general literature on supervision, consideration is given to the factors involved in selecting a supervisor (e.g. Hawkins and Shohet, 2000). We suspect that the issues may be different for clinical psychologists working within the NHS. Whilst there is little known about clinical psychologists' supervision arrangements currently, organizational constraints are likely to be influential, and the question remains: to what extent can and do clinical psychologists *choose* their supervisor(s) and supervision arrangements?

With regard to choice of supervisor, the BPS, DCP *Professional Practice Guidelines* state:

> If no clinical psychologist is available with the necessary expertise and skill to provide specialist supervision for key aspects of work, clinical psychologists should seek supervision from an appropriately qualified psychologist in a neighbouring authority or from a related discipline.
>
> (BPS, 1995b: section 1.2.2)

This leads to a consideration of *who* provides supervision for clinical psychologists. As implied in the above statement, the expectation is that the supervisor will be someone working in the same service as the supervisee. Interestingly, in Sue Wheeler's (Chapter 2) survey of experts, there were mixed views expressed as to whether or not the supervisor should work in and have knowledge of the service context. With regard to professional relationship, in our experience it is not unusual for a person's line manager to also provide supervision. In some professions, however (for example, counselling psychology), there is an explicit expectation that 'the supervisory relationship is clearly distinguished from any line-management responsibilities' (BPS, 2001d: 8).

Given what is known about non-disclosure in supervision (see Chapter 2 for a full discussion of this), it would appear that choice of supervisor is an important issue and one that needs to be balanced with the constraints of the work context.

Recognizing that post-qualification supervision is a relatively new concept for clinical psychologists, and referring back to the BPS statement cited at the start of this section, we should be mindful of the need to evaluate supervisory practice on a regular basis.

Multi-professional training

As mentioned in several of the chapters of this book, the concepts of shared learning and multi-professional training are being accorded prominence within the NHS and the education of health professionals. As noted in Chapter 4 of this book, for example, at the undergraduate level 'several innovative schemes are being established to support inter-professional learning across medical, allied health care professions and social work education'.

With regard to supervision within clinical psychology, during pre-qualification training, to date, there has been a general expectation that clinical psychology trainees will 'normally be supervised by a clinical psychologist' (BPS, 1995a: section 1.1). At the time of writing, however, there is a move towards recognizing that the supervision of specific aspects of a trainee's work could be provided by 'an appropriately qualified and experienced member of another profession' (BPS, 2002a: section 8.2, p. 14).

With regard to post-qualification supervision, the concept of inter-professional working and training has particular relevance, as clinical psychologists both provide supervision for and receive supervision from members of other professions.

Sue Wheeler, in Chapter 2 of this book, described the generic supervisor training courses that attract members from a range of professional groups (including clinical psychologists); as mentioned in Chapters 5 and 6, however, to date the supervisor training provided by clinical psychology programmes has not tended to be organized on a multidisciplinary basis.

In view of the aforementioned developments within both the NHS and the profession, it will be interesting and important to gain a clearer picture of the ways in which this aspect of multi-professional training develops in clinical psychology.

What should clinical psychologists do next?

Carry out research in order to evaluate both supervision and supervisor training

Bernard and Goodyear (1992) make the point that the first research into supervision was carried out as recently as 1958. Since then, there has been a mushrooming in research, and Ellis *et al.*, in a review published in 1996, referred to 32 empirically based studies of supervision.

Nonetheless, one of the main themes in much of the general literature on clinical supervision, and one that has been highlighted in most of the chapters in this book, is the need for more research in the area.

Whilst acknowledging the importance of supervision and training in the psychotherapies, for example, one of the concluding comments in Roth and Fonagy's (1996) review of psychotherapeutic interventions is:

> [T]here is relatively little research on the impact of these processes, particularly in a form that examines the progress made by individual therapists over time . . . A longitudinal rather than a cross-sectional methodology might be more useful for assessing the impact of training and supervision on the development of and outcomes from, clinical practice.
> (Roth and Fonagy, 1996: 376)

There are a number of important and pressing areas for research. These include identifying the particular skills necessary for effective supervision in clinical psychology, evaluating the most effective means of training supervisors, and identifying whether clinical psychologists can use different models in supervision to those used predominantly in their clinical work.

In relation to supervisor training, Ian Fleming (Chapter 5) reported that the forms of evaluation used by the majority of training programmes are currently quite limited; he concluded by stating that more research into supervisor training is needed. In a similar vein, David Green concluded his chapter by stating: 'There is probably enough professional consensus and research expertise within the clinical psychology training community in the UK to mount larger-scale and more formally evaluated programmes than have as yet been reported.' It is to be hoped that the profession will rise to this challenge.

Consider the most important tasks for supervision within clinical psychology, both pre-qualification and post-qualification

In Chapter 1, it was noted that within clinical psychology there has not been much explicit discussion of supervisory tasks to date. Similarly, as reported in Chapter 5, whilst there was found to be agreement amongst clinical psychology trainers about the content of supervisor training, it was acknowledged that this did not necessarily shed any light on whether there was agreement about supervisory tasks and skills.

In the general literature on supervision, there is a good deal of agreement about the functions and tasks of supervision; as was mentioned in Chapters 1 and 2, Carroll (1996) describes seven main tasks of supervision and, in general, these accord with other writers' descriptions.

With regard to pre-qualification supervision, there is some evidence both from the data presented in Chapter 5 and from the wider clinical psychology literature, that many, if not all, of these tasks are seen as having relevance to clinical psychology supervision. As stated earlier, however, there is a need to discover more about both the perceived functions and the practice of post-qualification supervision within clinical psychology and, in doing so, to find out whether, and if so in what ways, the tasks are different to those of pre-qualification supervision.

Consider the material that should be included in training for clinical psychology supervisors

Sue Wheeler concluded her chapter by stating: 'There is now a vast literature on supervision that can be consulted when a training programme for supervisors is planned.' Similarly, as reported in Chapter 5, Carroll (1996) describes six elements of a 'model curriculum' for training supervisors. Unsurprisingly, perhaps, given that much of the content of clinical psychology supervisor training derives from work carried out in counselling and other professions, there is a good deal of agreement between the content of supervisor training currently provided by clinical psychology training programmes and that suggested in the wider supervision literature. As discussed previously, however, there is an urgent need for more research in this area.

What we do know about good practice in supervisor training is that the way in which the training is delivered is very important. Milne and Howard (2000), amongst others, remind us that good supervisor training should mirror the process of supervision and contain a mixture of symbolic, iconic and enactive methods (Milne and James, 1999) Thus, advocating the use of Kolb's (1984) model of experiential learning in supervision, Milne and Howard (2000) suggest that supervisor training should enable participants to work round the learning cycle themselves. Sue Wheeler (Chapter 2) makes the same point when she states that good teaching should mirror the model of supervision; 'didactic teaching will reinforce the idea that supervision is a didactic experience'. It is not known how many training programmes refer to Kolb's model in their supervisor training, but we do know (Chapter 5) that programmes use more than just didactic teaching.

Much of the literature on supervisor training has focused solely on training provided to supervisors. As noted in the Introduction and in several of the ensuing chapters, however, there is a growing recognition that any discussion of supervisor training also needs to consider the training provided for supervisees. The literature suggests that by training supervisees they will be empowered to use the supervisory relationship in order to maximize their opportunities for learning in supervision (Inskipp, 1999). Training should help supervisees both to make the best use of supervision and to recognize their rights and responsibilities.

In Chapter 6, David Green described an initiative within nursing in which supervisees are provided with training in supervision.

Within clinical psychology, Graham Turpin, Joyce Scaife and Peter Rajan (Chapter 4) suggested that clinical psychology training programmes could introduce training in supervision as a core skill throughout the three years of training. The recently revised accreditation criteria (2002) certainly pave the way for this by having as one of the objectives for clinical psychology training:

> Using supervision to reflect on practice, and making appropriate use of feedback received.
>
> (BPS, 2002a: B.1.3.7)

Whilst we know that many clinical psychology programmes do already provide this type of training within the curriculum, there is no systematic information about this.

Delia Cushway and Jacky Knibbs concluded their chapter by listing trainees' roles and responsibilities in supervision, and these could certainly be used as a starting point for training supervisees. In Chapter 5 it was reported that there have been some initiatives for jointly training supervisors and trainees; this would seem to be an ideal way of emphasizing that supervision is a joint venture.

In Chapters 1 and 5 we referred to the support and spirit of collaboration that can be found within the Group of Trainers in Clinical Psychology (GTiCP), the body within the British Psychological Society that comprises and represents the interests of those involved in clinical psychology training. Members of the GTiCP already share some supervisor training materials and resources; it is not uncommon, for example, for clinical psychology programmes to invite trainers from other programme teams to deliver supervisor training. The survey reported upon in Chapter 5 is a first attempt at gaining a view of supervisor training for clinical psychology supervisors in the UK. It is likely this will lead to further collaboration and sharing of resources in the future.

Finally, much of the discussion about content of supervisor training to date has focused on pre-qualification supervision. Whether, and the extent to which, the needs of post-qualification supervisors are different is unknown at the time of writing. If the links between CPD, supervision and accreditation become formalized in the ways suggested earlier in this chapter, these issues will need to be examined in more detail.

Develop a professional structure through which quality of supervision can be monitored

Becoming a supervisor constitutes a milestone in a person's career since it is the primary validation of one's clinical experience. Recognition of this requires supervising to be seen as a critical element of CPD. This presentation of the importance of supervising may appear exaggerated. We would argue that it is not; the appearance is because historically the profession of clinical psychology has not awarded the role and practice of supervision the training and support that it is due. The profession is in a position to change this situation, possibly in the ways suggested previously.

Consider research supervision

Whilst this book has focused exclusively on supervision of clinical work, any discussion of supervision within both clinical psychology in general and clinical psychology training in particular would not be complete without mention of research supervision.

For many qualified clinical psychologists, working either in clinical or academic settings, research is a key aspect of their work. Within the profession, supervision for research work is now seen as being just as important as supervision for clinical work, as is reflected in the following statement taken from the DCP Guidelines for CPD when referring to post-qualification supervision: 'an opportunity to reflect systematically on one's practice is a useful discipline and applies to all aspects of a clinical psychologist's work, e.g. research, consultancy, teaching, administration' (DCP, 2001a: 9).

In clinical psychology training, research plays a large part. In addition to trainees undertaking a series of clinical placements throughout the three years (as outlined in Chapter 4), there is a requirement for them to carry out both a small-scale project within a clinical placement setting and an independent ('large-scale') research project under supervision.

With regard to the 'large-scale' research project, the work usually begins in the second year and extends to the end of training. In general, trainees are able to choose both the area of research they want to pursue and the research supervisor(s) who will oversee this aspect of their training. Research supervisors are usually clinical psychologists who are chosen by trainees for their expertise in the particular field under study. It is interesting to consider how trainees make their decisions about their area of research and, in particular, whether the choice of research supervisor is guided by the supervisor's reputation as a supervisor or as a researcher.

Whilst there exist BPS *Guidelines on Clinical Supervision* (1995a) which specify minimum standards for certain aspects of placement (clinical) supervision during training – such as the need to draw up a placement contract, opportunities for trainees and supervisors to observe each other's clinical work and amount of time spent in supervision whilst on placement – until recently there has been no equivalent guidance from the BPS about the requirements for research supervision.

This situation has changed slightly, however, with the introduction of the revised *Criteria for the Accreditation of Postgraduate Training Programmes in Clinical Psychology* in which the following reference is made to research supervision:

> Each trainee must have a research supervisor who is competent in research supervision . . . There should be a research agreement between supervisor and trainee that covers matters such as a schedule of regular supervision meetings and progress reviews, written feedback on drafts and a timetable for the project.
>
> (BPS, 2002a: section 10.8)

This is the first time any formal guidance has been issued about both the practicalities of research supervision (e.g. the need for a research agreement) and the competence of the supervisor. The latter begs the question what skills and knowledge are needed to be a competent research supervisor? Many of the clinical psychologists who offer research supervision are the same people who provide clinical supervision on placements and it is interesting to reflect on whether or not the tasks of both types of supervision are similar and transferable.

That research supervision is considered important within clinical psychology training is reflected in the findings of the recent survey of supervisor training provided by clinical psychology training programmes, reported in Chapter 5, which indicate that nine of the 27 clinical training programmes that responded to the survey offer training in supervising research. As acknowledged in Chapter 5, the exact content of this training is unknown, which makes it difficult to draw any conclusions and to know whether the focus of these events is on the practicalities and requirements of the research or on the research supervision itself. This is clearly an area that would benefit from further examination.

Interestingly, in the wider academic arena too, there is an increasing acknowledgment of the importance of high-quality supervision for postgraduate research. The Quality Assurance Agency for Higher Education (QAA) recommend that in addition to having recognized subject expertise, supervisors 'should have the necessary skills and experience to monitor, support and direct research students' work' (1999: section 9B). Leading on from this, the QAA recommend that institutions should consider the 'provision of training for supervisors' (ibid.).

With this recommendation in mind, the Training and Accreditation Programme for Postgraduate Supervisors (TAPPS, 2002) was set up as a three-year pilot scheme through the Biotechnology and Biological Sciences Research Council (BBSRC). The aim of TAPPS is to provide improved training, recognition and support for postgraduate research supervisors by encouraging them to gain accreditation for their skills against set criteria. To gain accreditation, supervisors have to submit a portfolio of evidence demonstrating competence in the essential areas of postgraduate supervision.

The aforementioned developments are particularly interesting in view of the earlier discussion about accreditation of clinical supervisors.

Decide whether pre-qualification training programmes should have responsibility for post-qualification supervision

The increasing recognition of the importance of post-qualification supervision within clinical psychology has been discussed in several places throughout the book. At present, training for pre-qualification supervision is provided by clinical psychology training programmes. One question remaining at present is to what extent should the training required for post-qualification supervision be provided by pre-qualification programmes?

There is a wealth of knowledge and expertise about supervision amongst clinical psychology trainers, and it could be argued therefore that they would be ideally placed to provide the training. As mentioned in Chapter 5, however, there would be significant resource implications; at present, the majority of programmes do not have a designated budget for pre-qualification supervisor training.

As reported in Chapter 5, there are currently a small number of clinical psychology programmes that have responsibility for both pre-qualification training and CPD, which includes training of post-qualification supervisors. It will be interesting to monitor the extent to which this practice becomes more widespread in the future.

Consider whether there is a role for mentorship within clinical psychology

The concept of mentorship is one that is developing in the field of education; less has been written about mentoring in clinical professions within the NHS to date. One exception to this is in nursing, where mentoring exists within the training of student nurses. Described by Butterworth and Faugier (1992: 11) as 'an experienced professional nurturing and guiding the novitiate', the mentor is a qualified and experienced nurse whose role is to facilitate, guide and support the student in learning new skills, behaviour and attitudes. It is worthy of note that the concept of clinical supervision for qualified staff is relatively new in most areas of nursing, and it is interesting to reflect on the similarities and differences between mentoring and supervision (Fowler, 1998).

Within clinical psychology, a 'mentor scheme' for newly qualified clinical psychologists has been in existence in the north-west of England since 1991

(Verduyn *et al.*, 1994). The scheme was introduced as a way of systematizing the training needs of recently qualified clinical psychologists at a time when it had been established that not all newly qualified clinical psychologists were receiving supervision. It was envisaged that the mentor would be an experienced clinical psychologist whose role would be 'to work collaboratively with the recently qualified psychologist to develop a training plan' during the first three years of the 'mentee's' post-qualification practice (Verduyn *et al.*, 1994); mentoring was seen as being complementary to, rather than an alternative to, supervision. Since its introduction the mentor scheme has continued to flourish, and both authors have had experience of acting as mentors. From our experience, there are some similarities between mentoring and supervising: the need to establish and define the parameters of a supportive mentoring relationship, to set objectives and review them regularly, and to seek and receive feedback on the process. In contrast to supervision, however, whilst the mentor is, by definition, a more senior member of the profession, the relationship has less of a managerial feel than it does in pre-qualification supervision and the explicit evaluative component is removed. Whether there is a role for mentoring within clinical psychology remains to be seen. At the time of writing, more information is needed about both the extent to which the practice of mentoring exists elsewhere within clinical psychology and the role and functions of mentoring within this context.

Linked to the concept of mentoring is the idea of 'supervision for supervisors'. As discussed in Chapter 5, in our experience new supervisors in particular frequently state that they would like to receive supervision for their supervisory practice. Whilst this could occur within the context of their clinical supervision, we are aware that this does not happen very often. Milne and James (2002) describe a consultancy model for supervisor training and it would be interesting to consider whether such a model would serve the purpose described above and whether there is a role for programme team staff to provide this support.

Concluding comments

It would seem that British supervision is in a healthy, forward-moving state, characterised by rootedness in practice. There can be little doubt about the richness of supervision work taking place within counselling training as well as in the supervision of seasoned counsellors. Furthermore, British supervision is well on its way to providing excellent training for supervisors.

(Carroll, 1996: 21)

To what extent does Carroll's assertion apply to clinical psychology supervision? Throughout this book, one of the consistent themes has been that whilst we are beginning to gain an idea of the practice of supervision and supervisor training in clinical psychology in the UK, more research is needed to help us to develop a clearer picture.

These are exciting and challenging times for both clinical psychology as a profession and clinical psychology training. As has been discussed throughout the book, the profession has grown rapidly in recent years and is continuing to expand. Both receiving and providing supervision are becoming recognized as important parts of a clinical psychologist's work and are certainly high on the agendas of newly qualified clinical psychologists, whose choice of job is influenced, to some extent, by whether they will have access to supervision (Lavender and Thompson, 2000).

Much has changed in the 20 years since we both qualified, when there were no clear guidelines for pre-qualification supervision, and post-qualification supervision was sporadic, at best, and was usually only received when feeling 'stuck' with clinical work. Supervision now has a high profile within the profession, and the challenge that faces us is to learn from the supervision literature from other professions and to continue to carry out more research in order to 'develop more flexible and efficient methods of supervision' (Milne and James, 1999: 36).

In doing so, we need to remain mindful of the following, written from the viewpoint of counselling psychology, where post-qualification supervision has been mandatory for some time:

> Clinical supervision costs money, it has become increasingly mandatory for many, there is no convincing empirical evidence that it 'works', yet it seems to have few opponents.
>
> (Davy, 2002: 229)

With this in mind, some of the challenges that face us include: how to ensure good practice in supervision and to avoid 'supervision for supervision's sake' in post-qualification supervision; how to make supervising more attractive for those clinical psychologists who currently do not supervise or attend supervisor training; how to manage the resource implications of increasing and competing supervisory demands – supervision of assistant psychologists (Knight, 2002), other professionals, trainee clinical psychologists and peers.

Whilst remaining mindful of the need for more research evidence and more sharing of information, the contributions in this book have shown that there already exists a great deal of knowledge and expertise within the profession.

> We are at an exciting stage in which both the methods used to develop supervisory practice and the content of supervision are ready to enter new territory . . .
>
> (Milne and James, 1999: 36)

References

Adams, M. (2001) 'Working group on criteria for the accreditation of postgraduate courses in clinical psychology', *Clinical Psychology* 4: 41–44.

Aitken, G. (1996) 'The present absence/pathologised presence of black women in mental health services', in E. Burman, G. Aitken, P. Alldred, R. Allwood, T. Billington, B. Goldberg, C. Heenan, A. Gordo Lopez, D. Marks and S. Warner *Psychology, Discourse, Practice: From Regulation to Resistance*, London: Taylor & Francis.

Aitken, G. (1998) 'Working with, and through, professional and "race" differences: issues for clinical psychologists', *Clinical Psychology Forum* 118: 10–17.

Aitken, G. (2000a) 'Women working with women: difference and power relations in forensic therapy encounters', *Changes: An International Journal of Psychology and Psychotherapy* 18: 254–263.

Aitken, G. (2000b) 'Clinical psychology in a cold climate: towards culturally appropriate services', in J. Batsleer and B. Humphries (eds) *Welfare, Exclusion and Political Agency*, London: Routledge.

Alberts, G. and Edelstein, B. (1990) 'Therapist training: a critical review of skill training studies', *Clinical Psychology Review* 10: 497–511.

Alicke, M., Klotz, M., Breitenbecher, D., Yorak, T. and Vrebenberg, D. (1995) 'Personal contact, individuation and the better-than-average effect', *Journal of Personality and Social Psychology* 68: 804–825.

Allen, C. and Brazier, A. (1996) 'Support for clinical supervisors: from training to play space', *Clinical Psychology Forum* 85: 37–39.

Allen, G. J., Szollos, S. J. and Williams, B. E. (1986) 'Doctoral students' comparative evaluations of best and worst psychotherapy supervision', *Professional Psychology: Research and Practice* 17: 91–99.

Almeida, R. V. (1998) 'The dislocation of women's experience in family therapy', *Journal of Feminist Family Therapy* 10 (1): 1–21.

Anastasopoulos, D. and Tsiantis, J. (1999) 'Supervision of individual psychoanalytic psychotherapy in institutions: the setting, the dynamics and the learning process', *Psychoanalytic Psychotherapy* 13 (2): 167–183.

Andersen, T. (1987) 'The reflecting team: dialogue and meta-dialogue in clinical work', *Family Process* 26: 415–428.

Andersen, T. (ed.) (1990) *The Reflecting Team*, New York: W. W. Norton.

Aronson, M. L. (1990) 'A group therapist's perspectives on the use of supervisory groups in the training of psychotherapists', *Psychoanalysis & Psychotherapy* 8 (1): 88–94.

Ashcroft, J. and Callanan, M. (1997) 'Clinical psychology training: the end of core placements', *Clinical Psychology Forum* 108: 41–42.

Ashcroft, J., Callanan, M., Adams, M., Roth, T., Gray, I. and Lavender, T. (1998) 'Clinical psychology training and the core placement issue: ways forward', *Clinical Psychology Forum* 112: 50–52.

Atkinson, D. R., Marten, G. and Sue, D. W. (eds) (1993) *Counseling American Minorities: A Cross-cultural Perspective* (4th edition), Dubuque, IA: Brown & Benchmark.

Bacon, H. (1992) 'Supervision in clinical training: the intregrative model, or meddling through', *Clinical Psychology Forum* 45: 24–28.

Bahrick, A. S., Russell, R. K. and Salmi, S. W. (1991) 'The effects of role induction on trainees' perceptions of supervision', *Journal of Counseling and Development* 69 (5): 434–438.

Bandura, A. (1965) 'Influence of models' reinforcement contingencies on the acquisition of imitative responses', *Journal of Personality and Social Psychology* 1: 589–595.

Banks, A. (2001) 'Tweaking the Euro-American perspective: infusing cultural awareness and sensitivity into the supervision of family therapy', *The Family Journal: Counseling and Therapy For Couples and Families* 9 (4): 420–423.

Bartram, D. (1995) 'National Vocational Qualifications and professional development', *Clinical Psychology Forum* 81: 38–40.

Beck, A. T., Epstein, N., Brown, G. and Steer, R. A. (1988) 'An inventory for measuring clinical anxiety: psychometric properties', *Journal of Consulting and Clinical Psychology* 56: 893–897.

Beckwith, J. (ed.) (1999) 'Power between women', Special feature, *Feminism & Psychology* 9 (4).

Beinart, H. (2002) 'An Exploration of the Factors which Predict the Quality of the Relationship in Clinical Supervision', Unpublished D.Clin.Psych. dissertation, Open University/British Psychological Society.

Bell, L. (1995) 'Cognitive analytic therapy: its key strengths and some concerns', *Clinical Psychology Forum* 84: 27–30.

Bennett, E. and Dennis, M. (2000) 'Adult mental health', pp. 89–108 in N. Patel, E. Bennett, M. Dennis, N. Dosanjh, A. Mahtani, A. Miller and Z. Nadirshaw (eds) *Clinical Psychology and 'Race' and Culture: A Training Manual*, Leicester: BPS.

Bepko, C., Almeida, R. V., Messineo, T. and Stevenson, Y. (1998) 'Evolving constructs of masculinity interviews with Andres Nazario, J. Williams Doherty and Roberto Font', *Journal of Feminist Family Therapy* 10 (1): 49–79.

Bernard, J. M. (1979) 'Supervisor training: a discrimination model', *Counselor Education and Supervision* 19: 60–68.

Bernard, J. M. (1997) 'The discrimination model', pp. 310–327 in C. E. Watkins (ed.) *Handbook of Psychotherapy Supervision*, New York: Wiley.

Bernard, J. M. and Goodyear, R. K. (1992) *Fundamentals of Clinical Supervision*, Boston, Mass.: Allyn & Bacon.

Bernard, J. M. and Goodyear, R. K. (1998) *Fundamentals of Clinical Supervision* (2nd edition), London: Allyn & Bacon.

Bickman, L. (1999) 'Practice makes perfect and other myths about mental health services', *American Psychologist* 54: 965–978.

Binder, J. (1993) 'Is it time to improve psychotherapy training?', *Clinical Psychology Review* 13: 301–318.

Binder, J. and Strupp, H. (1997) 'Supervision of psychodynamic psychotherapies', in C. E. Watkins Jnr (ed.) *Handbook of Psychotherapy Supervision*, New York: Wiley.

Bion, W. (1959) 'Attacks on linking', *International Journal of Psycho-Analysis* 40: 308–315. Republished (1967) in W. R. Bion, *Second Thoughts*, London: William Heinemann, pp. 93–109. (Republished 1984, London: Karnac.)

Bion, W. (1962) *Learning from Experience*, London: Heinemann (republished 1984, London: Karnac).

Bion, W. R. (1970) *Attention and Interpretation*, London: Maresfield.

Bishop, V. (1994) 'Clinical supervision questionnaire', *Nursing Times* 90 (11): 392–394.

Blocher, D. (1983) 'Towards a cognitive developmental approach to counseling supervision', *The Counseling Psychologist* 11: 27–34.

Bollas, C. (1994) 'Aspects of the erotic transference', *Psychoanalytic Inquiry* 14 (4): 572–590.

Bond, M. and Holland, S. (1998) *Skills of Clinical Supervision for Nurses*, Buckingham: Open University Press.

Borders, L. D. (1990) 'Developmental changes during supervisees' first practicum', *The Clinical Supervisor* 8: 157–167.

Borders, L. D., Rainey, L. M., Crutchfield, L. B. and Martin, D. W. (1996) 'Impact of a counseling supervision course on doctoral students' cognitions', *Counselor Education and Supervision* 35 (3): 204–217.

Bordin, E. (1979) 'The generalisability of the psychoanalytic concept of the working alliance', *Psychotherapy Theory, Research and Practice* 16: 252–260.

Bordin, E. S. (1983) 'A working alliance model of supervision', *Counseling Psychologist* 11: 35–42.

Bostock, J. (1997) 'Knowing our place: understanding women's experiences and cause of distress', *Feminism & Psychology* 7 (2): 239–247.

Boud, D. (1985) *Reflection: Turning Experience into Learning*, London: Kogan Page.

Boyd, J. (1978) *Counselor Supervision: Approaches, Preparation and Practices*, Muncie, IN: Accelerated Development.

Bradley, L. J. and Whiting, P. P. (2001) 'Supervision training: a model', in L. J. Bradley and N. Ladany (eds) *Counselor Supervision: Principles, Process, and Practice* (3rd edition), Philadelphia, PA: Brunner-Routledge.

Bramley, W. (1996) 'The supervisory couple in broad-spectrum psychotherapy', London: Free Association Books. (Cited in E. Holloway and M. Carroll (eds) (1999) *Training Counselling Supervisors*, London: Sage.)

British Association for Counselling and Psychotherapy (BACP) (1996) *What Is Supervision? Information Sheet 6*, Rugby: BACP.

British Association for Counselling and Psychotherapy (BACP) (2001) *The BACP Directory of Counselling and Psychotherapy Training in Britain*, Rugby: BACP.

British Association for Counselling and Psychotherapy (BACP) (2002) *Ethical Framework for Good Practice in Counselling and Psychotherapy*, Rugby: BACP.

British Psychological Society (BPS) (1995a) *Guidelines on Clinical Supervision*, Leicester: British Psychological Society.

British Psychological Society (BPS) (1995b) *Division of Clinical Psychology Professional Practice Guidelines*, Leicester: British Psychological Society.

British Psychological Society (BPS) (1995c) *Clinical Psychology Training: Meeting Health Service Demand*, Leicester: British Psychological Society.

British Psychological Society (BPS) (1996) *Criteria for the Accreditation of Postgraduate Training Courses in Clinical Psychology*, Leicester: British Psychological Society.

British Psychological Society (BPS) (1998a) *Guidelines for Continuing Professional Development*, Leicester: British Psychological Society.

British Psychological Society (BPS) (1998b) *National Occupational Standards in Applied Psychology*, Leicester: British Psychological Society.

British Psychological Society (BPS) (1998c) *Guidelines for Clinical Psychology Services*, Leicester: British Psychological Society.

British Psychological Society (BPS) (2001a) *Expanding Clinical Psychology Training to Achieve the National Plan Workforce Requirements: Options for Innovation and Development*, Leicester: British Psychological Society.

British Psychological Society (BPS) (2001b) *Guidance on Clinical Psychology Workforce Planning*, Division of Clinical Psychology Information Leaflet No. 6, Leicester: British Psychological Society.

British Psychological Society (BPS) (2001c) *Review of National Occupational Standards for Applied Psychology* (online). Available from: http://www.bps.org.uk/documents/nosDoc01.pdf (accessed 6 September 2002).

British Psychological Society (BPS) (2001d) *Division of Counselling Psychology. Guidelines for Professional Practice in Counselling Psychology*, Leicester: BPS.

British Psychological Society (BPS) (2002a) *Criteria for the Accreditation of Postgraduate Training Programmes in Clinical Psychology*, Leicester: British Psychological Society.

British Psychological Society (BPS) (2002b) http://www.bps.org.uk ('Frequently asked questions').

British Psychological Society (BPS), DCP (2003) *Policy Guidelines on Supervision in the Practice of Clinical Psychology*, Leicester: British Psychological Society.

Brown, M. T. and Landrum-Brown, J. (1995) 'Counselor supervision: cross-cultural perspectives', in J. G. Ponterotto, J. M. Casas, L. A. Suzuki and C. M. Alexander (eds) *Handbook of Multicultural Counseling*, Thousand Oaks, Calif.: Sage.

Burke, W. R., Goodyear, R. K. and Guzzard, C. (1998) 'Weakenings and repairs in supervisory alliances: a multiple-case study', *American Journal of Psychotherapy* 52 (4): 450–462.

Burns, D. (1980) *Feeling Good: The New Mood Therapy*, New York: New American Library.

Burton, M., Henderson, P. and Curtis-Jenkins, G. (1998) 'Primary care counsellors' experiences of supervision', *Counselling* 9 (2): 122–133.

Butterworth, T. and Faugier, J. (eds) (1992) *Clinical Supervision and Mentorship in Nursing*, London: Chapman and Hall.

Butterworth, T. (2001) 'Clinical supervision and clinical governance for the twenty-first century. An end or just the beginning?', in J. R. Cutcliffe, T. Butterworth and B. Proctor (eds) *Fundamental Themes in Clinical Supervision*, London: Routledge.

Byng-Hall, J. (1995) *Reviewing Family Scripts – Improvisation and Change*, New York: Guilford.

Carey, J. C., Williams, K. S. and Wells, M. (1988) 'Relationships between dimensions of supervisors' influence and counselor trainees' performance', *Counselor Education and Supervision* 28: 130–139.

Carifio, M. S. and Hess, A. K. (1987) 'Who is the ideal supervisor?', *Professional Psychology: Research and Practice* 18: 244–250.

Carpenter, J. and Treacher, A. (1989) *Problems and Solutions in Family and Marital Therapy*, Oxford: Blackwell.

Carroll, M. (1988) 'Counselling supervision: the British context', *Counselling Psychology Quarterly* 1: 387–396.

Carroll, M. (1996) *Counselling Supervision: Theory, Skills and Practice*, London: Cassell.

Carroll, M. (1999) 'Training in the tasks of supervision', in E. Holloway and M. Carroll (eds) *Training Counselling Supervisors*, London: Sage.

Carter, B. and McGoldrick, M. (1999) *The Expanded Family Life Cycle – Individual, Family and Social Perspectives*, Boston, Mass.: Allyn & Bacon.

Carter, P., Everitt, A. and Hudson, A. (1992) 'Malestream training? Women, feminism and social work education', in M. Day and L. Langon (eds) *Women, Oppression and Social Work*, London: Routledge.

Carter, R. (1995) *The Influence of Race & Racial Identity in Psychotherapy: Towards a Racially Inclusive Model*, London: John Wiley & Sons Inc.

Casement, P. (1988) *On Learning from the Patient*, London: Routledge.

Cassell, C. and Walsh, S. (1993) 'Being seen but not heard: barriers to women's equality in the workplace', *The Psychologist* 16 (3): 110–114.

Caves, R. (1988) 'Consultative methods for extracting expert knowledge about professional competence', pp. 199–229 in R. Ellis (ed.) *Competence in the Caring Professions*, London: Croom Helm.

Cecchin, G., Lane, G. and Ray, W. (1993) *Irreverence: A Strategy For Therapists' Survival*, London: Karnac.

Cheesman, G. (2001) *Practice Placements – A Discussion Paper*, London: Department of Health.

Cherry, D. K., Messenger, L. C. and Jacoby, A. M. (2000) 'An examination of training model outcomes in clinical psychology programs', *Professional Psychology: Research and Practice* 31: 562–568.

Chesler, P. (1972) *Women and Madness*, London: Allen Lane.

Clarkson, P. (1996) *The Bystander (An End to Innocence in Human Relations)*, London: Whurr.

Clarkson, P. and Gilbert, M. (1991) 'The training of counsellor trainers and supervisors, in W. Dryden and B. Thorne (eds) *Training and Supervision in Action*, London: Sage.

Clayton, M. (1997) 'Delphi: a technique to harness for critical decision-making tasks in education', *Educational Psychology* 17 (4): 373–386.

Collins, P. H. (1990) *Black Feminist Thought: Knowledge Consciousness and the Politics of Empowerment*, Boston, Mass.: Unwin Hyman.

Constantine, M. G. (1997) 'Facilitating multicultural competency in counselling supervision', in D. B. Pope-Davis and H. L. K. Coleman (eds) *Multicultural Counselling Competencies: Assessment, Education, Training and Supervision*, Thousand Oaks, Calif.: Sage.

Cooke, M. and Kipnis, D. (1986) 'Influence tactics in psychotherapy', *Journal of Consulting and Clinical Psychology* 54: 22–26.

Copeland, S. (1998) 'Counselling supervision in organisational contexts: new challenges and perspectives', *British Journal of Guidance & Counselling* 26 (3): 377–386.

Couchon, W. D. and Bernard, J. M. (1984) 'Effects of timing and supervision on supervisor and counselor performance', *The Clinical Supervisor* 2: 3–20.

Cross, W. E. (1971) 'The Negro-to-Black conversion experience: toward a psychology of Black liberation', *Black World* 20: 13–19.

Cross, W. E. (1995) 'The psychology of nigrescence: revising the cross model', in J. G. Ponterotto, J. M. Casas, L. A. Suzuki and C. M. Alexander (eds) *Handbook of Multicultural Counseling*, Thousand Oaks, Calif.: Sage.

Cushway, D. (1992) 'Stress in trainee clinical psychologists', *British Journal of Clinical Psychology* 31: 169–179.

Cutcliffe, J. (2001) 'An alternative training approach in clinical supervision', in J. Cutcliffe, T. Butterworth and B. Proctor (eds) *Fundamental Themes in Clinical Supervision*, London: Routledge.

Dallos, R. and Draper, R. (2000) *An Introduction to Family Therapy*, Milton Keynes: Open University Press.

D'Andrea, M. and Daniels, J. (1997) 'Multicultural counseling supervision: central issues, theoretical considerations, and practical strategies', in D. B. Pope-Davis and H. L. K. Coleman (eds) *Multicultural Counseling Competencies: Assessment, Education, Training and Supervision*, Thousand Oaks, Calif.: Sage.

Davey, G. (2002) 'Clinical research – worth our support', *The Psychologist* 15: 331.

Davies, H. (1987) Cited on p. 61 in P. Hawkins and R. Shohet (1994) *Supervision in the Helping Professions*, Milton Keynes: Open University Press.

Davis, D., Thompson, M., Oxman, A. and Haynes, B. (1992) 'Evidence of the effectiveness of CME. A review of 50 randomized controlled trials', *Journal of the American Medical Association* 268: 1111–1117.

Davy, J. (2002) 'Discursive reflections on a research agenda for clinical supervision', *Psychology and Psychotherapy* 75 (2): 221–238.

Dennis, M. (1998) 'Is there a place for diversity within supervision? An exploration of ethnic and cultural issues', *Clinical Psychology Forum* 118: 24–32.

Dennis, M. (2001) 'An integrative approach to "race" and culture in supervision', in M. Carroll and M. Tholstrup (eds) *Integrative Approaches to Supervision*, London: Jessica Kingsley.

Department of Health (DH) (1993) *A Vision for the Future*, London: HMSO.

Department of Health (DH) (1998a) *A First Class Service: Quality in the New NHS*, Health Services Circular 1998/113, London: HMSO.

Department of Health (DH) (1998b) *National Service Frameworks*, Health Services Circular 1998/074, London: HMSO.

Department of Health (DH) (1999) *National Service Framework for Mental Health: Modern Standards and Service Models*, London: HMSO.

Department of Health (DH) (2000a) *A Health Service of All the Talents: Developing the NHS Workforce. Consultation Document on the Review of Workforce Planning*, London: HMSO.

Department of Health (DH) (2000b) *Modernising Regulation – The New Health Professions Council: A Consultation Document*, London: Department of Health.

Department of Health (DH) (2001a) *Mental Health National Service Framework (and the NHS Plan). Workforce Planning, Education and Training. Underpinning Programme: Adult Mental Health Services. Final Report by the Workforce Action Team*, London: Department of Health.

Department of Health (DH) (2001b) *Working Together – Learning Together. A Framework for Lifelong Learning for the NHS*, London: Department of Health.

Department of Health (DH) (2001c) *Interdisciplinary Education and Training Development Programme '99–2001*. http://www.doh.gov.uk/swro/0501.htm

Department of Health (DH) (2002) *Workforce Development Confederations – Functions, Accountabilities and Working Relationships*, London: Department of Health.

Division of Clinical Psychology (DCP) (1998) *Briefing Paper No. 16, Services to Black and Minority Ethnic People: A Guide for Commissioners of Clinical Psychology Services*, Leicester: BPS.

Division of Clinical Psychology (DCP) (1999) *Guiding Principles for Continuing Professional Development*, Leicester: BPS.

Division of Clinical Psychology (DCP) (2001a) *Division of Clinical Psychology. Guidelines for Continuing Professional Development*, Leicester: BPS.

Division of Clinical Psychology (DCP) (2001b) *The Core Purpose and Philosophy of the Profession*, Leicester: BPS.

Dodenhoff, J. T. (1981) 'Interpersonal attraction and direct–indirect supervisor influence as predictors of counsellor trainee effectiveness', *Journal of Counseling Psychology* 28: 47–52.

Doehrman, M. J. G. (1976) 'Parallel processes in supervision and psychotherapy', *Bulletin of the Menninger Clinic* 40 (1): 9–57.

Dooley, C., Revell, J., Gessler, S., Liao, L.-M. and Winchurch, E. (2002) *Clinical Psychology Placement Project Report*, London: North Central London Workforce Development Confederation, Clinical Psychology Sub-Group.

Dowling, S. (1984) 'Clinical evaluation: a comparison with self, self with videotape, peers and supervisors', *Clinical Supervisor* 2 (3): 71–78.

Dreyfus, H. and Dreyfus, S. (1986) *How We Think – A Restatement of the Relation of Reflective Thinking to the Educative Process*, Boston, Mass.: Basil Blackwell.

Dryden, W. (1991) *Training and Supervision for Counselling in Action*, London: Sage.

Dryden, W. and Hunt, P. (1985) 'Therapeutic alliances in marital therapy', in W. Dryden (ed.) *Marital Therapy in Britain*, Vol. 1, London: Harper & Row.

Duan, C. M. and Roehlke, H. (2001) 'A descriptive "snapshot" of cross-racial supervision in university counseling center internships', *Journal of Multicultural Counseling and Development* 29 (2): 131–146.

Edwards, D. (1997) 'Supervision today: the psychoanalytic legacy', in G. Shipton (ed.) *Supervision of Psychotherapy and Counselling*, Buckingham: Open University Press.

Efstation, J. F., Patton, M. J. and Kardash, C. M. (1990) 'Measuring the working alliance in counselor supervision', *Journal of Counseling Psychology* 37 (3): 322–329.

Ekstein, R. and Wallerstein, R. (1972) *The Teaching and Learning of Psychotherapy*, Madison, WI: International Universities Press.

Ellis, M. V., Dell, D. M. and Good, G. E. (1988) 'Counselor trainees' perceptions of supervisor roles: two studies testing the dimensionality of supervision', *Journal of Counseling Psychology* 35: 315–324.

Ellis, M. V. and Ladany, N. (1997) 'Inferences concerning supervisees and clients in clinical supervision: an integrative review', in C. E. Watkins, Jnr (ed.) *Handbook of Psychotherapy Supervision*, New York: Wiley.

Ellis, M. V., Ladany, N., Krengel, M. and Schult, D. (1996) 'Clinical supervision research from 1981 to 1993: a methodological critique', *Journal of Counselling Psychology* 43 (1): 35–50.

Engel, A., House, R., Pearson, C. and Sluman, S. (1998) 'Report of a supervisors' workshop', *Training Link* 28 (1–2), Sheffield: University of Sheffield.

English National Board/Department of Health (ENB/DH) (2001) *Placements in Focus: English National Board for Nursing, Midwifery and Health Visiting and the Department of Health*, London: Department of Health.

Eraut, M. (1994) *Developing Professional Knowledge and Expertise*, London: The Falmer Press.

Eraut, M. (2000) 'Non-formal learning and tacit knowledge in professional work', *British Journal of Educational Psychology* 70: 113–136.

Erwin, W. J. (2000) 'Supervisor moral sensitivity', *Counselor Education and Supervision* 40 (2): 115–127.

Evans, M. (1998) 'Supervision: a developmental relational approach', *Transactional Analysis Journal* 28: 288–298.

Eysenck, H. (1952) 'The effects of psychotherapy', *Journal of Consulting and Clinical Psychology* 16: 319–324.

Fernando, S. (ed.) (1995) *Mental Health in a Multi-Ethnic Society: A Multi-Disciplinary Handbook*, London: Routledge.

Fleming, I. and Burton, M. (2001) 'Teaching about the individual and society links on the Manchester Clin.Psy.D course', *Clinical Psychology* 6: 28–33.

Fleming, I. and Steen, L. (2001) 'Supervisor training with the Manchester Clin.Psy.D. course', *Clinical Psychology* 8: 30–34.

Fleming, J. (1953) 'The role of supervision in psychiatric training', *Bulletin of The Menninger Clinic* 17: 157–159.

Fleming, R. K., Oliver, J. R. and Bolton, D. M. (1996) 'Training supervisors to train staff: a case study in a human service organisation', *Journal of Organizational Behaviour Management* 16: 3–25.

Flemons, D., Green, S. and Rambo, A. (1996) 'Evaluating therapists' practices in a postmodern world: a discussion and scheme', *Family Process* 35: 43–56.

Font, R., Dolan-Delvecchio, K. and Almeida, R. V. (1998) 'Finding the words: Instruments of therapy of liberation', *Journal of Feminist Therapy* 10 (1): 85–97.

Fordham, A., May, B., Boyle, M., Bentall, R. and Slade, P. (1990) 'Good and bad clinicians: supervisors' judgements of trainees' competence', *British Journal of Clinical Psychology* 29: 113–114.

Forman, D. and Nyatanga, L. (1999) 'The evolution of shared learning: some political and professional imperatives', *Medical Teacher* 21 (5): 489–496.

Foucault, M. (1977) *Discipline and Punish: The Birth of the Prison*, New York: Vintage Books.

Foucault, M. (1988) 'Power and strategies', in C. Gordon (ed.) *Power/Knowledge: Selected Interviews and Other Writings 1972–1977 by Michel Foucault*, New York: Pantheon Books.

Fowler, J. (Ed.) (1998) *The Handbook of Clinical Supervision: Your Questions Answered*, Salisbury, Wiltshire: Mark Allen Publishing Ltd.

Frawley-O'Dea, M. and Sarnat, J. (2001) *The Supervisory Relationship – a Contemporary Psychodynamic Approach*, New York: Guilford.

Friedlander, M. L. and Snyder, J. (1983) 'Trainees' expectations for the supervisory process: testing a developmental model', *Counselor Education and Supervision* 22: 342–348.

Friedlander, M. L. and Ward, L. G. (1984) 'Development and validation of the supervisory styles inventory', *Journal of Counseling Psychology* 31: 541–557.

Fukuyama, M. A. (1994) 'Critical incidents in multicultural counseling supervision: a phenomenological approach to supervision research', *Counselor Education and Supervision* 34: 142–147.

Gabbay, M., Kiemle, G. and Maguire, C. (1999) 'Clinical supervision for clinical psychologists: existing provision and client needs', *Clinical Psychology and Psychotherapy* 6: 404–412.

Gardner, R. M. D. (2001) 'Cultural perspectives of the supervisory relationship in the training of counselor education graduate students', *Dissertation Abstracts International Section A: Humanities & Social Sciences* 61, 8, 3050.

Garrett, T. (1998) 'Sexual contact between patients and psychologists', *The Psychologist* 11 (5): 115–127.

Garrett, T. (1999) 'Sexual contact between clinical psychologists and their patients: qualitative data', *Clinical Psychology and Psychotherapy* 6: 54–62.

Gatmon, D., Jackson, D., Koshkarian, L., Martos-Perry, N., Molina, A., Patel, N. and Rodolfa, E. (2001) 'Exploring ethnic, gender, and sexual orientation variables in supervision: do they really matter?', *Journal of Multicultural Counseling & Development Special Issue* 29 (2): 102–113.

Gilligan, C. (1982) *In a Different Voice: Psychological Theory & Women's Development*, Cambridge, Mass.: Harvard University Press.

Glaser, R. and Thorpe, J. (1986) 'Unethical intimacy: a survey of sexual contact and advances between psychology educators and female graduate students', *American Psychologist* 41: 43–51.

Golding, L. (2003) 'Report of the continuing professional development survey of clinical psychologists in the northwest of England', *Clinical Psychology* 26: 23–27.

Gopaul-Nicol, S. and Brice-Baker, T. (1998) *Cross Cultural Practice: Assessment, Treatment and Training*, New York: John Wiley.

Granello, D. H., Beamish, P. H. and Davis, T. E. (1997) 'Supervisee empowerment: does gender make a difference?', *Counselor Education and Supervision* 36: 305–317.

Gray, I. (1997) 'A follow-up survey of clinical psychology training resources carried out by the Group of Trainers in Clinical Psychology', *Clinical Psychology Forum* 108: 36–40.

Gray, I. (2001) 'Training numbers in England 2001–4', *Clinical Psychology* 2: 47.

Green, D. (1995) 'Supervision for qualified clinical psychologists', *Clinical Psychology Forum* 80: 40–41.

Green, D. (1997) 'Credit where credit's due', *Clinical Psychology Forum* 104: 28–31.

Green, D. and Gledhill, K. (1993) 'What ought a qualified clinical psychologist be able to do? Consulting the oracle', *Clinical Psychology Forum* 60: 7–11.

Green, D. and Sherrard, S. (1999) 'Developing an evidence base for post-qualification supervision', *Clinical Psychology Forum* 133: 17–20.

Green, D. R. (1998) 'Investigating the Core Skills of Clinical Supervision: A Qualitative Analysis', Unpublished D.Clin.Psych. dissertation, University of Leeds.

Green, R. J. (1998) 'Traditional norms of masculinity', *Journal of Feminist Family Therapy* 10 (1): 81–83.

Hagan, T. and Smail, D. (1997) 'Power-mapping – 1. Background and basic methodology', *Journal of Community and Applied Social Psychology* 7: 259–264.

Hall, J. and Firth-Cozens, J. (2000) *Clinical Governance in the NHS: A Briefing*, Leicester: British Psychological Society.

Harding, S. (1986) *The Science Question in Feminism*, Milton Keynes: Open University Press.

Harris, T., Moret, L. B., Gale, J. and Kampmeyer, K. L. (2001) 'Therapists' gender assumptions and how these assumptions influence therapy', *Journal of Feminist Family Therapy* 12 (2/3): 33–59.

Hart, G. M. (1982) *The Process of Clinical Supervision*, Baltimore, Md.: University Park Press. (Cited in D. Milne and F. Howard (2000) 'An introductory workshop for supervisors', *Clinical Psychology Forum* 136: 29–34.)

Hawkins, P. and Shohet, R. (1989) *Supervision in the Helping Professions*, Milton Keynes: Open University Press.

Hawkins, P. and Shohet, R. (2000) *Supervision in the Helping Professions* (2nd edition), Buckingham: Open University Press.

Helms, J. E. (1995) 'An update of Helms' white and people of color racial identity models', in J. G. Ponterotto, J. M. Casas, L. A. Suzuki and C. M. Alexander (eds) *Handbook of Multicultural Counseling*, Thousand Oaks, Calif.: Sage.

Helms, J. E. and Cook, D. A. (1999) 'Using race and culture in therapy supervision', in J. E. Helms and D. A. Cook, *Using Race and Culture in Counseling and Psychotherapy: Theory and Process*, Needham Heights, Mass.: Allyn & Bacon.

Helms, J. E. and Richardson, T. Q. (1997) 'How "multiculturalism" observes race and culture as differential aspects of counseling competency', in D. B. Pope-Davis and H. L. K. Coleman (eds) *Multicultural Counseling Competencies: Assessment, Education and Training and Supervision*, Thousand Oaks, Calif.: Sage.

Henwood, K. and Phoenix, A. (1999) ' "Race" in psychology, teaching the subject', in M. Bulmer and J. Solomos (eds) *Ethnic and Racial Studies Today*, London: Routledge.

Heppner, P. P. and Handley, P. G. (1981) 'A study of the interpersonal influence process in supervision', *Journal of Counseling Psychology* 28: 437–444.

Heppner, P. P. and Handley, P. G. (1982) 'The relationship between supervisory expertness, attractiveness or trustworthiness', *Counselor Education and Supervision* 22: 23–31.

Herbert, J. T., Ward, T. J. and Hemlick, L. M. (1995) 'Confirmatory factor analysis of the Supervisory Style Inventory and the Revised Supervision Questionnaire', *Rehabilitation Counseling Bulletin* 38: 334–349.

Hess, A. K. (1986) 'Growth in supervision: stages of supervisee and supervisor development', *The Clinical Supervisor* 4: 51–67.

Hess, A. K. (1987) 'Psychotherapy supervision: stages, Buber, and a theory of relationship', *Professional Psychology: Research and Practice* 18: 251–259.

Hewson, D. (1999) 'Empowerment in supervision. Special feature: Power between women', *Feminism & Psychology* 9 (4): 406–409.

Hilderbrand, E. T. (1989) 'Cognitive differences between experts and novices: implications for group supervision', *Journal of Counseling and Development* 67: 293–296.

Hill Collins, P. (1990) *Black Feminist Thought: Knowledge, Consciousness, and the Politics of Empowerment*, London: HarperCollins Academic.

Hingley, S. (1995) 'Applied psychology and BPS structure: issues for clinical psychology training', *Clinical Psychology Forum* 77: 40–43.

Hitchen, J., Gurney-Smith, B. and King, C. (1997) '"Perspectives on supervision. Opening the dialogue": a workshop for supervisors run by trainees', *Clinical Psychology Forum* 109: 21–25.

Hoffman, L. (1993) *Exchanging Voices: A Collaborative Approach to Family Therapy*, London: Karnac.

Hoffman, L. W. (1994) 'The training of psychotherapy supervisors: a barren scene', *Psychotherapy in Private Practice* 13: 23–42. (Cited in J. M. Bernard and R. K. Goodyear (1998) *Fundamentals of Clinical Supervision* (2nd edition), London: Allyn & Bacon.)

Hogan, R. (1964) 'Issues and approaches in supervision', *Psychotherapy: Theory, Research, and Practice* 1: 139–141.

Holland, S. (1990) 'Psychotherapy, oppression and social action: gender, race and class in black women's depression', in R. Perelberg and A. Miller (eds) *Gender and Power in Families*, London: Routledge.

Holland, S. (1992a) 'From social abuse to social action', in J. Ussher and P. Nicolson (eds) *Gender Issues in Clinical Psychology*, London: Routledge.

Holland, S. (1992b) 'From social abuse to social action: a neighbourhood psycho-therapy and social action project for women', *Changes: International Journal of Psychology and Psychotherapy* 10: 146–153.

Holland, S. (1995) 'Interaction in women's mental health and neighbourhood development', in S. Fernando (ed.) *Mental Health in a Multi-Ethnic Society: A Multidisciplinary Handbook*. London: Routledge.

Holloway, E. L. (1982) 'Interactional structure of the supervision interview', *Journal of Counseling Psychology* 29: 309–317.

Holloway, E. (1984) 'Outcome evaluation in supervision research', *Counseling Psychology* 12: 167–174.

Holloway, E. L. (1987) 'Developmental models of supervision: is it development?', *Professional Psychology: Research and Practice* 18: 209–216.

Holloway, E. L. (1995) *Clinical Supervision: A Systems Approach*, Thousand Oaks, Calif.: Sage.

Holloway, E. L. (1997) 'Structures for the analysis and teaching of supervision', in C. E. Watkins (ed.) *Handbook of Psychotherapy Supervision*, Chichester: Wiley.

Holloway, E. L. (1999) 'A framework for supervision training', in E. L. Holloway and M. Carroll, *Training Counselling Supervisors*, London: Sage.

Holloway, E. L. and Neufeldt, S. A. (1995) 'Supervision: its contribution to treatment efficacy', *Journal of Consulting and Clinical Psychology* 63: 207–213.

Holloway, E. L. and Poulin, K. (1995) 'Discourse in supervision', pp. 245–273 in J. Siegfried (ed.) *Therapeutic and Everyday Discourse on Behavior Change: Towards a Microanalysis in Psychotherapy Process Research*, New York: Ablex.

hooks, b. (1981) *Ain't I a Woman: Black Women and Feminism*, Boston, Mass.: South End Press.

hooks, b. (1990) *Yearning: Race, Gender, and Cultural Politics*, Boston, Mass.: South End Press.

hooks, b. (1993) *Sisters of the Yam: Black Women and Self-Recovery*, Boston, Mass.: South End Press.

Houston, G. (1995) *Supervision and Counselling*, London: The Rochester Foundation.

Hunt, P. (1976) 'Supervision', *Marriage Guidance* (Spring): 15–22.

Inskipp, F. (1999) 'Training supervisees to use supervision', in E. L. Holloway and M. Carroll (eds) *Training Counselling Supervisors*, London: Sage.

Inskipp, F. and Proctor, B. (1989) *Skills for Supervising and Being Supervised* ('Principles of Counselling' audiotape series), St Leonards-on-Sea, East Sussex: Alexia Publications.

Inskipp, F. and Proctor, B. (1993) *Making the Most of Supervision*, Twickenham: Cascade Pubs.

Inskipp, F. and Proctor, B. (2001a) *Making the Most of Supervision* (2nd edition), London: Cascade.

Inskipp, F. and Proctor, B. (2001b) *Becoming a Supervisor*, London: Cascade.

Izzard, S. (2001) 'The responsibility of the supervisor supervising trainees', in S. Wheeler and D. King, *Supervising Counsellors: Issues of Responsibility*, London: Sage.

Jacobs, D., David, P. and Meyer, D. J. (1995) *The Supervisory Encounter*, New Haven, CT: Yale University Press.

Jones, G. (2000) 'Group supervision: what can go wrong?', *Counselling* 11 (10): 648–649.

Jones, J. and Hunter, D. (1995) 'Consensus methods for medical and health services research', *British Medical Journal* 311: 376–380.

Kadushin, A. (1968) 'Games People Play in Supervision', *Social Work* 13 (July): 23–32.

Kadushin, A. (1992) *Supervision in Social Work* (3rd edition), New York: Columbia University Press.

Kauderer, S. and Herron, W. G. (1990) 'The supervisory relationship in psychotherapy over time', *Psychological Reports* 67 (2): 471–480.

Kavanaugh, K. H. and Kennedy, P. H. (1992) *Promoting Cultural Diversity: Strategies for Health Care Professionals*, Newbury Park, Calif.: Sage.

Kelvin, F. (1987) Cited in P. Hawkins and R. Shohet (2000) *Supervision in the Helping Professions* (2nd edition), Buckingham: Open University Press.

Kennard, B. D., Stewart, S. M. and Gluck, M. M. (1987) 'The supervision relationship: variables contributing to positive versus negative experiences', *Professional Psychology: Research and Practice* 18: 172–175.

Killian, K. D. (2001) 'Differences making a difference in cross-cultural interactions in supervisory relationships', *Journal of Feminist Family Therapy* 12 (2/3): 61–103.

Kilminster, S. M. and Jolly, B. C. (2000) 'Effective supervision in clinical practice settings: a literature review', *Medical Education* 34 (10): 827–840.

Kinderman, P. (2001) 'The future of clinical psychology training', *Clinical Psychology* 8: 6–11.

King, D. (2001) *Supervising Counsellors: Issues of Responsibility*, London: Sage.

King, D. and Wheeler, S. (1999) 'The responsibilities of counsellor supervisors: a qualitative study', *British Journal of Guidance & Counselling* 27 (2): 215–229.

Kingston, P. and Smith, D. (1983) 'Preparation for live consultation and live supervision when working without a one-way screen', *Journal of Family Therapy* 5: 219–234.

Kiresuk, T., Smith, A. and Cardillo, J. (1994) *Goal Attainment Scaling: Applications, Theory and Measurement*, Hillside, NJ: Lawrence Erlbaum.

Kitzinger, C. (1991) 'Feminism, psychology and the paradox of power', *Feminism & Psychology* 1 (1): 111–130.

Kleintjes, S. and Swartz, L. (1996) 'Black clinical psychology trainees at a "white" South African university: issues for clinical supervision', *Clinical Supervisor* 14: 87–109.

Knapp, S. and Vandecreek, L. (1997) 'Ethical and legal aspects of clinical supervision', pp. 589–602 in C. Watkins (ed.) *Handbook of Psychotherapy Supervision*, New York: Wiley.

Knight, A. (2002) *How to Become a Clinical Psychologist: Getting a Foot in the Door*, Hove: Brunner-Routledge.

Knight, P. and Llewelyn, S. (2001) 'Recruitment and retention in clinical psychology', *Clinical Psychology* 5: 32–35.

Kolb, D. A. (1984) *Experiential Learning: Experience as a Source of Learning and Development*, Englewood Cliffs, NJ: Prentice-Hall.

Krause, A. A. and Allen, G. J. (1988) 'Perceptions of counselor supervision: an examination of Stoltenberg's model from the perspectives of supervisor and supervisee', *Journal of Counselling Psychology* 35: 77–80.

Kruger, J. and Dunning, D. (1999) 'Unskilled and unaware of it: how difficulties in recognizing one's own incompetence lead to inflated self-assessments', *Journal of Personality and Social Psychology* 77 (6): 1121–1134.

Ladany, N. and Friedlander, M. L. (1995) 'The relationship between the supervisory working alliance and trainees' experience of role conflict and role ambiguity', *Counselor Education and Supervision* 34: 220–231.

Ladany, N. and Lehrman-Waterman, D. E. (1999) 'The content and frequency of supervisor self-disclosures and their relationship to supervisor style and the supervisory working alliance', *Counselor Education and Supervision* 38: 143–160.

Ladany, N. and Melincoff, D. S. (1999) 'The nature of counselor supervisor nondisclosure', *Counselor Education and Supervision* 38 (3): 161–176.

Ladany, N., Constantine, M. G. and Hofheinz, E. W. (1997) 'Supervisee multicultural case conceptualisation ability and self-reported multicultural competence as functions of supervisee racial identity and supervisor focus', *Journal of Counseling Psychology* 44: 284–293.

Ladany, N., Ellis, M. V. and Friedlander, M. L. (1999a) 'The supervisory working alliance, trainee self-efficacy, and satisfaction', *Journal of Counseling and Development* 77 (4): 447–455.

Ladany, N., Hill, C. E., Corbett, M. M. and Nutt, E. A. (1996) 'Nature, extent, and importance of what psychotherapy trainees do not disclose to their supervisors', *Journal of Counselling Psychology* 43: 10–24.

Ladany, N., Marotta, S. and Muse-Burke, S. L. (2001) 'Counselor experience related to complexity of case conceptualization and supervision preference', *Counselor Education and Supervision Special Issue* 40 (3): 203–219.

Ladany, N., Lehrman-Waterman, D., Molinaro, D. E. and Wolgast, B. (1999b) 'Psychotherapy supervisor ethical practices: adherence to guidelines, the supervisory working alliance, and supervisee satisfaction', *The Counseling Psychologist* 27 (3): 443–475.

Lago, C. and Thompson, J. (1997) 'The triangle with curved sides: sensitivity to issues of race and culture in supervision', in G. Shipton (ed.) *Supervision of Psychotherapy and Counselling*, Buckingham: Open University Press.

Laing, R. D. (1965) Cited in S. A. Spleen (1993) 'Safe supervision', *Interactions* (Autumn) 93: 8, and on p. 82 of J. Fowler (ed.) (1998) *The Handbook of Clinical*

Supervision: Your Questions Answered, Salisbury, Wiltshire: Mark Allen Publishing Ltd.

Lambert, M. J. (1980) 'Research and the supervisory process', in A. K. Hess (ed.) *Psychotherapy Supervision: Theory, Research and Practice*, New York: Wiley.

Lambert, M. J. and Arnold, R. C. (1987) 'Research and the supervisory process', *Professional Psychology: Research and Practice* 18: 217–224.

Lambert, M. J. and Ogles, B. M. (1997) 'The effectiveness of psychotherapy supervision', pp. 421–446 in E. Watkins (ed.) *Handbook of Psychotherapy Supervision*, New York: Wiley.

Larkin, J. and Popaleni, K. (1994) 'Heterosexual courtship, violence and harassment: the public and private control of young women, *Feminism and Psychology* 4: 213–227.

Lavender, T. and Thompson, L. (2000) 'Attracting newly qualified clinical psychologists to NHS Trusts', *Clinical Psychology Forum* 139: 35–40.

Lawton, B. and Feltham, C. (eds) (2000) *Taking Supervision Forward*, London: Sage.

Leary, K. (1997) 'Race, self-disclosure and "forbidden talk": race and ethnicity in contemporary clinical practice', *Psychoanalytic Quarterly* LXVI: 163–189.

Leary, T. (1957) *Interpersonal Diagnoses of Personality: A Theory and a Methodology for Personality Evaluation*, New York: Ronald Press.

Leathard, A. (1994) *Going Inter-Professional. Working Together for Health and Welfare*, London: Routledge.

Ledwith, S. and Stowers, C. (2001) Letter, *Clinical Psychology* 7: 5.

Leigh, J. (1984) 'Empowerment strategies for work with multi-ethnic populations', Paper presented at the Annual Meeting of the Council on Social Work Education, Detroit, Michigan. (Cited in C. Ridley (1995) *Overcoming Unintentional Racism in Counselling and Therapy*, London: Sage.)

Lenihan, G. O. and Kirk, W. G. (1992) 'Conjoint supervision with beginning trainees: the model and its effectiveness', *Clinical Supervisor* 10 (1): 35–50.

Leong, F. T. L. and Wagner, D. A. (1994) 'Cross-cultural counseling supervision: What do we know? What do we need to know?', *Counselor Education and Supervision* 34 (2): 117–131.

Lerner, G. (1986) Cited in J. McLean-Taylor, C. Gilligan and A. M. Sullivan (1994) *Between Voice and Silence, Women and Girls, Race and Relationship*, Cambridge, Mass.: Harvard University Press.

Lerner, S. (1999) 'Interactions between the therapist's and the client's life cycle stages', in B. Carter and M. McGoldrick (eds) *The Expanded Family Life Cycle*, Boston, Mass.: Allyn & Bacon.

Leslie, C. A. and Clossick, M. L. (1996) Cited in T. Harris, L. B. Moret, J. Gale and K. L. Kampmeyer (2001) 'Therapists' gender assumptions and how these assumptions influence therapy', *Journal of Feminist Family Therapy* 11 (2/3): 33–59.

Lichtenberg, J. W. and Goodyear, R. K. (1996) 'The structure of supervisor–supervisee interactions', ERIC: *Resources in Education*, ED., 387–759.

Liddle, H., Breunlin, D. and Schwartz, R. (eds) (1988) *Handbook of Family Therapy Supervision*, New York: Guilford.

Liddle, H. A., Becker, D. and Diamond, G. M. (1997) 'Family therapy supervision', in C. E. Watkins (ed.) *Handbook of Psychotherapy Supervision*, New York: Wiley.

Liese, B. S. and Alford, B. A. (1998) 'Recent advances in cognitive therapy supervision', *Journal of Cognitive Psychotherapy* 12: 91–94.

Liese, J. and Beck, J. S. (1997) 'Cognitive therapy supervision', in C. E. Watkins (ed.) *Handbook of Psychotherapy Supervision*, New York: Wiley.

Littrell, J. M., Lee-Bordin, N. and Lorenz, J. A. (1979) 'A developmental framework for counseling supervision', *Counselor Education and Supervision* 19: 119–136.

Loganbill, C. and Hardy, E. (1983) 'Developing training programmes for clinical supervisors', *The Clinical Supervisor* 1: 15–21.

Loganbill, C., Hardy, E. and Delworth, U. (1982) 'Supervision: a conceptual model', *The Counseling Psychologist* 10: 3–42.

Long, J. K., Lawless, J. J. and Dotson, D. R. (1996) 'Supervisory styles index: examining supervisees' perceptions of supervisor style', *Contemporary Family Therapy* 18: 589–606.

Lopez, S. (1997) 'Cultural competence in psychotherapy: a guide for clinicians and their supervisors', pp. 570–588 in C. E. Watkins (ed.) *Handbook of Psychotherapy Supervision*, New York: Wiley.

Lorber, J. and Farrell, S. (eds) (1991) *The Social Construction of Gender*, London: Sage.

Lorde, A. (1984) *Sister/Outsider: Essays and Speeches*, New York: Crossing Press.

Lowe, D. (1991) 'How to do it: set a multiple choice question (MCQ) examination', *British Medical Journal* 302: 780–782.

McGoldrick, M. and Gerson, R. (1985) *Genograms in Family Assessment*, New York: Norton.

McGuire, B. and Bekker, A., Green, D. and Keogan, C. (2001) 'The statement of equivalence in clinical psychology: problems and prospects', *Clinical Psychology* 6: 34–35.

McLean-Taylor, J., Gilligan, C. and Sullivan, A. M. (1994) *Between Voice and Silence, Women and Girls, Race and Relationship*, Cambridge, Mass.: Harvard University Press.

McKay, N. (1992) 'Remembering Anita Hill and Clarence Thomas: what really happened when one black woman spoke out', in T. Morrison (ed.) *Race-ing, Justice, En-gendering Power*, New York: Pantheon Books.

McNeill, B. W. and Worthen, V. (1989) 'The parallel process in psychotherapy supervision', *Professional Psychology: Research and Practice* 20: 329–333.

McQueen, C. (ed.) (2000) 'Women and power', Special feature for special issue of *Changes: An International Journal of Psychology and Psychotherapy* 18 (4).

Magnuson, S., Wilcoxon, S. A. and Norem, K. (2000a) 'A profile of lousy supervision: experienced counselor's perspectives', *Counselor Education and Supervision* 39: 189–202.

Magnuson, S., Wilcoxon, S. A. and Norem, K. (2000b) 'Exemplary supervision practices: retrospective observations of experienced counselors', *Texas Counseling Association Journal* 28 (2): 93–101.

Management Advisory Service (MAS) (1989) *Review of Clinical Psychology Services and Staffing*, London: MAS to the NHS.

Marikis, D. E., Russell, R. K. and Dell, D. M. (1985) 'Effects of supervisor experience level on planning and in-session supervisor verbal behaviour', *Journal of Counseling Psychology* 32: 410–416.

Marteau, T., Johnston, M., Wynne, G. and Evans, T. (1989) 'Cognitive factors in the explanation of the mismatch between confidence and competence in performing basic life-support', *Psychology and Health* 3: 278–282.

Martinez, R. P. and Holloway, E. L. (1997) 'The supervision relationship in multi-cultural training', in D. B. Pope-Davis and H. L. K. Coleman (eds) *Multicultural*

Counseling Competencies: Assessment, Education, Training and Supervision, Thousand Oaks, Calif.: Sage.

Marziali, E. (1984) 'Three viewpoints on the therapeutic alliance. Similarities, differences and associations with psychotherapy outcome', *Journal of Nervous and Mental Disease* 172 (7): 417–423.

Maslow, A. (1943) 'A theory of human motivation', *Psychological Review* 50: 370–396.

Mattinson, J. (1977) *The Reflection Process in Casework Supervision*, London: Tavistock Institute of Human Relations.

Miller, C., Freeman, M. and Ross, N. (2001) *Interprofessional Practice in Health and Social Care*, London: Arnold.

Miller, F. E. and Rogers, L. E. (1976) *Explorations in Interpersonal Communications*, Beverly Hills, Calif.: Sage.

Miller, G. M. and Larrabee, M. J. (1995) 'Sexual intimacy in counselor education and supervision: a national survey', *Counselor Education and Supervision* 34 (4): 332–343.

Miller, J. (1976/1986) *Toward a New Psychology of Women*, Boston: Beacon Press (Reprinted 1986, London: Penguin).

Miller, J. B. (1991) 'Women and power', pp. 197–205 in J. V. Jordan, A. G. Kaplan, J. B. Miller, I. P. Stiver and J. L. Surrey (eds) *Women's Growth in Connection*, New York: Guilford.

Milne, D. (1994) 'A "quality supervision" refresher workshop', *Clinical Psychology Forum* 74: 18–20.

Milne, D. and Britton, P. (1994) 'A workshop on skilled supervision', *Clinical Psychology Forum* 67: 4–6.

Milne, D. and Gracie, J. (2001) 'The role of the supervisee: 20 ways to facilitate clinical psychology supervision', *Clinical Psychology* 5: 13–15.

Milne, D. and Howard, F. (2000) 'An introductory workshop for supervisors', *Clinical Psychology Forum* 136: 29–34.

Milne, D. and James, I. (1999) 'Evidence-based clinical supervision: review and guidelines', *Clinical Psychology Forum* 133: 32–36.

Milne, D. and James, I. (2000) 'A systematic review of effective cognitive-behavioural supervision', *British Journal of Clinical Psychology* 39 (2): 111–127.

Milne, D. and Oliver, V. (2000) 'Flexible formats of supervision: description, evaluation and implementation', *Journal of Mental Health* 9 (3): 291–304.

Milne, D., Oliver, V., Ellis, F., Collerton, D. and Milne, J. (2001) 'Placement accreditation: a regional initiative', *Clinical Psychology Forum* 149: 37–39.

Milne, D. L. and James, I. (2002) 'The observed impact of training on competence in clinical supervision', *British Journal of Clinical Psychology* 41: 55–72.

Mitchell, J. (1974) *Psychoanalysis and Feminism*, Harmondsworth: Penguin.

Montalvo, B. (1973) 'Aspects of live supervision', *Family Process* 12: 343–359.

Morrison, T. (ed.) (1992) *Race-ing, Justice, En-gendering Power*, New York: Pantheon.

Morrison, T. (1993) *Staff Supervision in Social Care*, London: Longman.

Moskowitz, S. A. and Rupert, P. A. (1983) 'Conflict resolution within the supervisory relationship', *Professional Psychology: Research and Practice* 14: 632–641.

Mueller, W. J. and Kell, B. L. (1972) *Coping with Conflict: Supervising Counselors and Psychotherapists*, Englewood Cliffs, NJ: Prentice-Hall.

Nadirshaw, Z. (1999) 'Clinical Psychology', in K. Bhui and D. Objide (eds) *Mental Health Service Provision for a Multi-Ethnic Society*, London: WB Saunders.

Nadirshaw, Z. (2000) 'Professional and organisational issues', in N. Patel, E. Bennett, M. Dennis, N. Dosanjh, A. Mahtani, A. Miller and Z. Nadirshaw (eds) *Clinical Psychology, 'Race' and Culture: A Training Manual*, Leicester: BPS Books.

Nadirshaw, Z. (in press) *Transcultural Clinical Supervision in Healthcare Practice*, London: Department of Health/University of Bradford.

Najavits, L. M. and Strupp, H. H. (1994) 'Differences in the effectiveness of psycho-dynamic therapists: a process outcome study, *Psychotherapy* 31: 114–123.

National Audit Office (NAO) (2001) *Educating and Training the Future Health Professional Workforce for England. Report by the Comptroller and Auditor General*, London: HMSO.

National Health Service Executive (NHSE) (1995) *EL(95)27 Education and Training in the New NHS*, London: HMSO.

Nelson, G. L. (1978) 'Psychotherapy supervision from the trainee's point of view: a study of preferences', *Professional Psychology* 9: 539–550.

Nelson, M. E. (1997) 'An interactional model for empowering women in supervision', *Counselor Education and Supervision* 37 (2): 125–140.

Nelson, M. L. and Holloway, E. L. (1990) 'Relation of gender to power and involvement in supervision', *Journal of Counseling Psychology* 37 (4): 473–481.

Nelson, M. L., MacDonald, G., Blume, A., Coulon, A. E., Elliott, E., Rodriguez, J. and Milo, M. (1996) 'Development of 4 supervision relationships over time'. (Cited in S. Neufeldt, L. Beutler and R. Banchero (1997) 'Research on supervisor variables in psychotherapy supervision', pp. 508–524 in C. E. Watkins (ed.) *Handbook of Psychotherapy Supervision*, New York: Wiley.)

Neufeldt, S., Beutler, L. and Banchero, R. (1997) 'Research on supervisor variables in psychotherapy supervision', pp. 508–524 in C. E. Watkins (ed.) *Handbook of Psychotherapy Supervision*, New York: Wiley.

Newnes, C. (1996) 'The development of clinical psychology and its values', *Clinical Psychology Forum* 95: 29–35.

NHS Scotland (2002) *Clinical Psychology Workforce Planning Report*, Edinburgh: NHS Education for Scotland.

Nickell, N. J., Hecker, L. L., Ray, R. E. and Tarcik, J. (1995) 'Marriage and family therapists' sexual attraction to clients: an exploratory study', *American Journal of Family Therapy* 23 (4): 315–327.

Nisbet, R. and Wilson, T. (1977) 'Telling more than we can know: verbal reports on mental processes', *Psychological Review* 84 (3): 231–259.

Norcross, J., Brust, A. and Dryden, W. (1992) 'British clinical psychology: a national survey of the BPS Clinical Division', *Forum* (February): 19–24.

Nordlund, M. D. (1999) *Developmental Changes Among Beginning Psychotherapy Supervisors*, Oregon: George Fox University Press.

Olk, M., and Friedlander, M. L. (1992) 'Trainees' experience of role conflict and role ambiguity in supervisory relationships', *Journal of Counseling Psychology* 39: 389–397.

Orlans, V. and Edwards, D. (2001) 'A collaborative model of supervision', in M. Carroll and M. Tholstrup (eds) *Integrative Approaches to Supervision*, London: Jessica Kingsley.

Osborn, C. J. and Davis, T. E. (1996) 'The supervision contract: making it perfectly clear', *Clinical Supervisor* 14 (2): 121–134.

Osgood, C., Suci, C. and Tannenbaum, P. (1957) *The Measurement of Meaning*, Urbana, IL: University of Illinois.

Overholser, J. C. and Fine, M. A. (1990) 'Defining the boundaries of professional competence: managing subtle cases of clinical incompetence', *Professional Psychology: Research and Practice* 21: 462–469.

Padesky, C. (1996) 'Developing cognitive therapist competency: teaching and supervision models', in P. Salkovskis (ed.) *Frontiers of Cognitive Therapy*, New York: Guilford Press.

Page, S. and Wosket, V. (1994) *Supervising the Counsellor: A Cyclical Model*, London: Routledge.

Page, S. and Wosket, V. (2001) *Supervising the Counsellor: A Cyclical Model* (2nd edition), Philadelphia, PA: Brunner-Routledge.

Parry, A. and Doan, R. E. (1994) *Story Re-visions: Narrative Therapy in the Postmodern World*, New York: Guilford.

Patel, N. (1998) 'Black therapist/white clients: an exploration of experiences in cross-cultural therapy', *Clinical Psychology Forum* 118: 18–23.

Patel, N. and Fatimilehin, I. A. (1999) 'Racism and mental health', in C. Newnes, G. Holmes and C. Dunn (eds) *This is Madness. A Critical Look at Psychiatry and the Future of Mental Health Services*, Ross-on-Wye: PCCS.

Patel, N., Bennett, E., Dennis, M., Dosanjh, N., Mahtani, A., Miller, A. and Nadirshaw, Z. (2000) *Clinical Psychology, 'Race' and Culture: A Training Manual*, Leicester: BPS Books.

Patterson, C. H. (1983) 'Supervision in counseling II. Contemporary models of supervision: a client-centered approach to supervision', *Counseling Psychologist* 11: 21–25.

Patton, M. J. and Kivlighan, D. M. (1997) 'Relevance of the supervisory alliance to the counseling alliance and to treatment adherence in counselor training', *Journal of Counseling Psychology* 44 (1): 108–115.

Peterson, D. R. (1995) 'The reflective educator', *American Psychologist* 50: 975–983.

Pickvance, D. (1997) 'Becoming a supervisor', In G. Shipton (ed.) *Supervision of Psychotherapy and Counselling*, Buckingham, Open University Press.

Pidgeon, N., Turner, B. and Blockley, D. (1991) 'The use of grounded theory for conceptual analysis in knowledge elicitation', *International Journal of Man–Machine Studies* 35: 151–173.

Pilgrim, D. and Treacher, A. (1992) *Clinical Psychology Observed*, London: Routledge.

Pinderhughes, E. (1989) *Understanding, Race, Ethnicity and Power: The Key to Efficacy in Clinical Practice*, New York: Free Press.

Polanyi, M. (1967) *The Tacit Dimension*, Garden City, NY: Doubleday.

Ponterotto, J. G. and Pedersen, P. B. (1993) *Preventing Prejudice: A Guide for Counselors and Educators*, Newbury Park, Calif.: Sage.

Pope, K., Levenson, H. and Schover, L. (1979) 'Sexual intimacy in psychology training: results and implications of a national survey', *American Psychologist* 34: 682–689.

Pope, K. S. (1989) 'Sexual intimacies between psychologists and their students and supervisees: research, standards, and professional liability', *Independent Practitioner* 9 (2): 33–34.

Prevention of Professional Abuse Network (POPAN) (1994) *Development Plan 1994–1997*, London: POPAN.

Priest, R. (1994) 'Minority supervisor and majority supervisee: another perspective of clinical reality', *Counselor Education and Supervision* 34 (2): 152–158.

Prieto, L. R. (1996) 'Group supervision: still widely practiced but poorly understood', *Counselor Education and Supervision* 35 (4): 295–307.

Prilletensky, L. (1989) 'Psychology and the status quo', *American Psychologist* 10: 11–15.

Proctor, B. (1997) 'Contracting in supervision', in C. Sills (ed.) *Contracts in Counselling*, London: Sage.

Proctor, B. (2000) *Group Supervision: A Guide to Creative Practice*, London: Sage.

Proctor, G. (2001) 'CBT: the obscuring of power in the name of science', Paper presented at Northern & Yorkshire Regions' PQT 10th Joint Clinical Conference, Ambleside, 18–20 April.

Putney, M. W., Worthington, E. L. and McCullough, M. E. (1992) 'Effects of supervisor and supervisee theoretical orientation and supervisor–supervisee matching on interns' perceptions of supervision', *Journal of Counseling Psychology* 39: 258–265.

Quality Assurance Agency (QAA) (1999) *Code of Practice for the Assurance of Academic Quality and Standards in Higher Education: Postgraduate Research Programmes*, London: QAA.

Quality Assurance Agency (QAA) (2001a) 'Review of programmes in nursing and the professions allied to medicine', *Higher Quality* 8: 7.

Quality Assurance Agency (QAA) (2001b) *Code of Practice for the Assurance of Academic Quality and Standards in Higher Education: Placement Learning*, London: QAA.

Rabinowitz, F. E., Heppner, P. P. and Roehlke, H. J. (1986) 'Descriptive study of process and outcome variables of supervision over time', *Journal of Counseling Psychology* 33: 292–300.

Raichelson, S. H., Herron, W. G., Primavera, L. H. and Ramirez, S. M. (1997) 'Incidence and effects of parallel process in psychotherapy supervision', *Clinical Supervisor* 15 (2): 37–48.

Rajan, P., Scaife, J. and Turpin, G. (2002) *Trent Clinical Psychology Placement Project: Enhancing Placement Availability and Quality*, Trent Workforce Development Confederation, April.

Ravenette, T. (1997) 'The exploration of consciousness. Personal construct theory and change', in T. Ravenette, *Selected Papers*, Farnborough: EPCA.

Reeves, D., Culbreth, J. R. and Greene, A. (1997) 'Effect of sex, age and education level on the supervisory styles of substance abuse counselor supervisors', *Journal of Alcohol and Drug Education* 43: 76–86.

Rice, L. N. (1980) 'A client-centered approach to the supervision of psychotherapy', In A. K. Hess (ed.) *Psychotherapy Supervision: Theory, Research and Practice*, New York: Wiley.

Ricketts, T. and Donohoe, G. (2000) 'Clinical supervision in Cognitive Behavioural psychotherapy', in B. Lawton and C. Feltham (eds) *Taking Supervision Forward*, London: Sage.

Ridley, C. R. (1995) *Overcoming Unintentional Racism in Counseling and Therapy: A Practitioner's Guide to Intentional Intervention*, Thousand Oaks, Calif.: Sage.

Robinson, V. (1936) *Supervision in Social Casework*, Chapel Hill, NC: University of Carolina Press.

Rogers, C. (1961) *On Becoming a Person*, Boston, Mass.: Houghton Mifflin.

Rogers, C. R. (1957) 'The necessary and sufficient conditions of therapeutic personality change', *Journal of Consulting Psychology* 21: 95–103.

Ronnestad, M. H., Orlinsky, D. E., Parks, B. K. and Davis, J. D. (1997) 'Supervisors of psychotherapy: mapping experience level and supervisory confidence', *European Psychologist* 2 (3): 191–201.

Rosenblatt, A. and Mayer, J. E. (1975) 'Objectionable supervisory styles: students' views', *Social Work* 20: 184–189.

Roth, A. and Fonagy, P. (1996) *What Works for Whom?: A Critical Review of Psychotherapy Research*, London: Routledge.

Russell, R. K. and Petrie, T. (1994) 'Issues in training effective supervisors', *Applied and Preventive Psychology* 3: 27–42.

Ryde, J. (2000) 'Supervising across difference', *International Journal of Psychotherapy* 5 (1): 37–49.

Sainsbury Centre for Mental Health (SCMH) (2001) *Capable Practitioner*, London: Sainsbury Centre for Mental Health.

Samec, J. R. (1995) 'Shame, guilt, and trauma: failing the psychotherapy candidate's clinical work', *The Clinical Supervisor* 13: 1–18.

Sayal-Bennett, A. (1991) 'Equal opportunities: empty rhetoric', *Feminism and Psychology* 1 (1): 74–77.

Scaife, J. (2001a) *Supervision in the Mental Health Professions: A Practitioner's Guide*, Hove: Brunner-Routledge.

Scaife, J. (2001b) 'The contracting process and the supervisory relationship, avoiding pitfalls and problems', in J. Scaife, *Supervision in the Mental Health Professions: A Practitioner's Guide*, Hove: Brunner-Routledge.

Scaife, J. and Walsh, S. (2001) 'The emotional climate of work and the development of self', in J. Scaife, *Supervision in the Mental Health Professions: A Practitioner's Guide*, Hove: Brunner-Routledge.

Scanzoni, J. (1970) *Opportunity and the Family*, New York: Free Press.

Schein, E. H. (1980) *Organisational Psychology*, Englewood Cliffs, NJ: Prentice-Hall.

Schon, D. (1983) *The Reflective Practitioner: How Professionals Think in Action*, New York: Basic Books.

Schon, D. (1986) *Educating the Reflective Practitioner*, San Francisco: Jossey-Bass.

Schulte, H. M., Hall, M. J. and Bienenfeld, D. *et al.* (1997) 'Liability and accountability in psychotherapy supervision – a review, survey, and proposal', *Academic Psychiatry* 21 (3): 133–140.

Scott, K. J., Ingram, K. M., Vitanza, S. A. and Smith, N. G. (2000) 'Training in supervision: a survey of current practices', *Counseling Psychologist* 28 (3): 403–422.

Scott, L. (1999) 'The nature and structure of supervision in health visiting with victims of child sexual abuse', *Journal of Advanced Nursing* 29: 754–763.

Searles, H. F. (1955) *The Informational Value of the Supervisors' Experience. Collected Papers on Schizophrenia and Related Subjects*, London: Hogarth Press.

Shanfield, S. B. and Matthews, K. L. (1993) 'What do excellent psychotherapy supervisors do?', *American Journal of Psychiatry* 150: 1081–1084.

Shanfield, S. B., Hetherly, V. and Matthews, K. L. (1993) 'Excellent supervision: the residents' perspective', *Journal of Psychotherapy Practice & Research* 10: 23–27.

Shanfield, S. B., Mohl, P. C., Matthews, K. L. and Hetherly, V. (1992) 'Quantitative assessment of the behavior of psychotherapy supervisors', *American Journal of Psychiatry* 149 (3): 352–357.

Shillitoe, R., Eltringham, S. and Green, D. (2002) 'Clinician, update thyself: assessing the value of local training courses', *British Journal of Therapy and Rehabilitation* 9 (5): 166–170.

Shipton, G. (ed.) (1997) *Supervision of Psychotherapists and Counsellors: Making a Place for Thinking*, Millton Keynes: Open University Press.

Skovholt, T. M. and Ronnestad, M. H. (1992) 'Themes in therapist and counselor development', *Journal of Counseling and Development* 70: 505–515.

Skovholt, T. and Ronnestad, M. (1995) *The Evolving Professional Self: Stages and Themes in Therapist and Counselor Development*, New York: Wiley & Sons.

Sloan, G. (1999) 'Good characteristics of a clinical supervisor: a community mental health nurse perspective', *Journal of Advanced Nursing* 30 (3): 713–722.

Smith, D. and Kingston, P. (1980) 'Live supervision without a one way screen', *Journal of Family Therapy* 2: 379–387.

Stein, D. and Lambert, M. (1995) 'Graduate training in psychotherapy: are therapy outcomes enhanced?', *Journal of Consulting and Clinical Psychology* 63 (2): 182–196.

Stenack, R. J. and Dye, H. A. (1983) 'Practicum supervision roles: effects of supervisee statements', *Counselor Education and Supervision* 23: 157–168.

Stevens, D. T., Goodyear, R. K. and Robertson, P. (1998) 'Supervisor development: an exploratory study in changes in stance and emphasis', *Clinical Supervisor* 16 (2): 73–88.

Steward, R. J., Breland, A. and Neil, D. M. (2001) 'Novice supervisees' self-evaluations and their perceptions of supervisor style', *Counselor Education and Supervision* 41: 131–141.

Stoltenberg, C. (1981) 'Approaching supervision from a developmental perspective: the counselor complexity model', *Journal of Counseling Psychology* 28: 59–65.

Stoltenberg, C. and Delworth, U. (1987) *Supervising Counselors and Therapists: A Developmental Approach*, San Francisco: Jossey-Bass.

Stoltenberg, C. D., McNeill, B. and Delworth, U. (1998) *IDM Supervision: An Integrated Developmental Model for Supervising Counsellors and Therapists*, San Francisco: Jossey-Bass.

Stonefish, L. and Busby, D. (1996) 'The Delphi method', pp. 469–482 in D. Sprenkle and S. Moon (eds) *Research Methods in Family Therapy*, New York: Guilford Press.

Surrey, J. L. (1991) 'The "self-in-relation": a theory of women's development', pp. 51–66 in J. V. Jordon, A. G. Kaplan, J. B. Miller, I. P. Stiver and J. L. Surrey (eds) *Women's Growth in Connection*, New York: Guilford.

Sweeney, G., Webley, P. and Treacher, A. (2001) 'Supervision in occupational therapy. Part 1: The supervisor's anxieties', *British Journal of Occupational Therapy Special Issue* 64 (7): 337–345.

TAPPS http://www.iah.bbsrc.ac.uk/TAPPS/index.html (accessed 9/11/02)

Taylor, C. (1984) 'Foucault on freedom and truth', *Political Theory* 12: 152–183.

Taylor, M. (1994) 'Gender and power in counselling and supervision', *British Journal of Guidance and Counselling* 22 (3): 319–327.

Temperley, J. (1984) 'Our own worst enemies: unconscious factors in female disadvantage', *Free Association*, Pilot Issue: 23–38.

The Concise Oxford Dictionary of Current English (1990) Eighth edition edited by R. E. Allen, Oxford: Clarendon Press.

Thomas, G. V., Turpin, G. and Meyer, C. (2002) 'Clinical research under threat', *The Psychologist* 15: 286–289.

Thomas, L. and Harri-Augstein, E. (1985) *Self-Organised Learning: Foundations of a Conversational Science for Psychology*, London: Routledge.

Tomlinson, P. D. (1999) 'Conscious reflection and implicit learning in Teacher Preparation: 1 Recent light on an old issue', *Oxford Review of Education* 25 (3): 405–424.

Tomm, K. (1988) 'Interventive interviewing, Part III. Intending to ask linear, circular strategic or reflexive questions', *Family Process* 27: 1–15.

Tomm, K. and Wright, L. (1979) 'Training in family therapy: perceptual, conceptual and executive skills', *Family Process* 18: 278–302.

Townend, M., Iannetta, L. and Freeston, M. H. (2002) 'Clinical supervision in practice: a survey of UK Cognitive Behavioural psychotherapists accredited by the BABCP', *Behavioural and Cognitive Psychotherapy* 30: 485–500.

Tracey, T. J., Ellickson, J. L. and Sherry, D. (1989) 'Reactance in relation to different supervisory environments and counsellor development', *Journal of Counseling Psychology* 36: 336–344.

Turpin, G. (1995) 'A survey of clinical placements and supervisors involved in clinical psychology postgraduate training', *Clinical Psychology Forum* 86: 36–40.

Turpin, G. (1997) 'Options for expanding training: update and farewell', *Clinical Psychology Forum* 99: 47.

Turpin, G. (2002) 'Fostering clinical research', *The Psychologist* 15: 505–506.

United Kingdom Central Council for Nursing, Midwifery and Health Visiting (UKCC) (1996) *Position Statement on Clinical Supervision for Nursing and Health Visiting*, London: UKCC.

Universities UK/DH (2002) *Funding Learning and Development for the Healthcare Workforce*, London: Department of Health.

Ussher, J. (1991) *Women & Madness: Misogyny or Mental Illness*, London: Harvester Wheatsheaf.

Ussher, J. and Nicolson, P. (eds) (1992) *Gender Issues in Clinical Psychology*, London: Routledge.

Vetere, A. and Gelsthorpe, S. (eds) (1994) 'The gender issue', *Clinical Psychology Forum*, no. 64 (February).

Verduyn, C., Steen, L. and Marriott, A. (1994) 'The North Western Region mentor scheme', *Clinical Psychology Forum* 63: 17–20.

Wachtel, E. and Wachtel, P. (1986) *Family Dynamics in Individual Psychotherapy – A Guide to Clinical Strategies*, New York: Guilford.

Walker, G. and Goldner, V. (1995) 'The wounded prince and the women who love him', in C. Burck and B. Speed (eds) *Gender Power and Relationships*, London: Routledge.

Wampold, B. E. and Holloway, E. L. (1997) 'Methodology, design, and evaluation in psychotherapy supervision research', in C. E. Watkins (ed.) *Handbook of Psychotherapy Supervision*, Chichester: Wiley.

Watkins, C. E. (1995) 'Psychotherapy supervisor and supervisee: developmental models and research nine years later', *Clinical Psychology Review* 15: 647–680.

Watkins, C. E. (1997a) 'Some concluding thoughts about psychotherapy supervision', pp. 603–616 in C. E. Watkins (ed.) *Handbook of Psychotherapy Supervision*, New York: Wiley.

Watkins, C. E. (1997b) *Handbook of Psychotherapy Supervision*, Chichester: Wiley.

Weaks, D. (2002) 'Unlocking the secrets of "good supervision": a phenomenological exploration of experienced counsellors' perceptions of good supervision', *Counselling and Psychotherapy Research* 2 (1): 33–39.

Webb, A. and Wheeler, S. (1998) 'How honest do counsellors dare to be in the supervisory relationship? An exploratory study', *British Journal of Guidance and Counselling* 26 (4): 509–524.

Wells, J. A. (2001) 'Gender roles, racial and gender attitudes, and training level influences on perceptions of the supervision experience', *Dissertation Abstracts International: Section B: The Sciences & Engineering* 61: 5013.

Wheeler, D., Avis, J., Miller, L. and Chaney, S. (1986) Cited in A. Prouty (2001) 'Experiencing feminist family therapy supervision', *Journal of Feminist Family Therapy* 12 (4): 171–203.

Wheeler, S. (2002) 'A Systematic Review of Supervision Research', Presentation at BACP Research Conference, London, May.

Wheeler, S. and King, D. (2001) *Supervising Counsellors: Issues of Responsibility*, London: Sage.

White, M. (1995) *Re-authoring Lives*, Adelaide: Dulwich Centre Publications.

White, M. and Epston, D. (1991) *Narrative Means to Therapeutic End*, New York: Norton.

White, M. and Russell, C. (1995) 'The essential elements of supervisory systems: a modified Delphi study', *Journal of Marital and Family Therapy* 21 (1): 33–53.

White, V. E. (2000) 'Contribution of supervisor and supervisee personal well-being characteristics to the supervisory working alliance', Ph.D. thesis, University of Akron, OH.

Whiting, P. P., Bradley, L. J. and Planny, K. J. (2001) 'Supervision-based developmental models of counselor supervision', pp. 125–146 in L. J. Bradley and N. Ladany (eds) *Counselor Supervision: Principles, Process and Practice*, Philadelphia, PA: Brunner-Routledge.

Whittington, A. and Burns, J. (2001) 'Statement of Equivalence developments', *Clinical Psychology* 8: 3–4.

Wilkins, P. (1995) 'A creative therapies model for the group supervision of counsellors', *Counselling* 23 (2): 245–247.

Wilkinson, S. and Kitzinger, C. (1996) *Representing the Other: A Feminism and Psychology Reader*, London: Sage.

Williams, A. (1995) *Visual and Active Supervision: Roles, Focus, Technique*, New York: W. W. Norton.

Williams, J. and Watson, G. (eds) (1991) 'Clinical psychology training: training in oppression', Open Forum, *Feminism & Psychology* 1: 55–109.

Williams, P. and Webb, C. (1994) 'Clinical supervision skills: a Delphi and critical incident study', *Medical Teacher* 16: 139–157.

Wilner, P. and Napier, B. (2001) 'The Statement of Equivalence: further problems and a modest proposal', *Clinical Psychology* 8: 2–3.

Wilson, R. and Keil, F. (2000) 'The shadows and shallows of explanation', in F. Keil and R. Wilson (eds) *Explanation and Cognition*, Cambridge, Mass.: MIT Press.

Working Paper 10 (1989) *Education and training: Working Paper 10*, London: HMSO.

Worthen, V. and McNeill, B. W. (1996) 'A phenomenological investigation of "good" supervision events', *Journal of Counseling Psychology* 43: 25–34.

Worthington, E. L., Jnr (1984) 'An empirical investigation of supervision of counselors gain experience', *Journal of Counseling Psychology* 31: 63–75.

Worthington, E. L., Jnr (1987) 'Changes in supervision as counselors and supervisors gain experience: a review', *Professional Psychology: Research and Practice*, 18: 189–208.

Worthington, E. L. and Roehlke, H. J. (1979) 'Effective supervision as perceived by beginning counselors-in-training', *Journal of Counseling Psychology* 26: 64–73.

Yourman, D. B. and Farber, B. A. (1996) 'Nondisclosure and distortion in psychotherapy supervision', *Psychotherapy* 33 (4): 567–575.

Yuval Davis, N. (1994) 'Women, ethnicity and empowerment', *Feminism and Psychology* 4 (1): 179–198.

Zarski, J., Sand-Pringle, C., Greenbank, M. and Cibik, P. (1991) 'The invisible mirror: in-home family therapy and supervision', *Journal of Marital and Family Therapy* 17: 133–143.

Index

abuse 149

accreditation: of clinical psychology training programmes 16, 53–5, 57, 62, 68, 73, 76, 84–5, 96, 179, 223, 225; of placements 62, 66, 71; of supervisors 10, 19–20, 74–6, 81, 85–6, 212–13, 222–3, 226

Allied Health Professions 52, 74

American Psychological Association 27

anti-oppressive practice 137

anxiety 156, 161

attachment theory 19, 45, 191

Beck Anxiety Inventory (BAI) 155

biological factors 151

boundaries *see* supervision

Bristol 189

British Association for Behavioural and Cognitive Psychotherapies (BABCP) 219

British Association for Counselling (BAC) 16

British Association for Counselling and Psychotherapy (BACP) 1–2, 16, 19, 21, 84, 212

British Psychological Society (BPS) 3, 9, 16, 52–7, 59, 63, 69, 96, 131; Committee for the Scrutiny of Individual Clinical Qualifications (CSIQ) 66; Committee on Training in Clinical Psychology (CTCP) 9, 53, 55–6, 73, 75, 84; BPS Guidelines: Expanding Clinical Psychology Training 55; Criteria for Accreditation of Postgraduate Training Programmes in Clinical Psychology 9, 76, 151, 179, 220, 225; Equal Opportunities Statement 151; Guidelines for Continuing Professional Development 4, 75, 135; BPS Options Project 54–5; National Occupational Standards 56–7, 69, 76; BPS Statement of Equivalence 65–6

CASCADE 19

clinical governance 3, 5, 11, 15, 68, 74, 88, 208

clinical psychology: chartered status 116; development of supervision in 2–5, 7–8, 52, 67–8, 110; Diploma in Clinical Psychology 187; doctoral qualification in (Clin.Psy.D.) 9–10, 72–3, 75–81, 83–6, 90–2, 100, 104, 189, 212–17, 221–3, 225; gradings 150; heads of clinical psychology services 12, 67, 98; professional development 5; trainee clinical psychologists 13, 55–6, 58, 68, 96, 213, 220, 224–5

clinical psychology training: clinical tutors 3–4, 11, 50, 54, 68, 98, 188, 212; commissioning of 54, 66 (*see also* workforce planning); competence models of training 55–8, 65, 97, 120, 182; expansion of 3, 51–2, 54–5, 58–9, 64, 69–71, 73, 91, 208, 228; training options 55–6; training programmes in 3–4, 6, 10, 12–13, 50–4, 66, 70, 96–7; training programme directors 98

cognitive analytic therapy (CAT) 201

cognitive-behaviour therapy (CBT) 26, 86, 88, 91–2, 176, 186–8, 190–1, 194–7, 201, 203, 266

Cognitive Therapy Adherence and Competence Scale (CTACS) 200

PART 1

LEADING, MANAGING AND NEW PROFESSIONAL IDENTITIES

(Continued)

and management, that of EYP is essentially that o
not inherently carry a wider management remit.

A number of key theorists and researchers, includ
United Kingdom, have contributed to our current
leadership. In particular, I discuss how the European
has helped shape that of the EYP and suggest a ne
practice', though I also consider some of the con
employment for EYPs. Equally, the challenge of mana
is noted, with the focus here on multi-professional wo
istics of leader and manager, particularly those of su
model and instigator of change. Three case studies a
offer appropriate contextualization of the theoretical

Defining leadership and management

The terms 'leadership' and 'management' are often use
within early years. This is both unhelpful and confusing
often misunderstood across a range of professional dis
cited in Rodd, 2006) offer helpful insights into the c
roles. They encourage an understanding of manager
decisions, organizes and clarifies work roles, coordinat
ally takes responsibility for monitoring its effectiven
role is to give direction, offer inspiration, build teamv
the respect and acceptance of other practitioners. F
separate leadership from management; indeed, Hall':
headteachers shows them to be simultaneously leaders
to the conclusion that 'management without leadersh
without management irresponsible' (p. 11). Whilst disc
on the roles of managers/leaders in private, voluntary
settings, I intend that there will also be some relevance
ership in early years provision within maintained schoo

Learning from research

For the past couple of decades, there has been a gro
relating to leadership and management in the early yea
bal but within the UK since 1997, it has been driven –
priority and huge financial investment of the governme
status of early years practice and provision (Moss, 2001
In developing the Effective Leadership and Mana
Moyles (2006) draws on several years of research into ea

Musgrove, 2003; Moyles et al., 2002). In the ELMS-EY, she uses the metaphor of a tree with four distinct, but commonly rooted, branches:

- leadership qualities
- management skills
- professional attributes
- personal characteristics and attitudes.

It is interesting to see leadership and management listed separately here. Leadership includes: accountability for quality, setting a culture's 'vision' and shared values; the ability to lead and manage change; and the ability to take responsibility for the needs of children, staff and families. Management skills include ensuring: effective human resource management, curriculum management and administration; effective interaction, involvement and intervention at setting, national and international levels; effective decision-making and strategic planning (adapted from Moyles, 2006: 21–4). Here, with the subtle distinction between leadership *qualities* and management *skills*, Moyles raises the age-old argument about whether leadership can be 'learned' or is a set of inherent characteristics. This is discussed later in the chapter.

Aubrey et al.'s 2005 research study (Aubrey, 2007; Aubrey et al., 2006) offers key insights into contemporary understanding of leadership practice in the early years. Drawing on participant practitioners' own reflections on their leadership and management roles, a picture emerges that highlights the diversity of roles and responsibilities across different types of setting (full day care, voluntary, foundation stage classes in schools, integrated children's centres); but what also emerges is a commonality of understanding about the significance of these. Aubrey's quest for a grounded theory model of early childhood leadership focuses on Spillane et al.'s (2001: 28) concept of 'distributed leadership'. Although originally applied to school leadership, Ebbeck and Waniganayake (2003) argued that early childhood leadership required a paradigm shift towards such a model and Aubrey's findings indicate that a shared core vision, collegial way of working and a climate of trust and openness are integral to effective early childhood leadership. With a growing emphasis on integrated provision, the concept of distributed leadership is one that has strong resonance.

Rodd's work (1997, 2006) is seminal to contemporary understanding of leadership in the early years and points to a clear correlation between effective leadership and quality childhood services (Waniganayake, 2006: xii). Her original study concluded with practitioners' identifying their need for leadership and management training and Rodd developed a typology of an early childhood leader which suggests a staged developmental process from 'novice' leader to leading through 'indirect care', each stage characterized by a set of personal traits, professional skills and roles and responsibilities. The professional skills – including pedagogical and curriculum leadership, conceptual ability (which involves critical thinking and advocacy) and interpersonal skills – are elements which Rodd believes can be developed through training.

Siraj-Blatchford and Manni's study (2007) was undertaken in response to the ongoing investment in early years leadership within the Children's Workforce and aimed to address significant questions about effective leadership of this expanded provision. Drawing on insights from wider leadership theory, they conclude that the role of leadership in early years is essentially that of 'leadership for learning' where the fundamental requirements for the role are:

- **contextual literacy** – situational leadership, engaging with the specific place, time and people she is leading
- **commitment to collaborative practice** – with effective partnerships with families and other professionals
- **commitment to the improvement of outcomes for all children** – taking a holistic view of children's development, where individual needs are identified and met (adapted from Siraj-Blatchford and Manni, 2007: 12).

The cultural context: international perspectives on leadership in early childhood settings

Although space does not allow for further expansion, I acknowledge the contribution of theories of leadership and management which, although belonging more appropriately to the worlds of finance, commerce, business and government, have nonetheless informed and shaped understanding of leadership and management roles in all organizations. Bolman and Deal's (1997) concept of 'transformational leadership' has particular resonance for early years. The transformational leader, who is seen as a 'change agent', will 'move (colleagues) towards higher and more universal needs and purposes' (p. 314).

The majority of leadership and management theories have come from North America, or are strongly influenced by its culture, thus raising the issue of possible cultural bias. There are, in fact, wide cultural variations in how people address and talk to each other, carry out and respond to different leadership styles and behaviours. Some cultures are more individualistic or value family systems as against more bureaucratic models. Chakraborty's study (2003) suggests that leadership in the East is dominantly 'feminist-intuitive' whereas in the West it is 'masculine-rational'. Other writers (such as Marshall, 1994) have explored different patterns of leadership linked to gender, with the suggestion that women develop a leadership style that is nurturing, caring and sensitive while male leadership is more often characterized by control, power, domination and competition. There is a danger of stereotyping here, for evidence indicates that the leadership styles of men and women may be influenced as much by the situation as by gender (Rodd, 2006). For example, women are more likely to be in management positions in people-oriented sectors so the nurturing style is likely to be emphasized. The theme of women in early years leadership and management is revisited later in this chapter.

The influential work of Rodd, Moyles, Aubrey and Siraj-Blatchford within the UK has been acknowledged, but all four have also gained international respect. There is limited research available internationally though I will briefly consider Muijs et al.'s

(2004) review of the available literature on early childhood leadership which offers a more comprehensive global perspective and draws together some key themes for exploration. Clear links are made between effective leadership and the quality of early childhood provision (Rodd, 1997; Sylva et al., 2004). Further, a number of studies are cited which suggest a link between effective leadership and low staff turnover which in turn relates to a higher-quality learning environment (Hayden, 1997). Studies from the Head Start Program in the United States of America (USA) indicate that competent and stable leadership is essential for the effectiveness of new programme implementation (Ramey et al., 2000).

From Hujala's (2004) study in Finland, there is convincing evidence that, within the Scandinavian context at least, early years leadership is determined by factors specific to a particular setting, ranging from the leader's perception of her role, to the way she is viewed within the community, to national legislation relating specifically to early years services. In the review of the literature carried out by Muijs et al. (2004), a strong picture emerges that leaders in early years settings have a 'multiplicity of roles which are context specific' (p. 161). Siraj-Blatchford and Manni's 2007 study concurs with this concept of 'contextual literacy'.

From the Muijs et al. review, too, interesting insights emerge from studies of the experience of leaders in New Zealand (Hatherley and Lee, 2003) and the USA (Kagan and Hallmark, 2001), which highlight 'community leadership', and show the role of the leader/manager as that of developing a community of learners and strengthening links between setting and community. This links to the concept of 'distributed leadership' (Spillane et al., 2001) considered earlier and which Ebbeck and Waniganayake (2003) suggest should be applied in early years leadership. However, they also express concern about the almost universal lack of leadership training and argue strongly that this is essential for effective 'distribution' of leadership tasks. The Muijs et al. review concludes with reference to Bloom's (2000) study which identifies three core areas of competence required by leaders and managers in early years settings, whatever the context:

- **knowledge** – including child development, pedagogical principles, group dynamics and organizational theory
- **skills** – including technical, human and conceptual skills (including budgeting)
- **attitudes** – including a sense of moral purpose and inspiring confidence and respect.

The challenges of leadership and management in integrated settings

The government in England recognizes that the quality of services for children and young people depends above all on the quality of the workforce and, 'in particular, on the quality of the leadership' (NCSL, 2007: 1). This is true of all settings, whatever their size and contexts. Social and political drivers within the UK context have resulted in a new emphasis on integrated working which involves everyone who works with children and young people. This is a central part of the Every Child Matters reforms (DfES, 2003, 2004a, 2004b, 2006a), the Children's Plan (DCSF, 2007) and Children's Workforce Strategy (CWDC, 2008a, 2009) and is aimed at ensuring that everyone involved in supporting children and young people works together effectively to 'put the child at the centre, meet their needs and improve their lives' (CWDC, 2008b: 2). Although there is historical evidence of services working together (Pugh, 2007), this multi-disciplinary/professional way of working is one that is increasingly impacting on all practitioners working with young children, but has particular implications for those leading and managing early years settings (see Chapter 6).

The development of Sure Start Children's Centres since 2004, bringing together childcare, early education, health and family-support services for families with children from birth to 5 and for parents-to-be, continues to be the cornerstone of the government's drive to tackle child poverty, social exclusion and inequalities in order that all children can flourish at home and continue to do so when they get to school. By 2010, a Children's Centre should be established in every community – about 3,500 in total across the country (DfES, 2005), with further targets for 2015. There are wide regional variations in how such centres are organized but the NPQICL was introduced alongside Children's Centre provision as a nationally recognized qualification aimed at supporting leaders in providing 'seamless high quality, integrated services for babies, children and families' (NCSL, 2007: 4). Children's Centre leaders/managers embarking on the NPQICL normally hold an honours degree and achieving it is generally considered by higher education institutions to be equivalent to approximately one-third credit for a Master's degree. Thus, it has equivalency to the National Professional Qualification for Headship in schools.

The six standards for the NPQICL (DfES, 2007) identify the knowledge, skills and attributes which are required by the Integrated Centre Leader (ICL). The standards also have application in informing job descriptions, person specifications and performance management. Usually, the job title associated with the role is 'Children's Centre Manager' although the emphasis in the NPQICL is on *leadership*. In particular, the characteristics of the Integrated Centre Leader role are:

- providing vision, direction and leadership vital to the creation of integrated services
- establishing and sustaining an environment of challenge and support for children
- leading the work of the centre to secure success, accountability and continuous improvement
- working with and through others to design and shape flexible services
- ensuring that all staff understand children's developmental needs
- collecting and using all relevant data to gain a better understanding of its local community to inform how services should be organized (adapted from DfES, 2007: 5).

Amanda is a Children's Centre manager and describes how she sees her role:

 Case study: Amanda, Children's Centre manager

Since early in my initial training as a nursery nurse, I have had an interest in young children as part of families and communities and my first post was with Social Services in a large urban local authority. I moved to a development post with a local Sure Start Project within an Early Excellence Centre, during which time I completed a Sector Endorsed Foundation Degree in Early Years and then went on to achieve the BA Hons in Childhood Studies. My own 'learning journey' was taking place as Sure Start Children's Centres were evolving and I was appointed as manager of a Phase 1 Children's Centre in an area of significant social disadvantage. This was a challenging but exciting time as the concept of integrated Children's Centre provision began to be consolidated and I was able to complete the NPQICL during this initial post which helped me to root my leadership experience in both grounded theory and in a reflective approach to the role. I then decided to take on a fresh challenge as I was appointed to manage Phase 2/3 Children's Centre provision in a large town. Initially I was a 'team of one', with actual provision only at the 'ideas' stage. Over the past two years, I have led and managed the establishment of three sites across the town and now manage a team of 13 staff, coordinating flexible multi-agency provision which includes family support and training, health visiting, midwifery services, early years provision, speech and language and various voluntary sector activities. Provision is thriving – though there are daily challenges and many critical incidents! For me, the key to being effective in the ICL role is keeping the child and family at the heart of what we do. It is important to maintain a positive outlook as so often the families we support have not engaged with 'professionals' for one reason and another. Leadership for me is about creating an ethos where all the above happens; it's about encouraging an environment where all staff sign up to a shared vision and children and families feel valued.

Amanda's approach to leadership here shows both her own commitment to learning and to the learning and development of the families she serves. Indeed, the initial review of the NPQICL (Williams, 2006) was generally very positive and highlights some excellent examples of effectiveness in ICL. However, in much Children's Centre provision there remain challenges and potential barriers to effective inter-professional communication and collaboration, including confusion about parameters of roles and responsibilities, frustration about slowness or lack of change and conflicting priorities and work practices (Anning et al., 2006). Clearly, a shared multi-professional focus on 'the child and family' is critical here.

Leadership of practice: the role of the Early Years Professional

Few of the texts on leadership and management in early childhood settings focus clearly on the role of 'leader of practice', though Siraj-Blatchford and Manni's concept of 'leadership for learning' comes close. In 2005, the role of Early Years Professional was introduced as a 'strategic leadership role ... with a set of core skills, knowledge and values' (DfES, 2006b). The emergence of the graduate EYP role is fundamental to the government's agenda to improve workforce skills, knowledge and competencies (CWDC, 2007) and particularly in leading effective practice across the Early Years Foundation Stage for children from birth to 5 (EYFS) (DCSF, 2008).

Unlike the NPQICL, EYP is a graduate 'status' and not in itself a qualification – thus having some comparability to Qualified Teacher Status. Candidates seeking validation for EYPS not only have to demonstrate that they can meet the 39 EYP Standards through their own practice but also provide evidence that they can lead and support others in these (CWDC, 2007). It is this 'leadership of practice' which is the defining aspect of the EYP role and which distinguishes it clearly from that of leader or manager of a setting. The EYP's main role is to lead and support the learning and development of the children and to lead and improve the practice of others. The challenge is that this model of leadership is one that must fit generically across all types, sizes and locations of early years settings – private, voluntary, independent and maintained (though not maintained schools).

In developing the EYP role, the CWDC acknowledges the influence of the continental European model of the 'social pedagogue' – mooted as one of the possible titles for the new role (CWDC, 2005). In countries such as Denmark and Sweden, it is social pedagogues (or, simply, 'pedagogues') who are the lead workers in pre-school settings. This is a graduate professional role, with favourable comparability in status, pay and conditions to that of teachers in schools in these countries. The role of the pedagogue has its roots in 19th-century Germany and was developed in response to what became known as the 'transmission' model of learning (Bottery, 1990), with the child as 'passive recipient' and the educator as 'active transmitter' of knowledge. Knowledge and experience of young children's learning and development – at different rates and in different ways – do not sit easily with this model and the concept of the pedagogue has evolved to emphasize the relationship of the adult with the child as a whole being – with a body, mind, emotions, creativity, history and social identity (Moss and Petrie, 2002). The pedagogue, thus, supports all aspects of the child's development equally, working individually with each child to establish positive dispositions for learning. Boddy et al. (2005) offer further insights into and understanding of the pedagogue role, describing it as one of strategic leadership, especially in managing change.

Following wide consultation, the government in England rejected the title of 'social pedagogue' for the new professional role of leading practice in favour of Early Years Professional. This writer worked with a group of newly validated EYPs to define a new paradigm of leadership which best fits the new professional status. Arguably, this emerging definition offers some parallels with the Scandinavian social pedagogue role in suggesting that the EYP demonstrates:

- a reflective and reflexive practice
- skills in decision-making
- sound knowledge and understanding of: early years pedagogy; the holistic needs of all children from birth to 5; and competence in planning, implementing and monitoring within the Early Years Foundation framework (DCSF, 2008)
- a strong sense of the intrinsic worth of each child and all those in her/his world
- the ability to role-model, lead and support others in effective practice
- the ability to define a vision for practice within a setting
- competence as an agent of change
  (Whalley, 2008: 12–13).

Claire, a newly validated Early Years Professional, offers an account of her role which exemplifies many of the above skills and traits.

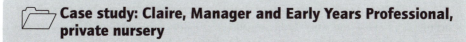

Case study: Claire, Manager and Early Years Professional, private nursery

In the past year, I have gained a BA in Childhood Studies degree *and* achieved Early Years Professional Status and I am only 26! From the age of 16 to 18, I completed a level 3 Diploma in Early Years and then explored the opportunity of completing a degree full-time. However, what I really wanted to do was begin work with young children so I worked initially as a nanny and then in day nursery provision, working my way up to posts as senior nursery nurse and then deputy manager. When I was 21, I returned to the same college where I had gained my diploma and started a Sector Endorsed Foundation Degree in Early Years. During the time I was doing the FD, not only did I acquire much more in-depth knowledge and understanding but I was also able to critically reflect on my own practice. In April 2008, I moved to a deputy manager post at a new nursery and six months later was appointed manager. I have come to realize the importance of effective leadership in early years settings and am grateful for a manager, in my early posts, who role-modelled for me an approachable but confident style of leadership where each team member felt a valuable part of the whole. I have been able to build a new team, plan and organize the learning environment, work very closely with prospective (many now actual!) parents and – most importantly for me – lead on planning a child-led approach to provision for the children, in partnership with their families. This for me is the essence of my pedagogy. I am delighted that early years is now viewed as a profession and am very proud that my achievements are now being recognized.

Claire's experience has been positive, both in terms of her own career development and in the way she is being able to carry out her role as an EYP. Other EYPs' experiences are not so positive. A key issue for many is the lack of clear infrastructure for the role. A recent survey by Aspect (2009) indicates growing discontent, particularly relating to pay and conditions. Although the government has earmarked funding for EYP training and salary increases, it is up to local authorities to decide how much is allocated to individual settings and the Aspect survey found huge funding variations between local authorities. Murray (2009) cites the situation of a pre-school leader in the voluntary sector who has not had any additional pay since achieving EYPS and feels her status is unrecognized both in the value placed on her work and in her pay. Another EYP discovered a significant difference in her salary when she moved to a post in a neighbouring local authority and learned that she had a greater entitlement there to a pay rise. Such inequalities become even more apparent in private and voluntary settings which are finding it hard to compete with salaries in maintained settings and better-paid careers elsewhere in the early years workforce (Tanuka, cited in Murray, 2009).

In introducing EYPS as a 'graduate leader' role (DfES, 2006b), the government made comparisons with the graduate role of Qualified Teacher Status (QTS). A statement from CWDC describes the two as 'both professional statuses, but ... based on a different set of skills and knowledge ... and ... not interchangeable' (CWDC, 2008c). Historically, it took some time for teaching to become firmly embedded as a graduate profession and, thus, it may be too early to ascertain longer-term outcomes for EYPS. The huge investment in training and funding for EYPs through the graduate leader fund mirrors that directed towards the teaching profession from the late 1960s. However, at the present time, few EYPs consider themselves to be recognized at the same level as qualified teachers, and terms and conditions for the vast majority of EYPs remain very poor (Alexander, cited in Murray, 2009). Anecdotally, many EYPs find that it is schools which are demonstrating a particularly unhelpful attitude to their roles. One EYP in a private setting found the teachers in her local school to be condescending about and uninterested in the EYP role.

Indeed, the EYP role itself is proving much more difficult to define than previously anticipated and, with around 4000 EYPs already in England at the time of writing (Murray, 2010), a more complex picture is emerging nationally. Whilst the role has always been intended to be contextualized to different types of settings – private, voluntary and independent (including childminders) as well as in maintained Children's Centres – the reality is that there is no consistency in the type of role the EYP has. In addition to the anticipated graduate leader role in early years settings, EYPs are employed in roles as diverse as a teaching assistant in the preparatory department of an independent school and a family outreach worker in a Children's Centre. This development can be viewed positively, as it allows the EYPs themselves to shape and establish the role in public consciousness and to 'restructure, rethink and re-envision the future workforce' (Moss, 2006: 31). However, with the challenge to establish a new professional identity, such ambiguity can also be considered unhelpful.

Within the early years workforce itself, there are a number of concerns. The pathways initially offered to EYPS assumed a significant level of experience in early years practice but, since 2008, the full pathway training route has been introduced which allows a graduate from any discipline, whether or not they have any early years experience, to undertake a full-year programme which includes some taught sessions and placements in two settings covering the birth to 5 age range. To a large extent, such a programme mirrors the full-year postgraduate certificate in initial teacher education (ITE). However, such comparisons are limited because in ITE a candidate is understood to be a 'novice' amongst highly experienced and qualified colleagues. With the full pathway route to EYPS, the candidate is often the most highly qualified academically but the *least* experienced practitioner; yet, within a relatively short space of time, is required to be leading the practice of others. Whilst there are some examples of this route being followed successfully and in the context of positive staff relationships, there are also ripples of resentment amongst many staff. Crucial here are the roles of the full pathway trainee's tutor and setting mentor and the way information is shared with staff about the training pathway. Connie describes her experience here:

 Case study: Connie, full pathway EYPS candidate

I had a degree in modern languages with business studies but became increasingly interested in early years practice and provision and when I read about the EYP full pathway programme I was immediately drawn to it. In my first placement, I was very eager to learn – which I understood to be the main purpose of the placement! However, it soon became apparent that the staff perceived my questions to them to be threatening and over-challenging. One colleague described it as 'feeling like we're being "Ofsted-ed" [a process of inspection in England] every day'. I was quite upset by this but, with the support of my tutor, we were able to re-establish a relationship and by the end of that placement, I was able to look back and believe I had both learned a great deal and contributed significantly to the setting. In fact, my mentor acknowledged that my questioning had made her think too! For me, it helped me to understand something of the complexity of change management.

Clearly, within the early years workforce, there is some way to go in developing understanding of the EYP role and the different routes to it, though, as Connie shows, such challenges need not be insurmountable.

Currently, there are wider concerns about the lack of clear infrastructures for EYPs and confusions about the role itself. Moreover, there is much uncertainty about the future of the role given the change of government in the UK and the overall sustainability of the EYP programme (Gordon-Smith, 2009). Arguably, there remains something of a gulf between the rhetoric of this 'world class transformational early years sector, with a high quality, fairly paid workforce' (Cooke and Lawton, 2008) and the reality for many EYPs. Questions are rightly being asked about how such transformation can be delivered with existing levels of spending through the current market model which dominates early years provision in the UK.

Towards a new professional understanding of early years leadership and management

At the outset of the chapter, I noted a new sense of professionalism within early years provision and practice. Historically, the early years workforce has been prima-rily female, with low pay, low status, basic qualification requirements and little or no career structure (Miller and Cable, 2008), reflecting the general position of women and young children in society. Through enhanced knowledge and under-standing of the critical importance of the first five years of a child's life, early years practitioners are becoming passionate about and empowered by their own distinc-tive contribution to children's services. In the past, there may have been some reluctance from a predominantly female workforce to embrace roles of leadership and management (Hennig and Jardim, 1976, cited in Rodd, 2006) though, arguably, this is no longer the case (McGillivray, 2008). Paradoxically, while the glass ceiling remains a barrier to aspiring women leaders in many professions, the great major-ity of EYPs and ICLs to date are women and there is a growing call to encourage more male leaders and managers in early years to counterbalance the perceived 'feminized culture' by which it is currently characterized (Early Years Stakeholder Group (EYSG), 2008).

Final thoughts

There remain anomalies and inequalities in many aspects of early years practice and provision (EYSG, 2008) which extend to differences in the way settings are led and managed. Yet, despite these, there is a groundswell of welcome for the raised status and opportunities for career development within the early years workforce. Effective leadership and management are critical to this new understanding of 'professionalism'. The government's vision remains the creation of a 'world class workforce in the early years to improve outcomes for children' (CWDC, 2007: 4) through developing a trained bank of graduate workers whose knowledge and competences will be key to effective leadership of integrated services and of EYFS provision. The roles of ICL and EYP are distinct but complementary within this vision. However, there are significant challenges to this vision becoming reality.

Summary

- A number of influential contemporary writers and studies have significantly informed our understanding of issues relating to leadership and management in the early years.
- Insights from international perspectives on leadership of early childhood services identify some common global themes and the need for cultural perspectives on leadership to be taken into account.
- Two specific roles of Integrated Children's Centre leader and Early Years Professional have emerged which are seen to be key to transforming early years provision and practice.

 Questions for discussion

In the context of contemporary early years provision and practice:

1. How important is it to make distinctions between 'leadership' and 'management'? What are the main responsibilities within each role?
2. How has the European model of 'social pedagogue' shaped and informed the role of Early Years Professional?
3. What are the key issues for the early years workforce in establishing the EYP role?
4. What are the challenges of developing 'distributed leadership' practices, particularly within integrated service provision? *(Higher level question)*

Further reading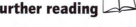

Levels 5 and 6

Boardman, M. (2003) 'Changing times: changing challenges for early childhood leaders', *Australian Journal of Early Childhood*, 28(2): 20–5. Available from: http://eprints.utas.edu.au/1829/

Rodd, J. (2006) *Leadership in Early Childhood.* Maidenhead: Open University Press.
Drawing both on her own role in leadership and her earlier research, Jillian Rodd offers a very useful discourse on the early childhood leader in practice. Particularly useful are the first-person accounts from a range of practitioners.

Whalley, M.E. (2008) *Leading Practice in Early Years Settings.* Exeter: Learning Matters.
The writer here focuses particularly on the role of Early Years Professional in leading practice and being an agent of change. Case study examples, reflective tasks and self-assessment exercises support individual reflection on the leadership role.

Levels 6 and 7

Aubrey, C. (2007) *Leading and Managing in the Early Years.* London: Sage.
Offering a detailed report of the study she led with colleagues, Carol Aubrey investigates many different models of early childhood leadership and raises significant implications for leadership preparation and continuing professional development.

Cooke, G. and Lawton, K. (2008) *For Love or Money: Pay, Progression and Professionalism in the 'Early Years' Workforce.* London: Institute for Public Policy Research.
A helpful analysis of the inequalities in early years provision for children and families and on the low status, pay and conditions of early years practitioners. Recommendations are based on addressing the correlation of these.

Websites

www.cwdcouncil.org.uk/early-years
Provides detailed information on the role of the Early Years Professional including the training, preparation and assessment processes.

http://nationalstrategies.standards.dcsf.gov.uk/earlyyears
Lists resources and publications relating to early years provision and practice – both statutory and guidance – issued by the government in the UK. Many of these are downloadable.

http://onechildrensworkforce.cwdcouncil.org.uk/about
This website provides information about the development of a tool to help Children's Trusts in England to develop a more effective integrated children's workforce.

www.teachernet.gov.uk/management/atoz/e/earlyyearsandchildcare/
On this website, you will find up-to-date information relating to key legislation and other initiatives relating to early years provision and practice in England.

References

Anning, A., Cottrell, D., Frost, N., Green, J. and Robinson, N. (2006) *Developing Multiprofessional Teamwork for Integrated Children's Services.* Maidenhead: Open University Press.
Aspect (2009) *In Their Own Words: EYPs Speak Out (Aspect's EYP Survey, 2009).* London: Aspect. Available from: www.aspect.org.uk/eyp/wp-content/uploads/2009/04/eyp-p-survey-report.pdf (accessed 12 December 2009).
Aubrey, C. (2007) *Leading and Managing in the Early Years.* London: Sage.
Aubrey, C., Godfrey, R., Harris, A. and Dahl, S. (2006) 'How do they manage? An investigation of early childhood leadership', Symposium at British Educational Research Association Conference, University of Warwick, 9 September.
Bloom, P.J. (2000) 'How do we define director competence?', *Childcare Information Exchange,* 138: 13–18.
Boddy, J., Cameron, C., Moss, P., Mooney, A., Petrie, P. and Statham, J. (2005) *Introducing Pedagogy into the Children's Workforce: Children's Workforce Strategy – A Response to the Consultation.* London: Thomas Coram Research Unit/Institute of Education, University of London.

Bolman, L.G. and Deal, T.E. (1997) *Reframing Organisations: Artistry, Choice and Leadership*, 2nd edn. San Francisco, CA: Jossey-Bass.

Bottery, M. (1990) *The Morality of the School*. London: Cassell.

Chakraborty, D. (2003) 'Leadership in the East and West: a few examples', *Journal of Human Values*, 9: 29–52.

Children's Workforce Development Council (CWDC) (2005) *Children's Workforce Strategy: A Consultation*. Leeds: CWDC.

CWDC (2007) *Early Years Professional Status: Handbook*. Leeds: CWDC.

CWDC (2008a) *One Children's Workforce – A Journey to the End of the Rainbow*. Available from: www.cwdcouncil.org.uk?whats-new/news/1126 (accessed 14 May 2009).

CWDC (2008b) *Integrated Working Explained*. Leeds: CWDC.

CWDC (2008c) *EYPS: Frequently Asked Questions*. Available from: www.cwdcouncil.org.uk/about/faq#Q_425 (accessed 18 November 2009).

CWDC (2009) *One Children's Workforce Tool*. Available from: http://onechildrensworkforce.cwdcouncil.org.uk/about (accessed 22 July 2009).

Cooke, G. and Lawton, K. (2008) *For Love or Money: Pay, Progression and Professionalism in the 'Early Years' Workforce*. London: Institute for Public Policy Research.

Department for Children, Schools and Families (DCSF) (2007) *The Children's Plan: Building Brighter Futures*. Nottingham: DCSF.

DCSF (2008) *The Early Years Foundation Stage*. Nottingham: DCSF.

Department for Education and Skills (DfES) (2003) *Green Paper: Every Child Matters*. Nottingham: DfES.

DfES (2004a) *Every Child Matters: The Next Steps*. Nottingham: DfES.

DfES (2004b) *Every Child Matters: Change for Children*. Nottingham: DfES.

DfES (2005) *A Sure Start Children's Centre for Every Community: Planning Guidance*. Available from: www.dcsf.gov.uk/everychildmatters/earlyyears/surestartchildrenscentres/childrenscentres (accessed 12 August 2009).

DfES (2006a) *Championing Children: A Shared Set of Knowledge Skills, Knowledge and Behaviours for Those Leading and Managing Integrated Children's Services*. Nottingham: DfES.

DfES (2006b) *Children's Workforce Strategy: The Government's Response to the Consultation*. Nottingham: DfES.

DfES (2007) *National Standards for Leaders of Children's Centres*. Nottingham: DfES.

Early Years Stakeholder Group (EYSG) (2008) *Report to the Children's Minister*. Available from: www.teachernet.gov.uk/_.../Early_Years_Stakeholder_Report_FINAL2.doc (accessed 12 July 2009).

Ebbeck, M. and Waniganayake, M. (2003) *Early Childhood Professionals: Leading Today and Tomorrow*. Sydney: Maclennan and Petty Ltd.

Gordon-Smith, P. (2009) 'Analysis: Conservative Party policy – time for the sector to talk to the Tories', *Nursery World*, 21 January. Available from: www.nurseryworld.co.uk/.../Analysis-Conservative-Party-Policy-Time-sector-talk-Tories/ (accessed 26 November 2009).

Hall, V. (1996) *Dancing on the Ceiling*. London: Paul Chapman.

Hatherley, A. and Lee, W. (2003) 'Voices of early childhood leadership', *New Zealand Journal of Educational Leadership*, 18: 91–100.

Hayden, J. (1997) 'Directors of early childhood services: experience, preparedness and selection', *Australian Research in Early Childhood*, 1(1): 49–67.

Hennig, M. and Jardim, A. (1976) *The Managerial Woman: The Survival Manual for Women in Business*. New York: Pocket Books.

Hujala, E. (2004) 'Dimensions of leadership in the childcare context', *Scandinavian Journal of Educational Research*, 48(1): 53–71.

Kagan, S.L. and Hallmark, L.G. (2001) 'Cultivating leadership in early care and education', *Child Care Information Exchange*, 140: 7–10.

Law, S. and Glover, D. (2000) *Educational Leadership and Learning: Practice, Policy and Research*. Buckingham: Open University Press.

Leithwood, K. and Levin, B. (2004) 'Approaches to the Evaluation of Leadership Programs and Leadership Effects', paper presented to the DfES, March.

Marshall, J. (1994) 'Revolutionising organisations by developing female values', in J. Boot, J. Lawrence and J. Morris (eds) *Managing the Unknown by Creating New Futures*. London: McGraw-Hill.

McGillivray, G. (2008) 'Nannies, nursery nurses and early years professionals: professional identity in the Early Years workforce', *European Early Childhood Research Journal*, 16(2): 242–54.

Miller, L. and Cable, C. (2008) *Professionalism in the Early Years*. London: Hodder Arnold.

Moss, P. (2001) 'New Labour's record: end of term report', *Nursery World*, 3 January. Available from: www.nurseryworld.co.uk/news/727177/New-Labours-record-End-term-report (accessed 19 July 2009).

Moss, P. (2006) 'Structures, understandings and discourses: possibilities for re-envisioning the early childhood worker', *Contemporary Issues in Early Childhood*, 7(1): 31–41.

Moss, P. and Petrie, P. (2002) *From Children's Services to Children's Spaces*. London: Taylor and Francis.

Moyles, J. (2006) *Effective Leadership and Management in the Early Years*. Maidenhead: Open University Press.

Moyles, J. and Musgrove, A. (2003) *EEPES (EY) Essex Effective Pedagogy Evaluation Scheme (Early Years)*. Chelmsford: APU/Essex County Council.

Moyles, J., Adams, S. and Musgrove, A. (2002) *SPEEL: Study of Pedagogical Effectiveness in Early Learning*, Report No. 363. London: DfES.

Muijs, D., Aubrey, C., Harris, A. and Briggs, M. (2004) 'How do they manage? A review of the research in early childhood', *Journal of Early Childhood Research*, 2: 157–69. Available from: http://sagepub.com/cgi/content/abstract/2/2/157 (accessed 21 June 2009).

Murray, J. (2009) 'The poor professionals', *Education Guardian*, 28 April.

Murray, J. (2010) 'Shaping the future: caring and learning are inextricably linked', *Society Guardian*, in association with the Children's Workforce Development Council, 17 February.

National College for School Leadership (NCSL) (2007) *Guidance to the Standards for Leaders of Sure Start Children's Centres*. Nottingham: NCSL.

Pugh, G. (2007) 'Foreword', in I. Siraj-Blatchford, K. Clarke and M. Needham (eds) *The Team Around the Child: Multi-agency Working in the Early Years*. Stoke-on-Trent: Trentham Books.

Ramey, S.L., Ramey, C.T., Philips, M.M., Lanzi, R.G., Brezausek, C., Katholi, C.R., Snyders, S.A and Lawrence, F.L. (2000) *Head Start Children's Entry into Public School: A Report on the National Head Start/Public School Early Childhood Transition Study*. Birmingham, AL: Curtan International Research Centre.

Rodd, J. (1997) 'Learning to be leaders: perceptions of early childhood professionals about leadership roles and responsibilities', *Early Years*, 18(1): 40–6.

Rodd, J. (2006) *Leadership in Early Childhood*, 3rd edn. Maidenhead: Open University Press.

Siraj-Blatchford, I. and Manni, L. (2007) *Effective Leadership in the Early Years Sector: The ELEYS Study*. London: Institute of Education, University of London.

Spillane, J., Halverson, R. and Diamond, J.B. (2001) 'Investigating school leadership practice: a distributed perspective', *Educational Researcher*, 30(3): 23–8.

Sylva, K., Melhuish, E.C., Sammons, P., Siraj-Blatchford, I. and Taggart, B. (2004) *The Effective Provision of Pre-School Education (EPPE) Project: Final Report*. London: DfEE/Institute of Education, University of London.

Waniganayake, M. (2006) 'Foreword', in J. Rodd *Leadership in Early Childhood*, 3rd edn. Maidenhead: Open University Press.

Whalley, M.E. (2008) *Leading Practice in Early Years Settings*. Exeter: Learning Matters.

Williams, S. (2006) *Evaluation of the NPQICL Rollout Programme*. Henley-on-Thames: Henley Management College. Available from: www.ncsl.org.uk/media-fd5-c3-final-evaluation-npqicl.pdf (accessed 25 June 2009).

CHAPTER 3

CHALLENGING IDENTITIES
A Case for Leadership

Christine Woodrow

Overview

This chapter traces some emerging and dominant policy trends in early childhood provision to consider their impact on discourses of professionalism and implications for professional identity and leadership in the field. Using the concept of a 'case' as an instance of a policy intervention or outcome, the chapter documents three 'cases' of recent policy directions or policy outcome in Australia. Each case includes a description, some analysis and discussion of implications for professional identity. Across the cases, the potential impact of increasing market-based approaches to early childhood provision, intensification of regulation and accountability, and contradictions within the Australian early childhood reform agenda are canvassed. These discussions are informed by Australian research involving document and policy analysis, surveys and interviews with early childhood teachers, and personal experience as a policy actor and participant in the development of a new national curriculum framework for early childhood education in Australia. The chapter concludes with a discussion of the implications for leadership and the possibilities for new resources for leadership in the intersections of emerging discourses of professionalism and traditional and established understandings of professionalism in these new and ever-changing contexts.

Introduction

Across the OECD countries, and beyond, early childhood provision has become sub-ject to fervent policy attention in recent times. Research findings from within and across fields as diverse as psychiatry, economics, education, neuro-psychology and epidemiology have contributed to the establishment of an evidence-based argument which many governments and policy-makers have found compelling. A significant cross-national study of early childhood policy within and across the OECD has also been a significant catalyst for action (OECD, 2001, 2006). This increasing recognition of the economic and social importance of 'investing' in early childhood and the result-ing policy responses have contributed to a rapidly changing socio-political context in which early childhood professionals understand and undertake their work. For exam-ple, a 'market-based' approach to childcare provision rapidly emerged to dominate the Australian policy landscape culminating in over 25% of childcare provision being in the hands of one single for-profit, publicly listed corporation, ABC Learning. At its peak, ABC Learning employed 17,000 people and was responsible for the care and education of over 100,000 young children in Australia. The subsequent collapse of that company exposed some problematic aspects of policies reliant on a market model to meet social policy objectives (Brennan, 2007), but other, perhaps more subtle impacts of such a trend have remained relatively hidden from view (Press and Woodrow, 2009). For example, questions arise about the impact of such develop-ments on the professional practices of educators and discourses of professionalism within the field of early childhood. How might the statutory obligation of returning profit to shareholders mediate the relationships between staff, children and parents and what forms of professional identity might be produced, privileged or suppressed in corporate culture?

Similarly, questions emerge about the resilience of traditional forms of early child-hood professional identity and their appropriateness in contemporary contexts for resourcing leadership in the field when many of the emerging discourses of early childhood provision include narratives of human capital formation, child rescue and salvation, and economic prosperity (Dahlberg and Moss, 2008; Prentice, 2009), and where emerging policy trends foreground integrated service provision and inter-disciplinarity (Siraj-Blatchford et al., 2007).

Gaining a better understanding of discourses of professional identities and their role in resourcing leadership in the field of early childhood becomes particularly sig-nificant in the context of this new policy environment, in which there is a pressing need to expand and up-skill the early childhood workforce. Typically, the policy envi-ronment is characterized by an expectation of rapid change, swift achievement of policy objectives and political imperatives in the short-term – as is undoubtedly the case in countries like Australia and England. Experience tends to suggest that policy trajectories are often underpinned by simplistic assumptions about the inputs required to mobilize change without an appreciation of the complexities of human agency, the role of field-based leadership and the relationship between existing pro-fessional discourses and the new conditions created by policy initiatives. Some research highlights how teacher identity influences not only how teachers 'teach' but also their development as professionals and how they approach change (Nias, 1989; Ortlipp, 2009). Other research on teacher identity exposes conflicts between societal expectations and what teachers desire and experience as good teaching (Beijaard et al., 2004; Korthagen, 2004). Clearly, teacher professional identity emerges as a key consideration in any change agenda for early childhood provision. Current national and international policy trajectories indicate a need for new, expanded and multiple professional identities to implement and sustain a change agenda (Sumsion, 2006, 2007a), and although the political interest in early childhood provision is welcome, its advent significantly reconfigures the policy landscape and expands the range of policy actors, producing a more complex socio-political environment in which the desired change is to occur. It is thus timely to consider how policy discourses and their inter-sections might constrain, affirm or expand understandings of professionalism and the perspectives on professional identity.

Case study 1: a market-based model of early childhood provision

The recent international experience of the rapid and aggressive expansion of the Australian-based company ABC Learning as a global provider of early child-hood care and education has demonstrated just how readily the private, for-profit sector can respond to favourable policy conditions to meet demand for the provision of human services. Such responsiveness contributes to rendering market-based solutions to social policy objectives very palatable to many governments as they attempt to address a burgeoning need for childcare (Brennan, 2007). At the peak of its expansion activities, the ABC Learning 'family' were involved in the provision of early childhood services across the world, in countries that included Australia, USA, UK, Indonesia, Hong Kong, The Philippines, China and New Zealand (Sumsion, 2007b), making ABC Learning the second largest provider of childcare in the USA and the largest listed childcare company in the world (Brennan, 2007). Its dominance of the Australian childcare landscape led one social policy researcher to observe that through allowing the rapid expansion of one company to dominate the 'market', Australia effectively 'embarked on a vast national experiment' (Brennan, 2007). Whilst the subsequent spectacular fall of ABC Learning has drawn international attention to issues of possible market failure, corporate governance and fiscal impropriety, there has been little serious examination in the wake of the company's collapse of the endemic risks in the market model and the broader implications and impact of corporate provision.

(Continued)

(Continued)

As some countries continue to pursue market approaches to early childhood, including Canada, England and the Netherlands (Lloyd, 2009), and the extensive vertical and horizontal integration business practices in the ABC Learning company continue to reputedly be used as an exemplar of an effective business model in Business Studies courses, it continues to be significant to explore questions relating to the impact of corporate provision on the early childhood field itself. Relevant issues include the possible impact on quality of provision, staff conditions, professionalism and discourses of professional identity that may emerge, be privileged, constrained or suppressed. Of particular interest in a discussion of professionalism in early childhood are the ways enterprise culture might be privileged in corporate childcare and how this might influence professional practices and shape professional identity.

Whilst the following analysis highlights issues identified though researching the Australian experience of corporate childcare in which, because of its dominance, ABC Learning and corporate childcare were almost synonymous, the insights possible from existing research provide a signpost to possible issues of concern in other contexts.

An Australian study exploring the possible impact of corporate provision on quality (Rush, 2006) revealed that on some well-established indicators of quality at least, there were significant differences between centres operated by corporate chains and other categories of provision. For example, in her study Rush found only 25% of staff working in corporate chains believed that they had time enough to form relationships with children, compared to 54% of staff in community-based centres and 49% in independent private centres (Rush, 2006: 30). Equally significant was how staff responded to a survey/interview question asking if they would be happy to enrol their own child in the centre in which they worked, or one of similar quality. Twenty-one per cent of staff working in corporate childcare indicated they would not be happy to do so, compared with only 4% of staff in community-based centres and 6% of staff working in private, independent centres. This suggested a high level of discomfort with the standard of corporate care by employees working in these contexts. The findings regarding adequate time for relationships is particularly pertinent in a context where relationships and relationality are such strong discourses in early childhood professionalism (Dahlberg and Moss, 2005). It is reasonable to conclude from the study findings that there was some basis for concern about the constraints on quality practice and, by extension, a tension between desired modes of professional practice and identity and a perceived reality within corporate childcare. The study was relatively small in scale and clearly such links warrant further investigation.

(Continued)

(Continued)

Another Australian study involved the tracing and cross-referencing of an extensive range of documents relating to the ABC Learning 'family' of companies and enabled the researchers to discern and disentangle a complex web of corporate relationships, leading them to conclude that aspects of children's learning and experiences, family relationships and professional identity were indeed mediated through commercial relationships and a commodified curriculum (Press and Woodrow, 2009). This study was undertaken at a time when ABC Learning was near its peak and provided approximately 25% of government subsidized childcare places across Australia, catering for more than 100,000 children. The study revealed, for example, how the in-house 'Life-Smart' curriculum, centre furniture, toys and annual photographic services for children and families were supplied by companies in which the parent ABC Learning company had a financial relationship through the mechanisms of vertical and horizontal integration, either as wholly owned or subsidiary companies (Press and Woodrow, 2009; Woodrow, 2008), although this was not transparent and almost certainly not known by most parents. It became evident through this study that 'many aspects of the daily curriculum that children experience, and that early childhood professionals implemented (were) mediated through corporate relationships designed to maximize shareholder profit' (Woodrow, 2008: 272). Similarly, the research revealed a number of features of the companies' operations which had the potential to significantly shape professional discourse and perspectives on professional identity. For example, the National Institute of Early Childhood Education (NIECE), a wholly owned company of ABC Learning which through its status as Registered Training Organization (RTO) was able to provide training up to Diploma level, quickly grew to become the main vehicle for staff training, thus becoming an effective mechanism for 'authorizing' the dispositions, attributes or capacities which early childhood professionals should have. This was not insignificant given the company's dominance of the market and the size of its workforce (17,000 at the time of the study). When combined with typical branding practices (logos and staff uniforms), exuberant marketing ('Our spirit of fun runs as deep as our spirit of competition') and a staff loyalty scheme involving an employee share plan, questions arise as to how and whether a collective identification with the company might become stronger for employees than identification with the profession and its values. The analysis surfaced issues about how corporate childcare might promote material concerns about shareholder profits being placed over concerns about values and issues such as equity in the curriculum, resulting in a possible advancement of privatized concerns over a communal discourse, and considerations of how a 'culture of production and profit ' (Ball, 1994) might replace discourses of community, traditionally more

(Continued)

(Continued)

prominent in the discourses of the early childhood profession (Press and Woodrow, 2009).

The study findings raise questions about how normalized practices of corporate culture as they are exhibited in these emerging 'corporatized' early childhood contexts might promote discourses of private benefit, competition, individualism and entrepreneurship and how these might intersect with, or over-ride, values of caring, collectivism and collegiality that appear emblematic of early childhood professional identity, where they are clearly expressed through such artefacts as state curriculum statements, codes of ethics and research accounts of teachers' work. The elements of marketization in corporate childcare illuminated by the study clearly reflected characterizations of 'the entrepreneurial professional' and enterprise culture evident in the research literature (McWilliam et al., 1999).

Whilst the evidence at this point about the impact of corporate provision on professional discourse is indicative rather than conclusive, the issues of poorer quality and reduced time for relationships which were raised by the Rush study, and the evidence assembled in the analysis by Press and Woodrow (2009), were reflected in yet another small 'case' study (Ortlipp and Woodrow, 2008). The research found that former employees of corporate providers of childcare interviewed for the study highlighted issues of inadequate resourcing, limited professional development opportunities that were primarily linked to statutory requirements (first-aid, occupational health and safety, etc.) and minimal staffing levels and that these were often influential in their decision to leave their employment. Clearly, larger-scale research about corporate provision is urgently required to further investigate the issues that the current studies have surfaced. As this chapter was being written, a new variation on corporate provision emerged in the Australian landscape under the banner of 'Good Start': an alliance of four Australian-based charity organizations that had purchased 678 childcare centres with a view to running good quality childcare services that also operate at a profit (www.missionaustralia.com.au/news/media-releases, accessed 17 January 2010), suggesting that strategies for early years provision will continue to be complex and diversify.

 Case study 2: a national early childhood policy agenda

The election of a new government in 2007 signalled a new era for early childhood policy at a national level in Australia. A 'new agenda' (ALP, 2007; Rudd and Macklin, 2007), widely promoted during the election campaign, and

(Continued)

(Continued)

comprehensive in its scope, foreshadowed significant new initiatives, including national standards, attention to workforce issues, universal pre-school access in the year before formal schooling, and the articulation of a 'quality' policy discourse, reflecting international trends (Dahlberg and Moss, 2008). For early childhood to have such a high political profile supported by a well articulated 'agenda' at the national level was unusual in the Australian context. The subsequent election of the Rudd government has been followed by a period of fervent policy activity, involving new forms of inter-government co-operation and culminating in mid-2009 in the release of a comprehensive framework for national policy and strategic initiatives in early childhood across the country. As the agenda of the new government has unfolded, implications for the field of such a wide-ranging policy agenda have begun to emerge. A comprehensive analysis of the framework, now known as *Investing in the Early Years – A National Early Childhood Development Strategy* (DEEWR, 2009), is beyond the scope of this chapter. However, there are a number of emerging issues relevant to any discussion of early childhood professionalism, professional identity and leadership. For example, some analyses have highlighted the 'scientific discourse' focused on brain research and the appeals to medicine-based authority that have dominated the public policy announcements (Bown et al., 2008; MacNaughton, 2004), raising questions about the diminishing importance attached to alternative rationales for policy action (children's rights or social change, for example). Similarly, a human capital discourse is frequently deployed to sustain arguments about the importance of 'investing' in early childhood, with the two key concerns of this discourse being: (1) ensuring workplace participation of women; and (2) the economic returns from investing/intervening early in young children's lives to prevent later possible learning and social difficulties and thus ensuring the development of a 'productive' citizenry. These readings of the dominant discourses argue that these trends privilege health perspectives and economic knowledge over an educational discourse, with likely effects of marginalizing and diminishing the knowledge claims of a field that is both highly feminized, and suffers from low status and poor working conditions, also leading to what has been described as a pervasive 'pedagogical silence' in Australian early childhood social policy (Cheeseman, 2007). Further, reflecting the often paradoxical nature of policy development (Bown et al., 2008), these concerns intersect with a 'quality' discourse about raising the quality of provision through enhanced, university-level teacher qualifications to highlight issues associated with the extensive shortfall in suitably qualified people. On the one hand, the broad policy trajectory might contain the potential to influence public perceptions about the professional nature of early childhood work and contribute to raising the status of

(Continued)

(Continued)

this work. However, on the other hand, the policy-based strategies developed to increase the qualified workforce by expanding funded university places and offering fee rebates to graduates taking up employment in certain specified locations has not been matched or supported by strategies to increase pay and conditions of early childhood personnel. The issues of status, pay and conditions have been publicly recognized by the government (Rudd and Macklin, 2007). In a recent speech to a well-informed audience, the Minister of Education, Employment and Workplace Relations, Ms Julia Gillard referred to raising the status of the early years workforce as a 'critical' issue, identifying staff training, development and retention as the key components of developing a national professional early years workforce and calling all stakeholders to address these issues whilst omitting any further reference to pay and conditions as an issue of equal importance (Gillard, 2008).

It is not hard to see how current and potential early childhood educators may perceive mixed and contradictory messages about the status of early childhood work and be reluctant to embrace participation in the prior-to-schooling early childhood workforce. Thus, in the absence of substantive action on salary and conditions, and in the context of ongoing mixed messages about the position of early childhood in a perceived knowledge hierarchy, ongoing staff shortages, now well documented in the Australian context (Sumsion, 2007a) have little prospect of abating. Similarly, such contradictory messages do little to interrupt common misconceptions about work in early childhood contexts as intellectual work that is of equal importance and status to that of teaching in school settings: issues that are again taken up in the third case described in this chapter.

The development and production of Australia's first national framework for curriculum and pedagogy in early childhood settings: Belonging, Being and Becoming: The Early Years Learning Framework for Australia (EYLF), launched in July 2009 for immediate implementation, has been another significant early outcome from the new government's agenda. The development of this framework was perceived by many to present a unique opportunity for the creation of new discourses of early childhood, rich with 'transformational possibilities' (Sumsion et al., 2009) and the articulation of a vision for the role of early childhood education in promoting social inclusion and equity. The compressed timeframe for its development (nine months compared to the six years of development for the New Zealand early childhood curriculum Te Whāriki) and the political compromises necessary to achieve quick consensus from the many stakeholders, have undoubtedly truncated the opportunities for dialogue about what matters in early years education, and limited the conceptual space for the creation of new discourses of early years education and the work of those undertaking its leadership.

(Continued)

(Continued)

The account by Sumsion et al. (2009) of some of the necessary compromises by the development team and the kinds of challenges to, and erasures from, early versions of the EYLF by risk-averse political gatekeepers provide sobering reading and salutary lessons about the political and contested nature of the curriculum. They also provide telling insights into the significant challenges that must be overcome if the field is to advance robust new images of professional identity and early childhood leadership. For example, the reported institutional resistance to the use of the term 'pedagogy', explicitly chosen by the writers to communicate complex ideas involving the centrality of relationships and the importance of intentionality in teaching in early childhood contexts where this is not always visible, together with erasure of reference to power relationships in play, could be read as maintaining the hegemony of childhood innocence and developmental frameworks. These frameworks have not been seen to be empowering to the profession in recent times and a robust critique exists to highlight their dangers in reinforcing the care and nurturing dimension and minimizing the intellectual character of early childhood work. Thus conflicting images of the early childhood professional have emerged during the implementation of the government's 'new agenda', that both constrain and expand possibilities for strengthening professional identities within the field. It is at least encouraging to see politicians locating early childhood provision within a 'professional' discourse. Arguably, the activation of strong and effective field-based leadership will play a significant role in how these opportunities and challenges ultimately play out. As Osgood (2006), Miller (2008) and others have suggested, early years educators can 'harness their own agency' (2008: 260) and exert power over their professional identity and positioning to resist the disempowering potentials inherent in many of the policy discourses.

 Case study 3: regulation of teacher knowledges and performance

As 'quality' discourses have intensified over the last decade, numerous agencies, structures, policies and protocols have been created to assure teacher 'quality' and regulate teacher education. Regulating for teacher quality is a policy arena in which early childhood's uneasy and ambiguous positioning 'between the conceptual and jurisdictional framework of education, health and social welfare' (Press, 2007: 192) has been problematic in perpetuating the care–education dichotomy, and disruptive to the broader project of improved recognition of the pedagogical dimensions and professional status of working in early childhood contexts.

(Continued)

(Continued)

In Australia, the treatment of specialist early childhood teachers within these regulatory emerging frameworks has been inconsistent, leading to widespread ambiguity about the place of early childhood within an educational discourse and an education system. For example, in some jurisdictions, the regulatory bodies, variously known as 'Institutes' (New South Wales) or 'Colleges of Teaching' (Queensland) have developed standards for teachers and content requirements for teacher education courses that promote generic school-based teacher identities and either exclude qualified teachers working in the prior-to-school sector, or leave little space for the 'threshold' knowledges typically associated with early childhood, including, for example, childhood and family studies. In some cases, accrediting of early childhood courses has been relocated in welfare and community service portfolios. I have argued elsewhere that these policies and practices continue to privilege and promote narrow and outdated constructions of teacher identity as deriving only from the compulsory schooling sector, thereby relegating early childhood teaching to the margins of educational legitimacy (Woodrow, 2007, 2008). It is perhaps ironic that these trends are intensifying in Australia at a time when a flourishing of robust early childhood professional identities might otherwise be expected from the current policy trajectories, evident, for example, in the legislative requirements for some jurisdictions for the employment of early childhood teachers in non-school early childhood settings, and a 'workforce reform' agenda promoting university-level teacher preparation for early childhood professionals, as previously described. Further momentum might also be expected from the strengthening of international research studies implicating the significance of high-level qualifications in quality early childhood provision and outcomes for children's development and learning (Bueno et al., 2010), and the development of curricular frameworks for the early childhood sector.

In contrast to the frequent subordination of early childhood interests to those of the schooling sector, extensive advocacy efforts within the early childhood sector have been successful in gaining the support of the Australian Institute for Teaching and School Leadership (AITSL) in developing specialized advanced teaching standards for early childhood teachers working across the 3–8 years age range. The institute is a recently established national statutory authority responsible for 'promoting excellence in the profession of teaching' (www.aitsl. edu.au/ta/go, accessed 20 March 2010). The development of these standards has been seen as '... aspirational, grounded in a deep knowledge of teaching', and there are expectations that: '... they will contribute to building a stronger early childhood profession [and] be a powerful tool for increasing public recognition and increasing the status of the early childhood profession' (Early Childhood Australia, 2009).

(Continued)

(Continued)

Whilst the process of development of standards for early childhood teachers in advance of the development of national professional standards for teachers in schools might be viewed positively as a strategic opportunity, the relationship between the two sets of standards being developed and their implications for enforcement is not yet clear. Since both sets have a brief to cover teachers of children between 5 and 8 years in school settings, this is another example of the discontinuities and ambiguities in desired and/or officially sanctioned professional identities and how these are perpetuated institutionally. My more recent experiences of involvement in the development of the national Early Years Learning Framework and experience and readings of the state-based regulatory institutions suggest that the often narrowly conceived perspective of the schooling sector will almost always prevail when dissonance exists, reflecting seemingly intractable traditional hierarchies of knowledge and status, even within the teaching profession.

Early childhood identity discourses

Of course, all kinds of meanings can be attached to the nomenclature 'teacher' and the discourses that its use might produce, reflect and perpetuate. One implication of the above discussion is that teacher identity discourses are appropriate to the complex work of early childhood professionals. Undoubtedly, there is a widespread perspective that the designation 'teacher' invokes desirable images and discourses relevant to the early childhood context. Whilst this view is not universally shared either in Australia or internationally, it reflects current positive trends in the Australian policy landscape to raise the qualification requirements of those working with young children by locating these requirements within frameworks of teaching, even though counter-flows within the policies and practices of teacher regulation institutions might be seen as obstructive. In the Australian context at least, associating early childhood work with 'teacher identities' has been seen as important in raising the status of early childhood professionals and gaining improved pay and conditions for those working in non-school early childhood contexts (Burton and Lyons, 2000). A further imperative for privileging 'teacher' identities is the possibility it offers to more robustly locate early childhood conceptually as a pedagogical space (Cheeseman, 2007; Woodrow, 2007). However, the fields of knowledge on which early childhood policy and practice draw are diverse and include those of health and community welfare development, as well as education, and many of the current trajectories call for the integration of service provision across traditional discipline boundaries. In the current climate of teacher accountability and regulation of teacher education, there may well be risks of too narrow an understanding of pedagogy and teaching deriving from a regulation-focused schooling perspective associated with drawing exclusively on discourses of 'teaching'. Internationally, diverse traditions and historical antecedents have led to different trajectories for early childhood professional identity and associated nomenclature. For example, the terms 'pedagogue' and 'social pedagogue' have been adopted with some success in Europe to communicate the relationship focus of early childhood work and the interdependence of care and education (Oberhuemer, 2005). The extent to which the creation of 'Senior Practitioner' and 'Early Years Professional' roles in England have been similarly successful in capturing and communicating the complexity of this work, and in so doing strengthening early childhood professional identities, remains a matter of debate requiring further research (Miller, 2008).

Strengthening leadership identities: some provocations

This chapter has provided a snapshot of some emerging policy trajectories in the rapidly changing landscape of early childhood provision in Australia. The ensuing discussion has identified some possible implications for early childhood professional identity arising from these circumstances and indicated aspects that might be problematic in building multiple, expanded and robust professional identities across the field. There are a number of reasons why such a discussion might be of international significance. These include widespread concerns about the way technicist discourses and regulatory approaches to quality concerns provide limited frames within which to construct the early childhood project (Dahlberg and Moss, 2005; Moss, 2007). These limitations also potentially constrain related discourses and practices including the expectations and understandings of the role of the professional, the kind of professional preparation implied and the status and positioning of the work. The Australian experience provides one southern hemisphere perspective on the impact of regulatory trends on shared concerns about early childhood professionalism, and in this case the emergence of an exclusionary discourse related to 'teacher' identities in which early childhood discourses are constructed as subordinate, and by implication, lesser than, those of school-based teachers through institutional structures and accountability requirements. Further points of international interest include the recent national experience of codifying early years curriculum in a context where pressure for such codification is intensifying internationally. Finally, and of significant international interest, is the Australian experience of childcare provision dominated by large corporations in which the imperatives to operate for profit and the taken-for-granted commercial practices might have a role in reshaping professional identities within an entrepreneurial discourse.

A growing international literature highlights many common features that contribute to persistent issues of low status and vulnerable identities across the early childhood sector (Woodrow, 2008; Woodrow and Busch, 2008). These issues, which include the role of hegemonic developmental discourses, characterizations of a feminized profession, and associations with mothering discourses, for example, have now been well rehearsed in the literature (Grieshaber, 2001; Moyles, 2001). In this chapter, I have identified other challenges to the development of robust identities that emerge from current policy directions, informed by an understanding of the role discourses play in making possible certain constructions of early childhood professionalism, and excluding others. Whilst acknowledging that professional identities are seldom fixed entities, and as social constructions are representations and manifestations resulting from the complex interplay of factors in a dynamic, ever-changing context, there are sufficient indications that traditional identities for early childhood have not served the interests of equity and justice very effectively. There is a timely intersection of conceptual space, and policy and ethical imperatives, to create opportunities for new and different identities for early childhood professionals to emerge, nationally and internationally. Identity emerges from intersections between concepts of self, and the broader conceptions and expectations of others. Understanding these broader contexts, expectations and institutional imperatives is an important element of understanding the current situation and a necessary ingredient for 'harnessing of agency' (Miller, 2008) and the creation of new identity possibilities. Of course, exercising agency is a challenging task and questions will always arise about the capacity educators have to select which discourses to take up, resist or subvert: a capacity in which leadership is strongly implicated.

Locating early childhood professional identity within discourses of leadership

A strong theme to emerge in this chapter relates to the powerful influences in the current policy landscape and their potential to direct and narrow constructions of early childhood professional identity, particularly within human capital and free-market-entrepreneurial discourses. Where discourses of leadership within the field are weak, there is likely to be greater risk that these dominant discourses prevail. Taking inspiration from the work of Miller (2008), Oberhuemer (2008) and others who advocate resistance to dominant discourses by encouraging early childhood professionals to participate in the creation of their own discourses of professional identity, the final part of this chapter is directed to considering how early childhood professional identity might be more strongly located within discourses of leadership. This line emerges from recognition of several intersecting issues or concerns. The first consideration relates to the generally accepted problematic state of leadership in the field. Whilst some significant advances are occurring in relation to researching leadership and the development of conceptual resources relevant to the field (for example, the work of Pen Green and the National Qualification in Integrated Centre Leadership), this work is at best emergent, and research continues to identify worrying silences in relation to leadership identities in the field (Goffin and Washington, 2007).

A second strand relates to the timeliness of undertaking renewed identity work in a context where early childhood is more prominent in the policy agendas of nations, communities and the academy. A further imperative relates to ethical and moral concerns about the purposes of the early childhood project and the possibilities of them contributing more to communities than the safe-keeping of children and their education in human capital terms. These lead to difficult questions with sometimes uncomfortable answers about whose interests are privileged and whose are discounted by the current arrangements.

It is clear that new philosophies and approaches involving holistic and integrated delivery across disciplinary boundaries are capturing the attention of policy-makers and creating new imperatives for different kinds of professionals to work in these contexts. Similarly, new imaginings of the potential for early childhood institutions to be sites of regenerating democracy, community-building and community transformation seem to be moving in from the margins. A recent personal experience in Chile shows how powerful these conceptions can be in mobilizing communities, but also how confronting to traditional notions of 'professionals as experts' (Woodrow, 2009). In the intersections of these lines, strengthened imperatives and new opportunities to reconceptualize professional identities more closely affiliated with discourses of leadership, alliance-building and communities are implicated. Recent research about leadership capacity in the field in North America led researchers to conclude that there was a dangerous void of leadership capacity that demanded a response beyond resourcing the development of individual leaders and instead creating a 'field-wide community of diverse leaders' (Goffin and Washington, 2007: 3). Recognizing the current policy interest in early childhood as a unique moment, the researchers argue the need to 'build coherent leadership *for* the field ... networked, field-wide leadership capable of envisioning, advancing and executing complex systemic change ... ' (Goffin and Washington, 2007: 10). Notions of networked leadership interrupt traditional constructions of leadership as a privatized concept pertaining to the individual, and resonate strongly with concepts of participative democracy and engaged citizenry advocated by Sumsion as characteristics of a 'new activist professionalism' (2006). These constructions demand stronger engagement with communities than many constructions of professional identity currently allow room for. Values and discourses of collaboration and community are more likely to be constitutive of professional identities responding to these challenges than the market-driven practices and conformity promoted through many of the current policy regimes and the practices and structures they inspire. Activating and sustaining these discourses will undoubtedly require a great deal of courage and a much stronger research literature about change and activism in the field than currently exists.

Final thoughts

This chapter highlights the dynamic state of the early childhood field and the complex flows and counter-flows of policy trajectories and some of their effects: intended and unintended. In such a state lie many challenges, some risks and many opportunities. Issues of professional identity seldom feature in policy debates, and associated issues largely remain invisible, yet how people think about and construct their work, and the expectations and understandings that others have of the role of the professional who will carry the work forward, are critical considerations affecting the achievement of policy intentions. This chapter raises some of these issues in the expectation that it will stimulate debate and discussion which are productive for clarifying understandings and contesting taken-for-granted or unexamined assumptions. These activities form important foundations for reflection and considered action.

☐ Summary

- Emerging and dominant policy trends in early childhood provision in Australia (and elsewhere) are having an impact on discourses of professionalism and this has implications for professional identity and leadership.
- Three 'cases' are used to consider the potential impact of increasing market-based approaches to early childhood provision, intensification of regulation and accountability, and contradictions within the Australian early childhood reform agenda.
- Early childhood education is perceived as an area for investment, particularly in human capital terms, and this has implications for provision, views of professionalism and professional identities.
- The notion of 'networked leadership' is discussed as a means of bringing together individuals around values and discourses of collaboration and community and enabling engagement with complexity and change.

Questions for discussion

1. What nomenclature and concepts are used in your context to describe early childhood professionals and their work? Are they helpful to the advancement of the status of the profession? What other nomenclature might be appropriate?
2. This chapter identifies a number of challenges to the establishment of a robust early childhood professional identity. In what ways do these issues resonate with your context? What other issues or factors shape or construct identity for early childhood professionals? What is an ideal professional identity in early childhood?
3. The author describes leadership in the field as being somewhat problematic. How do you see leadership being practised in the field? What understandings do you have of what makes a good early childhood leader?
4. What would a 'networked, field-wide leadership' look like in practice? What would be important to building this? How would the resources be mobilized? *(Higher level question)*

Further reading

Levels 5 and 6

Cheeseman, S. (2007) 'Pedagogical silences in early childhood social policy', *Contemporary Issues in Early Childhood*, 8(3): 244–54.

This article considers a range of discourses that contribute to shaping contemporary early childhood programmes. The author discusses a perceived absence of early childhood teachers' voices in the design and delivery of social policy initiatives for young children. The article calls for pedagogical leadership to overcome these barriers and promote the democratic rights of children to high-quality early childhood education and care programmes.

Press, F. and Woodrow, C. (2009) 'The giant in the playground: investigating the reach and impli-cations of the corporatisation of childcare provision', in D. King and G. Meagher (eds) *Paid Care in Australia: Profits, Purposes and Practices.* Sydney: University of Sydney Press.
This chapter traces a complex set of interrelationships that characterizes the operations of a corporate childcare provider. The authors interrogate issues raised by their research and con-sider what is at stake for children, families and staff when early years provision is dominated by large for-profit organizations. The examination includes consideration of the children's daily experience through the 'corporate' curriculum, and constructions of early childhood professional identity.

Levels 6 and 7

Fenech, M., Sumsion, J. and Shepherd, W. (2010) 'Promoting early childhood teacher profes-sionalism in the Australian context: the place of resistance', *Contemporary Issues in Early Childhood*, 11(1): 89–105.
This article is concerned with how teacher professionalism can be re-imagined and practised within an ECE setting in ways that uphold children's rights and interests and emancipate early childhood teachers from technical, deprofessionalizing constraints. The article extends think-ing about teacher activism and promotes resistance-based professionalism as one way of pro-ducing an alternative habitus about quality ECE and the integral role early childhood teachers play in such provision.

Goffin, S. and Washington, V. (2007) *Ready or Not: Leadership Choices in Early Care and Education.* New York: Teachers College Press.
This book discusses recent research about leadership perceptions in the early childhood field to raise concerns about resistance to change and a lack of leadership capacity. The authors outline some strategies and resources contributing to building 'field-wide' leadership capacity and repositioning it more favourably as leading, rather than responding to change.

Websites

www.earlychildhoodaustralia.org.au
This is a website for early years practitioners in Australia.

References

Australian Labor Party (ALP) (2007) *Labor's Plan for Early Childhood*. Available from: www.alp.org.au/download/now/early_childhood_policy.pdf (accessed 30 December 2009).
Ball, S.J. (1994) '"... and this little piggy has none": education goes to market', *Education Today and Tomorrow*, 46(1): 2–4.
Beijaard, D., Meijer, P.C. and Verloop, N. (2004) 'Reconsidering research on teachers' professional identity', *Teaching and Teacher Education*, 20: 107–28.

Bown, K., Sumsion, J. and Press, F. (2008) 'Influences on politician's decision making for early childhood education and care policy. What do we know? What don't we know?', paper presented at the Australian Association for Research in Education (AARE) International Conference: Changing Climates: Education for Sustainable Futures, Queensland University of Technology, Brisbane, Australia.

Brennan, D. (2007) 'The ABC of child care politics', *Australian Journal of Social Issues*, 42(2): 213–26.

Bueno, M., Darling-Hammond, L. and Gonzales, D. (2010) *A Matter of Degrees: Preparing Teachers for the Pre-K Classroom*. Available from: www.preknow.org/documents/teacherquality_march2010.pdf (accessed 20 March 2010).

Burton, C. and Lyons, M. (2000) 'When does a teacher teach? The Queensland early childhood profession on trial', in J. Hayden (ed.) *Landscapes in Early Childhood Education*. New York: Peter Lang. pp. 271–91.

Cheeseman, S. (2007) 'Pedagogical silences in early childhood social policy', *Contemporary Issues in Early Childhood*, 8(3): 244–54.

Dahlberg, G. and Moss, P. (2005) *Ethics and Politics in Early Childhood Education*. London: RoutledgeFalmer.

Dahlberg, G. and Moss, P. (2008) 'Beyond quality in early childhood education and care: languages of evaluation', CESifo (Ifo Institute for Economic Research at the University of Munich) DICE Report 2/2008: 21–6.

DEEWR (2009) *Investing in the Early Years – A National Early Childhood Development Strategy*. Canberra, Australia: Department of Education, Employment and Workplace Relations.

Early Childhood Australia (2009) 'Advanced teaching standards forums', *Early Childhood News*. Available from: www.earlychildhoodaustralia.org.au/early_childhood_news/june_2009_advanced_teaching_standards_forums.html (accessed 20 March 2010).

Gillard, J. (2008) Opening speech, Launch of LHMU Big Steps in Childcare Campaign. Available from: www.deewr.gov.au/Ministers/Gillard/Media/Speeches/Pages/Article_081023_112358.aspx (accessed 31 December 2009).

Goffin, S. and Washington, V. (2007) *Ready or Not: Leadership Choices in Early Care and Education*. New York: Teachers College Press.

Grieshaber, S. (2001) 'Advocacy and early childhood educators: identity and cultural conflicts', in S. Grieshaber and G. Cannella (eds) *Embracing Identities in Early Childhood Education*. New York: Teachers College Press.

Korthagen, F. (2004) 'In search of the essence of a good teacher: towards a more holistic approach in teacher education', *Teaching and Teacher Education*, 20: 77–97.

Lloyd, E. (2009) *Childcare Markets in England and The Netherlands: A Comparative Study*. International Centre for Study of the Mixed Economy of Childcare (ICMEC), University of East London. Available from: www.uel.ac.uk/icmec (accessed 28 December 2009).

MacNaughton, G. (2004) 'The politics of logic in early childhood research: a case of the brain, hard facts, trees and rhizomes', *The Australian Education Researcher*, 31(3): 87–104.

McWilliam, E., Hatcher, C. and Meadmore, D. (1999) 'Corporatising the teacher, new professional identities in education', article presented at the Australian Association for Educational Research (AARE) Annual Conference, 30 November–2 December, Melbourne.

Miller, L. (2008) 'Developing professionalism within a regulatory framework in England: challenges and possibilities', *European Early Childhood Research Journal*, 16(1): 255–68.

Moss, P. (2007) 'Bringing politics into the nursery: early childhood education as a democratic practice', *European Early Childhood Education Research Journal*, 15(1): 5–20.

Moyles, J. (2001) 'Passion, paradox and professionalism in early years education', *Early Years*, 21(2): 81–95.

Nias, J. (1989) 'Teaching and the self', in M.L. Holly and C.S. McLoughlin (eds) *Perspectives on Teacher Professional Development*. London: Falmer Press. pp. 151–71.

Oberhuemer, P. (2005) 'Conceptualising the early childhood pedagogue: policy approaches and issues of professionalism', *European Early Childhood Research Journal*, 13(1): 5–15.

Oberhuemer, P. (2008) 'Who is an early years professional? Reflections on policy diversity in Europe', in L. Miller and C. Cable (eds) *Professionalism in the Early Years.* London: Hodder Arnold. pp. 131–41.

Organisation for Economic Co-operation and Development (OECD) (2001) *Starting Strong: Early Childhood Education and Care.* Paris: OECD.

Organisation for Economic Co-operation and Development (OECD) (2006) *Starting Strong II: Early Childhood Education and Care.* Paris: OECD.

Ortlipp, M. (2009) 'Becoming and being an early childhood teacher: what difference does a degree make?', unpublished paper.

Ortlipp, M. and Woodrow, C. (2008) 'Professionalism and professional identity in corporate child-care', paper presented to the AARE International Education Research Conference – Changing Climates: Education for Sustainable Futures, Brisbane.

Osgood, J. (2006) 'Deconstructing professionalism in early childhood education: resisting the regulatory gaze', *Contemporary Issues in Early Childhood*, 7(1): 5–14.

Prentice, S. (2009) 'High stakes: the "investable" child and the economic reframing of childcare', *Signs: Journal of Women in Culture and Society*, 34(3): 687–710.

Press, F. (2007) 'Public investment, fragmentation and quality early education and care: existing challenges and future options', in E. Hill, B. Pocock and A. Elliott (eds) *Kids Count: Better Early Childhood Education and Care in Australia*. Sydney: Sydney University Press. pp. 181–97.

Press, F. and Woodrow, C. (2009) 'The giant in the playground: investigating the reach and implications of the corporatisation of childcare provision', in D. King and G. Meagher (eds) *Paid Care in Australia: Profits, Purposes and Practices*. Sydney: University of Sydney Press.

Rudd, K. and Macklin, J. (2007) *New Directions for Early Childhood Education*. Sydney: Australian Labor Party.

Rush, E. (2006) 'Childcare quality in Australia', *Discussion Paper No 84*. Canberra: The Australia Institute.

Siraj-Blatchford, I., Clarke, K. and Needham, M. (2007) *The Team Around the Child: Multi-agency Working in the Early Years*. London: Trentham Books.

Sumsion, J. (2006) 'From Whitlam to economic rationalism and beyond: a conceptual framework for political activism in children's services', *Australian Journal of Early Childhood*, 31(1): 1–9.

Sumsion, J. (2007a) 'Sustaining the employment of early childhood teachers in long day care: a case for robust hope, critical imagination and critical action', *Asia Pacific Journal of Teacher Education*, 35(3): 311–27.

Sumsion, J. (2007b) *Corporate Child Care in Australia: Is it in the Public Interest?*, invited presentation to the International Centre for Study of the Mixed Economy of Childcare (ICMEC), University of East London.

Sumsion, J., Barnes, S., Cheeseman, S., Harrison, L., Kennedy, A. and Stonehouse, A. (2009) 'Insider perceptions on developing Belonging, Being and Becoming: The Early Years Learning Framework for Australia', *Australian Journal of Early Childhood*, 34(4): 4–13.

Woodrow, C. (2007) 'W(h)ither the early childhood teacher: tensions for early childhood professional identity between the policy landscape and the politics of teacher regulation', *Contemporary Issues in Early Childhood*, 8(3): 233–43.

Woodrow, C. (2008) 'Discourses of professional identity in early childhood: movements in Australia', *European Early Childhood Research Journal*, 16(2): 269–80.

Woodrow, C. (2009) *Futuro Infantil Hoy: A Project of Quality Experiences Integrating Early Childhood. Phase 2 Report*. University of Western Sydney, September.

Woodrow, C. and Busch, G. (2008) 'Repositioning early childhood leadership as action and activism', *European Early Childhood Education Research Journal*, 16(1): 83–93.

CHAPTER 4

EARLY YEARS PROFESSIONALISM
Issues, Challenges and Opportunities

Dorothy McMillan and Glenda Walsh

Overview

In this chapter, we explore the notion of professionalism within the context of early years provision in Northern Ireland. The policy and practice background is sketched alongside an outline of the history of early years services in the province. It is clear that within Northern Ireland (NI) there is a strong aspiration towards integrated services but, as yet, the reality is that of a 'split system' of provision and training. The early years workforce today is diverse and fragmented in terms of qualifications, training, status and financial reward. Perhaps one of the few uniting factors is its gender: the workforce is almost exclusively female. We consider theoretical and philosophical perspectives on these issues and address some pertinent 'dominant discourses'. As early years professionals await the publication of a long delayed Early Years Strategy for Northern Ireland, the question arises: what is to be done? We conclude this chapter by considering three potential courses of action: maintaining the status quo, introducing a 'dual degree' approach or pursuing, as in England, the route of a new profession.

Early years provision in Northern Ireland

Almost all children of pre-school age in Northern Ireland spend one year in a pre-school setting. Around half of these are statutory sector settings (nursery schools and nursery classes within primary schools) and half are voluntary/private sector settings (playgroups and daycare facilities) which are funded by the Department of Education (Education and Training Inspectorate (ETI), 2009). Children in Northern Ireland start primary school in the September following their fourth birthday. The first two years of primary education constitute the recently introduced Foundation Stage (Council for the Curriculum, Examinations and Assessment (CCEA), 2007). This is intended to provide 'a more developmentally, play-based and child-led approach to teaching and learning' (Walsh, 2007: 67) for the youngest pupils by developing their skills and confidence and introducing them to formal learning when they are ready. The Foundation Stage is followed by Key Stage 1 (Years 3–4) and Key Stage 2 (Years 5–7). Walsh (2007: 68) refers to the introduction of the less formal Revised NI Curriculum (CCEA, 2007) as a 'huge landmark in the education system of Northern Ireland' which has long been known for its conservatism and traditional methods. In this context, we now retrace our steps to examine the historical development of early years professionalism.

An historical perspective

The first nursery school in Northern Ireland opened in 1928. The earliest nursery schools were situated in areas of social and economic need and so their aims were expressed in terms of health and welfare. Nursery school 'superintendents' were trained in England, since no training facilities were available in Northern Ireland. In 1947, nursery tutors were appointed for the first time in the two local teacher training colleges so that nursery teachers could be trained within Northern Ireland. This option was only open to women students, in keeping with the attachment theory of Bowlby (1951) prevalent at the time, which maintained that a continuous mother figure was essential to the wellbeing of the young child. There was, therefore, no question of training men to fulfil such a role.

Although nursery and infant school teachers were trained together, graduate status for nursery school teachers was not offered by the Colleges of Education until 10 years after the Bachelor of Education (BEd) degree was introduced for primary and secondary level teachers. This indicated a level of ambivalence around the issue of early years professionalism: did nursery school teachers really belong to the teaching profession? Was it appropriate to award a degree for work in a pre-compulsory stage of education? In the end, degree status was granted to nursery students, thus situating early years professionalism in Northern Ireland within the realm of the nursery teaching profession, where it has remained until recent days. Postgraduate nursery education study is possible through the Masters in Education (MEd) course and through the Postgraduate Certificate in Education (PGCE) Early Years option, which enables graduate students to attain 'eligibility to teach' status at pre-school, Foundation Stage and Key Stage 1 levels, as an alternative route to the BEd degree.

Nursery and infant teachers were, for the most part, autonomous professionals – deciding for themselves what and how to teach – until the advent of the Education Reform Order (Great Britain, 1989) which introduced a prescribed curriculum, the Northern Ireland version of the National Curriculum, to be delivered in all primary schools. Although this curriculum did not apply to the (non-compulsory) nursery stage, in the same year the *Nursery Education Guidelines* were published, including a booklet on *The Curriculum* (NI Curriculum Council (NICC), 1989). This was the first centrally produced curriculum document in 60 years of nursery education in Northern Ireland and marked a transition for nursery education from a mainly care-based approach to a more structured 'preparation for school' approach. Some writers – for example, Oberhuemer (2005) – interpret the introduction of curricular frameworks as the beginning of a journey for early years professionals towards closer state accountability and away from professional autonomy. Moss (2006) has a similar fear that prescriptive curricula or practice guidelines may reduce early years professionals to the role of technicians. This debate continues today, when the 'regulatory gaze' (Osgood, 2006) of externally imposed standards and regulations has gone far beyond curricular guidance.

The rapid growth of the voluntary/private early years sector in Northern Ireland, from the formation of the Northern Ireland Preschool Playgroups Association (NIPPA) in 1965, was accompanied by a strong emphasis on staff/volunteer training. Due to poor funding, training was usually paid for by the participants themselves and short courses were attended outside working hours. There was no suggestion that playgroup staff might be regarded as professionals in the same sense as nursery school teachers; in fact, as Griffin (2008) suggests, some early years workers might have wanted to avoid being called 'professional' because they felt the term conflicted with the caring, intimate nature of the work they carried on with young children. Nevertheless, whether or not early years practitioners perceived themselves to be professionals, there were clear indications of a desire to *act professionally* in their work – to think of professionalism in terms of *what they do* rather than *who they are* (Osgood, 2006). Thus demand for training in the voluntary/private sector increased, so that by 1996 NIPPA offered training to over 1,200 students, with a particular commitment to National Vocational Qualifications (NVQ) courses (NIPPA, 1996), although at this stage there were no qualification requirements for childcare staff in this sector. This situation was to change when the Labour government came to power in England in 1997, and in the next section we examine rapid changes in early years policy over the past decade.

Recent developments

With the launch of the Pre-School Education Expansion Programme (PEEP) (Department of Education for NI (DENI) and Department of Health and Social Services (DHSS), 1998) and the Northern Ireland Childcare Strategy (DHSS, DENI and Training and Employment Agency, 1999), came a new emphasis on quality in early years services. Urban (2008) notes the proliferation of national policy documents on quality during the late 1990s (for example, in Ireland, Germany and Flanders) and highlights the tendency to equate quality with professionalism: policies aim to *professionalize* the workforce by raising qualification levels in order to achieve higher quality standards. This approach has been supported by research such as the Effective Pre-School Provision in Northern Ireland (EPPNI) study which found that overall quality was higher in nursery schools and classes than in playgroups and daycare centres. The researchers concluded that this was 'likely to be related to higher staff qualifications' (DE, 2006b: 7). This finding mirrored the findings of the English study EPPE (Sylva et al., 2004).

Consistent with this analysis, the PEEP sought to begin the professionalization of the early years voluntary/private sector by requiring that funded playgroups/daycare in this sector should have a leader qualified to National Vocational Qualifications (NVQ) Level 3 (or equivalent). There was also a stipulation that each setting must 'buy in' the part-time advice and support of an Early Years Specialist (EYS) qualified to diploma or degree level in Early Childhood Studies or Education (DE, 2003). The EYS support role is unique to the Childcare Strategy for Northern Ireland and its success has been variable; the most recent ETI Chief Inspector's Report (ETI, 2009: 29) states that in almost a quarter of cases the EYS support is 'not as effective as it needs to be'. The exact reasons for this lack of effectiveness are not rehearsed, but the Report points to a 'variation in the level and quality of professional external support available to the preschool sector' (ETI, 2009: 26). The implication from the Chief Inspector's Report is that having a Level 3 qualification and receiving graduate support and advice leads to less effective provision than having a degree-level qualification. Statutory sector nursery, Foundation Stage and Key Stage 1 teachers are required to be qualified to degree level and to have qualified teacher status – either through the BEd or PGCE route. The ETI Chief Inspector's Report (ETI, 2009) shows clearly that the overall effectiveness of pre-school settings – including the quality of provision for learning and of leadership/management – is much higher in the statutory sector than in the voluntary/private sector. This indicates that degree-level training leads to higher quality provision, as the EPPNI study (DE, 2006b) had previously concluded. In 1997, in preparation for the new 'pre-school sector' to be created by the Childcare Strategy, the *Nursery Education Guidelines* (NICC, 1989) were replaced by a new curriculum document *Curricular Guidance for Pre-School Education* (DHSS, CCEA and DENI, 1997) to be followed by all settings in receipt of government funding. This was later updated in 2006 (DENI, DHSSPS and CCEA, 2006).

In 1996, Stranmillis University College launched one of the first BA (Hons) in Early Childhood Studies (ECS) part-time degree programmes in the UK, out of a recognition that early years services had outgrown the field of nursery education. There is a widely accepted association between professionalism and a body of 'domain-specific knowledge' (Karila, 2008: 211) and the rationale for the degree, as explained by Calder, was to establish a distinct academic field of knowledge:

> The aim was to bridge the care and education divide and develop a degree which would form the basis of a potential education and training route for an early years professional, who would combine the knowledge, skills and education necessary for the upbringing, care and education of children from birth through to later childhood. (2008: 32–3)

A full-time ECS pathway was introduced in 1999. This coincided with the launch of the PEEP and was consistent with the Labour government's policy decision that early years services would move away from a promise of universal 'nursery education' (DHSS and DENI, 1994: 9) to one of 'pre-school education' (DHSS, DENI and T&EA, 1999: 14). In 2006, a Masters degree in ECS (MA) was introduced.

The pursuit of an integrated approach to children's services as set out in the agenda of *Every Child Matters* (DfES, 2003) has been followed in principle by the *Ten Year Strategy for Children and Young People in Northern Ireland* (Office of the First Minister and Deputy First Minister, 2006). This document comprised a strategy for children's services in Northern Ireland from 2006 to 2016 and focused particularly on issues of health and wellbeing. In the same year, the *Children and Young People Funding Package* (DE, 2006a) announced a pilot programme of 'extended schools' (8am–6pm) to be targeted, initially, on schools (including nursery schools) in disadvantaged areas. Over £10m was to be invested in the provision of breakfast clubs, after-school care/leisure activities, parent programmes and other innovatory schemes, including a pilot series of Full Service Extended Schools and Networks launched in Belfast (DE, 2009). The extent to which these opportunities are taken up by nursery schools and the extension of the schemes to pre-school settings in the voluntary/private sector may, in time, form the basis for integrated children's centres in Northern Ireland. A new Early Years Strategy to replace the 1999 Childcare Strategy is now two years overdue and so many vital questions remain unanswered: Is graduateness considered essential to early years professionalism? Which degree is appropriate for early years professionals? How will integrated early years provision be structured? With no clear answers to these questions, we turn our attention to defining the chief characteristics of today's early years profession in Northern Ireland.

Where we are now

A feminized profession

The early years workforce continues to be overwhelmingly feminized (Cable and Miller, 2008; Cameron, 2006). Despite an English government target of 6% male workers by 2006, the actual figure remains closer to 2%. In a wider context, men represent less than 1% of the Early Childhood Education and Care workforce across the 20 countries surveyed by the Organisation for Economic Co-operation and Development (OECD) report *Starting Strong II* (OECD, 2006).

The case study of Conor below focuses on a male nursery assistant in the early stages of his professional journey. It may be useful, having read the study, to compile a list of issues for Conor to raise at his review meeting. These may form the basis of a group discussion or role-play activity.

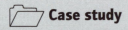 **Case study**

Conor has recently been appointed as a nursery assistant in a large nursery school. Having graduated with a Foundation Degree in Early Childhood Studies, he has now enrolled for the BA (Hons) part-time course and is looking forward to a successful career as an early years professional. During his first term in the nursery school, Conor has experienced mixed reactions to his appointment: one single mother told him how happy she was to have a 'good role model' in the nursery for her son; one father asked him why he should want to 'waste your time playing with kids all day'. A small group of parents spoke to the principal about their concern that Conor (the first male nursery assistant employed by the nursery school) should 'always be supervised by a female member of staff'. The young principal replied that Conor had as much right to the job as any female applicant, and that the school's Child Protection policy applied equally to all staff in the nursery. Conor was a little shaken to realize that not all parents were happy with his appointment. However, the children respond well to Conor and he feels that he is building positive relationships with them all. He also gets on fairly well with the other nursery assistants – two older women who have worked there for several years – though sometimes he is not sure whether they expect him to be more 'macho' in his interactions with the children or to show a gentler, more feminine approach. Next week, he will have his first term review with the principal to discuss his progress. At first, Conor thought he would have no issues to raise at the meeting; now he's not so sure.

The small number of men working in early years roles cannot be attributed to any one factor (see Chapter 9). Many writers and practitioners speak of a long-standing cultural unease in our society with the idea of men caring for young children. In line with this, research carried out in Northern Ireland (McMillan, 2008) found that parents who opposed the employment of men in early years roles spoke of their child protection concerns, men not being 'at children's level', and their view that children need a mother substitute at this stage of their lives. Another complicating factor is the ambiguity that exists around the meaning of 'male role model' within an early years setting. There are, according to Sargent (2005), three possible interpretations: being a model of traditional masculinity; being a model of discipline; and being a model of a gentler form of masculinity. Owen (2003) contends that male early years staff tend to see themselves in the more caring, gentler masculinity role, whereas parents tend to see them in the traditional masculinity, stereotypical 'macho' role. In any case, it will be problematic to match the expectations of employers, setting staff, parents and the male educator without open discussion of this issue. By contrast, Cooke and Lawton (2008) point to poor pay and conditions as possible reasons for low male participation, but this argument is rejected by Moss (2006), on the grounds that countries

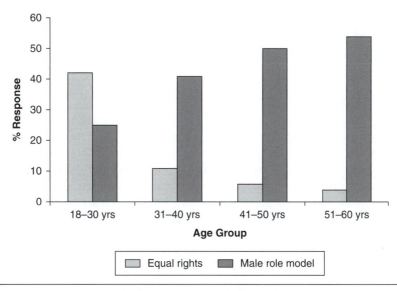

Figure 4.1   Practitioner reasons for employing male educators

such as Denmark, where the early years workforce has been restructured and enjoys favourable employment terms and conditions, still have low proportions of male staff (as discussed in Chapter 9 of this book).

In a study conducted in England by the Children's Workforce Development Council (CWDC, 2009), which involved an online survey of 1,009 parents of pre-school children, 55% of parents said they wanted a male childcare worker for their nursery-aged children. A questionnaire survey of 228 pre-school practitioners and 477 parents across Northern Ireland (McMillan, 2008) asked participants about their views on a range of issues relating to pre-school policy and practice. The study found that 88% of practitioners (across both sectors) and 75% of parents in Northern Ireland would welcome the employment of men in the early years profession. The most common reasons given in favour of employing men as educators were that they have equal rights and they provide male role models for children. Figure 4.1 indicates a noteworthy trend in these responses, whereby younger practitioners appeared to be more concerned with the equal rights of adults argument and older practitioners with the potential benefits for the children of having male role models in early years settings. This divergence in rationale indicates a need for radical discussion and negotiation of professional identity in early years settings, particularly in those settings where male staff are employed.

Although three-quarters of parents in the study cited above stated their approval for employing men in early years settings, several parents added conditional comments such as: 'as long as they are properly trained and vetted' or 'with proper training under female supervision'. Such comments indicated 'mental assent ... but emotional discomfort with the practice' (McMillan, 2008: 147). Overall, the percentage of male staff employed remains largely unaffected and it would appear that, despite the huge political, social and economic changes of the last century, early years education and care in Northern Ireland – and further afield – is still regarded as 'women's work'.

A divided profession

Northern Ireland has developed a 'split system' of 'childcare' and 'early education', alongside which evolved a 'split training system' of vocational training for staff in the voluntary/private sector (daycare and playgroup leaders) and graduate training for staff in the statutory sector (nursery school and class, Foundation Stage and Key Stage 1 teachers). Moss (2006: 31) refers to 'a clear and deep fault line between the two workforces' in terms of material conditions, qualifications, and employment terms and conditions. McMillan (2008: 287) found 'abundant evidence of inter-sectoral division in the form of discussion about inequalities and perceived inequalities'. The inequalities related mainly to the areas of adult:child ratios, salaries, capital funding, inspections and training opportunities, thus validating Moss's findings within the context of Northern Ireland.

It is not possible to move into a new era in early years professionalism in Northern Ireland without some recognition of the 'historical baggage' (Anning, 2004: 57) that is carried by both sectors. The statutory sector was the main provider of pre-school education for over half a century and has recently, through the expansion of pre-school services, been forced to yield that position of power through a largely unwanted alliance with the voluntary/private sector. Even before the PEEP (DENI and DHSS, 1998), representatives of the British Association for Early Childhood Education expressed 'grave concern at the prospect of early years education being delivered by other than qualified teachers' (Sutherland, 2006: 74). More recently, one local nursery principal wrote in a professional newsletter: 'Recently, teachers in nursery education have felt under threat as provision in the private/voluntary sector has gained a significant voice' (Beattie, 2009: 19).

The PEEP has, undoubtedly, raised the status of the care sector in Northern Ireland; however, it seems to have simultaneously produced a perception of being threatened within the pre-school education sector. This situation lends itself to analysis based on the theories of Foucault (1988), particularly in relation to the close connection between knowledge and power. From a Foucauldian perspective, power is diverse and pervasive, so that everybody is involved in power relations, both as 'vehicles of power, as well as the effects of power' (Dahlberg et al., 1999: 32). Thus the statutory early years sector has held power but now faces loss of power and experiences feelings of betrayal, since it is their own department – the Department of Education – which now holds responsibility for all pre-school services in Northern Ireland (since 2006). Osgood (2006) identifies a 'passive resistance' amongst early years practitioners, whereby they are overtly opposed to what she, from a poststructuralist feminist viewpoint, considers 'masculinist', managerialist policy change, yet feel powerless to resist. Cooke and Lawton (2008: 7) report a 'widespread sense of powerlessness: that changes are being "done to" the workforce, rather than in partnership with it'. At a local level, McMillan (2008) found similar evidence of practitioner apprehension about future changes to early years policy and provision – across both early years sectors – without any suggestion of their ability to shape these changes.

The 'dominant discourse' or 'regime of truth' (Moss and Petrie, 2002: 30) of early years services in Northern Ireland stated that nursery education delivered by trained teachers was always superior to playgroup/daycare provision, even when the latter was delivered by graduate (non-teacher trained) leaders. The issue at stake here is not the widely recognized link between professionalism and a body of knowledge (Oberhuemer, 2005; Urban, 2008), since both graduate groups (qualified teachers and BA in ECS graduates) have engaged with a body of knowledge, but rather the desire to retain power. However, dominant discourses need to be 'questioned and challenged, treated respectfully but not reverentially' (Moss and Petrie, 2002: 166) and the local early years discourse has been intentionally and gradually challenged and 'unmasked' by the voluntary/private sector through improved quality, staff training and, most significantly, through government funding and recognition in the last 10 years. Early Years (formerly NIPPA) is committed to a graduate early years profession, based on a pedagogue- rather than a teacher-led profession (Walsh, 2007). Voluntary/ private sector setting leaders are encouraged to exceed the qualification requirements of their sector by engaging in graduate early years courses. However, despite the professionalization of the workforce in terms of 'upgraded' qualifications and initial progress towards integrated structures, the new 'pre-school sector' which the government aimed to nurture through the PEEP has failed to thrive, due to continuing actual and perceived inequalities between the two sectors, added to a disabling 10-year policy vacuum. So, where do we go from here?

Future possibilities

The future of early years professionalism in Northern Ireland would appear to lie in one of three directions: a continuation of the status quo, a 'dual degree' approach, or the creation of a new profession. The continuation of the status quo would perpetuate a 'split system' based on nursery, Foundation and Key Stage 1 teachers who belong to the teaching profession and hold Level 6 qualifications working on a par with vocationally trained playgroup and daycare leaders who hold Level 3 qualifications (levels based on the National Qualifications Framework (QCA, QCAA and CCEA, 2006)). Whilst the ETI declare that similar inspection standards and procedures are applied to settings across both sectors, the Chief Inspector's most recent report (ETI, 2009) acknowledges the unfairness of this approach from the perspective of voluntary/ private sector settings. He cites lower levels of resourcing; variation in the level of EYS support; lower levels of qualifications and in-service training. In light of this, the Chief Inspector (ETI, 2009: 29) appeals to the Department of Education to 'review the discrepancies in the quality of provision' between the two sectors. Clearly this is not a level playing field and, if the current approach is continued, the inter-sectoral divisions already referred to by both Moss (2006) and McMillan (2008) might also be expected to persist.

The second option would be to 'upgrade' the qualifications of voluntary/private sector leaders to graduate level (Level 6) and those of assistants to Level 3, and to retain the structures of the current 'split system'. This would mean dispensing with the unsatisfactory EYS support scheme (ETI, 2009), out of a commitment to graduate leadership, which is widely supported as essential to the professionalization of the early years workforce (Alakeson, 2004; Eraut, 1994; McMillan, 2008). This option would produce an early years workforce based on Level 6 (teachers/leaders) and Level 3 (assistants) qualifications, with the possibility of other setting staff working towards these qualification levels, as proposed by OECD (2006) and by Boddy et al. (2005). The Foundation Degree, for example, would then be seen as a stepping stone towards graduateness. This move would have considerable financial implications, since graduate leaders with Level 6 qualifications would reasonably expect higher salaries than those with Level 3 qualifications. In support of this goal, the voluntary/private early years sector continues to lobby the Northern Ireland government for transformation funding as an essential means of funding a 'Graduate Recruitment Incentive' (NIPPA, 2007). Whilst this 'dual degree' approach would professionalize the early years workforce from the point of view of qualifications, it would not resolve the resourcing inequalities identified by the ETI Chief Inspector (ETI, 2009) or defuse the inter-sectoral perception divisions.

The third and more radical option for the future of early years professionalism in Northern Ireland is to abandon the 'split system' and to create a new early years sector with its own system of shared training. The advantages of creating an 'early years profession' distinct from the teaching profession have been promoted by several writers (Lumsden, 2005; Moss, 2006; OECD, 2006). Oberhuemer (2005) points out that, although some countries such as England have moved towards an integrated approach in recent years, only a few such as Denmark, Finland and Sweden have adopted a coherent approach to professional training. Miller (2008: 266) contends that the 'new profession' is 'a unique opportunity to influence the framing of the discourses around qualifications, training and leadership and the knowledge base that individuals who make up the profession need to draw on in their interactions with children and families'. This opportunity has been embraced in New Zealand, where integrated early years graduate training, integration of the teacher and childcare workforce unions and a new system of early years settings have led, within a quarter century, to the abolition of the education/care divide (Bennett, 2003; Dalli, 2010).

The financial implications for Northern Ireland of adopting this policy would mainly be in the area of staff costs, since these account for around 80% of the cost of early childhood services in most countries (OECD, 2006). Moss (2006) states that, in the Nordic countries, graduate pedagogues are paid only slightly less than teachers, and in New Zealand pre-school and school teachers are soon to be paid the same. The development of a system of shared graduate-level training and equalizing ratios and capital funding across the sectors would add considerable expense to the project. Alakeson (2004) proposes that the UK should adopt the New Zealand model, which aims to have an entire workforce of trained early years teachers by 2012. His proposal that the UK should aim, initially, for a target of 60% graduates by 2020 might usefully be considered by policy-makers in Northern Ireland. It is to be hoped that the imminent Early Years Strategy will take premature steps in that direction.

Final thoughts

Early years professionalism involves a blend of factors including values and attitudes, professional standards, a specific body of knowledge and practice, membership of a professional body and quality of action (Cable, 2008; Cameron, 2006; Cooke and Lawton, 2008; Griffin, 2008). In whatever ways these aspects of professionalism may be worked out in the future in the Northern Ireland context, Adams (2008: 208) reminds us of the central importance of early years professionals developing 'a sense of collective identity'. In this chapter, we have raised some issues which illustrate the considerable difficulties in this area. Westcott (2004) links this sense of professional identity to standards and quality. Only through a system which involves shared training and equality of resources can a shared professional identity be achieved. The creation of an early years profession based on a broad knowledge base, participatory relationships between staff (male and female) and parents, quality interactions with children and effective leadership – what Oberhuemer (2005) terms 'democratic professionalism' – seems a goal worth striving for in Northern Ireland.

 Summary

- In this chapter, we have attempted to paint a picture of early years professionalism in Northern Ireland, highlighting the main features of today's workforce against the background of the relevant historical and policy developments.
- The introductory question 'What is to be done?' recurs in various forms throughout the chapter. We hope that the reader will engage in personal and group reflection above and beyond the possibilities suggested here.
- The issues discussed in this chapter are not unique to Northern Ireland. The case study, questions for discussion and suggested readings aim to encourage debate and application to other contexts.

 Questions for discussion

1. What do you see as the connection between quality and professionalism?
2. Reflect on some of the implications for children, families and communities of an overwhelmingly feminized early years profession.
3. Which of the three 'future possibilities' (or an alternative) do you think would best serve early years professionalism in Northern Ireland and why?
4. Do you agree that Oberhuemer's concept of 'democratic professionalism' is 'a goal worth striving for'? How might it be worked out in the context of early years services in your particular situation? (*Higher level question*)

Further reading

Levels 5 and 6

Cable, C. and Miller, L. (2008) 'Looking to the future', in L. Miller and C. Cable (eds) *Professionalism in the Early Years.* Abingdon: Hodder Education.
In this final chapter, the editors review the main themes of the book – defining professionalism and identifying themes which underpin the concept – before posing some questions to encourage readers to make choices and engage in a process of professional transformation.

McMillan, D.J. (2009) 'Preparing for educare: student perspectives on early years training in Northern Ireland', *International Journal of Early Years Education*, 17(3): 219–35.
This paper explores the reflections of students from both graduate and vocational early years training courses on the content and effectiveness of their training. There is broad agreement on the issue of essential course content but weaknesses are revealed in terms of preparation for professional practice.

Walsh, G. (2007) 'Northern Ireland', in M. Clark and T. Waller (eds) (2007) *Early Childhood Education and Care.* London: Sage.
In this chapter, Glenda Walsh explores a number of key developments in Early Childhood policy and practice (including a section on professional development and training) within the context of Northern Ireland. Case studies are used to ground the issues raised in the lives of young children and their families.

Levels 6 and 7

Gasper, M. (2010) 'The "new professionals"', in M. Gasper *Multi-agency Working in the Early Years.* London: Sage.
Michael Gasper looks at the role of the 'new professional' in the context of integrated early years provision. He presents a personal view of the current and future skills and training needed for this demanding role and hopes, in the process, to 'provoke reflection and debate'.

Urban, M. (2008) 'Dealing with uncertainty: challenges and possibilities for the early childhood profession', *European Early Childhood Education Research Journal*, 16(2): 135–52.
Matthias Urban argues in his paper that a highly skilled, qualified and knowledgeable workforce is needed to achieve the ambitious policy goals of government. He explores a paradigm of professionalism that involves relationalism, openness and uncertainty – one which may not, controversially, always produce evidence on which to base practice.

Whalley, M. (2008) 'Professional development', in M. Whalley *Leading Practice in Early Years Settings.* Exeter: Learning Matters.
In the final chapter of her book on leading practice in the early years, Mary Whalley considers the gradual journey towards professionalism. She explores how professional development can redefine leadership through effective self-evaluation and nurturing the competence and confidence of others.

Websites

www.ci-ni.org.uk/
CiNI (Children in Northern Ireland) is the regional umbrella organization for the children's sector in Northern Ireland. It promotes the work of the children's sector and provides training,

policy, information and participation support to member organizations relating to their work with children and young people.

www.early-years.org/
Early Years (formerly NIPPA) is the organization which represents many voluntary and private sector childcare and education providers in Northern Ireland.

www.meninchildcare.com/
Men in Childcare (MIC) is an organization based in Edinburgh which provides childcare training for men.

www.niscc.info
The Northern Ireland Social Care Council website provides information about standards of training and practice for the social care workforce in Northern Ireland.

www.oecd.org/edu/earlychildhood
This is the website of the Organisation for Economic Co-operation and Development. This section of the site is dedicated to the OECD reviews of national early childhood policies and organization across 20 countries.

References

Adams, K. (2008) 'What's in a name? Seeking professional status through degree studies within the Scottish early years context', *European Early Childhood Education Research Journal*, 16(2): 196–209.

Alakeson, V. (2004) *A 2020 Vision for Early Years: Extending Choice, Improving Life Chances.* London: Social Market Foundation/Esmée Fairbairn Foundation.

Anning, A. (2004) 'The co-construction of an early childhood curriculum', in A. Anning, J. Cullen and M. Fleer (eds) *Early Childhood Education: Culture and Society.* London: Sage.

Beattie, S. (2009) 'Nursery school and unit provision: a unique experience', *Termtalk*, March, General Teaching Council for Northern Ireland.

Bennett, J. (2003) 'Starting Strong: the persistent division between care and education', *Early Childhood Research*, 1(1): 21–48.

Boddy, J., Cameron, C., Moss, P., Mooney, A, Petrie, P. and Statham, J. (2005) *Introducing Pedagogy into the Children's Workforce.* London: Thomas Coram Research Unit.

Bowlby, J. (1951) *Maternal Care and Mental Health.* Geneva: World Health Organization.

Cable, C. (2008) 'Teaching assistants in the early years', in L. Miller and C. Cable (eds) *Professionalism in the Early Years.* Abingdon: Hodder Education.

Cable, C. and Miller, L. (2008) 'Looking to the future', in L. Miller and C. Cable (eds) *Professionalism in the Early Years.* Abingdon: Hodder Education.

Calder, P. (2008) 'Early childhood studies degrees: the development of a graduate profession', in L. Miller and C. Cable (eds) *Professionalism in the Early Years.* Abingdon: Hodder Education.

Cameron, C. (2006) 'Men in the nursery revisited: issues of male workers and professionalism', *Contemporary Issues in Early Childhood*, 7(1): 68–79.

Children's Workforce Development Council (CWDC) (2009) 'Parents demand more male childcare workers'. Available from: www.cwdcouncil.org.uk/whats-new/1591 (accessed 25 March 2010).

Cooke, G. and Lawton, K. (2008) *For Love or Money: Pay, Progression and Professionalisation in the 'Early Years' Workforce.* London: Institute for Public Policy Research.

Council for the Curriculum, Examinations and Assessment (CCEA) (2007) *The Northern Ireland Curriculum: Primary.* Belfast: CCEA.

Dahlberg, G., Moss, P. and Pence, A. (1999) *Beyond Quality in Early Years Education and Care: Postmodern Perspectives.* London: Falmer Press.

Dalli, C. (2010) 'Towards the re-emergence of a critical ecology of the early childhood profession in New Zealand', *Contemporary Issues in Early Childhood*, 11(1): 61–74.

Department for Education and Skills (DfES) (2003) *Every Child Matters: The Green Paper.* London: The Stationery Office.

Department of Education (DE) (2003) *The Role of the Qualified Teacher or Early Years Specialist.* Belfast: Department of Education.

Department of Education (DE) (2006a) *Children and Young People Funding Package.* Belfast: Department of Education.

Department of Education (DE) (2006b) *Effective Pre-School Provision in Northern Ireland.* Research Briefing RB3/2006, Northern Ireland Statistics and Research Agency (NISRA).

Department of Education (DE) (2009) *Every School a Good School: A Policy for School Improvement.* Available from: www.deni.gov.uk/esags_policy_for_school_improvement_-_final_version_05-05-2009.pdf (accessed 10 March 2010).

Department of Education for Northern Ireland (DENI) and Department of Health and Social Services (DHSS) (1998) *Investing in Early Learning: Pre-School Education in Northern Ireland.* Belfast: The Stationery Office.

Department of Education for Northern Ireland (DENI), Department of Health, Social Services and Public Safety (DHSSPS) and Council for the Curriculum, Examinations and Assessment (CCEA) (2006) *Curricular Guidance for Pre-School Education.* Belfast: CCEA.

Department of Health and Social Services (DHSS) and Department of Education for Northern Ireland (DENI) (1994) *Policy on Early Years Provision for Northern Ireland.* Belfast: DHSS and DENI.

Department of Health and Social Services (DHSS), Department of Education for Northern Ireland (DENI) and Training and Employment Agency (T&EA) (1999) *Children First: The Northern Ireland Childcare Strategy.* Belfast: DHSS, DENI and T&EA.

Department of Health and Social Services (DHSS), Council for the Curriculum, Examinations and Assessment (CCEA) and Department of Education for Northern Ireland (DENI) (1997) *Curricular Guidance for Pre-School Education.* Belfast: NICCEA.

Education and Training Inspectorate (ETI) (2009) *The Chief Inspector's Report 2006–08.* Belfast: ETI.

Eraut, M. (1994) *Developing Professional Knowledge and Competence.* London: The Falmer Press.

Foucault, M. (1988) *Politics, Philosophy, Culture: Interviews and Other Writings, 1977–1984* (L. Kritzman, ed.). London: Routledge.

Great Britain (1989) *Education Reform (Northern Ireland) Order.* Belfast: HMSO.

Griffin, S. (2008) 'The "P" word and home-based child carers', in L. Miller and C. Cable (eds) *Professionalism in the Early Years.* Abingdon: Hodder Education.

Karila, K. (2008) 'A Finnish viewpoint on professionalism in early childhood education', *European Early Childhood Education Research Journal*, 16(2): 210–23.

Lumsden, E. (2005) 'Joined up thinking in practice: an exploration of professional collaboration', in T. Waller (ed.) *An Introduction to Early Childhood.* London: Paul Chapman Publishing.

McMillan, D.J. (2008) 'Education and care: implications for Educare training in Northern Ireland', unpublished PhD thesis, Queen's University, Belfast.

Miller, L. (2008) 'Developing professionalism within a regulatory framework in England: challenges and possibilities', *European Early Childhood Education Research Journal*, 16(2): 255–68.

Moss, P. (2006) 'Structures, understandings and discourses: possibilities for re-envisioning the early childhood worker', *Contemporary Issues in Early Childhood*, 7(1): 30–41.

Moss, P. and Petrie, P. (2002) *From Children's Services to Children's Spaces.* London: RoutledgeFalmer.

Northern Ireland Curriculum Council (NICC) (1989) *Nursery Education Guidelines: The Curriculum.* Belfast: NICC

Northern Ireland Preschool Playgroups Association (NIPPA) (1996) *Valuing Play, Valuing Early Childhood: Policy and Practice Guidelines for Early Years Practitioners.* Belfast: NIPPA – the Early Years Organisation.

Northern Ireland Preschool Playgroups Association (NIPPA) (2007) *Briefing Paper: Transformation Fund for Northern Ireland.* Belfast: NIPPA.

Oberhuemer, P. (2005) 'Conceptualising the early childhood pedagogue: policy approaches and issues of professionalism', *European Early Childhood Education Research Journal*, 13(1): 5–16.

Office of the First Minister and Deputy First Minister (OFMDFM) (2006) *Our Children and Young People – Our Pledge: A Ten Year Strategy for Children and Young People in Northern Ireland 2006–2016.* Belfast: OFMDFM.

Organisation for Economic Co-operation and Development (OECD) (2006) *Starting Strong II: Early Childhood Education and Care*. Paris: OECD.

Osgood, J. (2006) 'Deconstructing professionalism in early childhood education: resisting the regulatory gaze', *Contemporary Issues in Early Childhood*, 7(1): 5–14.

Owen, C. (2003) 'Men in the nursery', in J. Brannen and P. Moss (eds) *Rethinking Children's Care*. Buckingham: Open University Press.

Qualifications and Curriculum Authority (QCA), Qualifications, Curriculum and Assessment Authority for Wales (QCAA) and Council for the Curriculum, Examinations and Assessment (CCEA) (2006) *The National Qualifications Framework: Helping Learners Make Informed Decisions*. Available from: www.qca.org.uk/libraryAssets/media/qca-06-2298-nqf-web.pdf (accessed 12 March 2010).

Sargent, P. (2005) 'The gendering of men in early childhood education', *Sex Roles*, 53(3–4): 251–9. Available from: http://dx.doi.org/10.1007/s11199-005-1300-x (accessed 20 March 2010).

Sutherland, A. (2006) 'Including pre-school education', in C. Donnolly, P. McKeown and B. Osborne (eds) *Devolution and Pluralism in Education in Northern Ireland*. Manchester: Manchester University Press.

Sylva, K., Melhuish, E., Sammons, P., Siraj-Blatchford, I. and Taggart, B. (2004) *Effective Pre-School Provision (EPPE)*. London: Institute of Education.

Urban, M. (2008) 'Dealing with uncertainty: challenges and possibilities for the early childhood profession', *European Early Childhood Education Research Journal*, 16(2): 135–52.

Walsh, G. (2007) 'Northern Ireland', in M. Clark and T. Waller (eds) *Early Childhood Education and Care: Policy and Practice*. London: Sage.

Westcott, E. (2004) 'The early years workforce – towards professional status? An issues paper', unpublished paper presented at the Senior Practitioner Working Group, Department for Education and Skills (DfES).

CHAPTER 5

CHILDCARE PRACTITIONERS AND THE PROCESS OF PROFESSIONALIZATION

Jan Peeters and Michel Vandenbroeck

Overview

There is a large degree of consensus that higher staff qualifications are correlated with higher quality in early childhood provision and that reflection is the most important part of professionalism. However, the concepts of the 'reflective practitioner' and the 'reflexive practitioner' (see below for the elaboration of these terms), although frequently mentioned in the literature, remain rather underdeveloped and the apparent consensus on the need for reflection may very well disguise a lack of consensus on what it actually means. Moreover, concepts of professionalism in general and of reflective and reflexive professionalism in particular are overwhelmingly elaborated without the professionals themselves. In this chapter, analysis of narratives of professionals during 30 years of action research show how professionals who engage with pedagogic guidance can become actors of change and develop new pedagogic practices.

Introduction

Academic attention to the professionalization of the early years workforce is relatively new and is dominated by studies in the United States of America, Australia and the United Kingdom. As a result, the academic discussion on professionalism in early childhood is dominated by contexts, marked by a history of significant differences in staff qualifications, large shares of care work provided by private providers, and little government regulation regarding staff qualifications, though in the case of the UK this has recently changed (OECD, 2006; Unicef, 2008). Notwithstanding this bias in published research, some consensus emerges from the literature regarding the relationship between quality and professionalization. Higher levels of qualifications correlate positively with better childcare quality as well as with better developmental outcomes for children (e.g. Cameron and Moss, 2007; Fukkink and Lont, 2007; Sylva et al., 2004). Research also shows that in-service training (on the job) may be as important as pre-service (initial) qualifications, provided it is of sufficient length and intensity (e.g. Fukkink and Lont, 2007). However, this does not mean that qualifications can be considered in isolation, nor that the professionalization of the workforce is in itself sufficient to predict the quality of provision. First, it is important to note that educators with higher levels of qualification tend to choose to work in higher quality provision. Second, more highly qualified practitioners can bring about quality results only when the staff is supported in implementing the insights gained through training in their practice and when the working conditions (including salaries) do not jeopardize the continuity of the workforce (Early et al., 2007).

In addition, there is also a considerable degree of consensus on how this professionalism may be understood. There is general agreement that a specific body of knowledge, as well as a series of skills, are necessary but that these do not suffice. Indeed, reflection is considered by many writers to be the most important part of professionalism (Dunn et al., 2008; Urban, 2008). However, the concept of the 'reflective practitioner', although frequently mentioned in the literature, remains rather underdeveloped and the apparent consensus on the need for reflection may very well disguise a lack of consensus on what it actually means. We can distinguish between reflection-for-action (what will I do?); reflection-in-action (what am I doing?) and reflection-on-action (what have I done?) (Cheng, 2001). Overall, however, the concept of reflection that is most dominant in academic literature is about 'doing things right'. As Coussée, Bradt, Roose and Bouverne-De Bie (2008) rightly argue, this is quite different in nature to reflection on 'doing the right things'. The reflective practitioner moves towards becoming reflexive by questioning taken-for-granted beliefs and by understanding that knowledge is contestable (Kuisma and Sandberg, 2008; Kunneman, 2005; Miller, 2008; Urban and Dalli, 2008). While the first approach focuses on documenting and evaluating one's practice within a fixed paradigm, the second approach questions the very paradigms in which one is operating. A recent thematic monograph published by the *European Early Childhood Education*

Research Journal (Urban and Dalli, 2008), is one of the few international publications exploring this second approach. A second observation is that practitioners are virtually absent from the discussion about their reflexive professionalism. The result is that – paradoxically – the literature on reflexive practitioners risks reducing the practitioners to objects, rather than including them as reflexive and agentic subjects. According to Sorel and Wittorski (2005), it is essential that the individuals who are 'professionalizing' themselves are not reduced to the role of a 'consumer' of the knowledge that is presented to them. Yet, little is known about the practitioner's views on this emerging role transformation, with its new emphasis on negotiating and networking competencies (Oberhuemer, 2000). As a result, important questions of how individuals develop their professionalism remain. This may imply a need for participative action research in this field. Leitch and Day (2000) have argued that action research can play an important role in increasing professionalism, providing that it is oriented towards change, critical reflection and participation. Action research, as opposed to pragmatic research, raises the possibility of questioning the social position of research. According to Roose and De Bie (2003), participative research may be a driving force for cultural action, a process of searching for new definitions of reality, leading to a commitment to critical thinking.

Three decades of action research

Since the late 1970s, action research projects have been set up with early years workers by the Faculty of Psychology and Educational Sciences of Ghent University. Initially, these projects were theoretically inspired by social constructivism and by the notion of the 'teacher-as-researcher' (Stenhouse, 1975) and the Freirian notion of 'cultural action'. These frameworks were put into practice in adult education through democratic, participative and experiential training methods (as developed for instance in the Friedrich Ebert Stiftung) and theorized in the Frankfurter Schule. Some of the guiding principles included: avoiding the hierarchical dichotomy between researchers and practitioners; involving practitioners in debates on their everyday work; and documenting their experiences as actors of change. These action research projects may be viewed as 'communicative spaces' for practitioners and researchers (Dahlberg and Moss, 2005). Rinaldi (2005) argues from the rich experiences of the children's centres in Reggio Emilia, where a high level of professionalism has been developed since the 1960s, that the participation of the practitioners is an important factor in the process of professionalization: 'The staff member should be the first to nurture the pleasure of participation, to draw meaning from meetings, and find the opportunity to qualify and enrich his/her professionalism through participation' (Rinaldi, 2005: 51).

In this vein, 11 action research projects were set up within Ghent University, between 1979 and 2008, with the aim of increasing the level of professionalism of the childcare workforce. In each project, video documentaries were made to document the processes of participation that enriched the professionalism of the practitioners. All recordings from 1979 until 2006 were produced in the same way. The researchers used typical research methods (observations, interviews and questionnaires) to identify an issue (e.g. multiple conflicts between toddlers) and subsequently did a literature search in order to investigate possible framings of the issue. In addition, the researchers looked for parents, children and/or practitioners, willing and able to describe the problem concretely from their own experiences in the childcare centres. Then the researchers looked for practitioners who had reflected on the problematic situation and had experimented successfully with the problem. These practitioners were interviewed and their practice was documented on video. This sample of practitioners has therefore no claim whatsoever to represent the population or to be 'average' practitioners. On the contrary, they may be identified as 'actors of social change' (Urban, 2006) as they, together with the researchers, played an active role in a process of change that aimed to increase the level of professionalization over the past 30 years.

The last film, made in 2007, had a different framing. Three practitioners who participated in several of the projects (and thus have a long-standing career in childcare) and were still active in the field, were confronted with a video showing interviews from 1981. They were asked to comment on continuity and change over the last three decades, drawing on 'video-elicitation' methodology (Declercq, 2002), in which the videos themselves do not serve as data, but as triggers for the interview. Their interviews were again video-taped, transcribed and analysed.

In total, 30 documentaries, featuring 84 practitioners, 23 parents and six children were analysed by the researchers. The selected fragments focus on how childcare workers have interpreted their work from the 1970s to the present. The focus of the analysis is therefore on the 'little narratives' (Lyotard, 1979) of the actors of change themselves and may, therefore, convey multiple, even contradictory meanings. These contradictions, however, may be very useful, since it is dissensus, rather than consensus, that has the potential to create emancipation and greater equity (Dahlberg and Moss, 2005; Hughes and MacNaughton, 2000; Vandenbroeck, 2009). The analysis of these narratives formed part of a larger PhD study on evolutions in professionalism, both in practice and in policy, in Flanders, Denmark, France, New Zealand and England (Peeters, 2008).

Agentic practitioners looking for new possibilities

Thirty years ago, the childcare sector in Belgium was entirely dominated by a discursive medical-hygienic regime. It was common practice that parents were forbidden to enter the premises; childcare workers were seldom allowed to talk to parents, as this was the monopoly of their head, a hospital nurse; children were undressed, bathed and dressed in clothes provided by the centres upon their arrival; the staff wore white clinical uniforms; play materials were stacked out of the reach of children; a strict hierarchy was observed, with the doctor at the top, the nurse next and the childcare worker at the bottom; team meetings were scarce and it was most uncommon to discuss educational matters with the staff (Mozère, 1992; Peeters, 1993; Vandenbroeck, 2004).

The statements of the staff members talking in 2007 about the late 1970s illustrate the dominance of specific discursive regimes and how they influenced the image of the self. In this case, the testimonies give explicit examples of how their view of their profession was influenced by the medical-hygienic regime.

My training during the 1970s consisted exclusively of providing care and the nurseries paid an excessive amount of attention to what was 'healthy'. Children were dressed too warmly, so that their freedom of movement was severely curtailed. The children spent all of their waking and sleeping hours in the same room. For that reason, the room had to be aired and we would put on the hats and sweaters and open the window for 10 minutes. We then closed the window and waited until the room got back up to the correct temperature. Only then did we take off the hats and coats. Thus, the child was never given the chance to relax and could not sleep when tired. No one ever asked what that meant for the child. That is something that they would now never be able to have me do. But at that time, you are young, you don't have any experience, this is the way you learned it and you go along with it without question – until your eyes are opened. (Childcare worker, 2007)

Narratives by parents from 1980 make it clear how negatively this cool and distant way of dealing with children and parents was experienced:

One is not allowed to enter the playroom, they call the name of the child and the parent must wait in the hall until they give him to you. (Father, 1980)

You are not introduced to the childcare workers and you do not know their names. (Father, 1980)

I would like to have received information about what my child did during the day, but you never got that spontaneously. You had to ask explicitly and the reaction was generally very short. 'He has eaten and slept well'. Other than that, you didn't get any information. (Mother, 1980)

The 1980s were a period of major changes within the sector (Vandenbroeck, 2003). The medical-hygienic discourse was to a large extent abandoned and committed staff members (actors of change) engaged in action research experimented with more pedagogic interpretations of professionalism. The video images show how the childcare workers in this period expanded their interpretation of professionalism by becoming themselves actors in the innovations that were being implemented. Rinaldi summarized this participatory process succinctly: 'Participation nurtures professionalism' (Rinaldi, 2005: 51). The following short fragments from the narratives illustrate the positive impact of the participatory process.

I have experienced the change as extremely positive. We were given more space to determine for ourselves how to develop our activities.

In the past, if you had an idea about how to improve the activities, it was difficult to implement it. Now, we have a team meeting in which this is discussed, so that you get support from your colleagues and can achieve better results when improving the activity.

(Childcare workers, 1981/1982)

The staff members' narratives demonstrate that being involved in a process of change, in which they are agentic actors, gives them hope and self-confidence, and increases their job satisfaction. These participative action research projects provoked a major change in professional attitudes towards the parents. From the exclusion of parents in the 1970s, they gradually moved towards inviting parents to get to know the way the centre worked in order to increase the wellbeing of the children.

> If the parents stay a little bit longer in the playroom before they go to work, the children cry less. (Childcare worker, 1981)

> After seeing the video of a day in the life of the centre, parents are astonished about the many things their child is doing at the centre. They ask a lot of questions and they give information about how their child is at home. (Childcare worker, 1982)

> I do not replace the parents, but I take over as much as possible the habits of the parents, the way they interact with their child. I ask how they put their child to bed, how they feed their child, what their child likes and how they comfort it at home, in order to make the children feel as good here in the day care centre as at home. (Childcare worker, 1985)

These actors were very concerned with increasing the wellbeing and involvement of the children, by making the playroom into a more stimulating environment and by introducing activities that enhanced meaningful adult–child and peer interactions. They also developed a researching attitude. They reflected on pedagogic practice and constructed new pedagogic knowledge.

> Now we can choose the furniture of the play room ourselves and we have bought a second-hand lounge suite. I find it much more cosy. We are now reading a book together in the chair and the children like it. (Childcare worker, 1981)

> We have started to make play corners, and we position the play materials so that the children can take the toys they want to play with by themselves; and the children are now able to put away the toys themselves. (Childcare worker, 1981)

> In the beginning we have to work things out, such as: 'Is the baby tired?' or 'What is the matter with him?' But once he's been here a while we know that the baby has a certain rhythm that is repeated. And then the rhythm of the baby changes around 6–7 months. (Childcare worker, 1987)

The childcare workers emphasize that their initial training was inappropriate to reflect on these day-to-day problems and that they consequently had to look for answers themselves to the new complex problems they were facing.

> I think far too much is expected of nursery nurses, given their training. For some people, expectations are too high for us to be able to meet them. (Childcare worker, 1981)

> We have to learn on our own how to interact with children in the daily experience. (Childcare worker, 1985)

Respect for diversity: a paradigm shift

Our analysis of the narratives on continuity and change show that the discussions on respect for diversity in the 1990s played an important role in changing practitioners' conceptions of the profession. In 1995, with the support of the governmental organization Kind en Gezin (Child and Family), a large-scale action research project on respect for diversity in childcare was set up. This project was aimed at diversifying the workforce as well as adapting the pedagogy of childcare centres to the multicultural society (Somers and Peeters, 1998). The numerous narratives collected in this project show how it confronted the practitioners with a paradigm shift. Both ethnic minority and ethnic majority trainees testified about the difficulties in addressing diversity issues.

> Female Moroccan graduates like me have to be assertive at work and make eye contact with others, but in my home situation this is unheard of.

> I used to think that the purpose of criticism was to put you down. I now know that you can also learn from criticism, that criticism can also be constructive. Subjects also came up that were taboo for us, such as, for example, homosexuality.

> We used to do things simply because that was the way they were done. Now, however, we continually ask ourselves why we did this or that. In the beginning, we therefore had conflicts with our family and friends. They saw us change and we confronted them with their own norms and values.

> (Ethnic minority trainees, 1997)

Both the ethnic minority course members and their Flemish mentors spoke about this paradigm shift and about the difficulties of constructing an inclusive professionalism. Working with respect for diversity in early childhood presupposes a focus on respect for the uniqueness of the Other (Moss, 2007b). Dahlberg and Moss (2008: 64) state 'Putting everything one encounters into pre-made categories implies we make the Other into the Same ... To think another whom I cannot grasp is an important shift and it challenges the whole scene of Pedagogy'. This implies that in contexts of diversity, the focus may be on dealing with what we cannot understand, rather than on trying to understand or trying to 'grasp' the Other into our own frames of reference. This requires openness and flexibility and the recognition of multiple perspectives and paradigms, acknowledging and welcoming that there is more than one answer to most questions.

The narratives show that during the project, open discussions were held in the childcare centres on these issues, for example through discussions on practical matters such as whether or not a headscarf was an impediment to a professional approach. This search for the Other appeared to be extremely successful in developing, together with the parents, new practical knowledge.

> A baby [whose parents were from Zaire] had trouble sleeping in a bed and often wept. We talked to the parents and they said that they first rock their child before they put her in bed. We tried that in a hammock and it worked well.

> We ask the parents for pet words or nicknames that they use with their child. We try to say these words in the child's native language so that they hear familiar sounds when they are with us. We search for things that are recognizable for the child, such as music from their native country. This is extremely important if the child is still adjusting.

> (Flemish childcare workers, 1997)

The testimonies suggest that dealing with diversity presents the early years practitioners with complex problems that cannot be solved with a technical body of knowledge, since they ask for interpretations of professionalism based on continuous reflection on their practice as well as the need to move beyond reflection and develop the ability to be reflexive.

At the beginning of the new millennium, another aspect of diversity creates new possibilities for reflection and change. Fierce discussions emerge on the gender-specific interpretation of childcare professionalism. Our study suggests that, as in many other European countries, the childcare professions in Flanders are based on a female-oriented construction of professionalism and that this 'mother-like prac-tice' excludes both male staff and fathers (Peeters, 2003). When more men are part of the staff, new questions emerge that challenge traditional constructions of the early years professional as female, mother-like and 'naturally' caring (Cameron, 2006). However, in order to be able to realize a gender-neutral construction of professionalism, the atmosphere in the training courses and in the centres also needs to change (Vandenbroeck and Peeters, 2008). The focus on a narrow care con-cept needs to be abandoned as broader interpretations of professionalism are real-ized (Hauglund, 2005; Wohlgemuth, 2003), making a place for more social functions of childcare (Meleady and Broadhead, 2002; Vandenbroeck, 2004). By the social func-tions of childcare, we mean the multiple ways in which childcare is contributing to social justice, as part of the welfare system. This may include issues of tackling une-qual access, but also issues of how professionals relate to parents in reciprocal ways and how parents, children and local communities are involved in the decisions that affect their lives.

Children as active citizens

Since the end of the 1990s, the practitioners have become more interested in the way parents educate their young children at home and in questioning how the childcare centre could take on some of the practices of the parents. In this evolution, children are increasingly considered as active citizens who can decide upon important aspects of daily life in the childcare centre.

> I find it very important that the parents can stay for a while in the morning; that they have the time and the opportunity to talk about their child. Did he sleep well, what did he eat, what else happened in the family; for us all those things are important when we take over the [care of the] child. (Childcare educator, 2001)

> To say goodbye is not easy for the child or for the parent. When the parents are on the street they give their child a hand through the mailbox; the child sees the parent and touches their hand through the mailbox; this ritual makes saying goodbye easier for the parent and for the child. (Childcare educator, 2001)

> Children can decide themselves if they want to participate in the play and when they want to stop playing. How long and how frequently they want to participate in activities is up to the children to decide. (Childcare educator, 2001)

Possibilities of a close collaboration between research and practice

Several authors argue that there are no universal answers for the problems facing childcare workers and teachers in early childhood education (e.g. Cameron, 2008; Moss, 2007a; Urban, 2008). They therefore advocate for professionals who are able to continually reflect on their practice and who can, time and again, find new solutions for the complex situations they face. This raises timely questions on how to facilitate this process. The analysis of praxis in day-to-day working situations contributes, according to Favre (2008), to the construction of a professional identity that is focused on change. From his perspective, professionalism can only evolve if the institution allows it a discretionary space to do so. Early years practitioners should take up the challenge to question their work and be focused on the continual adjustment of their pedagogic practices on the basis of reflection. Annalia Galardina (2008) documents how, in Pistoia, the introduction of reflexivity to the work of the institution is developed by the *pedagogistas*. The task of these pedagogic counsellors consists of instigating a mutual dialogue between the centres and encouraging the professionals' ongoing reflection on their approach and their beliefs. In the action research projects from Ghent University, the childcare workers were also supported by researchers or pedagogic counsellors who fulfilled a similar role to the pedagogistas of Pistoia. Their task is to assist the early childhood workers in 'discovering what is possible' (Dalli, 2008: 17).

Pedagogic counsellors/researchers or pedagogistas can play an important role in the construction of new pedagogic knowledge by supporting the practitioners in the analysis of their practice. From our study of the narratives of the Flemish actors of change, we would argue that it is important that the childcare workers and staff members are given sufficient autonomy by the counsellors in their search for what is possible: practitioners must remain the main 'actors of change'. In this sense, a close collaboration of researchers and practitioners, blurring the boundaries between both, may be very useful.

Competencies for change

The action-oriented competencies that educators acquire through the process of engagement with action research and pedagogic counsellors, provide the staff with the possibility of changing existing pedagogic practices, and allow them to deal reflexively with complex situations and to construct practical knowledge in interaction with children, parents and colleagues.

> The intense collaboration with parents starts with the intake procedure when the parents show us how they deal with important things about their child. In the past we were explaining to the parents how we are working, now we ask the parents: how do you want us to care for your children? (Pedagogic counsellor, 2003)

There was a transition period, where we as parents showed the childcare workers how we dealt with Zoë; it was good to feel that they were interested in how we were dealing with our child, they do not see themselves as the experts. I expect that they will continue what we are doing at home. (Father, 2006)

We have a mother from Somalia here who is a political refugee, and her child cries a lot. We asked the mother to show us how she comforted her baby: she was singing for her child. The childcare worker recorded the song of the mother and now when the child is crying she plays the tape of the mother singing, and it helps a lot, the child calms down hearing the voice of his mother. (Pedagogic counsellor, 2003)

Discussion

As we have said, literature that unveils what is meant by reflective and reflexive professionalism is rather scarce and the voice of practitioners is often missing. The analysis of the narratives of professional actors of change in Flemish childcare settings, shows different evolutions over the last 30 years. Most importantly, there has been a notable evolution in the way childcare workers have viewed children since the 1980s: from the child as an object that needed to be cared for, to a child as subject and actor in the process of development. Interestingly, this shift coincides with a second evolution: a shift in how these professionals themselves are treated. The rigid hierarchy of the settings until the late 1970s prohibited professionals from speaking up (and prohibited parents or 'experts' from addressing the professionals directly). When professionals were observed by researchers, they were constructed as objects of study, rather than as agentic subjects. The narratives of these professionals document how a shift in the hierarchical view enabled them to reflect upon their practice and to reconstruct what it may be to 'do things right'.

A third shift – during the late 1990s – seems to be of another nature and occurred in the diversity projects that encouraged the professionals to also take parental opinions and views into account. The agentic childcare workers gradually conceptualized the education of the child in the centre as a shared responsibility between parents and childcare workers. In addition, they were confronted with questions of inclusion and exclusion and traditional power relations were challenged. These projects questioned taken-for-granted opinions in a much deeper way and invited the professionals to not only think about 'doing things right' but also about 'doing the right things'.

In a provisional attempt to further unravel and concretize this concept of reflexive professionalism, we formulate the hypothesis that practice, enabling reflection on 'doing things right' as well as 'doing the right things', asks for four categories of basic and generic competencies:

1. *The ability to look for (always provisional) solutions in contexts of dissensus.*
   The most significant results have been achieved in teams who displayed the ability to discuss different opinions intensively and where on the basis of these debates concrete decisions were taken and put into practice.

2. *The ability to focus on the meeting of the Other, the one we do not know.* The 'little' narratives in this study document that the orientation to try to understand the parent who is 'different' is a basic competence of working in childcare (Dahlberg and Moss, 2008).
3. *The ability to co-construct knowledge with others (colleagues, parents, children).* This study has given several examples of how the childcare workers developed, in collaboration with the researchers or the pedagogic counsellor, the competence of being able to construct new practical knowledge, new ways of working with children, parents and colleagues.
4. *The ability to act with a focus on change.* The participation in action research projects has created a belief in the possibilities of experimentation. The 'little' narratives document how the 'actors of change' have developed competences that help them to discover what is possible in working in early childhood education.

Ongoing research by the European DECET network (Diversity in Early Childhood Education and Training) will further elaborate this hypothesis.

Taking into account the experiences and the meaning making of the professionals, may also shed some light on the conditions that are necessary to let reflexive professionalism flourish. One of the more salient conditions is the creation of communicative spaces. Dahlberg and Moss (2005) advocate these 'communicative spaces' or 'islands of democracy' where researchers, policy-makers and staff work together to develop new knowledge. They use the concepts of minor and major politics, referring to Deleuze and Guattari (1980) and argue that:

> The two forms of politics should not be seen as in opposition. Each can provoke the other into creativity; minor politics may, for example, connect up with a whole series of other circuits and cause them to fluctuate, waver and reconfigure in wholly unexpected ways. (Dahlberg and Moss, 2008: 56)

Final thoughts

Action research projects combine some features of these communicative spaces, where minor and major politics meet. During the past 30 years, the most significant evolutions occurred when representatives of the sector, the academia and policy-makers collaborated in democratic ways to develop new types of professionalism. The most interesting project from this perspective was the action research on respect for diversity in the late 1990s. In the diversity project, representatives of childcare centres and community organizations working with ethnic minorities, together with researchers and policy-makers, discussed what professionalism was about and this brought about lasting and creative results. The professionalization process needs to be considered as a social practice and as a result of complex interactions between social evolutions (e.g. the growing diversity of families), policy measures (e.g. new legislation) and new scientific insights (e.g. the importance of men in the development of young children), interacting in turn with researchers or pedagogic counsellors, staff members and users (parents as well as children). These insights also point at the crucial role of pedagogic counselling. Many authors have already pointed to the fact that some pedagogic guidance is necessary to allow professionals to implement the knowledge, skills and attitudes from the initial training (e.g. Early et al., 2007). In addition, we argue that examples from practice show that this counselling, be it by action researchers or by pedagogistas (Galardina, 2008) may also help construct professionalism, in the case of insufficient initial training. This is not to say that initial training should be dismissed. Indeed, one needs to acknowledge that the projects presented here and the evolutions described are about a small sample of 'actors of change' and need to be considered as the fruition of long periods of sustained, intensive guidance and collaboration, rather than as 'products' of eclectic short-term interventions.

Summary

- Professionalism matters for children.
- Professionalism is not just a matter of knowledge, skills and attitudes but also a matter of becoming reflective *and* reflexive.
- Reflexive professionalism can be developed in practice, given sustained pedagogic counselling.
- Reflexive professionals move beyond applying pedagogy or psychology, and create new knowledge in complex and uncertain situations.

Questions for discussion

1. What do you consider are the critical factors in the process of transformation from reflective practitioner to reflexive 'actor of change'? Which are the critical conditions in the process of professionalization that help transform a practitioner into an actor of change?
2. How does an understanding of diversity enhance professional practice? Can you explain why working in contexts of diversity broadens the interpretation of professionalism?
3. Consider the four competencies that characterize reflexive professionalism outlined in this chapter. Can you provide examples of each from your own practice? (*Higher level question*)

Further reading

Levels 5 and 6

Craft, A. and Paige-Smith, A. (2008) 'Reflective practice', in L. Miller and C. Cable (eds) *Professionalism in the Early Years*. London: Hodder Education. pp. 87–97.

The authors are exploring here the growing place of reflection in, and on, professional practice in the work of the early years practitioner. The notion of community of practice and means of documenting children's learning are also put forward as ways of establishing common approaches.

Moss, P. (2008) 'The democratic and reflective professional: rethinking and reforming the early years workforce', in L. Miller and C. Cable (eds) *Professionalism in the Early Years*. London: Hodder Education. pp. 119–30.
In this article, Moss is offering an alternative direction for the weakness of the workforce in many countries; he is promoting a democratic and reflective professional, instilled with a number of core values.

Peeters, J. and Moss, P. (eds) (2008) 'Aiming high: a professional workforce for the early years', *Children in Europe*, 15(2). Published in 14 languages.
This special issue of the *Children in Europe* magazine, gives an overview of the professionalization discussion throughout Europe and New Zealand. It also contains a description of the core professionals in ECE in the EU-27.

Levels 6 and 7

Peeters, J. (2008) *The Construction of a New Profession: A European Perspective on Professionalism in Early Childhood Education and Care*. Amsterdam: SWP.
This book shows that the striving for the co-construction of a new profession in ECE is not an isolated event, but an international endeavour in which actors from various countries are deeply involved.

Urban, M. (2008) 'Dealing with uncertainty: challenges and possibilities for the early childhood profession', *European Early Childhood Education Research Journal*, 16(2): 135–52.
Drawing on the conceptual framework of hermeneutics, the article explores an alternative paradigm of a relational systematic professionalism that embraces openness and uncertainty, and encourages co-construction of professional knowledges and practices.

Vandenbroeck, M. and Peeters, J. (2008) 'Gender and professionalism: a critical analysis of overt and covert curricula', *Early Child Development and Care*, 178(7–8): 703–15.
This article presents three studies that unveil how professionalism is affected by both overt and covert gendered curricula. A first study interviewed 30 students in initial training, while a second study involved 16 men in adult education for caring professions. A third study examined 1,635 pages of textbooks on aspects of gender.

Websites

www.decet.org
This is the website of the European network Diversity in Early Childhood Education and Training. The site provides training material and background texts as well as information on ongoing international projects and local projects in different European countries.

www.vbjk.be/en/taxonomy/term/410/history
This is the website from the Resource and Research Centre in Early Childhood Education and Care in Flanders (Belgium). From this website, you can download the video clips relating to this chapter.

References

Cameron, C. (2006) 'Male workers and professionalism', *Contemporary Issues in Early Childhood*, 7(1): 68–79.

Cameron, C. (2008) 'What do we mean by "competence"?' *Children in Europe*, 15: 12–13.

Cameron, C. and Moss, P. (2007) *Care Work in Europe: Current Understandings and Future Directions*. London: Routledge.

Cheng, D.P.W. (2001) 'Difficulties of Hong Kong teachers' understanding and implementation of play in the curriculum', *Teaching and Teacher Education*, 17(7): 857–69.

Coussée, F., Bradt, L., Roose, R. and Bouverne-De Bie, M. (2008) 'The emerging social pedagogical paradigm in UK child and youth care: deus ex machina or walking the beaten path?', *British Journal of Social Work*, 40(3): 789–805.

Dahlberg, G. and Moss, P. (2005) *Ethics and Politics in Early Childhood Education*. London: Routledge.

Dahlberg, G. and Moss, P. (2008) 'Au-delà de la qualité, vers l'éthique et le politique en matière d'education préscolaire', in G. Brougère and M. Vandenbroeck (eds) *Repenser l'éducation des jeunes enfants*. Brussels: Peter Lang. pp. 53–78.

Dalli, C. (2008) 'Early childhood teachers in New Zealand', *Children in Europe*, 15: 16–17.

Declercq, A. (2002) 'Visuele sociologie: het gebruik van video, film en foto's als onderzoeksmateriaal'. Ongepubliceerde cursus. Universiteit Gent.

Deleuze, G. and Guattari, F. (1980) *Mille plateaux*. Paris: Editions de Minuit.

Dunn, M., Harrison, L.J. and Coombe, K. (2008) 'In good hands: preparing research-skilled graduates for the early childhood professional', *Teaching and Teacher Education*, 24(3): 703–14.

Early, D., Maxwell, K., Burchinal, M., Bender, R., Ebanks, C., Henry, G., et al. (2007) 'Teachers' education, classroom quality, and young children's academic skills: results from seven studies of preschool programs', *Child Development*, 78(2): 558–80.

Favre, D. (2008) 'Educateur de jeunes enfants in France', *Children in Europe*, 15: 20–1.

Fukkink, R.G. and Lont, A. (2007) 'Does training matter? A meta-analysis and review of caregiver training studies', *Early Childhood Research Quarterly*, 22: 294–311.

Galardina, A. (2008) 'Pedagogistas in Italy', *Children in Europe*, 15: 20.

Hauglund, E. (2005) 'Men in childcare in Norway', paper presented at the Men in Childcare Conference, National Children's Bureau, London, 20 September.

Hughes, P. and MacNaughton, G. (2000) 'Consensus, dissensus or community: the politics of parent involvement in early childhood education', *Contemporary Issues in Early Childhood*, 1(13): 241–57.

Kuisma, M. and Sandberg, A. (2008) 'Preschool teachers' and students preschool teachers' thoughts about professionalism in Sweden', *European Early Childhood Education Research Journal*, 16(2): 186–95.

Kunneman, H. (2005) 'Social work as a laboratory for normative professionalisation', *Social Work & Society*, 3(2): 191–200.

Leitch, R. and Day, C. (2000) 'Action research and reflective practice: towards a holistic view', *Educational Action Research*, 8(1): 173–93.

Lyotard, F. (1979) *La condition post-moderne*. Paris: Editions de Minuit.

Meleady, C. and Broadhead, P. (2002) 'Diversity: the norm, not the exception', *Children in Europe*, 2(2): 11–15.

Miller, L. (2008) 'Developing professionalism with a regulatory framework in England: challenges and possibilities', *European Early Childhood Education Research Journal*, 16(2): 255–68.

Moss, P. (2007a) 'Bringing politics into the nursery: early childhood education as a democratic practice', *European Early Childhood Education Research Journal*, 15(1): 5–20.

Moss, P. (2007b) 'Meetings across the paradigmatic divide', *Educational Philosophy and Theory*, 39(3): 229–45.

Mozère, L. (1992) *Le printemps des crèches: Histoire et analyse d'un movement*. Paris: L'Harmattan.

Oberhuemer, P. (2000) 'Conceptualizing the professional role in early childhood centres: emerging profiles in four countries', *Early Childhood Research & Practice*, 2(2). Available from: http://ecrp.uiuc.edu/v2n2/oberhuemer.html (accessed 14 January 2008).

Organisation for Economic Co-operation and Development (OECD) (2006) *Starting Strong II: Early Childhood Education and Care*. Paris: OECD.

Peeters, J. (1993) 'Quality improvement in the childcare centres with the support of the Bernard van Leer Foundation', in J. Peeters and M. Vandenbroeck (eds) *Working Towards Better Childcare: Report over Thirteen Years of Research and Training*. Gent: RUG, VBJK. pp. 39–79.

Peeters, J. (2003) 'Men in childcare: an action-research in Flanders', *International Journal of Equality and Innovation in Early Childhood*, 1(1): 72–83.

Peeters, J. (2008) *The Construction of a New Profession: A European Perspective on Professionalism in Early Childhood Education and Care*. Amsterdam: SWP.

Rinaldi, C. (2005) *In Dialogue with Reggio Emilia*. London: RoutledgeFalmer.

Roose, R. and De Bie, M. (2003) 'From participative research to participative practice: a study in youth care', *Journal of Community & Applied Social Psychology*, 13: 475–85.

Somers, A. and Peeters, J. (1998) *Diversiteit in de Kinderopvang*. Gent: VBJK.

Sorel, M. and Wittorski, R. (2005) *La Professionalisation en Actes et en Questions*. Paris: L'Harmattan.

Stenhouse, L. (1975) *An Introduction to Curriculum Research and Development*. London: Heinemann.

Sylva, K., Melhuish, E., Sammons, P., Siraj-Blatchford, I. and Taggart, B. (2004) *The Effective Provision of Preschool Education (EPPE) Project: Final Report*. Nottingham: DfES Publications – The Institute of Education.

Unicef Innocenti Research Centre (2008) *Report Card 8: The Child Care Transition*. Florence: Unicef.

Urban, M. (2006) *Strategies for Change. Gesellschafts- und fachpolitische Strategien zur Reform des Systems frühkindlicher Bildung*. Halle: Bertelsmans Stiftung.

Urban, M. (2008) 'Dealing with uncertainty: challenges and possibilities for the early childhood profession', *European Early Childhood Education Research Journal*, 16(2): 135–52.

Urban, M. and Dalli, C. (2008) 'Editorial', *European Early Childhood Education Research Journal*, 16(2): 131–3.

Vandenbroeck, M. (2003) 'From crèches to childcare: constructions of motherhood and inclusion/exclusion in the history of Belgian infant care', *Contemporary Issues in Early Childhood*, 4(2): 137–48.

Vandenbroeck, M. (2004) *In verzekerde bewaring. Honderdvijftig jaar kinderen, ouders en kinderopvang*. Amsterdam: SWP.

Vandenbroeck, M. (2009) 'Let's disagree', *European Early Childhood Education Research Journal*, 17(2): 165–70.

Vandenbroeck, M. and Peeters, J. (2008) 'Gender and professionalism: a critical analysis of overt and covert curricula', *Early Child Development and Care*, 178(7–8): 703–15.

Wohlgemuth, U. (2003) 'One for all: men on the pedagogue course', *Children in Europe*, 3(5): 22–3.

CHAPTER 6

WORKING IN MULTIDISCIPLINARY TEAMS

Sue Greenfield

Overview

The Children and Young People's Workforce Strategy (DCSF, 2008) recommends that everyone who works with children and young people should be committed to integrated working with other professionals in order to improve outcomes for children and young people. In this chapter, I look at the background to the move towards integrated working and measures that have been taken to promote this. I then explore some of the ways that professionals from different backgrounds are attempting to work together and consider how multidisciplinary working may be accomplished. I consider whether this way of working is possible and why it is so desirable. I then use the work of teams in Sure Start Children's Centres as a basis for discussion about multidisciplinary working.

Background

In 2007, the death of 'Baby Peter' in the United Kingdom (UK) as a result of abuse from his mother and stepfather highlighted the work of those professions who engage with families and young people. Lord Laming, who had led a previous inquiry in England in

2003, when another child, Victoria Climbié (aged 8), died from abuse, was asked to undertake a further review. For many years prior to this inquiry, agencies had been criticized for not sharing information available to them. In the UK in the 1970s, this was highlighted in the reports of the deaths of Maria Colwell and Jasmine Beckford due to abuse. The reviews from subsequent inquiries gave the impression that little had changed.

Laming's inquiry into Victoria's death led to an overhaul of children's services in the United Kingdom. This inquiry exposed a lack of communication between professionals working with children and stressed the importance of professionals from social services, education and health working together for the benefit of the child. As well as highlighting 'a gross failure of the system' (Laming, 2003), Laming also stated that: 'I am in no doubt that effective support for children and families cannot be achieved by a single agency acting alone. It depends on a number of agencies working well together. It is a multi-disciplinary task' (Laming, 2003: para. 1.30).

Following this report, the Green Paper *Every Child Matters* (DfES, 2003) was published which highlighted the need for an increased focus on supporting families and carers through common assessment systems, shared working practices and shared goals for all early childhood professionals. The document stated: 'we want to put children at the heart of our policies, and to organise services around their needs. Radical reform is needed to break down organisational boundaries' (DfES, 2003: 9).

The importance of all organizations working together as multidisciplinary teams to provide services for children is stressed in *Every Child Matters* as one of the main factors to consider if children's needs are to be paramount. As Sloper (2004: 572) suggests '... [c]hildren and their families have a range of needs which do not fall neatly into separate segments'. The 2004 Children Act in England built further on this by legislating for integrated children's services and the establishment of Children's Trusts, combining the new services with health and other childhood services.

Following the Laming report (2003), all members of organizations related to children's needs (health, education and social services) were expected to be accountable for their actions and Local Authorities were obliged to establish Local Safeguarding Children's Boards. Workforce reform was considered crucial to this initiative and the newly created Children's Workforce Development Council (CWDC) was given the job of 'ensuring that a "common core" of skills and knowledge exists amongst the children's workforce' (Charles and Horwath, 2009: 371). The new Lead Graduate Early Years Professional (EYP) role in England arose partly to enable workers at all levels to promote work in multidisciplinary and multi-agency contexts, such as Children's Centres. However, whilst being considered essential by some, this initiative has been much criticized by others (Moss, 2006; Osgood, 2006) and is discussed in detail elsewhere (Miller and Cable, 2008) (see also Chapter 2).

Bringing about change

In order to bring about the proposed changes and recommendations discussed above, a number of initiatives were put in place which I briefly outline below.

Sure Start Children's Centres

Sure Start, a preschool intervention initiative was committed to reducing educational, social and health inequalities. The first Sure Start Centres were set up in 1999 in the UK in areas of deprivation, to provide services for children from birth to 4 and their families, with the intention of giving children a better start in life and to lift them out of poverty. One of the main intentions of Sure Start was to provide a multi-agency approach to service delivery in which professionals would listen to families and so provide the services they needed. The range of services for each geographical area would not be identical but would be provided according to the specific needs of each area. All services would be brought together under one roof to help parents access them and to provide more joined-up working. This was intended to reduce travelling time for parents, prevent duplication of services and obviate the need for parents to provide information to many different professionals (Weinberger et al., 2005).

The Common Assessment Framework

One important feature arising from the publication of *Every Child Matters* is the Common Assessment Framework (CAF). Children with additional needs frequently require support from more than one agency and possibly from more than one local authority. The CAF has been conceived to encourage integration of services and the CAF form is completed by all those working with a child, in conjunction with the child's parent/carer. The purpose and rationale for the CAF is set out on the government's Every Child Matters website (www.everychildmatters.gov.uk). Duplication should be avoided as there is a named lead professional who is the main point of contact for the family and who is responsible for ensuring that agencies provide the appropriate services. All information gathered is in one place so that anyone working with a family can have access to it. In principle, this idea seems sound but in reality has created problems, as the case study below illustrates, because in some local authorities: 'CAF assessments are at severe risk of being based on the unspecified and possibly unjustified priorities of individual practitioners and agencies' (Gilligan and Manby, 2008: 185).

 Case study: Anna

Anna is a newly qualified teacher working in a nursery. The parent of one of the children is very late collecting her child. Anna is worried as the family is known to Social Services and the older children are on the 'at risk' register. She decides that she should complete a CAF form, which she does with the child's mother

(Continued)

(Continued)

when she finally arrives. Anna then tries to contact the social worker to ask her to be the lead professional, as the family is known to her, but she is not available. Anna is very worried as she does not know what to do next and decides to leave the form for another day.

As the case study of Anna illustrates, professionals sometimes demonstrate reluctance to make use of the CAF because they do not wish to take on the role of Lead Professional (LP). This is highlighted by a health visitor in an evaluation by Brandon et al. (2006) who says:

> I think the frustration, certainly in the team that I work in, is that there is a lot of work and they tend to end up as the LP by default, they don't always feel that it's appropriate and that impacts on their workload as well – if I end up being the LP for 4 families that's a heck of a lot of work and for 3 of those families someone else could have taken on the LP role. (Brandon et al., 2006: 43)

Negative consequences may also arise where professionals are uncertain of their roles and responsibilities, often because of a blurring of professional boundaries as in the above vignette. Anna's inexperience is an additional issue as there appear to be no clear guidelines about working with the CAF form. Gilligan and Manby (2008: 179) suggest that 'clear structures for relevant processes' are essential as well as a history of good multi-agency working because then professionals feel confident about working together. In this case, Anna does not have personal links with other professionals in the multi-disciplinary team who would have supported her. Interestingly, Brandon et al. (2006) also found that it was mostly practitioners from education and health who were undertaking CAF work as social workers were dealing with child protection issues and had no time for preventative work.

The Healthy Child Programme

This Healthy Child Programme (DoH, 2009) (formerly known as the Child Health Promotion Programme) is an early intervention and prevention public health programme, lying at the heart of the UK's universal service for children and families and is closely related to the goals of *Every Child Matters* (DfES, 2003), with an emphasis on improving the health and wellbeing of all children. It is part of an integrated approach to supporting children and families and the document stresses the importance of health, education and social services working together. Health visitors may be based in a General Practitioner Practice or in a Children's Centre, but in either case they are expected to work with other professionals to provide a multi-agency approach. The programme emphasizes the importance of multi-agency working, especially in Children's Centres, and is increasingly being delivered through integrated services that bring together Children's Centre staff, General Practitioners, midwives, health visitors and other professionals. As part of the programme, Children's Centres are expected to provide a range of services including breast feeding clinics, healthy eating advice and parenting programmes.

Working together

The following quote from a parent from Pen Green Centre, one of the first Early Excellence Centres in England and now a Children's Centre, refers to the situation before the beginning of the millennium when multidisciplinary working was not usual practice:

> Social workers are the welfare, they take your kids away ... health visitors tell you what's supposed to be good for your child ... and teachers tell you in five minutes what it's taken you five years to find out about your child! (Parent quoted in Whalley, 1994: 15)

This quote demonstrates one parent's perception of how separately agencies functioned at that time.

All agencies involved in working with children and families claim to want what is best for each child. It may seem surprising therefore that practitioners needed encouragement to work together. Brandon et al. (2006) highlight the fact that the Common Assessment Framework and Lead Professional role promote a way of working that has fostered trust between different professionals and improved multi-agency relationships. They suggest this is as a result of concentrating on the needs of the child. Leadbetter et al. state:

> We are all working to a common aim. We can all see it's about working with young people to improve their life chances. If you focus on the child, the barriers between health and social work or whatever don't seem to be a problem. (2007: 95)

However, social services, education and health include professionals who have a range of different training backgrounds. When they work together, they have to work to understand each others' roles and to begin to have a shared knowledge of what professionalism means in different contexts. A Director of Children's Services explains how professionals perceive each other's role:

> If you talk to a teacher ... very quickly they will start telling you about the impact on the class, school, on the curriculum. What they won't do is tell you what it's doing for that child. And if you talk to the social worker about the child they will start off by focusing on the child and then will move away to the impact on the family, and on the service they are trying to provide. And if you talk to the health visitor you will quickly get on to 'and my role isn't to do that'. And that's in all of us. (Brandon et al., 2006: 23)

Professional characteristics

Professionals who are expected to work together within multidisciplinary teams come from a wide range of backgrounds. Below I consider the characteristics of the various professions and what this might mean for multi-agency working.

Health professionals

A large and diverse range of health professionals work to provide services for children and their families, including health visitors, nurses, midwives, speech therapists, occupational therapists, psychologists, psychotherapists and nursery nurses, and aim to provide appropriate services in response to their needs. All families are entitled to personalized access to a well-trained early intervention and prevention team led by a health visitor, during pregnancy and the first years of life. The emphasis is on health promotion rather than treatment of ill health. Health visitors provide a universal service and so are in a unique position because they have contact with all families and children, from women in pregnancy through to the elderly. The Healthy Child Programme (DoH, 2009) highlights the importance of the neurological development of infants and greater emphasis has been placed on the emotional wellbeing of both mother and infant.

Social welfare professionals

The roles of social workers have been highlighted in cases of child abuse and neglect and their safeguarding role is the most well known. However, social workers also have considerable responsibilities as enablers, using their skills to help vulnerable families and prevent problems arising. For example, social workers are now based in schools and work closely with vulnerable and disadvantaged children to ensure that their needs are met. These professionals work as advocates for children, especially 'looked after' children, and their preventive work aims to reduce the number of children deemed to be 'at risk'. Social workers represent the Local Authority in court proceedings involving families on a range of issues.

Education professionals

The roles of professionals from education include: teachers, nursery nurses, nursery officers and teaching assistants. Understanding these roles is complicated by the phenomenon that most people have their own ideas of how schools function, often based on their own experience of schooling. Each individual has their own memories of their own school experience and this knowledge can influence the ways that people interact with schools and teachers. In England, as I noted earlier in this chapter, the relatively new role of Early Years Professional has been introduced as part of an initiative to upskill and professionalize the early years workforce and encourage multi-agency working. The EYP is 'intended to be a change agent who will raise standards in early years settings, in particular to lead practice in the Early Years Foundation Stage (EYFS)' (Miller, 2008: 23). However, as Miller (2008: 24) points out, 'increased professional recognition' is required in terms of a pay and conditions framework for this initiative to be successful, particularly in the context of successful team work.

A holistic approach

In an ideal shared community of practice, professionals such as those working both with and for young children and their families, should be able to work to their own strengths and make use of the strengths of others, thus sharing expertise from other areas of practice. As Graham and Machin (2009: 32) maintain, it is important that 'the team culture is one that facilitates shared learning and working but values the unique contributions that are made by different contributors'. They stress the importance of interaction and collaboration between all organizations and the individuals within the organizations. However, this requires work by the collaborators and some consider that interprofessional working may have a negative impact on professional identity (Graham and Machin, 2009). Below I consider some theoretical perspectives and discuss how groups of professionals may become multi-agency teams.

The way forward: communities of practice and activity theory

Sociocultural and activity theorists have used Wenger's (1998) work on communities of practice and Engeström's (1999) work on activity theory to try to understand the practices and learning that develop within the different professions involved in working with children and families (e.g. Anning et al., 2009; Leadbetter et al., 2007). As discussed above, there are considerable barriers to overcome in working together as each profession has its own identity, its own language and its own procedures. Wenger's (1998) notion of 'communities of practice' illustrates how professionals from different backgrounds and training routes construct their identities in shared practices when they have to work together. When faced with a problem to solve, such professionals view the situation from the perspectives of their own professions. Wenger's basic premise is that human knowing is a social act and he suggests that by working together in a team and becoming active participants who interact with each other, team members can create their own shared language and ways of working; including developing shared goals and a shared vision for the future. Processes included in developing a 'community of practice' are further proposed by Anning et al. (2006: 10) as: '... mutual engagement (co-participation), a joint enterprise (shared accountability) and shared repertoire (common discourses and concepts)'.

Activity theory (Engeström, 1999) provides a theoretical framework for scrutinizing ways that multidisciplinary teams work in creating and exchanging knowledge, as it focuses on the study of human activity in social groups. The professional characteristics of those working in teams may change as individuals come to know each other better. At the same time, in working together, practitioners may become defensive about their own profession and fight to keep the power they hold. Engeström (1999) sees conflict as inevitable, as members of a multidisciplinary team work together and make use of their different knowledge to achieve common goals. Each profession may consider that they hold more of this power and that therefore their voices should be listened to more than other agencies. They may not wish to relinquish anything by working and sharing together but would like to work together on their own terms. As Anning states:

> In an early years setting where multi-agency teams operate together, professionals may use the tool of language in different ways, depending on their training, personal histories and beliefs and the meanings embedded in their daily actions. (2009: 71–2)

As teams work together regularly, they share expertise and 'cross boundaries' therefore entering areas unknown to them. In doing so, they face obstacles caused by different trainings and personal beliefs; these obstacles can cause disagreement and discussion. However, once confrontation and argument is over, they may be able to discuss problems with each other and explore professional similarities and differences.

Working together in Children's Centres

Children's Centres can be seen as a microcosm of working together and provide an example of the ways that services are becoming more seamless and integrated. Barker (2009: 195) highlights the 'significance of Children's Centres as actual and potential vehicles for responding to the challenge of making all tiers of services accessible to children and families'. *Every Child Matters* (DfES, 2003) highlights the importance of a common core of skills competence and knowledge for those working with young children and Moss (2008: 125) the need for those working together using this knowledge to be 'democratic and reflective practitioners'.

It is essential that there is a great deal of trust between professions, otherwise there is little chance that confidential information will be shared. Sachs (2003: 6) suggests that 'poor morale, bad press, problems in recruitment and retention can all be seen as indicators of a profession in trouble'. Although Sachs is writing of the teaching profession, this could be said to be true of both health and social services as all these professions recently demonstrate 'the development of a culture of suspicion where increased regimes of accountability and audit are meant to reduce risk and improve trust' (Sachs, 2003: 6). The training of both social workers and health visitors is currently 'under the spotlight' with the government suggesting that social workers may be asked to gain a 'licence to practise'.

Leading multidisciplinary teams

The appointment of leaders of multidisciplinary teams such as those operating in Children's Centres may be contentious and the skills of such leaders are crucial. Pound (2008: 78) suggests that 'many organisations are too complex to be in the hands of a single leader' and highlight the importance of the relationship between the leader and the team. The ability to find solutions rather than problems and to reflect on practice is also central to successful leadership. The National Professional Qualification in Integrated Centre Leadership (NPQICL) supports those who are already working as leaders in integrated centres to develop their reflective and democratic skills and a diverse range of practitioners are undertaking this qualification.

Training and qualifications

The training of all professionals working together in a Children's Centre is important and different professions have their own long histories of practice. These histories can be considered as part of their 'community of practice'. Ideally, however, working in multi-agency teams requires changes in training so that, for some of the time at least, professionals are trained together or share common elements of training, as with the training and education of pedagogues in Denmark and Germany. For example, if such professionals shared the first year of training and then specialized in the profession of their choice, they would have the opportunity to build up shared knowledge and understanding.

A multi-agency approach that worked

Research by Bagley et al. (2004) illustrates one Sure Start project where the partnership multi-agency approach worked for four main reasons:

1. It encompassed a commitment to this way of working by ensuring that everyone who worked there had this commitment and acknowledged the scheme would be subject to external scrutiny.
2. Only individuals who shared 'the vision' of this way of working were recruited. As in many of the Sure Start areas, all the staff had to re-apply for the jobs available and those who saw this way of working as problematic were encouraged not to apply.
3. Team members possessed the common aim of enabling and empowering local communities by working together to make sure that this happened.
4. The management structure was built on mutual respect and shared problem solving which was further promoted by the team being located in a single office. This is not always possible, but in this case the fact that people saw each other every day promoted more sharing of information.

Of course, documentation and legislation do not mean that multi-agency work with children will necessarily have positive outcomes. The main benefit and purpose of this way of working must be better outcomes for children through making advice and services easily accessible. Where one professional does not have the answer, there should be another professional who can help. As professionals gain a better understanding of each other's roles, this should lead to the breaking down of professional barriers. This is demonstrated by a participant in research by Leadbetter et al. (2007: 96): 'I'm not interested in creating grey, generic Children's Services Professionals. You can't make social workers into nurses and you can't make nurses into social workers, but it is possible to develop a better understanding of other agencies'.

A 'united' multiprofessional perspective is needed (DfES, 2004) which requires that all those working together have access to a shared language so that discussion can take place, but this does not mean that professions should lose their individual identities.

Final thoughts

It is clearly important that professionals working within services for young children and their families, do not become 'grey' and 'generic'. Edwards (2004) suggests that in the past, the strength of the individual operational teams dictated what was offered and separate providers were co-located but did not always work together. Each profession has its own language and jargon that others often find difficult to understand. Professionals may use different language as evidence of their professionalism, relying on it even more when they feel uncertain and insecure. Uncertainty and suspicion may make them question their professional identity and there may be a lack of shared objectives because of different perceptions, different values and different priorities. A shared language makes communication easier and brings down barriers, easing boundary crossing. This shared language, however, is not intended to overshadow the importance of maintaining professional identities. Anning et al. (2006: 74) stress that: 'Professionals, then, can emerge from challenges to their identity with a new and positive sense of their professional self'.

It is far too simplistic to assume that because different professionals are co-located they will become a team. As Leadbetter et al. note:

> It's co-working rather than co-location. Co-location isn't everything ... we've got co-located teams in Area Partnerships ... but when we put them together they weren't co-working they were co-located. So everybody thought that's good, that's integrated – no it isn't because nobody was doing any work together. (2007: 97)

If professionals keep the child at the centre of their thinking and view the child holistically, as proposed in *Every Child Matters* (2003), then professionals will work together as a team. The different 'parts' of the support services described by the parent from Pen Green quoted earlier in this chapter may then be put together to form a unified whole. However, as another participant in Leadbetter et al.'s research notes, working together is not something that is easily established:

> I think there are signs that we are working together, but I think there's a lot of work to do about bringing organizations out of the box they exist in ... about being protective about their qualifications and skills base they think is theirs. I think that's one of the biggest problems we have. (2007: 97)

The participants in this research show a willingness to work together but express concerns about losing their professional identities, especially as the leader will be from a profession and that may not be their own. Another participant in the same study considers:

> People are going to have to learn to take direction and advice from people who haven't traditionally been involved with their services. People who've been educational psychologists or social workers for twenty years might find that difficult but you don't just magically become a partner, you actually have to learn to work with other agencies. (Leadbetter et al., 2007: 97)

Professionals in multi-agency teams will have to work together with skill, commitment and trust which will take time, training and reflection.

 Summary

- In this chapter, Sure Start has been used as an example of multidisciplinary working.
- From 2004, Sure Start Local Programmes and the Neighbourhood Nurseries programme formed the basis of Sure Start Children's Centres. Now in 2010 there are Centres available to many young children and their families in England.
- *Every Child Matters* (DfES, 2003, 2004) and the 'Healthy Child Programme' (DoH, 2009) stress the importance of multidisciplinary working.
- The Common Assessment Framework was introduced to be used by all those working in Children's Services and a Lead Professional role was established.
- Communities of practice (Wenger, 1998) and activity theory (Engeström, 1999) are used as theoretical frameworks to discuss ways that multidisciplinary teams can evolve.
- There are three main professions involved in working with young children who have three different professional trainings. It is the professionalism of these individuals that is most important and the practice of these roles must include reflection and democracy.

Miller, L. and Cable, C. (eds) (2008) *Professionalism in the Early Years*. London: Hodder Education.

Moss, P. (2006) 'Bringing politics into the nursery: early childhood education as a democratic practice', paper presented at the 16th EECERA Conference, University of Reykjavik, 1 September.

Moss, P. (2008) 'The democratic and reflective professional: rethinking and reforming the early years workforce', in L. Miller and C. Cable (eds) *Professionalism in the Early Years*. London: Hodder Education.

Osgood, J. (2006) 'Deconstructing professionalism in early childhood education: resisting the regulatory gaze', *Contemporary Issues in Early Childhood*, 7(1): 5–14.

Pound, L. (2008) 'Leadership in the early years', in L. Miller and C. Cable (eds) *Professionalism in the Early Years*. London: Hodder Education.

Sachs, J. (2003) *The Activist Teaching Profession*. Buckingham: Open University Press.

Sloper, P. (2004) 'Facilitators and barriers for co-ordinated multi-agency services', *Child Care, Health and Development*, 30(6): 571–80.

Weinberger, J., Pickstone, C. and Hannon, P. (eds) (2005) *Learning from Sure Start*. Maidenhead: Open University Press.

Wenger, E. (1998) *Communities of Practice*. Cambridge: Cambridge University Press.

Whalley, M. (1994) *Working with Parents*. London: Hodder & Stoughton.

PART 2

TOWARDS A NEW PROFESSIONALISM IN THE EARLY YEARS

CHAPTER 7

CONSTRUCTIONS OF PROFESSIONAL IDENTITY

Gill McGillivray

Overview

Through this chapter, I aim to explore some of the multiplicity of influences that contribute to the construction of professional identity in the early years workforce arising from influences such as personal histories, spaces and places of work, dominant discourses related to children and families and political ideologies. I start with setting the scene in terms of what is known about the early years workforce against the backdrop of workforce reform in England. Similarly, the historical legacy in its shaping of the current early years workforce will also be considered and may deepen an understanding of potential struggles and tensions, an influence acknowledged by Dent and Whitehead: 'The new professional that is given birth is identified by the discourses that usher it into existence' (Dent and Whitehead, 2002: 4).

I also include some theoretical and philosophical perspectives that may contribute to the construction of professional identities, such as communities of practice, self identity and power. Those working with young children from birth to 8 years in early years settings are located in a multiplicity of places (Nicholson et al., 2008), with a multiplicity of roles (Cameron, 2004), titles (Adams, 2008) and responsibilities. To be effective in their work with children, it is claimed that the workforce needs

(Continued)

(Continued)

to be better qualified and trained (Ball, 1994; Daycare Trust, 2008; DCSF, 2008; DfES, 2005; HM Treasury, 2004, for example), which may suggest a message of 'not good enough' for the workforce. Such pressures, particularly in the face of low pay and status (Cooke and Lawton, 2008; Daycare Trust, 2008), create difficulties for early years workers, their managers and those who aspire to early years work. A profile of the workforce provided in the next section sets the scene.

Profile of the workforce

Most recent early years workforce data have been collated from surveys undertaken in 2007 by Nicholson et al. (2008). They note that data were collected separately from childcare and early years provision, and have been 'drawn together to highlight similarities and differences across the sectors, as well as providing details of the whole childcare and early years workforce' (Nicholson et al., 2008: 1; see Table 7.1). This reinforces the continuing divide between childcare and early years provision, a point that is challenged by the Daycare Trust report (2008: 1): 'the Early Years Foundation Stage (EYFS, DfES, 2007) has expanded the role of early childhood care and education workers by merging the concepts of care and education'. However, the divide between care and education has existed for many decades, and it is likely to take more than the merging of curriculum and daycare standards within the EYFS to close the divide. Some data from the workforce survey undertaken by Nicholson et al. (2008), the most recent available, have been summarized in Table 7.1 in order to illustrate features of those who work in the early years sector.

Table 7.1   Summary of key workforce data (2007)

- 1 in 3 staff in the private sector was aged under 25 years; school-based early years workforce had an older profile.
- There were 165,200 paid and unpaid staff working in full daycare provision; 123,000 paid and unpaid staff working in schools and nursery schools (but equivalent numbers were not available for those working in sessional care, after school care, informal care or holiday clubs).
- 98% of the workforce were women.
- Approximately 50% worked part-time.
- In 2007, average hourly pay for full daycare was £5.90 for staff without supervisory duties; £7.10 for equivalent staff in Children's Centres; £8.70 for equivalent staff in school-based early years provision.
- In 2008, the median take-home hourly pay for women was £10.90; minimum wage was raised in 2006 to £5.30.
- 61% of the workforce in childcare provision had a level 3* qualification.

Note: *equivalent to A' levels; a school leaving qualification at 18 years, and the level required to work without supervision. For early years, qualified staff are required to have a National Vocational Qualification (NVQ) at level 3, a BTEC National Diploma, a CACHE level 3 Diploma or equivalent.

You may wish to consider the data in Table 7.1 and reflect on the following questions: what are the apparent differences across the early years sector and what impact might they have on members of the workforce? The intention to make a level 3 qualification a requirement for all those working in early years has been stated by the government

(DCSF, 2009), but for now, one in three staff require supervision because they do not have a level 3 qualification. What are the implications of this for management and leadership in early years settings? Finally, what are the implications of these data for aspiring early years workers?

Workforce reform, since the introduction of the National Childcare Strategy (DfEE, 1998), has attempted to integrate social services daycare and nursery education as well as expand access to qualifications, vertically and horizontally. Attempts to introduce vertical structures in order to create clearer progression routes for early years workers beyond level 3 qualifications was limited for the following reasons. Firstly, the title of Senior Practitioner conferred on those who achieved the Early Years Sector Endorsed Foundation Degree (a work-based degree that conferred 240 credits up to level 5 in higher education) was never established in practice or in its status, so no additional pay or associated roles and responsibilities were attached to it. Miller (2008b) explains and evaluates some of the issues related to Senior Practitioner status as part of the Foundation Degree sector endorsement by Sure Start, the government department in England that had responsibility for early years provision at that time. Also, the increasing numbers in the workforce were mostly located in the private sector where employers were unable to afford rates of pay equal to those in the statutory sector. Secondly, there was no one union or professional association for both teachers and those who were not teachers who worked in early years. Union membership for early years workers was generally low (Cohen et al., 2004), and the position of teaching unions seeks to protect early years work for those with Qualified Teacher Status (QTS) as well as excluding membership of those undertaking support or assistant work (Goff, 2008; NUT, 2006). Other unions were vocal in their advocacy for more equal pay and conditions (GMB, 2003; UNISON, 2006). Thirdly, changes in children's services were made at local, not national, level, and local authorities' reconfiguration of education, health and social care departments were dependent on local needs and resources. The devolved responsibilities for children's services from central to local government was an intentional shift in policy in an attempt to develop local services to meet local needs (DCSF, 2007). This policy however exacerbated the position of no national agreement as to what pay and conditions could be agreed as a minimum standard for those working in childcare.

Penn (2000: 104) contended that 'recruitment into childcare training in the UK is aimed at a particular group of women with low academic achievements and from mainly disadvantaged socio-economic backgrounds'. She continues, 'childcare students in training tend to see themselves as "naturals", building on their personal experiences in looking after children, and see their strength as lying in their everyday practice, rather than in the acquisition and application of knowledge about children' (Penn, 2000: 104).

Penn's argument remains compelling and is reinforced by Colley (2006); most recent data suggest that trends established decades ago are proving stubborn to shift in terms of gender and academic achievement. Cooke and Lawton (2008) reinforce Penn's proposition as to why young women choose the profession. The profile in Table 7.1 maps out a workforce where there are inequalities in pay by sector, variability in terms of a basic level of qualification, a gender imbalance and an age imbalance by sector. Such trends, traditions, expectations and perceptions have existed for decades. An interrogation of texts that relate to the early years workforce spanning the 1970s to the first decade of the millennium (McGillivray, 2008) reveals that the gender stereotypes of 'kind' and 'loving' were attached to those working with young children as recently as 1984. The historical trajectory of the early years workforce has been shaped by events such as the Second World War and the need for women to work and therefore have access to childcare (Bertram and Pascal, 2001). I would argue that the influence of changing societal and psychological expectations of the role of women, particularly those who work, since the 1960s (Crompton, 1997) and by the ideologies and policies of the governing political party (Baldock et al., 2009) perpetuate the stereotype of what it means to be an early years worker and thus the professional identities of the workforce.

I will now consider some ideas as to how such a varied and inequitable profile contributes to professional identities within the early years workforce with a focus on recent policy that sets out the vision for reform.

Workforce reform

When Labour became the party of government in 1997, the publication of the National Childcare Strategy (DfEE, 1998) laid out strategies for local authorities for early years provision. The government began to compile information on the activity, scope and scale of the early years landscape as it had not previously been available in any substantive form. During the intervening years, the rationalization of qualifications has been one part of workforce reform (see Baldock et al., 2009; Sauve Bell, 2004). The policy documents that set out children's workforce reform (DCSF, 2007; DfES, 2005, 2006; HM Treasury, 2004) state the intention for graduates to lead early years provision in all settings with children from birth to 5 by 2015 (in Children's Centres by 2010) as another aspect of reform. A consultation of the proposals for the early years workforce reform took place between February and July 2005 (DfES, 2005) and the government's response (DfES, 2006) claims support for the vision.

The benchmark of a level 3 qualification for a member of staff working in early years to be accepted as 'qualified' is a current goal for the government (DCSF, 2009) and along with the graduate Early Years Professional Status (EYP) (see Miller, 2008a; Miller and Cable, 2008; Nurse, 2007) suggest that changes will need to be made in schools, further education colleges and higher education institutions to accommodate new qualifications. However, Dent and Whitehead (2002: 4) caution that 'Despite the allure of professional status, the pressures driving this new identity formation are clearly not entirely benign', and, in the context of early years, becoming a professionalized workforce brings with it 'macro-systems' that promote standardization and measures of accountability such as the processes of assessment, inspection and regulation of the workforce. The creation of an Integrated Qualifications Framework (IQF) and the Functional Map (CWDC, 2009) are, at the time of writing, intended to rationalize qualification requirements and progression (the IQF), and define shared responsibilities across the children's workforce (the Functional Map). These developments further illustrate the ways in which government generally, but the Children's Workforce Development Council (CWDC) specifically, is continuing to invest in systems and measures that provide a structural overlay across relevant workforces. These initiatives may perpetuate a level of 'passive resistance' and disillusionment if members of the early years workforce do not feel connected to, consulted on or informed of such changes, or feel that the issues of pay and status are not taken seriously (Carey et al., 2009; CYPN, 2009; Murray, 2009). The post-structuralist ideas of Foucault are helpful in understanding the context of resistance. Foucault (1982) saw power as the means by which individuals enact or perform to reinforce their individuality. He suggests that 'These struggles are not exactly for or against the "individual", but rather they are struggles against the "government of individualization"' (Foucault, 1982: 212). In other words, resistance may already exist, or may emerge, from a model of imposed requirements to acquire specific statuses or qualifications.

So, in terms of imposed government requirements, we can ask ourselves who benefits from such workforce reform. Is the status of early years graduates one that is embraced by all those who currently work with young children (as well as those who are considering such a career)? What are the financial rewards of study and 'professionalization' if any? The purpose of this chapter is not to offer responses to such questions; rather, the questions serve to illustrate some of the potential struggles that may arise from workforce reform, and responses can contribute to an understanding of identities, decisions and aspirations within the workforce. The increase in 'professions' (NSO, 2009) reflects the shift, certainly in England, and the inherent government strategies associated with the 'professionalization' of workforces. Similar reform is underway in nursing, youth work, social work and social care. The measures may reinforce a 'culture of performativity: the belief in the veracity of apparently objective systems of accountability and measurement' (Dent and Whitehead, 2002: 2). The processes of inspection, audit, information storing and managing with decreasing resources are commonplace in the public sector; such practices sustain regimes of regulatory gaze and surveillance (see Osgood, 2006a; Penna, 2005). The ideas of Foucault in relation to power and regimes of truth are again relevant in this context. Dahlberg and Moss (2005: 142) interpret regimes of truth as the 'means by which the ethical and political are transformed into the technical and managerial'. Issues of gender and feminist ideologies (Colley, 2006; Gilligan, 1982; Goldstein, 1998; Osgood, 2006b), the hegemony of 'outcomes', 'effective practice', 'flexible childcare' become the regimes of truth that underpin the reform of the early years workforce. How aspects of these ideas shape the construction of professional identities, alongside the analysis of research, is the focus of the next section.

Professional identity

Tucker (2004) proposes that any framework that attempts to assist reflection on matters of professional identity construction must be able to:

1. explore the impact of 'ideological effects' on the socio-political terrain and the conditions of existence for those working with young people;
2. assist analysis of those forms of discourse that are used to define particular forms of work;
3. show how ideas are struggled over and contested at various levels of experience;
4. demonstrate how such matters directly impact upon the professional identities which individuals and groups adopt in their everyday work (Tucker, 2004: 84).

I have noted some of the debates about socio-political terrain and dominant discourses already, but Tucker's propositions point to how aspects of self, people and places are influential.

Self identity, personal identity and their potential interface with professional identities is therefore pertinent in this context. Giddens (1991) acknowledges the role of media, mass communication and globalization against a backdrop of modernity in the narratives we construct about 'the reflexive project of the self' (Giddens, 1991: 5). He argues that the self is not passive, but is reflexively constructed in response to external and internal influences as a narrative, or auto-biography. Thus, the phenomenological sense of who we are cannot be dissociated from our professional identities.

Similarly, Beijaard et al. (2000) and Lave and Wenger (1991) recognize the role that contexts, experiences and situations have to play in constructing identities. The interpretation of experience is important but it requires individuals to have the agency and motivation to undertake it. This may be determined by expectations of the self but also others in the workplace. The role of mentors, managers, leaders and other colleagues who work alongside early years workers becomes critical here. There needs to be a critical mass of early years staff who are able to undertake these roles; how individuals create narratives for interpretation and re-interpretation may be determined by a multiplicity of factors such as space, skills and support. The notion of agency is apparent here, and needs to be examined in terms of the extent to which early years workers and their colleagues have a sense of agency in order to facilitate change.

Kelchtermans (1993) suggests that significant aspects of the professional self are: self-image; self-esteem; job motivation; task perception; and future perspectives. There is some congruence here with Giddens (1991) and Williams (2007); how we see ourselves in the workplace and the influence of others in creating a self-image are both significant. The role of mentors, supervisors, managers, leaders, peers and colleagues once again, as well as family and wider society, therefore become apparent in the construction of how we perceive ourselves at work as part of our professional identities. A consideration of how media portray early years work is pertinent, particularly when television programmes in England such as *Supernanny* are at risk of perpetuating a stereotypical image not far removed from a Victorian governess.

Berry et al. (2007) acknowledge how professional identities are shaped by knowledge from a range of different sources but point to stories about ourselves as well. These stories are shaped and told by individuals as 'expressions of cultural values, norms and structures' (Berry et al., 2007: 137). Stories about our professional selves are constructed and evolve. The stories constructed by our families, communities, careers advisers sustain stereotypical images of working with young children, informed by historical and sociological influences. These narratives are the starting point for some entering the workforce, and they will be continued by the working communities and practices they become members of.

Therefore, the place, as well as the people where early years practitioners work, is significant in contributing to professional identities; the notion of place (the physical environment, its resources, its symbolism, its architecture and design) can have an impact on how we construct ourselves as employees within the workplace. Thus those early years workers who undertake sessional work in shared premises, for example, have significant constraints in terms of time, space and resources, and thus on how they perceive themselves as having permanence, ownership and status. Stronach et al. (2002) examine identities of teacher and nurse, suggesting that they are 'located in a complicated nexus between policy, ideology and practice' (Stronach et al., 2002: 109). The deconstruction of professionalism and professional identities as presented in their paper is helpful as it confirms the ephemeral complexity of what is meant by professional identities. They also articulate how 'economies of performance' (as manifested in the dominant discourses of standards, audit and accountability) interact with 'ecologies of practice' (practices, knowledge, beliefs adopted, acquired and implemented by those undertaking specific professional roles) to create a position, or nexus, in which the professional is caught between. This position recurs within the themes of policy, professionalization and professional knowledge and can be compared to what Dahlberg and Moss (2005: 15) propose as the subjectification of the early years workforce, 'whereby we are created as a particular type of subject'.

Similar influences on professional identities have been proposed by Kuisma and Sandberg (2008) who suggest that language is important in identity formation for early years practitioners in Sweden. They suggest that:

> a potential risk is that pre-school teachers can become private if they do not share a common understanding of professional language. To obtain status and legitimacy in society, professional competencies need to be articulated and communicated to the public. (Kuisma and Sandberg, 2008: 193)

Being private in this context contrasts with confidently articulating knowledge to others, and being able to 'concretely describe their professional area with the help of language and professional concepts' (Kuisma and Sandberg, 2008: 192). Reasons for becoming private as reported by Kuisma and Sandberg (2008) were suggested to be limited opportunities to learn from close colleagues, limited self-knowledge and limited knowledge of the role they are expected to undertake, arguably similar to 'cultural values, norms and structures' suggested by Berry et al. (2007: 137). Kuisma and Sandberg (2008) help us think about what early years workers need to do to become visible, and how status and legitimacy will be achieved through having the confidence, power and opportunity to be heard in society. Their research also reinforces the need for a professional community of learning and confidence to describe to others the nature of their work. The existence of communities of learning traditionally have proved a challenge for early years practitioners in England (Hargreaves and Hopper, 2006; Siraj-Blatchford, 1993) as well as Sweden.

In England, formal strategies of support exist for some groups such as mentoring for newly qualified teachers. The closest early years has achieved in terms of formal support for newcomers to the workforce was the attempt to introduce induction standards for early years workers in 2007–2008. However, issues such as sustainability were identified for their successful implementation in private daycare settings (Owens, 2009). Sustainability, resourcing and capacity are essential for effective mentoring, and the day-to-day demands of frontline early years work creates significant pressures for staff. When we think about newcomers, or apprentices, and how they begin to construct professional identities, concepts of communities of practice and legitimate peripheral participation, developed by Wenger (1998) and Lave and Wenger (1991) respectively, are also helpful.

Within communities of practice (Wenger, 1998), apprentices become included through 'legitimate peripheral participation' (Lave and Wenger, 1991) and thus through observing the ways in which the community operates, who operates within it, and how. For an individual to be on a trajectory that takes them towards the community of practice as opposed to being on the periphery, Wenger (1998) states the prerequisites as 'being useful, being sponsored, being feared, being the right kind of person, having the right birth' (Wenger, 1998: 101). It is worth comparing the notion of legitimate peripheral participation with other models of learning in the workplace, which I consider next.

The notion of movement from novice to apprentice, as suggested by Dreyfus and Dreyfus (1986, cited in Eraut, 1994), focuses on experiential learning in a professional context, with less emphasis on theoretical learning. Both take on a uni-dimensional form, and thus do not take account of the interruptions, multi-dimensional influences and uncertainty of the reality of being a newcomer to a profession. The early experiences as one enters a profession can be critical in the co-construction of professional identities as we shape ourselves through interactions with others (children, parents, colleagues, other professionals), with physical spaces and places and through the imposed structures at meso-, micro- and macro-levels of influence. The notions of micro-, meso- and macro-systems derive from the work of Bronfenbrenner (1979), and suggest systems arranged rather like a Russian doll, that exert influences on individuals as well as individuals exerting influences themselves. The level of micro-system is the immediate community within which an individual exists, surrounded by a meso-system of local community. In the context of this chapter, I am referring to the workplace as the meso-system. The macro-system encompasses the wider influences of government, society, culture, history and so on. The way in which early years workers undertake frontline work and the notion of discretion and interpretation of their work, as suggested by Lipsky (1980), contributes to the complexity of factors that interact with each other to influence ways in which individuals within the workforce, but also groups of workers, continually shape, and have shaped for them by others, their professional identities. Indeed, Frost (2005), in a review of research into frontline working with children and families, demonstrated how professional territories, identities (and I would argue professional cultures too) are dynamic, in a constant state of flux and reconstruction. These are particularly exacerbated by relatively new ways of inter-agency working that have been promoted through the reconfiguration of children's services as a result of Every Child Matters (DfES, 2003).

Finally, what factors, implicit or otherwise, *bind* early years workers together to create a community? How do they contribute to personal stories and professional identities? The point made earlier relating to micro-systems in communities of practice at the level of individual settings, and tensions that can emerge from macro-levels of influence, can be applied too in terms of who has right of entry to a workforce; what do they do when they are part of a workforce at micro-level, and how has this any form of interface with macro-levels of knowledge and expectation? If we consider the cultures of practice that may exist in individual settings, how these may be similar or different to other settings, and ask questions about 'why' and 'how', then we can see how professional identities are shaped by others and self and by the stories that are created and narrated in our day-to-day work. Gender is a significant factor in this debate when attributed to the ideologies and values already noted; there seems to be an expectation that those who undertake early years work are caring and loving – traditional prerequisites for entering the workforce (Colley, 2006; Goldstein, 1998). This is an over-generalization, but a point that still needs to be made and has some resonance with Bourdieu's (1993) notion of habitus in its proposition that symbolism and socialization practices perpetuate any constructions of reality and 'this is how it is'. Research shows that those entering the early years workforce are committed to working with children, and that recruits see their work as being rewarding (Cooke and Lawton, 2008), but data suggest that retention and recruitment are problematic in some provider types within the early years workforce (Nicholson et al., 2008) and that workers need to have access to progression opportunities in order to want to stay in the workforce (Cooke and Lawton, 2008). This returns us to the inequalities within the workforce, as noted near the beginning of the chapter, and reminds us of the challenges that those undertaking low-paid, low-status work face in their day-to-day lives, particularly in times of economic uncertainties. These cannot be ignored in any contemplation of the identities, aspirations and changes within the early years workforce.

Final thoughts

The aim of this chapter has been to offer perspectives that may have shaped and contributed to the construction of professional identities, specifically within the early years workforce, by drawing on a range of disciplines. I have argued that some of the significant factors that seem to have an influence on the construction of professional identities are the communities in which workers are located, and that includes the range of colleagues from leaders, parents, allied professionals, the places where they work, and their own families. Children are not too visible in this arena, however, but are significant from a sociological perspective. How children are sociologically constructed has a direct impact on the construction of identities of those who work with them. The impact of gender and the socialization of women into lower paid, lower status work is apparent not just in the early years sector, but these are other key influences on professional identities, as are notions of self and how we construct narratives about ourselves at work.

Looking forward, it might be optimistic to assert that as the early years workforce has increased access to higher level education and qualifications, then passivity and conformity could be replaced by explicit demands and shifted power bases. I suggest that this needs to be seen from a 'bottom up' perspective, starting with how young men and women in secondary education construct working with young children as a worthwhile career. Clear routes for progression for young people are essential, as well as opportunities to demonstrate values, skills, knowledge and a personal, pedagogical philosophy that respects the children and families they will be working with.

 Summary

- While there is no attempt to define professional identity in this chapter, the chapter is intended to provoke reflection and consideration of the complexity of influences that may contribute to any notion of professional identities that may exist or be emerging within the early years workforce, particularly in England as reform is under way.
- The chapter opened with the aims of exploring trajectories, spaces and places of work, discourses and ideologies as some of the influences but has really only touched on these.
- There are other influences yet to be explored (social and cultural capital, change and uncertainty, for example). The following discussion points and readings are intended to extend your understanding and promote further debate.

 Questions for discussion

1. What are your reflections on the impact of recent changes in children's services on individuals and groups who work with children, specifically early years practitioners?
2. How do you think dispositions, the expectations and influence of other people, career and personal biography influence how we construct our identity at work?
3. Do you agree that these influences *are* significant? Are there others that you consider should be drawn into the debate? (*Higher level question*)

Further reading

Levels 5 and 6

Colley, H. (2006) 'Learning to labour with feeling: class, gender and emotion in childcare education and training', *Contemporary Issues in Early Childhood*, 7(1): 15–29.
Helen Colley's paper explores research findings from work with childcare students in further education. Colley does not explore professional identities per se, but she provides readers with an engaging analysis of the discourses within curriculum and social practices, drawing on Marxist feminist thinking.

Moss, P. (2008) 'The democratic and reflective professional: rethinking and reforming the early years workforce', in L. Miller and C. Cable (eds) (2008) *Professionalism in the Early Years*. London: Hodder Education.
Peter Moss draws on policy and the values of democratic professionalism to explore the ongoing discussions about workforce reform and its implications for practitioners.

Levels 6 and 7

Hall, S. (2000) 'Who needs identity?', in P. du Gay, J. Evans and P. Redman (eds) *Identity: A Reader*. London: Sage with the Open University.
Stuart Hall has written the first chapter in this reader that includes contributions from Derrida, Foucault and Rose, among others, on the subject of identity. Hall's chapter alerts the reader to the inconsistencies, fissures and uncertainties that prevail in philosophical debates relating to identity.

Osgood, J. (2006) 'Deconstructing professionalism in early childhood education: resisting the regulatory gaze', *Contemporary Issues in Early Childhood*, 7(1): 5–14.
Jayne Osgood's paper problematizes the concept of professionalism within the context of workforce reform and dominant discourses articulated in regulatory, technical and similar initiatives in early years. The ideas of Foucault, Freire and Butler inform the writer's position and deconstruction of 'professionalism'.

Websites

The following websites provide information, links to policy initiatives, publications and reports relating to early years workforce reform:
www.cwdcouncil.org.uk
http://everychildmatters.gov.uk

The following website offers biographies and summaries of philosophers, for example, who have contributed to the debate about identity and self identity:
www.theory.org.uk

The following website has published research into life courses, transitions and professional histories, and thus offers the reader insight into personal, political and professional influences on individuals and, potentially, their identity:
www.tlrp.org

References

Adams, K. (2008) 'What's in a name? Seeking professional status through degree studies within the Scottish early years context', *European Early Childhood Education Research Journal*, 16(2): 196–209.

Baldock, P., Fitzgerald, D. and Kay, J. (2009) *Understanding Early Years Policy*, 2nd edn. London: Sage.

Ball, C. (1994) *Start Right: The Importance of Early Learning*. London: The Royal Society for the Encouragement of Arts, Manufacture and Commerce.

Beijaard, D., Verloop, N. and Vermunt, J. (2000) 'Teachers' perceptions of professional identity: an exploratory study from a personal knowledge perspective', *Teaching and Teacher Education*, 16(1): 749–64.

Berry, A., Clemans, A. and Kostogriz, A. (eds) (2007) *Dimensions of Professional Learning*. Rotterdam: Sense Publishing.

Bertram, T. and Pascal, C. (2001) *The OECD Thematic Review of Early Childhood Education and Care: Background Report for the UK.* Available from: www.oecd.org/ (accessed 30 October 2002).

Bourdieu, P. (1993) 'Structures, habitus, power: basis for a theory of symbolic power', in N. Dirks, G. Eley and S. Ortner (eds) *Culture/Power/History: A Reader in Contemporary Social Theory*. Princeton, NJ: Princeton University Press.

Bronfenbrenner, U. (1979) *The Ecology of Human Development: Experiments by Nature and Design*. Cambridge, MA: Harvard University Press.

Cameron, C. (2004) *Building an Integrated Workforce for a Long Term Vision of Universal Early Education and Care*. Policy Paper Number 3. Daycare Trust.

Carey, D., Cramp, A., Kendall, A. and Perkins, H. (2009) *Facilitating Progression: Towards a 'Fit for Purpose' Progression Model for Early Years Practitioners*. Birmingham Black Country and Solihull Lifelong Learning Network Report. HSCEYE 06-09.

Children's Workforce Development Council (CWDC) (2009) *Functional Map of the Children and Young People's Workforce in England*. Available from: www.cwdcouncil.org (accessed June 2009).

Cohen, B., Moss, P., Petrie, P. and Wallace, J. (2004) *A New Deal for Children?* Bristol: The Policy Press.

Colley, H. (2006) 'Learning to labour with feeling: class, gender and emotion in childcare education and training', *Contemporary Issues in Early Childhood*, 7(1): 15–29.

Cooke, G. and Lawton, K. (2008) *For Love or Money? Pay, Progression and Professionalisation in the 'Early Years' Workforce*. London: Institute for Public Policy Research.

Crompton, R. (1997) *Women who Work in Modern Britain*. Oxford: Oxford University Press.

CYPN (2009) 'Early years round up of the week', *Children and Young People Now*, 23–29 July.

Dahlberg, G. and Moss, P. (2005) *Ethics and Politics in Early Childhood Education*. Abingdon: RoutledgeFalmer.

Daycare Trust (2008) *Raising the Bar. What Next for the Early Childhood and Education and Care Workforce?* Available from: www.daycaretrust.org.uk/data (accessed 26 July 2009).

Dent, M. and Whitehead, S. (eds) (2002) *Managing Professional Identities*. London: Routledge.

Department for Children, Schools and Families (DCSF) (2007) *The Children's Plan: Building Brighter Futures*. London: DCSF.

Department for Children, Schools and Families (DCSF) (2008) *2020 Children and Young People's Workforce Strategy: The Evidence Base*. Available from: www.dcsf.gov.uk (accessed January 2009).

Department for Children, Schools and Families (DCSF) (2009) *Next Steps for Early Learning and Childcare*. Available from: www.cabinetoffice.gov.uk/media/120944/early_learning_childcare_main.pdf (accessed 12 May 2009).

Department for Education and Employment (DfEE) (1998) *Meeting the Childcare Challenge*. London: The Stationery Office.

Department for Education and Skills (DfES) (2003) *Every Child Matters*. London: DfES.

Department for Education and Skills (DfES) (2005) *Children's Workforce Strategy*. London: DfES.

Department for Education and Skills (DfES) (2006) *Children's Workforce Strategy: The Government's Response to the Consultation*. London: DfES.

Department for Education and Skills (DfES) (2007) *Early Years Foundation Stage*. London: DfES.

Eraut, M. (1994) *Developing Professional Knowledge and Competence*. London: RoutledgeFalmer.

Foucault, M. (1982) 'The subject and power: afterword', in H. Dreyfus and P. Rabinow, *Michel Foucault: Beyond Structuralism and Hermeneutics*. New York: Harvester Wheatsheaf.

Frost, N. (2005) *Professionalism, Partnership and Joined Up Thinking: A Research Review of Front-Line Working with Children and Families*. Available from: www.rip.org.uk (accessed 11 October 2007).

Giddens, A. (1991) *Modernity and Self Identity*. Cambridge: Polity Press.

Gilligan, C. (1982) *In a Different Voice*. Cambridge, MA: Harvard University Press.

GMB (2003) *Education's Hidden Professionals: GMB Survey of Teaching Assistants and Nursery Nurses*. London: GMB.

Goff, H. (2008) *Teachers Should Run Nurseries*. Available from: www.bbc.co.uk/go/pr/fr/-/1/hi/education (accessed December 2009).

Goldstein, L. (1998) 'More than gentle smiles and warm hugs: applying the ethic of care to early childhood education', *Journal of Research in Childhood Education*, 12(2): 244–62.

Hargreaves, L. and Hopper, B. (2006) 'Early years, low status? Early years teachers' perceptions of their occupational status', *Early Years*, 26(2): 171–86.

HM Treasury (2004) *Choice for Parents, The Best Start for Children: A Ten-year Strategy for Children*. London: HM Treasury.

Kelchtermans, G. (1993) 'Getting the story, understanding the lives: from career stories to teachers' professional development', *Teaching and Teacher Education*, 9(5/6): 443–56.

Kuisma, M. and Sandberg, A. (2008) 'Pre-school teachers' and student pre-school teachers' thoughts about professionalism in Sweden', *European Early Childhood Education Research Journal*, 16(2): 186–95.

Lave, J. and Wenger, E. (1991) *Situated Learning: Legitimate Peripheral Participation*. Cambridge: Cambridge University Press.

Lipsky, M. (1980) *Street-level Bureaucracy: Dilemmas of the Individual in Public Services*. New York: Russell Sage Foundation.

McGillivray, G. (2008) 'Nannies, nursery nurses and early years professionals: constructions of professional identity in the early years workforce in England', *European Early Childhood Education Research Journal*, 16(2): 242–54.

Miller, L. (2008a) 'Developing professionalism within a regulatory framework in England: challenges and possibilities', *European Early Childhood Education Research Journal*, 16(2): 255–68.

Miller, L. (2008b) 'Developing new professional roles in the early years', in L. Miller and C. Cable (eds) *Professionalism in the Early Years*. London: Hodder Education.

Miller, L. and Cable, C. (eds) (2008) *Professionalism in the Early Years*. London: Hodder Education.

Murray, J. (2009) 'The poor professionals', *The Guardian*, 28 April.

National Statistics Office (NSO) (2009) *The Jobs People Do*. Available from: www.statistics.gov.uk/cci/nugget.asp?id=11 (accessed 29 July 2009).

National Union of Teachers (NUT) (2006) *Early Years Campaigning Section*. Available from: www.teachers.org.uk/story (accessed December 2009).

Nicholson, S., Jordan, E., Cooper, J. and Mason, J. (2008) *Childcare and Early Years Providers Survey 2007*. Research Report DCSF RR047 BMRB. London: DCSF.

Nurse, A. (ed.) (2007) *The New Early Years Professional*. Abingdon: Routledge.

Osgood, J. (2006a) 'Deconstructing professionalism in early childhood education: resisting the regulatory gaze', *Contemporary Issues in Early Childhood*, 7(1): 5–14.

Osgood, J. (2006b) 'Professionalism and performativity: the feminist challenge facing early years practitioners', *Early Years*, 26(2): 187–99.

Owens, C. (2009) *CWDC Induction Standards Field Testing Project 07–08 Summary Report*. Available from: www.cwdcouncil.org.uk (accessed 8 August 2009).

Penn, H. (2000) 'Is working with children a good job?', in H. Penn (ed.) *Early Childhood Services: Theory, Policy and Practice*. Buckingham: Open University Press.

Penna, S. (2005) 'The Children Act 2004: child protection and social surveillance', *Journal of Social Welfare and Family Law*, 27(2): 143–57.

Sauve Bell (2004) *Sure Start Early Years Workforce Development Evidence Paper*. Bedford: Sauve Bell Associates.

Siraj-Blatchford, I. (1993) 'Educational research and reform: some implications for the professional identity of early years teachers', *British Journal of Educational Studies*, 41(4): 393–408.

Stronach, I., Corbin, B., McNamara, O., Stark, S. and Warne, T. (2002) 'Towards an uncertain politics of professionalism: teacher and nurse identities in flux', *Journal of Education Policy*, 17(1): 109–38.

Tucker, S. (2004) 'Youth working: professional identities given, received or contested?', in J. Roche, S. Tucker, R. Thomson and R. Flynn (eds) *Youth in Society*, 2nd edn. London: Sage.

UNISON (2006) *Qualifications, Pay and Quality in the Childcare Sector*. Report for UNISON prepared by the Centre for Economic and Social Inclusion. Available from: www.unison.org.uk/acrobat/B2773.pdf (accessed December 2009).

Wenger, E. (1998) *Communities of Practice*. Cambridge: Cambridge University Press.

Williams, J. (2007) 'Becoming a teacher', in A. Berry, A. Clemans and A. Kostogriz (eds) *Dimensions of Professional Learning*. Rotterdam: Sense Publishing.

CHAPTER 8

CONTESTED CONSTRUCTIONS OF PROFESSIONALISM WITHIN THE NURSERY

Jayne Osgood

Overview

In this chapter, which draws on a recent study (Osgood, 2011, forthcoming) with a sample of nursery staff from the private, voluntary and statutory sectors, I argue for 'professionalism from within' (Stronach et al., 2003). Discourse analytic methods have been employed to demonstrate that nursery staff reluctantly accept the dominance of government discourses. However, when questioned about the qualities and skills that equate to 'being professional' or 'doing professionalism', considerable dissonance is identified. Rationalism, accountability, measurability and other traits encompassed in neo-liberal discourses were notably absent (or qualified) from practitioners' self-definitions of professionalism in their work. Whilst performing hegemonic forms of professionalism involved adhering to external demands to demonstrate measurable outcomes or to, in effect, 'enact a fantasy' (Butler, 2004), claims to more authentic professional identities rested upon a set of different (and often competing) performances. It is to these alternative performances and counter discourses that I turn to argue for the promotion of the 'critically reflective emotional professional' in place of the 'competent technician'.

Introduction

I undertook a qualitative research study in three inner London nurseries. The study began in 2003 and ended in 2008. The aim of the study was to explore understandings and lived experiences of professionalism from the perspective of staff working directly with young children.

The contextual backdrop for the study was shaped by the unparalleled political attention that nurseries have received in the past two decades. The importance placed upon fostering greater professionalism amongst nursery staff is stressed throughout government policies and plans for further reform (Children's Workforce Development Council (CWDC), 2008; DfES, 2003, 2005, 2006). The study endeavoured to unearth the form(s) that professionalism takes within localized settings, and the forces that come to bear upon the ways in which Early Childhood Education and Care (ECEC) practitioners negotiate their professional identities. Ultimately, the goal was to identify constructions of 'professionalism from within' ECEC communities of practice and map their compatibility with those offered through authoritative discourses promoted through policy and other powerful sources such as the media. Throughout this chapter, I highlight the ambiguities that surround contemporary drives for standardization, accountability, measurability, transparency, and so on. The tactics employed by nursery staff to variously embrace, critique and resist dominant models of professionalism are explored. I conclude the chapter by offering the 'critically reflective emotional professional' as a conceptual means to envision a form of professionalism in ECEC that embraces subjectivity, autobiography and affectivity in place of technical competence.

Defining 'professionalism'

In public discourse, 'professionalism' commonly denotes an apolitical construct which is broadly defined as a combination of occupational specialism, high standards, self-regulation and autonomy. A recent search of the *Oxford English Dictionary* offered the following definition:

> A person who does something with a high level of competence, commitment, or expertise ... requiring special skill or training; that has or displays the skill, knowledge, experience, standards, or expertise of a professional; competent, efficient ... that has knowledge of the theoretical or scientific parts of a trade or occupation, as distinct from its practical or mechanical aspects; that raises a trade to a learned profession ... (OED, 2009)

Various commentators (Cannella, 1997; Fenech and Sumsion, 2007; Miller, 2008; Novinger and O'Brien, 2003), myself included (Osgood, 2004, 2005, 2006a, 2006b, 2006c, 2008a, 2008b, 2010, 2011), have troubled the idea that professionalism in ECEC is unproblematic, straightforward and apolitical. The academic debate surrounding professionalism within ECEC has usefully unsettled taken-for-granted assumptions that it is a straightforward process with an inevitably positive outcome. Rather, the prospect of professionalizing a highly gendered, classed and hitherto neglected workforce is fraught with difficulties and will be met with questioning resistance at each stage (as this chapter demonstrates).

Negotiating neo-liberal constructions of 'professionalism'

All participants in the study were asked to define what professionalism in ECEC meant to them. They were specifically asked what they felt made them good at their work and what skills/qualities were necessary to work effectively with young children in a nursery setting. The definitions offered indicated that 'professionalism' is a slippery concept that alters over time and in different contexts. Many recited details of their occupational journeys, highlighting the significance of training/ qualifications and accrued wisdom. All recounted that constant policy-driven reform had shaped their sense of professionalism in significant ways at different moments throughout their careers, for example Ruth (a Senior Practitioner with over 20 years experience in the voluntary sector) provided a retrospective account through which professionalism is presented as an evolving construct driven by external demands for better standards:

> About 23 years [ago] when I first started working [in nurseries] ... it was much more casual; very laid back ... There was some structure but not in the way there is now ... it wasn't so deep, we now have to measure and demonstrate and record ... in some ways that's an improvement ... in those days you didn't have to [keep records] and the children progressed just as well.

The increasing presence of an 'audit culture' (Ozga, 2000) is discernable in this quote which illustrates that (professional) expectations have altered over time. Others expressed scepticism about the developments to their practice; performativity discourses (Butler, 1990) were variously drawn upon to make sense of the ways in which practice has become refashioned through a range of policy developments designed to improve accountability, transparency and measurability. Most frequently discussed were Ofsted inspections. The participants came to view inspections as the embodiment of neo-liberal demands for accountability and the primary means of assessing quality. There was considerable ambiguity surrounding inspections; on the one hand they were viewed as offering the promise of heightened attention, comparability with schools, a form of quality assurance; and on the other as fostering a culture of competition, mistrust and ontological insecurity. The descriptions of and reflections given about Ofsted inspections were highly emotive and forcefully informed how the participants came to understand themselves as more or less professional at a given moment. Practitioners were actively engaged in performing professionalism in various ways throughout their daily lives in the nurseries. In discussions about the performance of professionalism, it was felt to rest upon an uncomfortable combination of personal/moral commitment and the embodiment of external definitions. For example, authoritative constructions of professionalism (and quality) encapsulated in

Ofsted assessment criteria were considered overly prescriptive and narrow in focus, denying space for subjective representations of professionalism:

> *Natalia*: I know that I am conscientious, well qualified, experienced and reflect on what I am doing, I also recognize that there is always room for improvement. If that was what Ofsted was about then great. But I just felt that there was an air of distrust; that my professionalism was being doubted and unfairly judged ... I would say that to get a sense of my professionalism and an understanding of what I am doing, then come and take a *good* look before making any sorts of assumptions ... It goes back to what I was saying before about your personal philosophy and working ethos and finding a balance between what you hold dear and what is expected of you from external agendas ... You always feel under scrutiny in this line of work but if judgements are being made they should be informed and considered.

The tension identified by Natalia between external agendas/public scrutiny and personal philosophy/working ethos offers a vital insight into the ways in which nursery staff wrestle with hegemonic discourses and practices designed to assess professional competence. Authoritarian discourses are constructed in multiple and contradictory ways; as necessary, affirming and legitimating, whilst simultaneously as unjust, partial and containing. The discursive landscape in which nursery staff are located, and to which they contribute, is inflected with neo-liberal technicist assumptions and expectations. Nevertheless, as Natalia's account testifies, investments are made to find space, to both challenge and refashion mechanisms designed to contain and control.

Professionalism as neo-liberal performance

The research participants demonstrated skilful negotiation of authoritative professionalism discourses, at certain times appearing to have taken them up in an accepting way, as demonstrated in the example of Ofsted inspections. However, there was acute awareness of the hegemonic discourses through and within which particular forms of professionalism are extolled at the expense of others. For example, the hegemony of the 'enterprising neo-liberal subject' (Walkerdine, 2003) within government discourses was identifiable within the data and the ways in which this played out in localized discursive practices, was reflected upon. There is an acute pressure to embody dominant forms of professionalism (i.e. the competent technician), and to, in effect, 'enact a fantasy' (Butler, 2004) through professional performance. Participants were busy demonstrating an approximation to hegemonic forms of professionalism whilst remaining unconvinced of either its appropriateness or authenticity to nursery work:

> *Gazala*: That is the way we need to be now, you have to sell yourself, you have to promote yourself as being a certain type of professional, hand over examples that demonstrate that, convince the powers that be that what we are doing is what is required ... but

then again, whether the powers that be really know what is best, you know for us, umm performing well during an inspection is a very different thing from being, well ... *knowing* ... that you are good at this sort of work ... that's a totally different ball game.

The rate and pace of policy developments and the sustained attention upon the children's workforce left many with a strong sense of ontological insecurity. In effect, nursery staff become rendered incapable of resisting (seemingly nonsensical) policy reform and are left feeling doubtful of their experiential wisdom and hands-on capabilities. Hegemonic discourses that promote certain forms of professionalism over others are embedded within and promoted by current ECEC policies designed to modernize, restructure and improve the workforce (CWDC, 2008; DfES, 2006). Located within this discursive landscape, educators are left to variously negotiate, resist and embrace hegemonic discourses whilst simultaneously creating, modifying and sustaining counter discourses from within their localized networks or communities of practice (Fleer, 2003).

'Professionalism from within'

Despite the apparent seduction of government discourses of professionalism in ECEC, this study revealed a considerable tension between performing hegemonic professionalism and retaining a tacit commitment to alternative constructions. When questioned about the qualities and skills that equated to 'doing professionalism', there was little reference to rationalism, accountability, measurability, standardization, and so on. It became obvious that whilst these women regularly 'enacted the fantasy' of hegemonic professionalism, they simultaneously laid claim to more authentic professional subjectivities which rested upon different (and often competing) performances.

The struggle to reconcile the necessarily emotional and affective aspects of ECEC practice with demands for more widely accepted constructions of professionalism occupied significant space in many of the narratives. Stronach et al. (2003: 125) 'criticise the reductive typologies and characterisations of current professionalism'; instead they argue that the 'professional self' is constituted by a series of contradictions and dilemmas. The authors offer an 'uncertain theory of professionalism' shaped by lived experience and characterized by plurality, tension, juggling, ambiguity and inconsistency. Applying an 'uncertain theory of professionalism' within the context of ECEC is particularly helpful to explore how competing discourses play out in the narratives, and to trace the emergence of counter discourses which then offer alternate versions of professionalism. Furthermore, it offers a chance to consider professionalism as shaped by biography and subjective experience. Professional identities come to be conceptualized as embodied performances shaped by subjective, life-long experiences of class, gender, 'race', and so on, rather than an externally constructed label conferred upon an occupational group.

This study was undertaken at about the same time that the Children's Workforce Development Council (CWDC) was introduced, in 2005. As a quasi independent government organization, the CWDC waged a deliberate and concerted effort to overhaul Early Childhood Education and Care (ECEC) services in the UK. The council was charged with creating order and clarity where there had been confusion, duplication and ambiguity surrounding career structures, training pathways and job titles. The council stated its aims as creating a clear hierarchy and achieving the goal of a graduate-led profession by 2015. In 2007, the 'Early Years Professional' became a credentialized status that could be conferred upon nursery workers (and others working with young children in ECEC) through a process of formal accreditation. This marked a significant moment; being 'professional' or having 'professional status' became an accolade attained through evidence of demonstrating a series of competencies.

The narratives recounted through this study, however, revealed complexity and tension regarding professional status in ECEC. Professional subjectivities or 'ways of being' come about from an active engagement and negotiation of the discourses through which individuals are shaped and in which they are positioned (Foucault, 1994). Whilst neo-liberal discourses place an overt emphasis on modernist rationalism, counter-discourses to emerge from this study tended towards an 'ethics of care' in the quest for a version of 'professionalism from within'. A substantial body of literature has established that emotionality is necessary and integral to ECEC practice since the nature of the work involves strong feelings towards children, a child's family, the wider community, and colleagues (see e.g. Dahlberg and Moss, 2005). The study reported here provides further evidence of the investment made within nurseries towards fostering caring communities of practice characterized by affectivity, altruism, self-sacrifice and conscientiousness.

Ethics of care

Interestingly, this recent study revealed that the most frequently cited and highly regarded attributes felt to represent 'professionalism in ECEC' were principally associated with the affective domain. In itself this is perhaps unsurprising, but becomes more so when contrasted to dominant notions of professionalism that promote rationalism and allow little or no space for emotion. Sevenhuijsen (1998) presents a 'feminist ethics of care' characterized by empathy, intuition, compassion, love, relationality and commitment; with the central tenets being responsibility and communication. Sevenhuijsen's model resonates loudly with the findings from this study. However, contradictions and ambiguities were also present in the insider constructions of professionalism which demonstrated that embodiment of an ethical and emotional professionalism involves careful management of the self and others to prevent 'burnout'. For example, a significant importance was attached to demarcating private/family life from work, and similarly the capacity to remain 'professionally detached' was considered crucial to sustaining commitment and enthusiasm for the work:

Francelle: I think that professionalism is about separating your social issues from your work, because in this job you can easily get too emotional and too much emotion can interfere with your work and that is where you have to know where, when and how to draw the line. But you can still be emotional, you have to be, you know? You need to show emotion to the children and to love them to be able to teach them and nurture them but you can do that so that they understand discipline, boundaries and so on, and it's possible to do that without losing balance and respect.

Others recounted the careful emotional balancing act required to work effectively. Allowing subjective experience (such as being a mother or memories of their own childhood) to inflect practice, whilst maintaining a safe distance between private and public, was central to constructions of 'professionalism from within'. The embeddedness of emotional labour to work within nurseries was recognized and understood as challenging. Whilst emotional labour is central to insider constructions of professionalism, for that labour to be credible and have a degree of status conferred upon it, emotions were understood to need skilful management and containment. Ashforth and Tomuik (2000: 195) argue that emotion management is constructed as integral to subjectivity – as a means of supporting authenticity and expressing identity. This position is borne out in the findings from this study. Participants spoke of the need to manage a caring self and emotionality 'in the right way', which is suggestive of a scripted performance (Hochschild, 1983). However, within nurseries 'the script' evolves from within a community of practice and is accompanied by 'ways of being' that rely upon performing commitment, genuineness and authenticity.

Orla: The type of caring that you do depends on how professional you are; what 'professional' means to you … you wouldn't come into this [nursery work] unless you were … emotionally committed … that you care and can be caring … but it boils down to doing it the right way … treat [children] with compassion and really mean it … children can tell if you're faking it, it has to be natural … If you come into nursery work and you 'get it', if you can genuinely do the sort of caring I'm talking about then you stay for life but if you can't – you won't last five minutes.

Hence, the emotional labour performed by nursery staff differs from the 'scripted performances' discussed by Hochschild (1983). An analysis of the narratives from this research indicates that the tensions between subjective authenticity and surface acting (identified by Hochschild) were incongruous in the nursery context. In effect, space and opportunities to 'fake' emotional labour in the nursery were denied. Interpretations of emotionality indicated that the occupational demands of nursery work amount to more than the mere execution of a set of preordained competencies.

The narratives were littered with examples of strong feelings towards protecting, supporting and engaging empathically with children (Elfer et al., 2003; Moyles, 2001). However, the emotional labour extends beyond meeting the exclusive needs of children to interactions with colleagues and parents. The biographies of the women in this study revealed that 'caring about' and 'caring for' people had shaped many childhood and adolescent identities. The 'fit between who I am and what I do' was a sentiment to run through much of the data collected from this occupational group. For many commentators, emotional labour is regarded negatively (as a means to position working-class women subordinately; for example, see Hochschild (1983), Skeggs (2003) and Colley (2006)). Yet in the context of ECEC, it becomes possible to conceive of meticulous management of emotional capital in their professional lives as holding agentic potential (Manion, 2006; Reay, 2000). The capacity to effectively manage emotions and deploy them in a range of ways (through pedagogical practices with children, in work with colleagues, and interaction with families) and potential opportunities to construct themselves as worthy, insightful, autonomous professionals are opened up.

'The fit between who I am and what I do'

> The emotional demands are great ... in a professional role she must develop a very personal and intimate relationship with each of the babies and children with whom she is working. There are bound to be some painful feelings involved as the work can not be done in an emotionally anaesthetised way ... Maintaining an appropriate professional intimacy, which every child needs in order to feel special, while keeping an appropriate professional distance requires emotional work of the highest calibre. (Elfer et al., 2003: 27)

Through a celebration of emotional labour opportunities to manage the self in ways that take account of the effects on others (children, parents, colleagues, the self), a discourse of professionalism emerges that represents a direct challenge to the limiting and containing version offered in neo-liberal government discourse. By way of example, a high degree of importance was placed on acting in non-judgemental and socially just ways, on working collegially and on being self-reflexive/critical. The professional subjectivities constructed through this study tended to run counter to neo-liberal discourses that promote standardization and individualist, publicly accountable approaches to assuring effectiveness, quality and hence professionalism. In attempts to 'stay true to your own belief system' (Natalia), 'be true to yourself and what you're about' (Debbie) and 'hold dear what you believe to be the right and proper way' (Bertrise), this study revealed that negotiating the dominance of more dispassionate modes of professionalism was fraught with tension and uncertainty.

Dominant conceptualizations of caring work often foreground the image of oppressed, docile bodies, routinely performing emotion in daily interactions by virtue of an externally imposed, gendered, professional script (Colley, 2006; Hochschild, 1983; Skeggs, 1997). This study exposes that emotional labour is, in many ways, empowering to nursery staff. The women were constantly negotiating and assessing the role and interplay of emotions in their work and demonstrating sophisticated emotion management.

Final thoughts

The aims of the study reported here were concerned to investigate multiple subjectivities and the implications of doing class, gender and 'race' (Butler, 1990) for professionalism in ECEC. The narrative methods allowed space for reflection upon aspects of life that are not readily assumed to shape professional subjectivities; delving into the personal to seek to understand the public identities of nursery workers informed new ways to theorize professionalism. The ways in which nursery workers come to conceive of themselves as more or less professional rests upon their (life-long, life-wide) subjective experiences and the wider discourses in which they are located and upon which they draw, reject and negotiate.

Subjective experiences drawn from autobiography and the prominence of 'the personal' are acutely significant to the ways in which 'professionalism from within' can be reconceptualized. By relating the significance of their autobiographies, nursery workers can experience greater authenticity in their pedagogical practices, and in their sense of professionalism. The emotional nature of nursery work is both acknowledged and valued within the community of practice. Pedagogical engagement with children, collegial working practices and the careful management of emotionally charged relationships with parents all require the sophisticated deployment of emotional capital (Reay, 1998). Recognizing the centrality of emotion in ECEC professionalism should be taken up and celebrated in public discourse rather than obscured and denigrated, as is currently the case.

 Summary

- This chapter has demonstrated that professionalism within ECEC is in many ways a performance. Practitioners take up and reject dominant modes of professionalism at different moments within their professional lives.
- Through my research, I have endeavoured to foreground aspects of professionalism that are readily dismissed or at least obscured in hegemonic understandings of professionalism – notably, promoting the significance of autobiography and subjective experiences that occur in the private lives of nursery practitioners is an important development for conceptualizing professionalism differently.
- Related to this is the importance of emotion in debates about professionalism in ECEC. It is my contention that professionalism from within the nursery is shaped by a commitment to an ethics of care and critical reflection.
- Whilst practitioners might appear to be adhering to demands for technical competence, there is a significant degree of subversion and resistance occurring at the local level within nursery settings.
- Through my research, I want to promote and celebrate a feminist reading of professionalism which sits in stark contrast to common-sense and dominant constructions which are currently promoted through policy discourses.

Questions for discussion

1. Do the views of the practitioners in this chapter speak to you and your feelings about how you currently view professionalism? Make a note of similarities and differences to discuss with a colleague.
2. What are your experiences of inspection? Can you summarize the positive and not so positive outcomes for you and other staff?
3. What do you consider are the parts played by training and subjective experience in developing your understanding of your own professionalism?
4. To what extent do you agree that ethics of care and the concept of emotional labour are missing from current and dominant discourses surrounding professionalism in the early years? (*Higher level question*)

Further reading

Levels 5–8

Fairclough, N. (2001) 'The discourse of New Labour: critical discourse analysis', in M. Wetherell, S. Taylor and S.J. Yates (eds) *Discourse as Data: A Guide for Analysis*. London: Sage with the Open University.
This chapter offers a guide on how to undertake critical discourse analysis of policies and other authoritative sources. The edited collection in which the chapter is located offers a range of alternate ways to approach discourse analysis (*Levels 7 and 8*).

Novinger, S. and O'Brien, L. (2003) 'Beyond "boring meaningless shit" in the academy: early childhood teachers under the regulatory gaze', *Contemporary Issues in Early Childhood*, 4(1): 4–18.
This journal paper offers the reader a critical appraisal of the ways in which ECEC training and practice has developed in neo-liberal times. It is written in an engaging and thought-provoking way that enables the reader to usefully trace the impact of policy on practice and a sense of professionalism (*suitable for all levels*).

Osgood, J. (2009) 'Government policy and childcare workforce reform: a critical discourse analysis', *Journal of Education Policy*, 24(6): 733–51.
This journal paper complements this chapter in numerous ways. As the title suggests, it offers a critical analysis of the policy discourses that construct nursery workers in particular ways (*suitable for all levels*).

Websites

CWDC (2007) *Be a Leader: Early Years Professional Status*. Available from: www.cwdcouncil.org.uk/pdf/Early%20Years/EYP_Prospectus_0407.pdf (accessed 5 August 2008).

CWDC (2008) *Early Years Professional Status*. Available from: www.cwdcouncil.org.uk/eyps (accessed 5 August 2008).
These online documents provide the reader with the primary sources outlining the CWDC's vision of professionalism in ECEC.

References

Ashforth, B.E. and Tomuik, M.A. (2000) 'Emotional labour and authenticity: views from service agents', in S. Fineman (ed.) *Emotion in Organizations*. London: Sage. pp. 184–203.

Butler, J. (1990) *Gender Trouble: Feminism and the Subversion of Identity*. London: Routledge.

Butler, J. (2004) *Undoing Gender*. London: Routledge.

Cannella, G.S. (1997) *Deconstructing Early Childhood Education: Social Justice and Revolution*. New York: Peter Lang.

Children's Workforce Development Council (CWDC) (2008) *Early Years Professional Status*. Available from: www.cwdcouncil.org.uk/eyps (accessed 5 August 2008).

Colley, H. (2006) 'Learning to labour with feeling: class, gender and emotion in childcare education and training', *Contemporary Issues in Early Childhood*, 7 (1): 15–29.

Dahlberg, G. and Moss, P. (2005) *Ethics and Politics in Early Childhood Education*. London: RoutledgeFalmer.

Department for Education and Skills (DfES) (2003) *Every Child Matters* (Green Paper) Cm. 5860. London: HMSO.

DfES (2005) *Children's Workforce Strategy: Building a World-Class Workforce for Children, Young People and Families*. London: DfES.

DfES (2006) *Children's Workforce Strategy: Building a World-Class Workforce for Children, Young People and Families. The Government's Response to the Consultation*. London: DfES.

Elfer, P., Goldschmied, E. and Selleck, D. (2003) *Key Persons in the Nursery: Building Relationships for Quality Provision*. London: David Fulton. pp. 1–82.

Fenech, M. and Sumsion, J. (2007) 'Early childhood teachers and regulation: complicating power relations using a Foucauldian lens', *Contemporary Issues in Early Childhood*, 8(2): 109–22.

Fleer, M. (2003) 'Early childhood education as an evolving "community of practice" or as lived "social reproduction": researching the "taken-for-granted"', *Contemporary Issues in Early Childhood*, 4(1): 64–79.

Foucault, M. (1994) *Power: Essential Works of Foucault 1954–1984*, vol. 3. J.D. Faubion (ed.) and R. Hurley (trans.). London: Penguin.

Hochschild, A. (1983) *The Managed Heart: The Commercialisation of Human Feeling*. Berkeley, CA: University of California Press.

Manion, C. (2006) 'Feeling, thinking, doing: emotional capital, empowerment and women's education', in I. Epstein (ed.) *Recapturing the Personal: Essays on Education and Embodied Knowledge in Comparative Perspective*. London: Sage.

Miller, L. (2008) 'Developing professionalism within a regulatory framework in England: challenges and possibilities', in L. Miller. and C. Cable (eds) *Professionalism in the Early Years*. London: Hodder Education.

Moyles, J. (2001) 'Passion, paradox and professionalism in early years education', *Early Years*, 21(2): 81–95.

Novinger, S. and O'Brien, L. (2003) 'Beyond "boring, meaningless shit" in the academy: early childhood teacher educators under the regulatory gaze', *Contemporary Issues in Early Childhood*, 4(1): 4–18.

Osgood, J. (2004) 'Time to get down to business? The responses of early years practitioners to entrepreneurial approaches to professionalism', *Journal of Early Childhood Research*, 2(1): 5–24.

Osgood, J. (2005) 'Who cares? The classed nature of childcare', *Gender and Education*, 17(3): 289–303.

Osgood, J. (2006a) 'Professionalism and performativity: the paradox facing early years practitioners', *Early Years*, 26(2): 187–99.

Osgood, J. (2006b) 'Editorial: rethinking "professionalism" in the early years: English perspectives', *Contemporary Issues in Early Childhood*, 7(1): 1–4.

Osgood, J. (2006c) 'Deconstructing professionalism in the early years: resisting the regulatory gaze', *Contemporary Issues in Early Childhood*, 7(1): 5–14.

Osgood, J. (2008a) 'Professionalism and performativity: the paradox facing early years practitioners', in E. Wood (ed.) *The Routledge Reader in Early Childhood Education*. London: Routledge.

Osgood, J. (2008b) 'Narratives from the nursery: negotiating professional identities', PhD thesis.

Osgood, J. (2010, forthcoming) 'Multi-professionalism and the early years professional: contested terrain', in R. Thompson (ed.) *Critical Practice in Work with Children and Young People*. Buckingham: Open University Press.

Osgood, J. (2011, forthcoming) *Professional and Social Identities in the Early Years: Narratives from the Nursery*. London: Routledge.

Oxford English Dictionary (OED) (2009) Available from: http://dictionary.oed.com/cgi/entry/50189445?query_type=word&queryword=professionalism&first=1&max_to_show=10&single=1&sort_type=alpha (accessed 8 September 2009).

Ozga, J. (2000) *Policy Research in Educational Settings: Contested Terrain*. Buckingham: Open University Press.

Reay, D. (1998) 'Rethinking social class: qualitative perspectives on class and gender', *Sociology*, 32(2): 259–75.

Reay, D. (2000) 'A useful extension of Bourdieu's conceptual framework? Emotional capital as a way of understanding mothers' involvement in their children's education', *The Sociological Review*, 4: 568–85.

Sevenhuijsen, S. (1998) *Citizenship and the Ethics of Care: Feminist Considerations on Justice, Morality and Politics*. London: Routledge.

Skeggs, B. (1997) *Becoming Respectable: Formations of Class and Gender*. London: Sage.

Skeggs, B. (2003) *Class, Self, Culture*. London: Routledge.

Stronach, I., Corbin, B., McNamara, O., Stark, S. and Warne, T. (2003) 'Towards an uncertain politics of professionalism: teacher and nurse identities in flux', *Journal of Education Policy*, 17(1): 109–38.

Walkerdine, V. (2003) 'Reclassifying upward mobility: femininity and the neo-liberal subject', *Gender and Education*, 15(3): 237–48.

CHAPTER 9

WHERE ARE THE MEN?
A Critical Discussion of Male Absence in the Early Years

Guy Roberts-Holmes and Simon Brownhill

Overview

Despite the rapid expansion of the early years labour market and cultural and policy shifts in favour of men working in the early years, 99% of the early years workforce remains female (Owen, 2003; Rolfe, 2006). This is despite an official commitment to increase the number of male childcare workers to 6% by 2004 (DfES, 2005). In this chapter, we seek to critically analyse why the early years workforce remains so gender imbalanced. Historically located discourses continue to locate early years work as naturally feminine. The effects of such historically situated discourses, combined with ever present fears of masculine sexuality, have had the effect of maintaining the early years workforce as almost totally female. An early years sector 'vocational habitus' is analysed in which stereotypical feminine traits are included whilst masculine traits are excluded. We argue that the increasing privatization of the early years sector, which maintains low wages, has compounded a gendered workforce. The thesis of the 'male role model' in the early years is critically discussed for both its perceived advantages and in the light of recent literature which questions the effect of the 'male

(Continued)

(Continued)

role model'. Despite popular discourses calling for more men in the early years sector, Carrington et al. (2007) maintain that the gender of the practitioner is 'largely immaterial'. We conclude the chapter with an examination of both United Kingdom (UK) based and international projects and initiatives that have successfully included men as early years practitioners. Such successful projects have at their heart a political desire to be inclusive of all difference, including the shortage of British Minority Ethnic (BME) early years practitioners, so that diversity is the norm and not the exception.

Historical construction of childcare as feminine

In this chapter, we understand gender from a social constructionist perspective. Such a perspective rejects biological understandings of there being a natural female or male behaviour, arguing instead that cultural and social conditioning is largely responsible for establishing male and female gender roles. Within this perspective, we argue that patriarchal gendered discourses, in which women occupy subordinate positions to men in terms of power and status, continue to have significant effects upon the gendered composition of today's early years workforce. The early years workforce, which is historically underqualified, underpaid and overwhelmingly female (Miller and Cable, 2008), can be critically analysed as being located within 19th-century patriarchal discourses which oppress women. Patriarchal discourses maintain that caring (paid and unpaid) is naturally women's work. Additionally, within some contexts, the continued reification of the Victorian idealized middle-class home, with a male breadwinner and a stay-at-home mother caring for children, remains persistent.

Moss and Petrie (2002) maintain that nurseries and pre-schools have historically been constructed as an extension of the home rather than as democratic children's spaces where communities engage in dialogue. Within such a construction, both the early childhood institution and the early childhood professional remain female. It can be argued that in a patriarchal society female nursery workers' poverty levels of pay can become justifiable and naturalized. Such arguments have added weight in the light of the increasing marketization of the early years (Roberts-Holmes, 2009a). The early years business model drives down staff costs (and thus qualifications) which is central to maintaining profit margins. Thus, the business model of the early years further legitimates the low wages of the underqualified female childcare worker (Roberts-Holmes, 2009a). In addition, Moss (2008) notes that there remains a continuing construction of children as immature and incomplete and who therefore have fairly simple developmental needs. According to Moss (2008), such a continuing deficit construction of children means that little training (and hence pay) is required of those who care for children (rather than teach children), once again legitimizing low qualifications and therefore pay.

Vincent and Braun (2009) argue that the early years profession remains firmly rooted within an exclusive feminine 'vocational habitus'. The concept of vocational habitus may be understood as:

> the process of orientation to a particular identity, a sense of what makes 'the right person for the job' … Vocational habitus proposes that the learner aspires to a certain combination of dispositions demanded by the vocational culture. It operates in disciplinary ways to dictate how one should properly feel, look and act, as well as the values, attitudes and beliefs one should espouse. (Colley et al., 2003: 473)

The early years vocational habitus tends to include stereotypical feminine qualities and at the same time tends to exclude male qualities. Furthermore, 'white working class girls are four times as likely as white middle class girls to expect to work in childcare' (EHRC, 2009: 29). Thus the vocational habitus offered to early years practitioners is constrained and limited by gendered and class discourses. Vincent and Braun (2009: 8) report on findings from childcare students who stated that the academic side of their course was to some extent 'a waste of their time'. The female students felt this because they were 'naturally born' with the ability to care for young children. Consequently, the academic creditionals needed to work in a nursery are, for some of these female students, deemed to be largely irrelevant. The students understood 'the right person for the job' as 'possessing highly gendered characteristics' (Vincent and Braun, 2009: 14).

Increasing participation of men in young children's lives

In some families, there has been a significant change in gendered patterns of childcare. These include the rise of male primary carers who are an increasingly common phenomenon in children's lives (Roberts-Holmes, 2009b). Sixty-six percent of mothers with children under five work (Kilkey, 2006) and hence working mothers are increasingly reliant upon their partners to share caring responsibilities. However, working mothers predominately work part-time and still carry out the majority of the childcare responsibilities. Twenty-first century British dads are expected to be 'accessible and nurturing as well as economically supportive to their children' (O'Brien, 2005: 1). The average time spent by fathers with their young children on childcare activities has increased eight-fold since the 1970s (O'Brien, 2005). However, despite the expectation that fathers will now take care of their own children, this has not been translated into an expectation that men will care for other people's children (Owen, 2003; Roberts-Holmes, 2009b).

Recent policy initiatives (HM Treasury/DfES, 2005, 2007) state a desire for the early years sector to engage in a positive 'culture shift' towards fathers (Roberts-Holmes, 2009b). Despite this rhetoric, Lister (2006) compares the fully paid and dedicated father quota or 'Daddy month' (in which a father has a protected paternity right of one month's paid leave) in Canadian Quebec and the Scandanavian countries with the 'meagre' UK two-week paternity leave which serves to reinforce traditional gendered childcare patterns. Rostgaard (2002) argues that a dedicated father quota helps to reconceptualize what 'normal' gender roles are for mothers and fathers.

The barriers to men working in the early years

Stereotypes of feminine and masculine roles exacerbate tensions when men decide to work in the early years sector. Owen (2003: 4) argues that men in the early years are constructed as 'managers in waiting; gay or paedophiles'. The questioning of the sexuality of men who work with young children is a major cultural barrier to encouraging more men into the early years workforce. Personal perceptions that '… you're gay because you're in … education' (King, 1998: 107) remain prevalent in the minds of many male early years practitioners (Cameron, 2001; Rolfe, 2005) and are largely the result of societal opinion. Such prejudices are evident in Mark's experiences below.

 Case study 1

Mark, 37, and a father of two teenagers, was in the sales division of an international company but got fed up with constant commuting and the threat of redundancy. He loved being at home with his own children and felt really confident with young children. Consequently, he made the bold decision to retrain as an early years teacher and did the Post Graduate Certificate in Education (PGCE) five years ago. He has taught in both Key Stage One (KS1) and the Early Years Foundation Stage.

'I'm really lucky to be working in a school where the kids are really motivated. Most of the time being a man in the early years is just not an issue at all. It makes no difference to the children or to what I do. I mean I'm good at my job because I work really hard – that's nothing to do with my being a man – that's because I find the job exciting and I'm motivated to do my best for the children and the school and the community. That's the same for my female colleagues. However, there are some issues as a man working in the Foundation Stage which I have to constantly negotiate and then that can be tedious.

'One senior older female teacher once patronizingly said to me "Don't worry – you'll be promoted up to Key Stage Two and then management". I think she was being sarcastic but it was very pointed. There's this pervasive expectation that because I'm a man I will naturally get promoted. I mean that's just terrible. I love where I am – I have no intention of promotion. As a man you're really watched too – you can't just 'be' – you're either brilliant and clearly on your way to a headship or rubbish and shouldn't be in the Early Years. You can't just be an

(Continued)

(Continued)

"ordinary" Foundation Stage teacher and I think that is gendered. For example, I have experienced one senior early years woman who deliberately excludes me from decision-making processes in team meetings. It's as if she is threatened by me working in what she sees as her female area. Just because I am a man she thinks I'm after promotion and her job! The problem is the head teacher is a man and I think people subconsciously look at me and wonder why I'm on not on headship training courses and the like. I want to stay in the classroom but there is the unwritten assumption that someday I will be a manager. Why should I fulfil these stereotypes?

'Most parents are really supportive of what I do in the class. It's because I'm a good teacher though not because I'm a man. However, I can sense that one or two of the dads are a bit wary around me. There's one dad in particular – I can feel him staring at me as he leaves his daughter in my class. Sometimes he even looks me up and down as if to say "I'm watching you" – it makes me a bit paranoid to tell the truth. Women don't have to put up with any of that nonsense. So, I'm really careful not to touch the children at all. I've noticed my teaching assistant with children sitting on her knees and she has given the children a cuddle on occasion. That's just a big "no no" for me – it would make me vulnerable to accusations.'

Working in the early years sector is synonymous with emotions, sensitivity, creativity and care, all of which are regarded as being 'feminine traits' (Browne, 2008: 73). Any male working with young children who emulates these characteristics is viewed as, at best, 'unusual' and, at worst, an object of 'suspicion' (Smedley, 2007). For many men, this threat to their masculinity acts as a real deterrent to them participating in the profession. For those actually in the workforce, unease is felt by male practitioners whose 'uncommon caring' (King, 1998) opposes accepted stereotypical notions of what it means to be a man (Mills et al., 2008). Coupled with the low status and perceived 'secondary' wage earned as an employee in the sector (Cushman, 2005), it is hardly surprising that many men do not consider employment in the early years as a viable and 'appropriate' option.

Nevertheless, there are men who do work in the sector, and their presence in the workforce is clearly regarded by policy-makers, recruitment agencies, employers and educationalists as being advantageous: 'Having more men working with the under fives [and above] would surely have a positive impact on children, parents, the dynamics of the workforce and society at large' (Cook, 2006, cited in Hirst and Nutbrown, 2006: 55).

One of the most commonly espoused reasons for advocating more male presence in the early years sector centres on the need for more 'role models' to be in the lives of children (Ashley, 2009), and it is a critical exploration of this argument which we now turn our attention to.

The male role model in the early years

Efforts to close the 'gender [attainment] gap' (Carrington et al., 2007: 397) have included a number of concerted government campaigns, aided by various media coverage in the United Kingdom (*Children Now*, 2004; DfES, 2002), urging men to consider working in the early years and primary sector. The suggestion is that children can benefit from seeing a man in a caring and responsible role, and that this will have a particular effect in terms of improving children's behaviour and their relationships with others (Rolfe, 2006).

Tinklin et al. (2001) argue that having more men in the sector will provide children with strong, positive male role models which will help meet the educational needs of boys, particularly those who are socially disadvantaged and generally disaffected with schooling. This disaffection is largely attributed to findings which show how settings continue to promote and adopt teaching styles and learning activities which are better suited to girls. These have been found to alienate and disadvantage boys who are seemingly encouraged to engage in 'quiet, co-operative, verbal, fine-motor, indoor, artistic and passive kinds of activities' (Biddulph, 1995: 145). As a consequence, it is claimed that boys become 'disaffected' in their schooling (Burn, 2002), thus resulting in poor engagement, behavioural difficulties and academic underachievement. It is believed that men in early years settings will complement the 'soft pedagogical practices' of women (Odih, 2002: 91) by bringing in alternative forms of provision which incorporate 'movement, vigour, "hands-on" [and] natural activity' (Mulholland and Hansen, 2003: 214), thus enticing boys to want to learn. A prevalent viewpoint in the 'missing men in education' argument (Thornton and Bricheno, 2006) centres on the notion of the father figure (Mills et al., 2008). By employing more male practitioners in the sector, it is believed that they will offer those children who come from homes where the father is absent a 'stable male role model' or substitute/surrogate dad/replacement father (Skelton, 2002: 82) who can relate better to them, providing them with a required level of stability which, in turn, will result in a rise in standards of academic attainment.

An argued advantage for having more male role models in the lives of young children relates to the anticipated notion of male practitioners modelling hegemonic masculinity (Connell, 1995) to those they work with. This has been promoted by government ministers hinting at conventional notions of what it means to be a male practitioner/teacher in the workforce, clearly presenting traditional images of men in educational employment (Carrington and Skelton, 2003).

Popular discourse suggests that having more male practitioners will actually help boys to envision masculinity differently as they will see men engage in a supportive, caring and nurturing role which, in turn, will encourage boys to 'value [learning] and develop an ethic of caring and allow them to envisage careers outside of traditional gender boundaries' (Ashcraft and Sevier, 2006: 130). Whilst Hutchings et al. (2007) highlight how practitioners and teachers of young children have an important role in offering children less stereotyped images, Davies (1989) is quick to stress how nursery children already have very rigid ideas of gender-appropriate behaviour by the age of 3. In light of this, one may question whether it is possible for male practitioners to demonstrate these 'alternative forms' of masculinity, particularly if they are expected to model qualities such as power, authority and aggression (Connell, 1995 cited in Cushman, 2008: 125) which primarily characterize 'man'. However, as has already been highlighted, these qualities appear unsuitable for the early years, seeing as working in the early years is synonymous with qualities normally associated as feminine: 'patience, empathy, flexibility, tolerance, kindness, compassion, gentleness and affection' (Balchin, 2002: 31).

Key challenges to the male role model argument

A number of key arguments challenge the male role model rhetoric, some of which are discussed below. Froude (2002) and Sabbe and Aelterman (2007) substantiate Bricheno and Thornton's (2002) claims that there is little to no evidence to suggest that boys' social or educational outcomes actually benefit from having a male practitioner; Ludowyke (2001) in fact suggests that the reverse is possibly true, particularly as underachievement is not simply the result of one factor, that is not having a male practitioner or a male role model, but is rather a complex interplay of factors including social class, poverty and ethnicity (Lingard, 1998; Tinklin et al., 2001).

Drexler (cited in Frankel, 2008) claims that 'there is no definitive research that says male [practitioners] improve academic achievement' of those that they work with, a notion supported by the recent research findings of Carrington et al. (2008: 321) who conclude that they were unable to draw strong evidence together to support claims that there is a tendency for male practitioners to significantly enhance the educational performance of boys. Sokal et al.'s (2007) research in fact suggests that boys' attitudes towards learning may actually be more positive when they are taught by female practitioners. Indeed, Carrington et al. (2005) showed that boys and girls taught by women 'were more inclined to show positive attitudes towards school [learning] than their peers taught by men' (p. 15). With no discernable impact on academic attainment, engagement, 'attitudes, behaviour … [or] motivation' (Bricheno and Thornton, 2002: 62), it would appear that the strength of the role model argument is weakened by these research findings.

Research by Carrington et al. (2007: 411) found that the gender of the practitioner has little bearing on children's level of academic engagement or the perceived quality – it is the practitioners' pedagogical and interpersonal skills that are vital in engaging children as learners, regardless of their gender (p. 412). As a result, it is argued that every practitioner has in fact the capacity of being a 'role model' (Carrington and McPhee, 2008: 114), particularly as Lahelma (2000) states that boys and girls alike 'value qualities that are not specifically male or female' (p. 181). Claims, therefore, that the qualities of a good early years practitioner are 'largely androgynous' (Cushman, 2005: 239) would appear well supported.

Ways forward?

In the UK, there have been some very successful initiatives and projects to encourage men into childcare. The Sheffield Children's Centre, for example, employs 25 male workers out of a total of 58 workers. The Sheffield Children's Centre is driven by the philosophy that 'diversity is the norm and not the exception'. This high number of male childcare workers is attributed to the management's deep commitment to inclusive and democratic participation with all members of the community, including fathers. In Scotland, the Men in Childcare project runs men-only childcare orientation programmes which are very successful. The Men in Childcare project had 900 men who followed some form of training after a men-only introduction course. In Charlie's experiences below, he felt isolated being the only man on the Early Childhood degree course and might have benefited from Edinburgh's men-only introduction course.

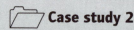 **Case study 2**

Charlie, 28, works in a Children's Centre as an Early Years Professional.

'Honestly, it's been a real struggle to get here. I left school at 16 with next to no qualifications and haven't really had a proper job since then. Then I started to look after my little cousins and found I was good at that. I wanted to make something of myself and to try to do better. I was fed up with no job and no future so I did an Early Childhood degree and then the Early Years Professional (EYP) training. This is a real chance for me now – working here as an EYP. I was the only man on the course (although it was great to see a male tutor) and I always felt that I had to do better than the girls simply because I was the only man. Some of the girls on the course tried to "mother" me 'cos they felt I couldn't cope. They were always asking why I was on the course and laughing – that was hard. Down the pub with my mates I even had to pretend I was doing engineering and stuff like that – even now I can't tell my dad what I do.

'Some of those private nursery managers are so prejudiced against men working that when I saw an advert I would phone up to ask more about the job. I did this to check their attitude to me. Some managers told me the job had gone. I knew this was a lie 'cos my female mates did the same and were encouraged to apply! I was lucky with this place though and I think that 'cos the manager is a man really helped me at the interview. I was looking at him and thought if you can do it so can I. Just seeing him here gives me confidence in what I am doing. I mean most people are really supportive of me here but one or two think I'm like the Christmas clown or something. They don't take me seriously and I have to be careful that I don't play up to them. I'm always really careful never to be in a room with children on my own. The manager has supported me in this and it's policy here for all staff that when changing nappies there is another member of staff present.

(Continued)

(Continued)

'It's interesting though 'cos I've noticed I'm usually the member of staff outside and I think that's 'cos I enjoy being outdoors – I mean I love sport myself so it kinda fits with what I do anyway. I'm gonna start up a dad's group too – I want to act as a positive role model for dads round here – they leave their kids at the gate and don't come in. They should stay and play and I reckon I can encourage them with that. There are some mums though who look at me in a strange way. I think that's 'cos they have had difficulties with men and they actually come here and don't want to see a man! But that's their problem, not mine. For some kids I think I'm a really good role model simply 'cos I don't shout and hit them.

'I love what I do here and feel that finally I'm able to do something really worthwhile with my life and move on. I want to earn more money and become a manager or something.'

Denmark, Sweden and Norway have achieved up to 9% male staff amongst their early childhood workforce (Peeters, 2007). This figure drops considerably, however, in settings for the under-3s (Rolfe, 2006). Within outdoor Norwegian pre-schools, there is an even higher percentage of male staff. Currently, within Norway's 300 outdoor forest pre-schools, 19% of the staff are men (Lysklett, 2007). It was found that these men were highly motivated to work with children outdoors because such outdoor work complemented men's existing interests (as with Charlie above). Additionally, the men saw themselves as being physically playful with the children and the outdoors suited such interactions with them (Lysklett, 2007). Some Norwegian pedagogue early childhood training courses have been made more attractive to men by incorporating sport and outdoor activities in their curriculum. In one Norwegian Pedagogue Seminarium, the number of male students who took a sports and outdoor activities course was 50% and the total number of male students in the institute rose from less than 15% to 24% (Peeters, 2007). However, Moss (2007) points out that the relatively high numbers of men in Scandanavian early childhood programmes actually confirms gender stereotypes because some of these men are either managers or owners of the early childhood institutions. Lysklett (2007) argues that in Scandinavian countries, increasing the level of professional training by making it more knowledge-based and pedagogical had a positive effect on raising the popularity of childcare work among men. In England, Miller and Cable (2008) raise the possibility as to whether the professionalization of the early years workforce through such initiatives as the Early Years Professional Status (DfES, 2005) will encourage more men into the early years workforce.

Final thoughts

Considering the contemporary changes and expectations between the genders, it is remarkable that the early years workforce remains so deeply segregated along gendered lines. Indeed over the past 20 years, the early years workforce has remained virtually gender segregated. In this chapter, we have begun to explore the historical, cultural and economic reasons why women should remain so numerically dominant in the early years workforce. Such factors include the maintenance of partriarchal Victorian discourses which (despite the development of the father primary carer) continues to locate many women as the 'natural' carers of young children. At the same time, these patriarchal discourses situate men out of the home and continue to legitimate men as breadwinners. In a similar way, we have shown that an early years 'vocational habitus' tends to include feminine qualities and sexuality whilst excluding masculine qualities and sexuality. We discussed arguments for and against the male role model, including recent evidence that gender seems to make little difference to the children themselves; rather it would seem that it is pedagogical and interpersonal skills that are important for children. Such evidence questions popular essentialist discourses that boys need male role models.

 Summary

- Despite significant cultural and economic shifts which have effected the construction of gender, historical discourses concerning the naturalized differences between men and women tend to maintain women as the natural carers for young children.
- Whilst such discourses encourage the inclusion of feminine stereotypical qualities, at the same time these discourses have a tendancy to exclude masculine stereotypical qualities (particularly masculine sexuality which is perceived as a risk and a threat to young children).
- This chapter has maintained that such discourses, combined with the effects of patriarchy (in which women occupy subordinate positions to men in terms of power and status), have resulted in the almost totally gendered segregation of the early years workforce.

 Questions for discussion

1. With reference to Ashley's (2001, 2009) research findings, what do you consider motivates and interests all children in terms of learning and teaching?
2. Do you think that early years settings and schools should have more male practitioners/teachers working in them? If so, why? If not, why not?
3. What barriers do you think tend to exclude men from working in the early years? Make some suggestions as to how these barriers might be overcome. (*Higher level question*)

Further reading 📖

Levels 5 and 6

Browne, N. (2008) *Gender Equity in the Early Years*. Maidenhead: Open University Press.
This book critically evaluates the extent to which current early years policies, provision and practice promote and foster gender equity. It explores the rationale for the drive to employ more men in the early years field and examines the link made between 'underachievement' in boys and the 'feminine' nature of early years provision. It also looks at the underpinning philosophy and impact of the Foundation Stage in early years provision.

Roberts-Holmes, G.P. (2003) 'Gender issues in education', in C. Alfrey *Understanding Children's Learning: A Text for Teaching Assistants*. London: David Fulton.
This chapter critically examines the reasons why historically located discourses concerning gender continue to impact upon the early years workforce. Additionally, popular discourses which focus upon the differential achievements of girls and boys are critiqued for their lack of a class and ethnic analysis.

Levels 6 and 7

Cameron, C., Moss, P. and Owen, C. (1999) *Men in the Nursery: Gender and Caring Work*. London: Paul Chapman.
This book is a study of gender in the workforce which compares the experience and views of men and women workers. The authors argue that the invisibility of men in childcare reflects and perpetuates a wider invisibility of gender and that gender issues need to be made visible and the subject of discussion and reflection.

Cushman, P. (2008) 'So what exactly do you want? What principals mean when they say "male role model"', *Gender and Education*, 20(2): 123–36.
This interesting journal article reports on the findings of a survey of 250 New Zealand primary school principals which set out to determine how they defined the term 'male role model' and what they considered to be the specific responsibilities and attributes of that role. The study found that the principals favoured men who exhibit a hegemonic masculinity couched in heterosexual, rugby-playing and 'real men' attributes.

Rolfe, H. (2006) 'Where are the men? Gender segregation in the childcare and early years sector', *National Institute Economic Review*, 195(1): 103–17.
Rolfe's paper provides an accessible and thorough overview of the literature and policy exploring men in childcare and the early years. Rolfe identifies benefits to men's participation in the workforce, the barriers to their entry and how these might be overcome. The paper is rich in historical and contemporary statistics illustrating that gender segregation in the early years is an historical and contemporary issue.

Websites 🖱

www.equalityhumanrights.com/
Equality and Human Rights Commission: this is a generic website that carriers recent research and initiatives to address a variety of discriminatory attitudes and practices, including the

gendered implications of the early years workforce. It is a good introductory website to the issues of discrimination, inclusion and exclusion and hence places the lack of men in the early years into a wider conceptual framework.

www.fatherhoodinstitute.org
The Fatherhood Institute is a portal website that collates and publishes international research on fathers, fatherhood and different approaches to engaging with fathers by public services and employers. There is a specialist early years section for professionals working within early years services. This section provides information on engaging successfully with fathers in the early years.

www.teachers.tv/video/24048
This very interesting Teacher's TV programme offers a series of frank accounts of what it is like to be a male practitioner in a female-dominated workplace.

References

Ashcraft, C. and Sevier, B. (2006) 'Gender will find a way: exploring how male elementary teachers make sense of their experiences and responsibilities', *Contemporary Issues in Early Childhood*, 7(2): 130–45.

Ashley, M. (2001) 'Caring for the boys: lessons from attachment theory', paper delivered at BERA Annual Conference 2001. Available from: www.leeds.ac. uk/educol/documents/00001857htm (accessed 10 October 2008).

Ashley, M. (2009) *Boys Who Dare Don't Care: Unwanted Men, the Performing Arts and Perplexing Disruptions to the Male Teacher Discourse*. Available from: www.leeds.ac.uk/educol/documents/183092.pdf (accessed 12 October 2009).

Balchin, T. (2002) 'Male teachers in primary education', *Forum*, 44(1): 28–33.

Biddulph, S. (1995) *Manhood*. Sydney, Australia: Finch Publishing.

Bricheno, P. and Thornton, M. (2002) 'Staff gender balance in primary schools', *Research in Education*, 68: 57–63.

Browne, N. (2008) *Gender Equality in the Early Years*. London: Open University Press.

Burn, E. (2002) 'Do boys need male primary teachers as positive role models?', *Forum*, 44(1): 34–40.

Cameron, C. (2001) 'Promise or problem? A review of the literature on men working in early childhood services', *Gender, Work and Organisation*, 8(4): 430–53.

Carrington, B. and McPhee, A. (2008) 'Boys' "underachievement" and the feminization of teaching', *Journal of Education for Teaching*, 34(2): 109–20.

Carrington, B. and Skelton, C. (2003) 'Re-thinking "role models": equal opportunities in teacher recruitment in England and Wales', *Journal of Education Policy*, 18(3): 253–65.

Carrington, B., Tymms, P. and Merrell, C. (2005) 'Role models, school improvement and the "gender gap" – do men bring out the best in boys and women the best in girls?', paper presented at the European Association of Research on Learning and Instruction, University of Nicosia, 22–27 August. Available from: www.cemcentre.org/publications/downloads/Earl:2005.pdf (accessed 24 November 2008).

Carrington, B., Tymms, P. and Merrell, C. (2008) 'Role models, school improvement and the "gender gap" – do men bring out the best in boys and women the best in girls?', *British Educational Research Journal*, 34(3): 315–27.

Carrington, B., Francis, B., Hutchings, M., Skelton, C., Read, B. and Hall, I. (2007) 'Does the gender of the teacher really matter? Seven- to eight-year-olds' accounts of their interactions with their teachers', *Educational Studies*, 33(4): 397–413.

Children Now (2004) 'Who says men can't care?', 1–7 December: 18–19.

Colley, H., James, D., Tedder, M. and Diment, K. (2003) 'Learning as becoming in vocational education and training: class, gender and the role of vocational habitus', *Journal of Vocational Education and Training*, 55(4): 471–96.

Connell, B. (1995) *Masculinities*. Sydney, Australia: Allen and Unwin.

Cook, C. (2006) '"It's not what men do": men in the early childhood workforce', in K. Hirst and C. Nutbrown (eds) *Perspectives on Early Childhood Education Contemporary Research*. London: Trentham Books.

Cushman, P. (2005) 'Let's hear it from the males: issues facing male primary school teachers', *Teaching and Teacher Education*, 21: 227–40.

Cushman, P. (2008) 'So what exactly do you want? What principals mean when they say "male role model"', *Gender and Education*, 20(2): 123–36.

Davies, B. (1989) *Frogs and Snails and Feminist Tales*. Sydney, Australia: Allen and Unwin.

Department for Education and Skills (DfES) (2002) *EYDCP Implementation Planning Guidance*. Nottingham: DfES.

DfES (2005) *Children's Workforce Strategy: A Strategy To Build A World-Class Workforce for Children and Young People*. Nottingham: DfES.

Equality and Human Rights Commission (EHRC) (2009) *Staying On*. London: EHRC.

Frankel, H. (2008) 'What's the problem here?', *Times Educational Supplement*, 5 December: 1.

Froude, L. (2002) 'Study defies the "boys need man" credo', *Times Educational Supplement*, 8 March: 2.

Hirst, K. and Nutbrown, C. (eds) (2006) *Perspectives on Early Childhood Education Contemporary Research*. London: Trentham Books.

HM Treasury/DfES (2005) *Support for Parents: The Best Start for Children*. Available from: www.hmtreasury.gov.uk/d/pbr05Supportparents391.pdf (accessed 19 December 2008).

HM Treasury/DfES (2007) *Aiming High for Children: Supporting Families*. Available from: www.everychildmatters.gov.uk/_files/HMT%20YOUNG%20CHILDREN.pdf (accessed 21 December 2008).

Hutchings, M., Carrington, B., Skelton, C., Read, B. and Hall, I. (2007) 'Nice and kind, smart and funny: what children like and want to emulate in their teachers', *Oxford Review of Education*, 34(2): 135–57.

Kilkey, M. (2006) 'New Labour and reconciling work and family life: making it fathers' business?', *Social Policy and Society*, 2: 167–75.

King, J.R. (1998) *Uncommon Caring: Learning from Men who Teach Young Children*. New York: Teachers College Press, Columbia University.

Lahelma, E. (2000) 'Lack of male teachers: a problem for students or teachers?', *Pedagogy, Culture and Society*, 8(2): 173–86.

Lingard, B. (1998) 'Contextualizing and utilizing the "What about the boys" backlash for gender equality goals', *Change: Transformations in Education*, 1(2): 41–50.

Lister, R. (2006) 'Children (but not women) first: New Labour, child welfare and gender', *Critical Social Policy*, 26(2): 315–35.

Ludowyke, J. (2001) 'Directing change: national enquiry into boys' education', *Professional Voice*, 1(3): 6–8.

Lysklett, O. (2007) 'What do 19% men among the staff in the outdoor pre-schools in Norway imply?', paper presented at the 17th EECERA Annual Conference, Exploring Vygotsky's Ideas: Crossing Borders, Prague, Czech Republic, 29 August–1 September.

Miller, L. and Cable, C. (eds) (2008) *Professionalism in the Early Years*. London: Hodder Education.

Mills, M., Haase, M. and Charlot, E. (2008) 'Being the "right" kind of male teacher: the disciplining of John', *Pedagogy, Culture and Society*, 16(1): 71–84.

Moss, P. (2007) *Changing the Gender Divide: Kindergarten, Family and Employment*. London: Thomas Coram Research Unit, Institute of Education, University of London. Presented at Tromso, Norway. Available from: www.fylkesmannen.no/PeterMoss (accessed 5 January 2009).

Moss, P. (2008) 'The democratic and reflective professional: rethinking and reforming the early years workforce', in L. Miller and C. Cable (eds) *Professionalism in the Early Years*. London: Hodder Education.

Moss, P. and Petrie P. (2002) *From Children's Services to Children's Spaces*. London: Taylor & Francis.

Mulholland, J. and Hansen, P. (2003) 'Men who become primary school teachers: an early portrait', *Asia-Pacific Journal of Teacher Education*, 31(3): 213–24.

O'Brien, M. (2005) *Shared Caring: Bringing Fathers into the Frame*. London: Equal Opportunities Commission. Available from: www.equalityhumanrights.com/Documents/EOC/PDF/Research/shared_caring_wp18.pdf (accessed 19 February 2007).

Odih, P. (2002) 'Mentors and role models: masculinity and the educational "underachievement" of young Afro-Caribbean males', *Race Ethnicity and Education*, 5(1): 91–105.

Owen, C. (2003) *Men's Work? Changing the Gender Mix of the Childcare and Early Years Workforce*. Daycare Trust. Available from: www.daycaretrust.org.uk/mod/fileman/files/facing_the_Future_Policy_Paper_6_–_Mens_Work_June_03.pdf (accessed 2 April 2009).

Peeters, J. (2007) 'Including men in early childhood education: insights from the European experience', *NZ Research in Early Childhood Education*, 10: 15–24.

Roberts-Holmes, G. (2009a) 'Towards an understanding of inclusive policies, cultures and practices in the early years', in T. Maynard and N. Thomas (eds) *An Introduction to Early Childhood Studies*. London: Sage.

Roberts-Holmes, G. (2009b) '"People are suspicious of us": a critical examination of father primary carers and English early childhood services', *Early Years*, 29(3): 281–91.

Rolfe, H. (2005) *Men in Childcare*. Occupational Segregation: Working paper Series, No. 35, National Institute of Economic and Social Research.

Rolfe, H. (2006) *Where are the Men? Gender Segregation in the Childcare and Early Years Sector*. National Institute Economic Review 195: 103.

Rostgaard, T. (2002) 'Setting time aside for the father: fathers' leave in Scandinavia', *Community, Work and Family*, 5(3): 343–64.

Sabbe, E. and Aelterman, A. (2007) 'Gender in teaching: a literature review', *Teachers and Teaching: Theory and Practice*, 13(5): 521–38.

Skelton, C. (2002) 'The "feminisation of schooling" or "Re-masculinising" primary education?', *International Studies in Sociology in Education*, 12(1): 77–96.

Smedley, S. (2007) 'Learning to be a primary school teacher: reading one man's story', *Gender and Education*, 19(3): 369–85.

Sokal, L., Katz, H., Chaszewski, L. and Wojcik, C. (2007) 'Goodbye Mr. Chips: male teacher shortages and boys' reading achievement', *Sex Roles: A Journal of Research*, 56(9/10): 651–9.

Thornton, M. and Bricheno, P. (2006) *Missing Men in Education*. Staffordshire: Trentham Books.

Tinklin, T., Croxford, L., Ducklin, A. and Frame, B. (2001) *Gender and Pupil Performance in Scotland's Schools*. Edinburgh: Centre for Educational Sociology, University of Edinburgh.

Vincent, C. and Braun, A. (2009) 'Learning to care for children: training, and the acquisition of a "vocational habitus"', Dissemination Seminar, Institute of Education, University of London, 22 September.

CHAPTER 10

TOWARDS PROFESSIONALISM/S

Iris Duhn

Overview

In this chapter, I argue that the meaning of professionalism in early childhood education is highly contestable, and I propose that the struggle for meaning can be a constructive feature. The first part of this chapter contextualizes professionalism by positioning the discourse in traditional and neoliberal meanings, while the second part of the chapter outlines how critical engagement, combined with an openness towards multiple and flexible meanings, can produce professionalism/s that are specific to context and supportive of democratic practices. Such a discourse offers constructive pathways for early childhood professionalism/s which emphasize specificity and fluidity over standardization and benchmarking: one professionalism does not fit all.

The changing discourse of professionalism

Over the past two decades, early childhood education has attracted the attention of policy-makers in New Zealand to the extent that childcare is now a 'major plank in government interest' (May, 2007: 133). This emerging political focus on early years education was not unique to New Zealand and has been observed in other member countries of the Organisation for Economic Co-operation and Development (OECD) (Woodrow, 2008). While the trend generally coincided with the emergence of neoliberal political rationalities in the 1990s in Western democracies, New Zealand stands out for the enthusiasm for drastic change which made New Zealand a 'textbook case' of neoliberal reform (Kelsey, 1995). Without doubt, much of the ensuing educational change has been driven by what John Codd (2008: 21) terms a 'commercial managerial culture preoccupied with performativity'. Teaching, like other professions in the throes of reform, has been shaped by the push into a culture of accountability, evidence-based practice and outcome-focused benchmarking (Brown and Hattie, 2003). Early childhood education, although differently affected by these shifts in political agendas (Duhn, 2006) than other streams within the teaching profession, is part of the ongoing trend towards the (re)professionalization of teaching (May, 2007).

Some of the effects are visible in government policy directives over the past two decades. The focus on the professionalization of early childhood education has generated an emphasis on teacher qualification benchmarks, with the target of creating a graduate profession of registered teachers. The current target aims for 80% of qualified early childhood teachers, with a minimum of a Diploma of Teaching, preferably a Bachelor of Teaching qualification, by 2012 (Ministry of Education, 2008). Both the 10-year strategic plan for early childhood education and the national curriculum are evidence of a push towards professionalization, and aim to offer leadership to the early childhood sector by providing frameworks and future directions (Duncan, 2008). The meaning of this new professionalism is complex: professionalism as a term of potential empowerment for the low-status early childhood practitioner (Miller, 2008) exists alongside the neoliberal 'regulatory gaze' that controls these emerging professionals (Osgood, 2006). Regardless of how professionalism in early childhood education is understood, it is clear that the neoliberal reconfiguration of professionalism has shaped early childhood discourses of professionalism in ways that make the discourse significantly different from, as well as align with, traditional models of professionalism.

The traditional discourse

Early childhood professionalism fits comfortably with some of the markers of the traditional professions. The hallmarks of professionalism in medicine, for example, have long been the responsibility of care and a commitment to 'doing no harm'. The principles and strands of the New Zealand early childhood curriculum Te Whāriki (Ministry of Education, 1996) underscore that a responsibility of care and a commitment to the child's wellbeing are paramount to early childhood professionalism in New Zealand. A second characteristic of traditional models is the regulation of conduct, generated and monitored internally by the profession, often through a code of ethics (Small, 2008). The policy-driven focus on qualification benchmarks and teacher registration for early childhood educators means that early childhood professionals in New Zealand are now guided by the Code of Ethics for Registered Teachers (New Zealand Teachers Council, 2004). For the early childhood profession in New Zealand, the commitment to a responsibility of care and the governance of this commitment through a code of ethics mark a continuity of traditional hallmarks of a profession (Small, 2008). However, when it comes to status, another hallmark of the traditional discourse, early childhood professionalism does not align easily with the traditional model (Miller, 2008).

Early childhood teaching is often seen as low-status in comparison to teaching in the school sector (King, 1998). In New Zealand, early childhood teachers' low status is compounded by the perception that the teaching profession in general has lost status (Codd, 2008). Although parents may turn frequently to early childhood teachers to seek advice, teachers' professional knowledge appears as an extension of dominant discourses of maternalism (Ailwood, 2008), and thus can be perceived as lacking 'real' expertise. Historically, professional status was derived from having expert knowledge and a responsibility of care towards the non-expert who seeks the professional's expertise. The high status assigned to traditional professions was based on the notion that 'the professional' was committed 'to the good of the person' and by extension 'to the good of society' which culminated in beliefs such as 'the doctor knows best'. This model of professionalism generates paternalism as its corollary (Rose, 1990).

While early childhood professionalism continues the emphasis on ethics of care of the traditional discourse, it differs markedly when it comes to status based on (paternalistic) authority. The erosion of a taken-for-granted belief in teachers' authority can be an advantage because it undercuts the traditional correlation between paternalism and ethics of care and opens spaces for the articulation of a specific early childhood 'professionalism'. Put into a wider context, the early childhood professional is not alone when it comes to ambivalence over the meaning of professionalism. With accelerated political and social change, often referred to as global neoliberalism (Peck, 2004), meanings of professionalism are subject to radical change which affects traditional and emerging professions alike.

The reformed discourse

For the past two decades, the traditional model of professionalism has been superseded by a discourse that emphasizes self-management as performativity (Larner, 2002) over the traditional emphasis on expertise and (paternalistic) responsibility of care for the other. In the traditional model, public trust in expert opinion was high, and being considered 'a professional' legitimated expertise and professional knowledge as valid and important. In a global neoliberal culture of accountability and performativity, 'being a professional' generates trust and status only on a contingent basis. Even a highly acclaimed surgeon is potentially subject to critical questioning by the patient and/or relatives: the professional is only as good as her/his last performance. In a culture where everything is considered potentially dangerous (Furedi, 2002), public trust in experts has waned considerably (Beck, 1992). With knowledge being easily accessible, expert knowledge can be contested, or at least questioned, by the lay-person who is aware that for every expert opinion, a range of opposing expert views can be found. In this radically changed landscape of professionalism, it is not self-evident what professionalism means for any profession, emerging or traditional.

Education as investment

A starting point for the re-configuration of teachers' professionalism in New Zealand is to consider Codd's (2008) concern that neoliberal educational reforms have heralded the de-professionalization of teachers. Codd argues that education is currently dominated by a free market ideology where notions of citizenship and democracy are less important than a continuous striving for the maximization of individual potential and choice. This ideological shift from a welfare state model to a global neoliberal model of governance has a huge impact on education which, according to Codd (2008), is now treated as a commodity. From a global neoliberal perspective, the state's investment in public education 'is viewed as an investment in the human and social capital of the new global economy' (Codd, 2008: 18). For the profession of teaching, the discourse of accountability puts pressure on teachers to provide evidence to the public that the state's investment in public education is warranted. Outcomes are measured and compared against global benchmarks, such as the OECD Programme for International Student Assessment (PISA) test result tables. The new (de)professionalization of teachers produces a discourse of mistrust – does the heavy financial investment in public education produce measurable, comparable results? Can we trust teachers to deliver? Or, more succinctly, as taxpayers, do we get what we pay for?

From this perspective, the increased investment in early childhood education indicates the state's interest in maximizing children's potential from birth, based on the rationale that the early investment will pay dividends by creating future 'global citizens' (Duhn, 2006) who will eventually contribute to the global economy. The professionalization of early childhood education is a necessary mechanism to ensure accountability for the state's investment. New Zealand's policy of 20 free hours of early childhood education for every child (May and Mitchell, 2009), introduced in 2007, indicates the government's ongoing commitment to invest in its human and social capital from birth. Access, availability and affordability of services is uneven; at this stage it seems that 'state-funded early childhood education for 20 hours a week has dramatically boosted the predominantly commercial all-day childcare industry' (Collins, 2010). This pushes the sector further towards a publicly funded, privately delivered model of education (LaRocque and Thorne, 2008). The corporatization of early childhood education leaves little doubt that education is a commodity, and early childhood teachers-as-professionals are accountable for its effective delivery (Duhn, 2010).

Professionalism and teacher agency

Early childhood teachers are positioned in a re-configured discourse of professionalism, where traditional meanings with an emphasis on expertise and expert care are in tension with neoliberal meanings which stress accountability, performance and benchmarks. Codd (2008) argues for a return to older models of professionalism as a way out of a culture of managerial performativity. He proposes a return to the liberal ideals of the welfare state and its traditional models of professionalism based on the correlation of paternalism, expertise and ethics of care. Structural analyses such as Codd's (2008) are powerful because they explain many of the issues that teachers face in their daily practice. This kind of analysis is also dangerous because it can have a paralysing effect: with these powerful structures in place, how can I as a teacher make a difference? Is it even worth trying to make a difference? I suggest that the global neoliberal analysis of the (de)professionalization of teachers tends to overlook the multifaceted and complex differences that exist *within* discourses. Even if teachers are accountable for effective delivery of early childhood education, what effective means and how accountability is achieved and documented, is currently (still) open to discussion and interpretation. For the primary school sector, this has changed with the advent of national standards, rolled out in February 2010 (Ministry of Education, 2009).

Reconfiguring the discourse

In the second section of this chapter, I argue for a more radical re-configuration of professionalism/s that takes account of potential for agency through a focus on the heterogeneous nature of discourse. No discourse is watertight – there are always run-offs, some of them easily detectable, others more hidden (Davies, 2005). Working within discourse to better understand its limitations and possibilities creates opportunities to identify and work with differences within. This is political work because it makes contradictions and tensions visible and disrupts monolithic, apparently seamless and overwhelmingly 'big' concepts, such as neoliberalism and, on a smaller scale, professionalism. Working with differences within discourse creates multiplicities – professionalism is not a given, it can take multiple forms and practices. Critical analysis of professionalism/s produces better understandings of how meaning is made – how does the discourse affect a sense of professional self and professional other? How are teachers performing a 'professional self'? What are the differences between professional conduct in different places? These kinds of questions begin the work of untangling the umbrella discourse of professionalism by paying attention to the multiple meanings and practices embedded within the discourse.

Similarly, global neoliberal political rationalities are diverse and contradictory: 'partnership', 'collaboration' and 'consultation' are now as much part of the (post) neoliberal vocabulary as are 'accountability', 'benchmarks' and 'management' (Larner, 2005). Larner argues that in this phase of (post) neoliberalism, oppositional voices have become integrated into professional roles within government structures. She emphasizes that this professionalization

> exemplifies an argument that neoliberal spaces and subjectivities are not simply imposed from above, nor is 'resistance' simply a bottom-up political response to macro-level structural processes. Rather, new governmental spaces and subjects are emerging out of multiple and contested discourses and practices. (Larner and Craig, 2005: 421)

There is no 'good' or 'bad' way of being a professional in (post)neoliberal times. Instead, there are always new and surprising ways of being and doing – these are the spaces and identities that are open because they are unpredictable and uncertain.

Political work, the work of critical analysis, involves engagement with a range of possibilities for meaning by exploring and imagining the 'lines of flight' (Deleuze and Guattari, 1988) or spaces for difference that are constitutive elements of all discourse. Liberal discourses, including paternalism, have been extensively analysed and critiqued for their limitations to account for differences and tensions within and between structures (see e.g. Brah et al., 1999; Braidotti, 2006). Making the tensions between tradition and reform visible, for instance, creates new spaces for debate. Working within the tensions, in the in-between spaces, enables critical engagement with what professionalism could mean for early childhood education.

Conceptualizing professionalism as a discursive construct with 'run offs', that is, with continuous possibilities for finding new and unexpected spaces and subjectivities, focuses attention by identifying 'professionalisms' within discourse. Such a perspective becomes possible when discourses are understood as assemblages, as made up from a wide range of ideas, practices, theories, all of which are held together by shared knowledges and practices (Cruikshank, 1999). The shared meaning of 'professionalism' in early childhood education is assembled out of traditional and neoliberal concepts and in this space individual teachers perform or enact their professional self. There is no space outside of discourse, no 'other' professionalism that is better, more autonomous, more free, which is only waiting to be discovered. The task of critical analysis is to challenge and play with the possibilities that exist when aspects of shared knowledge become contestable and teachers use diverse knowledges to change practices. Isn't it our professional responsibility to find ways 'to provoke insights into the conditions' (Todd, 2007: 593) of knowledge that we accept as 'true' or relevant, if we believe teaching is more than an implant or transfer of knowledge? Searching for an understanding of how, for instance, 'professionalism' is assembled can be a powerful tool to create change, in particular when the intention is to remain open to an ongoing search for insights into the conditions of meaning. This may involve provoking difficult questions and accepting that moments of unease can be indications of a shift in understanding how meanings of 'professionalism' are made. These are moments of 'becoming', where professionalism opens up to new meanings.

Close-up: towards 'professionalism/s'

Extending the argument that the contestable nature of contemporary discourses of professionalism creates spaces for a constructive reconfiguration, the final part of the chapter introduces moments of 'professionalism/s' as instances where teachers provoke questions that probe the basis for current understandings of professionalism. The teachers, Marina, Kate and Vanessa, teach in a privately owned, small inner-city centre, 'Collectively Kids' (CK), that participated in a two-year qualitative research project, Titiro whakamuri, hoki whakamua – Caring for Self, Other and the Environment in Early Years' Teaching and Learning (Ritchie et al., forthcoming). While the research context provided the opportunity to begin the process of tracing discursive shifts in how professionalism is performed and experienced by teachers, it is important to note that the project set out to investigate possibilities for ecological sustainability in early childhood education. The research was not concerned with professionalism as such. However, the research focus required a commitment to issues of professionalism and leadership because ecological sustainability has so far been a marginal topic for research and practice in early childhood education (Davis, 2009). Taking part in the project meant that teachers had to be open to the idea of exploring complex and challenging issues, and develop new pedagogical perspectives. The project depended on the leadership and professionalism of our teacher-participants.

Ecological sustainability and care for self and other are beginning to become closely entangled with notions of professionalism: in Australia, for instance, the National Professional Association for Early Childhood Educators (ECA) has recently updated its code of ethics to include 'the obligation for early childhood educators "to work with children to help them understand that they are global citizens with shared responsibilities to the environment and humanity"' (Davis, 2009: 230). This shift towards an integration of global issues into early childhood discourse is an example of how 'professionalism' is currently reassembled. Professional conduct, guided by the code of ethics, now involves teaching children how to become global, as well as national, citizens.

Collectively Kids was one of 10 participating centres in this nationwide project. Marina is the owner and a member of the teaching team. She had a personal interest in the research topic and used her leadership role in the centre to provoke insights into how professionalism creates possibilities for change. The Collectively Kids' centre philosophy statement emphasizes a commitment to community building and collaboration to 'extend the learning that goes on at the centre and beyond'. The statement acknowledges the importance of consultation and democratic practices to pedagogy. Professional expectations of teachers are that they foster and maintain responsive and reciprocal relationships with children, families, the wider community, and within the teaching team. Emphasis is placed on the concept of interrelationality as a basis for professional conduct. Being professional and demonstrating leadership in this environment demands that teachers are aware, or become progressively more aware, of complex interconnections. For Vanessa, this meant overcoming initial resistance to the research focus:

> We all have different levels of commitment, understanding and knowledge ... I have come from not knowing much at all [about ecological issues] to committing myself to the little things that I personally do at home, and to the larger commitment of our community and team at Collectively Kids. Being part of a team that is committed to the ecological sustainability approach has been a huge step for me but having us all take it on board has helped to make these changes worthwhile and work for us as a centre.

Vanessa's moment of provoking insights involved considering professionalism as a continuum which enabled her to see herself as 'a beginner' on this particular issue. She feels secure in the knowledge that others in the team can provide guidance for her, and that she is able to contribute to the best of her newly emerging ability and understanding. Vanessa has worked in this centre as a fully qualified teacher for many years. For her at least, two professional selves co-exist alongside each other: she can be a beginner when it comes to her contribution to developing practices, policies and pedagogies that address ecological sustainability. She also draws on her leadership abilities when she shared her insights of becoming aware of global and local interrelations at a large research hui (Māori word for meeting) with teachers from 10 other participating centres. Vanessa's sense of professionalism propelled her into a public space where she openly shared her insights into how she changed her professional self.

Leadership and professionalism: taking the difficult path

Vanessa was not the only one who initially had difficulties seeing the relevance of addressing a global topic. Ecological sustainability is potentially an area that creates unease for many early childhood teachers because the topic is seen as political. The notion that teachers are advocates for children, and in this role protect children from harm, including harm from complex knowledge and issues, dominates traditional early childhood discourse (Woodhead and Montgomery, 2003). Marina challenged this discourse: 'If, as teachers, we simply see our role as protecting children from harm, which we do constantly and often unnecessarily, are we meeting that goal if we do not address a very real threat to their future?' Marina's question highlights that for her professionalism means challenging ways of doing and thinking which leads to a changed understanding of self and others.

Children, for Marina, are foremost people who, like everyone else, have to deal with complex issues in an increasingly complex world. Her provocative question indicates that she is pursuing a different path in her teaching, a path that deviates from the emphasis on advocacy as a core element of early childhood professionalism. Ellsworth (2005: 16) suggests that learning means 'being in transition and in motion towards previously unknown ways of thinking and being in the world'. Following lines of flight or deviations within, the professionalism discourse is tied up with learning to transform the self as an effect of changed ways of relating to others and the world. Marina's ability to take risks and to pose uncomfortable questions is an indication of her willingness to learn to be a different teacher. It is a professionalism that embraces learning as motion and as being in transition towards uncertainty and the unknown.

Learning to be different

A discursive shift towards new and multiple meanings of professionalism evolved as the result of persistent leadership, and at times, forceful demands to reconsider well established practices and theories. Under Marina's leadership, the teaching team seemed to be able to develop open-mindedness about what it means to be a professional teacher. The teaching team began to consider that risk taking and creating opportunities to explore and accept uncertainty, especially for beginning teachers, was an important aspect of enabling multiple meanings of teaching, leadership and professionalism to emerge. Kate, who has worked in CK for many years, pointed out that the team had to learn to accept different views, even though they all were committed to change. She also highlights the importance of re-considering herself as teacher: 'My own feeling was that while we all agreed in principle the issues [changing practices] were serious and needed addressing, our own understandings and expectations regarding our role as teachers (and co-learners) differed'. Kate and Marina are shifting away from clear-cut definitions of what a teacher is towards an understanding of emerging professionalism/s as a continuous process of entanglement between self, others and the world. The discursive shift that is becoming noticeable may be described as a striving towards a professionalism of becoming, and as professional 'knowledge in the making' (Ellsworth, 2005: 1).

The professional self is the learning self

Ellsworth (2005) theorizes the learning self as movement or sensation rather than as a definable, describable entity. She considers the learning self in its materiality – learning is not a cognitive act but deeply experiential and sensory: 'We do not *have* experiences. We *are* experiences' (Ellsworth, 2005: 26). She proposes that learning happens in the encounter between inner self and other reality. In this encounter, neither inner self nor outer reality are fixed entities – inner and outer oscillate. Outer reality is 'in itself shaped in turn by what we bring to it from our inner realities' (Ellsworth, 2005: 37). For Marina, professionalism and leadership are closely interlinked with her learning self. Professional and personal self re-shaped each other in the ongoing process of professional 'knowledge in the making'.

Taking the risk of making her 'learning self' visible in the context of her personal experience was a core element of change for Marina. Reconnecting with her past self made it possible for her to make sense of how she experiences the present. It was a way of bringing the 'inner self' in interaction with the 'outer reality' to re-think how leadership and learning shaped leadership as an aspect of professionalism. Ellsworth (2005: 37) describes knowledge in the making as a moment of recognition, when the learning self 'has come to know [herself] differently'. Marina's professional self is re-made in the oscillation between past and present. Learning in this instance is the awareness that although the future remains unknowable, it is shaped by intentions that arise in the flux between past and present. Marina's moment of 'knowing herself differently' arises in the interplay between past, present and future, and shapes her professionalism and leadership. She takes the risk of making these interconnections visible as a driving force for agency.

> *Marina*: My growing up has involved several relocations over three continents. This background has given me rich experiences in community and sustainability and an understanding of how conflict and crisis can turn people's lives upside down. The key that used to hang above my grandfather's desk in Uruguay is a symbol for me of how our futures cannot be imagined. He locked the door of his family home, left the farm in eastern Prussia expecting to return in the not-too-distant future but that life was never possible again. The history of my family also makes me wonder how brave I would have been during those difficult times. This is a time to make a stand regardless of how uncomfortable or risky that might be for me.

Marina's professionalism is specific because it refers not only to the leadership, teaching and learning in the day-to-day encounters between teachers, children, parents and the wider community but also to a recognition of how the past is interwoven into who we are in the present, and how this weave shapes who we become in the future. How the self is imagined and lived makes a difference between paralysis and action, and creates a focus. Marina makes the indeterminable relationship between inner self and outer reality clear. Her professionalism, although specific, is not fixed but fluid and responsive. It arises in the in-between spaces and the interrelations between self, other, learner, teacher, global, local, the past, present, future – inner self and outer reality constitute each other. Such a conceptualization of the professional self can be invigorating as well as challenging.

> *Marina*: Kate and I discussed how easy it is to feel frustrated. I realized that my way of avoiding that is to try and stay focused on what I am able to do now and what I would like to see for children and adults at Collectively Kids and globally – vibrant, resilient, just, sustainable, critically reflective and engaged communities.

Professionalism and leadership as democratic practice

Hannah Arendt (1958), a political philosopher, argues that to act in the interest of others is a particularly challenging task because it means overcoming self-interest. Self-interest would dictate shelving complicated issues in the 'too hard' basket. As Marina points out, facing the incredible challenges to pedagogy and leadership of enormous problems, such as climate change, is uncomfortable, overwhelming and risky. It is easier to not address complicated questions to protect oneself from discomfort and uncertainty. The gesture of turning away denies experiencing the self in its complex relations with 'reality'. It is a refusal of learning, of becoming other-than-what-we-are. Without the willingness to experience the self differently to how it was before the moment of encounter, learning as transformative change is impossible.

Peter Moss's (2007) notion of early childhood education as democratic practice reiterates this point. Democratic practice flourishes if multiple meanings, knowledges and practices co-exist and if the difference that each person brings to meaning-making processes is recognized as an opportunity to change, to become different. 'Space to act', to transform the self in thought and practice is, Arendt argues, 'true freedom' (1958: 714). This 'freedom' to take action, to put the self in a potentially uncomfortable position, is essentially different from the 'freedom' associated with choice in consumer-driven meanings of the word. Early childhood education in New Zealand is not unfamiliar with calls to act democratically and to take a risk. Te Whāriki, with its bicultural emphasis and its challenge to teachers to act, can be interpreted as a deeply democratic document. It is a taonga (Māori for a treasured thing) that creates a space to act and to transform the present with intentions for a more just and sustainable future.

To be free to act requires the ability to have hope and faith in the future (Arendt, 1958). Enacting democratic practice may mean struggling for the freedom to act. Professionalism in this context refers to making connections with politics, history and policy to understand what makes agency currently possible, and what limits or endangers it. Marina is aware that freedom to act is a privilege and a responsibility:

> The freedom that still exists in the early childhood sector in NZ for the time being enables me to do this [act to create change]. Te Whāriki, our curriculum guidelines are broad and give us wide scope. We should guard this freedom fiercely and I would like to see the sector engage more consciously with the potential it provides for social change.

Final thoughts

The notion of professional knowledge-in-the-making and the learning self as a basis for professionalism/s requires ongoing engagement with people, things, ideas, policies and politics. It demands constant recognition of how 'professionalism/s' are made and re-made every moment, in encounters, in thought, in action, in contexts – knowledge is made and re-made by experiencing the self in relation to the world, and by provoking insights into how experiences shape knowledge and a sense of self. It involves the ability to take risks and live with uncertainty. Professional knowledge as meaning-making does not lead to measurable outcomes, nor does it provide useful benchmarks. It does, however, contribute new understandings of what professionalism/s in early childhood education may look like if it becomes the continuous process of experiencing and questioning the teaching and learning self in its relation to the world.

 Summary

- Professionalism/s are specific to people and contexts.
- Professionalism/s are responsive to people and contexts.
- Discourses of professionalism/s foster democratic practices and can provide alternatives to a culture of managerial performativity and to traditional models of professionalism.

 Questions for discussion

1. How does professionalism shape your sense of self as an early childhood educator?
2. How do you understand the relationship between a code of ethics and professionalism?
3. What is the relationship between learning and professionalism?
4. What does it mean to think of professionalism as a technology of government? How is professionalism governed? How does professionalism govern teachers? (*Higher level question*)

Further reading 📖

Levels 5 and 6

Burbules, N. and Torres, C. (2000) 'Globalization and education: an introduction', in N. Burbules and C. Torres (eds) *Globalization and Education: Critical Perspectives*. London: Routledge. pp. 1–26.
This chapter outlines how critical perspectives in education contribute to an understanding of change through an analysis of the politics of education. It provides background reading to the politics of professionalism.

Codd, J. (2008) 'Neoliberalism, globalisation and the deprofessionalisation of teachers', in V. Carpenter, J. Jesson, P. Roberts and M. Stephenson (eds) *Ngā Kaupapa Here: Connections and Contradictions in Education*. Melbourne, Australia: Centage. pp. 14–24.
This chapter provides a discussion of changes in the teaching profession. Although John Codd focuses on the New Zealand context, the chapter gives a good overview of the effect of neoliberal ideas on teaching in general.

Duhn, I. (2010) '"The centre is my business": neoliberal politics, privatisation and discourses of professionalism in New Zealand', *Contemporary Issues in Early Childhood*, 11(1): 49–60.
The article considers professionalism in light of the corporatisation of early childhood education. It argues that private centre ownership can create an environment for transformative practice in the current New Zealand ECE context but cautions against the limitations of corporate-defined notions of ECE professionalism.

Levels 6 and 7

Ellsworth, A. (2005) *Places of Learning: Media, Architecture, Pedagogy*. New York: RoutledgeFalmer.
The introductory chapter outlines Ellsworth's thoughts on pedagogy and learning as process. The interdisciplinary focus makes her work both relevant and challenging for education.

Rose, N. (1999) *Powers of Freedom: Reframing Political Thought*. Cambridge: Cambridge University Press.
The book is a carefully structured, powerful investigation of the relationship between politics and power. The introduction (pp. 1–14) outlines why it is important to reframe political thought at this point in time. Rose's argument makes it possible to consider professionalism as a technology of government.

Urban, M. (2008) 'Dealing with uncertainty: challenges and possibilities for the early childhood profession', *European Early Childhood Education Research Journal*, 16(2): 135–52.
The article questions the emphasis on expert knowledge in traditional understandings of professionalism. Urban argues that a discourse of professionalism as expert knowledge/practice is a hierarchical construct that is in tension with the interrelational focus of much early childhood theory and practice.

Websites 🖱

www.teacherscouncil.govt.nz/ethics/code.stm
Code of Ethics for Registered Teachers in New Zealand: this Code of Ethics currently guides professional conduct for teachers, including early childhood teachers, in New Zealand. It is interesting to read the code alongside Rose (1999).

www.tefanz.org.nz/
The Teacher Education Forum of Aotearoa New Zealand (TEFANZ) was officially launched on 12 July 1999 as the national voice for teacher education in Aotearoa New Zealand. It promotes the development of teaching as a graduate profession.

References

Ailwood, J. (2008) 'Mothers, teachers, maternalism and early childhood education and care: some historical connections', *Contemporary Issues in Early Childhood*, 8(2): 157–65.

Arendt, H. (1958) *The Origins of Totalitarianism*, 2nd edn. New York: Meridian Books.

Beck, U. (1992) *Risk Society: Towards a New Modernity*. London: Sage.

Brah, A., Hickman, M. and Mac an Ghaill, M. (eds) (1999) *Global Futures: Migration, Environment and Globalization*. New York: St Martin's Press.

Braidotti, R. (2006) *Transpositions*. Cambridge: Polity Press.

Brown, G. and Hattie, J. (2003) *A National Teacher-Managed, Curriculum-Based Assessment System: Assessment Tools for Teaching and Learning (Project AsTTLe)*. Auckland, NZ: The University of Auckland/The Ministry of Education.

Codd, J. (2008) 'Neoliberalism, globalisation and the deprofessionalisation of teachers', in V. Carpenter, J. Jesson, P. Roberts and M. Stephenson (eds) *Ngā Kaupapa Here: Connections and Contradictions in Education*. Melbourne, Australia: Centage. pp. 14–24.

Collins, S. (2010) 'State funds boost commercial part of industry', *The New Zealand Herald*, 26 January. Available from: www.nzherald.co.nz

Cruikshank, B. (1999) *The Will to Empower. Democratic Citizens and other Subjects*. Ithaca, NY and London: Cornell University Press.

Davies, B. (2005) 'The (im)possibility of intellectual work in neoliberal regimes', *Discourse: Studies in the Cultural Politics of Education*, 26(1): 1–14.

Davis, J. (2009) 'Revealing the research "hole" of early childhood education for sustainability: a preliminary survey of the literature', *Environmental Education Research*, 15(2): 227–41.

Deleuze, G. and Guattari, F. (1988) *A Thousand Plateaus: Capitalism and Schizophrenia* (B. Massumi, trans.). London: Athlone Press.

Duhn, I. (2006) 'The making of global citizens: traces of cosmopolitanism in the New Zealand early childhood curriculum, Te Whāriki', *Contemporary Issues in Early Childhood*, 7(3): 191–202.

Duhn, I. (2010) '"The centre is my business": neoliberal politics, privatisation and discourses of professionalism in New Zealand', *Contemporary Issues in Early Childhood*, 11(1): 49–60.

Duncan, J. (2008) *Notes on UNICEF Innocenti Research Centre Report Card 8: The Child Care Transition. A League Table of Early Childhood Education and Care in Economically Advantaged Countries*. Available from: www.unicef.org.nz/store/doc/MicrosoftWord-ExpertFeedback.pdf

Ellsworth, A. (2005) *Places of Learning: Media, Architecture, Pedagogy*. New York: Routledge Falmer.

Furedi, F. (2002) *Culture of Fear: Risk-taking and the Morality of Low Expectations*, revised edn. London and New York: Continuum.

Kelsey, J. (1995) *The New Zealand Experiment: A World Model for Structural Adjustment?* Auckland, NZ: Auckland University Press with Bridget Williams Books.

King, J.R. (1998) *Uncommon Caring: Learning from Men who Teach Young Children*. New York: Teachers College Press.

Larner, W. (2002) 'Globalisation, governmentality and expertise: creating a call centre labour force', *Review of International Political Economy*, 9(4): 650–74.

Larner, W. (2005) 'Neoliberalism in (regional) theory and practice: The Stronger Communities Action Fund in New Zealand', *Geographical Research*, 43(1): 9–18.

Larner, W. and Craig, D. (2005) 'After neoliberalism? Community activism and local partnerships in Aotearoa New Zealand', *Antipode*, 37(3): 402–24.

LaRocque, N. and Thorne, S. (2008) 'Early childhood education in New Zealand and Australia: lessons for policy design', paper presented at the World Bank Seminar. Available from: www.educationforum.org.nz/

May, H. (2007) '"Minding", "working", "teaching": childcare in Aotearoa/New Zealand, 1940s–2000s', *Contemporary Issues in Early Childhood*, 8(2): 133–43.

May, H. and Mitchell, L. (2009) *Strengthening Community-based Early Childhood Education in Aotearoa New Zealand: Report of the Quality Public Early Childhood Education Project.* Wellington, NZ: NZEI Te Riu Roa.

Miller, L. (2008) 'Developing professionalism within a regulatory framework in England: challenges and possibilities', *European Early Childhood Education Research Journal*, 16(2): 255–68.

Ministry of Education (1996) *Te Whāriki: He whāriki mātauranga mo ngā mokopuna o Aotearoa.* Wellington, NZ: Learning Media.

Ministry of Education (2008) *Education Report: Early Childhood Education Proposed Work Programme.* Available from: www.lead.ece.govt.nz/

Ministry of Education (2009) *National Standards: Information for Schools.* Wellington, NZ: Learning Media.

Moss, P. (2007) 'Bringing politics into the nursery: early childhood education as a democratic practice', *European Early Childhood Education Research Journal*, 15(1): 5–20.

New Zealand Teachers Council (2004) *Code of Ethics for Registered Teachers.* Available from: www.teacherscouncil.govt.nz/ethics/code.stm

Osgood, J. (2006) 'Deconstructing professionalism in early childhood education: resisting the regulatory gaze', *Contemporary Issues in Early Childhood*, 7(1): 5–14.

Peck, J. (2004) 'Geography and public policy: constructions of neoliberalism', *Progress in Human Geography*, 28(3): 392–405.

Ritchie, J., Duhn, I., Rau, C. and Craw, J. (forthcoming) *Titiro whakamuri, hoki whakamua – Caring for Self, Other and the Environment in Early Years Teaching and Learning. Final Report to the Teaching Learning Initiative.* Wellington, NZ: TLRI/New Zealand Council for Educational Research.

Rose, N. (1990) *Governing the Soul: The Shaping of the Private Self.* London and New York: Routledge.

Rose, N. (1999) *Powers of Freedom: Reframing Political Thought.* Cambridge: Cambridge University Press.

Small, R. (2008) 'Teaching, professionalism and ethics', in V. Carpenter, J. Jesson, P. Roberts and M. Stephenson (eds) *Ngā Kaupapa Here: Connections and Contradictions in Education.* Melbourne, Australia: Cengage. pp. 57–65.

Todd, S. (2007) 'Promoting a just education: dilemmas of rights, freedom and justice', *Educational Philosophy and Theory*, 39(6): 592–603.

Woodhead, M. and Montgomery, H. (2003) *Understanding Childhood: An Interdisciplinary Approach.* Hoboken, NJ: John Wiley & Sons.

Woodrow, C. (2008) 'Discourses of professional identity in early childhood: movements in Australia', *European Early Childhood Education Research Journal*, 16(2): 269–80.

CHAPTER 11

A NEW PROFESSIONALISM

Carrie Cable and Linda Miller

Overview

In this final chapter, we draw together some of the key themes and discussions from the chapters in this book.

The growth of interest in the early years in the United Kingdom (UK) and other countries over the last 10 years has generated significant policy developments which have been designed to impact on provision, practice, professional roles and ways of working. At the same time, there has been growing academic interest in the field and researchers, trainers and practitioners have engaged with these developments drawing on a number of different academic disciplines. Much of this discussion has aimed to challenge and problematize constructions of children and those working with children as 'docile bodies' who can be regulated, and to see them instead as active, responsive and agentive beings who live and work within complex, changing and unique environments. A central notion is that discussions of professionalism and of the roles of leaders and managers need to take account of the diversity and uniqueness of children, communities and contexts and that this involves openness and willingness to engage in a process of ongoing reconceptualization and reconstruction of professional practice and what it means to be a professional in the early years.

Introduction

The central focus of the chapters in this book has been to explore constructions of professionalism and what this means for those working in the early years, particularly for those who are involved in leading and managing provision and practice. The last few years have been seen as a period of considerable policy change in England with the introduction of new professional roles and statuses (CWDC, 2007), new qualification frameworks (CWDC, 2010), new curriculum initiatives (DfES, 2007a), and regulation and accountability measures (Ofsted, 2007). As Mary Whalley notes, many experts in the field of early years have been involved in contributing to these developments and have lent credibility to these initiatives. As we have noted elsewhere (Cable et al., 2007; Miller, 2008a, 2008b; Miller and Cable, 2008), these developments can also be seen as welcome and long overdue and as a necessary part of developing a coordinated rationale and approach to early years provision in England, through providing structures and systems for practitioners to evaluate their own provision and professional knowledge. They can be contextualized in terms of the overall drive by the English government to improve the quality of provision in the early years which has been closely related to the 'quality' of those working with children and families (Sylva et al., 2004). Dorothy McMillan and Glenda Walsh describe similar developments in Northern Ireland (Chapter 4). However, as a number of the contributors to this book note, the fast pace of change and neoliberal emphasis on accountability, performance and measurement can serve to undermine practitioners' own confidence in their practice and personal professional knowledge, leading to tension and confusion, a loss of autonomy and agency in decision making – and to what Moss (2007) refers to as a 'technicist' approach to practice.

The investment in the early years over the last decade has been considerable in a number of countries as well as England. However, although this investment has led to many positive developments for children, it is far from altruistic. It is perceived by governments as an investment in human and social capital, both that of future citizens and of their parents, as a means of moving children out of poverty and as a means of enabling parents and particularly mothers to engage in paid employment and the wage economy. Governments are persuaded by arguments that investment in the early years of children's lives can have an important impact on their later achievement. As Sue Greenfield discusses in her chapter, the establishment of Sure Start Children's Centres was one of the outcomes of this policy. However, as Iris Duhn points out, the drive to professionalize the early years workforce can also be seen as an accountability mechanism for this investment. 'Professionalism' must therefore be measurable; but even supposing it could be, would it be the kind of professionalism we would want in the early years or the kind of professionalism that practitioners would recognize?

Whose professionalism?

A key emerging question seems to be – do we want practitioners (and those who are leading and managing work) in the early years to be competent technicians who align themselves and their practice with external constructions of what it means to be an early years professional, or reflective, reflexive professionals who are able to respond to the variety and diversity of their individual contexts including the children and families they work with? But perhaps this is the wrong question. Perhaps one of the key problems is the tendency to see these positions as in opposition to one another rather than to see them as aspects of developing professionalism and professional identities. Perhaps, as many of the chapter authors note, it is the desire to have certainty through naming, labelling, compartmentalizing and categorizing that is at the root of our problem in understanding professionalism. A number of writers in this book and elsewhere (Dahlberg and Moss, 2005; Urban and Dalli, 2008; Stronach et al., 2002) suggest that we need to be more tentative and exploratory in our approach to professionalism in the early years, that we need to embrace uncertainty, difference, diversity, contradictions and tensions and see these as necessary and valuable in developing our understanding – 'that we need to develop an "uncertain" theory of professionalism' (Stronach et al., 2002: 116) and, as we note in the first chapter, one 'that is constantly under reconstruction' (Urban and Dalli, 2008).

Practitioner voices

Change, complexity and uncertainty are part of life in the 21st century and practitioners and those leading and managing practice need to be able to reflect on and respond to what this means for the children and families they work with and the environments in which they work, at both a micro and macro level. Structures, systems and standards can be useful in providing frameworks and benchmarks and can offer practitioners security and reassurance, but they are inclined to be viewed as static and given and, as a number of the authors of chapters in this book highlight, the authoritative discourses associated with these developments lend weight to this impression and can constrain and impede personal and professional development. A number of the chapter authors also note that because constructions of professionalism rarely include the voice of practitioners and fail to recognize their subjectivity, they present a picture which does not take account of difference, diversity or context or adequately consider how practitioners or leaders or managers develop professionalism.

Practitioner accounts provide important insights into how they grapple with contradictions, not in terms of resolving them but as a means of understanding their own practice and practice in their settings (see Simpson, 2010). The practitioners in Jan Peeters' and Michel Vandenbroeck's study clearly changed their practice over time as they were supported in reflecting on changing views of children and childcare and their role in working with children and families. Similarly, the practitioners involved in Jayne Osgood's study were supported in reflecting on their practice, through examining their personal histories and the tensions between what was required of them in terms of official policies and discourses and what they felt was important. Those in Iris Duhn's study were challenged through exploring an area (sustainability) they would not have immediately associated with early years provision. The ability to see oneself as a learner and to assume different roles and positions in different contexts seem to be significant factors both in leading and managing change and in participating in the process of change.

Personal histories play a particularly important part in these accounts. The ongoing construction of professional identities involves how practitioners view themselves and how others view them, both personally and professionally. Gill McGillivray discusses the range of influences including the different contexts in which people work, the people they work with and their experiences, and how these contribute at a point in time to their views of their professional selves. For many practitioners, initial and ongoing training contributes to this experience.

Troubling the concept – academic qualifications

Jayne Osgood talks about 'troubling' the concept of professionalism and we find this a useful way of approaching what it means to be a professional in the early years. Traditionally, professions and professionals are associated with academic qualifications which confer status and provide for a common means of identifying membership of a particular professional community. However, associating academic qualifications and graduate status with professionalism in the early years is a relatively new concept in England. The development of Early Childhood Studies Degrees was an important step as was the provision of Initial Teacher Education (ITE) courses for teachers working in the early years. The Early Years Professional Status (EYPS), a graduate-level award, and the National Professional Qualification for Integrated Centre Leadership (NPQICL), a postgraduate-level qualification, are significant moves towards associating academic qualifications with professionalism in England, although these levels of qualification are unlikely to be achieved by the majority of those working in the early years in the foreseeable future. Since 2002, intermediate-level qualifications at pre-degree level which combine elements of academic study with work- or practice-based learning (e.g. Foundation Degrees) have been available. However, these qualifications are now seen as stepping-stones to EYPS rather than as an intermediate-level qualification with an associated role, which only serves to reinforce a highly hierarchical structure in many early years settings.

This is in contrast to some European contexts where a graduate profession is more widely established, such as social pedagogues in Denmark and Sweden who have degree-level qualifications. The move in New Zealand to establish qualified teacher status for the majority of those working in the early years is a further example of an association between professionalism and academic qualifications. In England (and other parts of the UK), it has been more common to associate vocational qualifications at pre-university levels with early years practitioners, although as Gill McGillivray notes, one in three practitioners do not have a level 3 qualification, which is considered a basic level of qualification for someone working in the sector. Government difficulties in deciding what are appropriate academic or vocational qualifications for work in the early years are not confined to England, as Dorothy McMillan and Glenda

Walsh note in the context of Northern Ireland and Christine Woodrow notes in the Australian context. Differences and inequalities in terms of perceptions, training, conditions and pay between the private and maintained sectors are also evident across counties and serve to preserve and perpetuate tensions between those working in different types of provision.

Troubling the concept – variety and diversity

As we have outlined elsewhere (Miller and Cable, 2008), the early years workforce in the UK is diverse in terms of roles, titles, responsibilities and qualifications and practitioners work in a diverse range of settings in the private, voluntary, independent and maintained sectors. The gender, age and pay imbalances across the sector are starkly illustrated in Table 7.1 in Gill McGillivray's chapter and by other authors, including Guy Roberts-Holmes and Simon Brownhill in Chapter 9. Interpretations of leadership and management are also different in these different contexts. It is this variety and difference which makes it difficult to view early years practitioners (or for them to view themselves) as part of a unified or coherent profession or professional group. It also makes it difficult to see how imposing professionalism through standards and regulation can be considered a feasible option and lends strength to the argument that professionalism needs to be viewed through a different lens (or a number of different lenses) in order to take account of the ways in which practitioners view themselves and their changing professional identities. A number of new and useful ways of viewing and understanding professionalism are explored in the chapters in this book. For example, Jayne Osgood, drawing on the work of Stronach et al. (2002), argues for 'professionalism from within', which involves practitioners in an ongoing and recursive process of meaning making, in constantly moving backwards and forwards between top-down policy initiated views of knowledge, understanding and skills and their own personal and professional experiences in a creative and never-ending spiral of learning and exploration.

Troubling the concept – expert knowledge

Another aspect traditionally associated with being a professional is that of expert or specialized knowledge. But what should this knowledge encompass? In some areas of work, it may be relatively easy to define an appropriate body of knowledge; attempts have certainly been made for the early years (e.g. Thompson and Calder, 1998) but without consensus. However, traditionally conceptions of appropriate knowledge are often constructed as outside the individual and can be viewed as given and unchanging. Developmental stages might be an example here. However, our current understandings suggest that viewing development in this way does not take account of the complexity of the learning process, the socio-cultural context in which the learning is taking place or the multiple factors and influences that may be dominant at different points in time. Many of the authors who have contributed to this book have argued that knowledge of the latter is at least as important as knowledge of the former. But this knowledge develops through experience, through encounters and through reflection and is not given. Iris Duhn, drawing on the work of Ellsworth (2005), describes it as a 'professionalism of becoming' which takes account of 'knowledge in the making'.

Codes of ethics

Another aspect of professionalism is associated with a code of ethics, often a statement of the attitudes, beliefs and values that underpin professional practice in a particular area, considered especially important for those working with people; in effect ways of being and doing, ways of behaving and interacting that encompass respect for people as individuals and a commitment to respecting people's rights. Teachers in England have a Code of conduct and practice for registered teachers. The Chief Executive of the General Teaching Council for England (GTCE), Keith Bartley, says: 'Having a professional Code, *developed with and shared by members*, is a hallmark of a profession' (GTCE, 2009, our emphasis). Can a profession exist without such a code? Interestingly, there is no mention of a code of conduct and practice or a code of ethics on the Children's Workforce Development Council website (cwdcouncil.org) or in the standards for EYPS or NPQICL. Within the *Common Core of Skills and Knowledge for the Children's Workforce*, a definition of ethics as 'A code of behaviour agreed to be correct, especially that of a particular group, profession or individual' (DfES, 2005: 25) is provided, however what this means in practice is not explored. Rather, ethical considerations are assumed to underpin the standards that practitioners are required to demonstrate in their practice and through their work in achieving the outcomes specified for children and young people. These are outlined in *Every Child Matters* (DfES, 2003) – being healthy, staying safe, enjoying and achieving, making a positive contribution, economic wellbeing – and in the *Common Core of Skills and Knowledge for the Children's Workforce* (DfES, 2005) – effective communication and engagement, child and young person development, safeguarding and promoting the welfare of the child, supporting transitions, multi-agency working and sharing information.

Currently, practitioners in the early years in England lack the equivalent of a General Teaching Council or professional associations that would support the development of common frameworks with respect to professionalism and professional practice. In contrast, for example, Early Childhood Australia has a code of ethics generated through a consultative process (see www.earlychildhoodaustralia.org.au). It states that: 'it provides a framework for reflection about the ethical responsibilities of early childhood professionals'. It also acknowledges the changes that have taken place over the last 10 years in our knowledge and understanding of children and childhood and the increasing importance of a rights-based approach which includes viewing children as capable and competent. The code lists the following values and processes as central:

respect, democracy, honesty, integrity, justice, courage, inclusivity, social and cultural responsiveness and education. The protection and wellbeing of children is central in the code but 'speaking out and taking action in the presence of unethical practice' is seen as a professional responsibility. The onus is therefore placed on the practitioner to act and reflect on their own values and belief systems. This has to be a bottom-up and iterative process – a search for meaning and understanding, not a prescribed set of actions or responses which do not take account of the context, situation or people involved.

Ethics of care

An ethics of care is traditionally assumed to underpin early years practice although Jan Peeters' and Michel Vandenbroeck's chapter clearly illustrates how this is historically and culturally situated and how this can and does change over time (and will by implication continue to change). Jayne Osgood suggests that an ethics of care was a powerful emerging rationale for how practitioners perceived themselves and their work in her study. Dominant discourses tend to play down this aspect in terms of professional behaviours as it is seen as associated with emotions and emotional labour and therefore as behaviour that is not rational and as of lesser value as it cannot be categorized, regulated or measured. As a number of authors note, the work of Dahlberg and Moss (2005) and others has been important and influential in reinstating ethics and emotional labour as key and valid concepts and aspects of the work of early years practitioners and central to developing democracy and democratic practices. The practitioner voices the authors of chapters have drawn on in this book clearly indicate that, while there can be a tension between emotional involvement and responsiveness to children and families and maintaining distance and professional boundaries, they consider an understanding of the complexity of relationships and the balance that must be obtained as an essential part of their understanding of their role and responsibilities, and achievement of this contributes to what makes their jobs meaningful for them and, arguably, for children and parents.

Gender

Childcare, and therefore work in the early years, has long been perceived as the preserve of women and as requiring limited specific expertise in terms of knowledge, save that learnt through the experience of motherhood or relationships with siblings. This historical construction of women and women's role and the association with specific 'feminine' attributes and dispositions continues to inform modern discourses and perpetuate gender stereotypes and views of women as naturally caring. At the same time, the gendered nature of the workforce and the privatization and commercially orientated nature of much provision has served to keep wages low. In their chapter, Guy Roberts-Holmes and Simon Brownhill argue that this historical construction of gender also influences early years practitioners' views of themselves and is influential in their perceptions of experiential learning and natural feminine characteristics, such as kindness and caring, being seen as more important than formal knowledge or training. This view is endorsed through the media, personal and community histories, and fears about male sexuality and schooling, resulting in what they refer to as 'a vocational habitus' which excludes men. In their chapters, Guy Roberts-Holmes and Simon Brownhill and Dorothy McMillan and Glenda Walsh also explore the arguments for more male early years practitioners as providing 'role models' and the contradictory evidence from research, parents and practitioners themselves. The downplaying of an ethics of care and emotional labour is seen by many of the chapter authors, and particularly those who draw on feminist theories, as a means of attempting to align conceptions of professionalism in the early years with dominant rationalist and male-orientated views of professional behaviours. A reconceptualization of the significance of emotional labour and an ethics of care is clearly critical in any consideration of professionalism in the early years.

Reflection and spaces

A number of the authors who have contributed to this book have talked about, or referred to, the importance of life histories or autobiography in enabling practitioners to reflect on and understand their own learning process and come to new learning with curiosity and openness. However, many practitioners working in the early years are not used to this, or have had few opportunities to share their own experiences and to articulate their understandings and personal philosophies in spaces which are supportive and allow them to take risks. Spaces in which practitioners can reflect become key sites for developing personal and shared understandings.

The ability to reflect on one's own and others' actions, on policy and practices and on theoretical ideas is generally acknowledged as a key attribute in the development of personal and professional learning but unless it is linked to review, reconsideration and action, reflection may serve very little purpose. Reflexivity, the ability to understand one's own impact on a situation or event and one's contribution to meaning making, is an important aspect of developing professionalism. Linking this ability to a growing understanding that knowledge (and aspects of policy that may appear to be given) is contestable, is important for practitioners and for those who wish to lead and manage early years provision. The notion of communities of practice drawn from the work of Wenger (1998) can be seen as one means of enabling meaning making and shared understandings of practice and change. Many of the authors in this book describe projects, action research projects, research studies or courses of study which have supported practitioners in creating spaces for reflection linked to action, and there are many other examples in the literature (e.g. Anning and Edwards, 2006; Fleer, 2006; Mac Naughton, 2005; Moyles et al., 2002).

One of the key outcomes of involvement for practitioners appears to be the ability to articulate their understandings of what they do, why they do it and how change may be brought about. Variously described as 'dialogic spaces', 'communicative spaces' or 'democratic spaces' (Dahlberg and Moss, 2005), they can provide opportunities for reflection but also, and crucially, for critical participation. Jayne Osgood, in her chapter, argues for a perspective which sees the 'critically reflective emotional professional' as the way forward. Opportunities to engage in contexts where there is dissensus (rather than consensus) (Hughes and Mac Naughton, 2000), as for example in the development of multi-agency working or working across different types of early years setting, has the potential, if viewed positively, to open up new understandings and new ways of working. For some practitioners, this could mean moving from practice which focuses on conforming to external expectations, to practice which comfortably balances external requirements with context- and situation-specific knowledge and understanding, and where 'reflection-in-action' leads to changes in practice. For those leading and managing in the early years, this is a critical move in terms of their individual understanding and their ability to engage with others in their role as leaders or managers. However, the key features of a learning community and of successful leaders is dialogue and participation; not just an exchange of views but a process which enriches understanding and the capacity to interrogate ideas, challenge assumptions and provide the space for transformative learning. This space is neither sure, nor comfortable nor certain. It embodies the notion of criticality and reflects the complexity of modern society, the diversity of views and peoples and, most importantly, it is a space in which relations are foregrounded and in which knowledge is contestable.

Powerful discourses

The notion of powerful discourses is a recurrent theme in the chapters in this book. They have variously been described in terms of how professionalism is constructed and how these discourses can enable or limit and constrain action, agency and individual constructions of professionalism. Drawing on the work of Foucault, Dalberg and Moss (2005: 15, 142) describe these as 'regimes of truth' which appear to be given, incontestable and 'common sense'. However, as Christine Woodrow and others suggest, they can also be diverse and contradictory. As we noted above and as Iris Duhn comments in her chapter, the involvement of a range of early years experts in the development of official guidance documents means that language and concepts such as 'collaboration' and 'partnership' have become part of the dominant discourse. This is an example that suggests it may be possible to move away from the duality of viewing policy as being imposed from above, and resistance as coming from below, to see new spaces being opened up where new constructions of professionalism may be discussed. This has resonance with the view of professionalism as context-specific and in a constant process of reconstruction and suggests implications and possibilities for developing specific forms of leadership relevant to work in the early years.

The powerful discourses relating to accountability seek to ensure conformity and uniformity while at the same time embodying a range of contradictions and tensions.

For example, the centralized attempt to professionalize the workforce through practitioners meeting specified standards is coupled with a lack of standardization in terms of pay and conditions and a lack of accountability in terms of employers' obligations in this respect. Another example would be the introduction of regulation with respect to standards for provision but the obvious tension between their application in maintained and publicly funded settings and private, commercially orientated settings. Christine Woodrow's discussion of the development of a free market, entrepreneurial approach to childcare in Australia clearly identifies the inherent and pervasive contradictions and the resultant consequences.

It can also be argued that certain dominant discourses have served to enable a focus on the wellbeing of the child and to expose practices including the abuse of children by adults in homes and institutional settings and, for example, the forced movement of children from Britain to Canada and Australia up until 1967. Sue Greenfield highlights in her chapter that many of the changes proposed through the Every Child Matters agenda (DfES, 2003) have been a direct response to enquiries into child abuse and that greater inter-agency and multidisciplinary working is perceived as a means of reducing the incidence of such abuse or ensuring that it does not go undetected. Critics of the 'welfare' approach see it as being presented in an unquestioning way and as though it embodies universal truths (Cannella, 2005), and as attaching too much importance to the views of adults and not enough to the voices of children (Lansdown, 2010).

Some degree of regulation and coordination can be viewed as helpful and supportive in an environment characterized by diversity in terms of practitioner roles and settings. However, powerful discourses can also serve to suggest that there are simple solutions to problems and simple ways of achieving outcomes and fail to take account of diversity. The One Children's Workforce Framework (CWDC, 2008), aimed at supporting the development of multi-agency and inter-agency work, can be seen as one example of the government's attempt to standardize provision from above which fails to take account of the diversity of working practices. The Early Years Professional Status can be seen as another example. As Mary Whalley discusses in her chapter, the enactment of the role in practice has to take account of the complexities of relationships, of different regional interpretations, and its applications in a diverse range of settings including private and commercial settings and vast differentials in terms of pay and conditions. Diversity and complexity and the ability to live and work with diversity and complexity therefore also become key attributes for early years professionals and those leading and managing provision.

Revisiting competences

In England, the terms competences or standards are often used to describe the attributes, knowledge and understanding and skills that individuals are expected to demonstrate to obtain a recognized qualification in a particular professional area. There are standards or their equivalent for a range of different professional roles for those working in the early years in England, including guidance linked to the Common

Core of Knowledge and Skills for the Children's Workforce, for those obtaining Early Years Foundation Degrees (DfES, 2005), for EYPS (CWDC, 2007), for NPQICL (DfES, 2007b) for teachers (TDA, 2008) and for Higher Level Teaching Assistants (TDA, 2006).

However, the views of competence embodied in these documents with their focus on knowledge and understanding, skills and attributes, fail to take account of affective factors, personal histories, views, values and beliefs. They can be seen as narrow and performance related, part of the culture of audit and accountability and part of an approach which aims to standardize and reduce competence to a series of measurable outcomes, achievable at a point in time. Shared values are implicitly assumed and dispositions are subsumed within areas referred to as attributes. Emotionality is singularly missing, although it is clear from the practitioner accounts that it is a fundamental underpinning competence or capability that requires complex understandings and management by all those working with children and their parents. As Sue Greenfield outlines in her chapter, working successfully in multidisciplinary contexts requires new ways of thinking and interacting.

In the same way that an argument has been made for a view of professionalism that is more than, deeper and broader than, a defined set of knowledge and understanding, skills and attributes, a similar argument can be made for a broader set of competences that encompass the unknown and the yet to be known, the willingness to engage in ongoing learning, questioning, discussion and a readiness to respond and act – all critical for those leading and managing in the early years. Jan Peeters and Michel Vandenbroeck suggest four 'action orientated' competences including the willingness to look for solutions in contexts of dissensus, a willingness to meet the 'Other' (people outside one's own frame of reference), a willingness to co-construct knowledge with others and a willingness to focus on change and to discover how to do things differently. This approach resonates with that described in an OECD project report attempting to develop generic competences:

> A competency is more than just knowledge and skills. It involves the ability to meet complex demands, by drawing on and mobilising psychosocial resources (including skills and attitudes) in a particular context. For example, the ability to communicate effectively is a competency that may draw on an individual's knowledge of language, practical IT skills and attitudes towards those with whom he or she is communicating. (OECD, 2005: 4)

The importance of the 'particular context' is highlighted. The report suggests that the competences needed for full participation in the changing globalized society of the 21st century include: the ability to use tools (such as language, knowledge and information and technology) *interactively* (our emphasis), including the ability to recognize what is not known and identify, locate, access and evaluate information sources in terms of quality, appropriateness and value; the ability to interact in heterogeneous groups, including being able to relate well to others, cooperate and manage and resolve conflicts; and the ability to act autonomously within the big picture while being able to assert rights, interests, limits and needs. The abilities to reflect and to move beyond the simplistic binary of either–or are seen as critical in developing these competences (adapted from OECD, 2005).

These competences, together with those outlined by Jan Peeters and Michel Vandenbroeck in Chapter 5, invite a different interpretation of competence and one that is highly important for those leading and managing in the early years and for multidisciplinary working. These competences are rooted in affective factors and involve the individual in seeing themselves as a learner, as part of a learning community and as a relational agent in a situation of complexity, uncertainty and change. Importantly, these competences are not seen as finite or achievable or measurable at one point in time but as elements/aspects of lifelong learning.

> These categories, each with a specific focus, are interrelated and collectively form a basis for identifying and mapping key competencies. The need for individuals to think and act reflectively is central to this framework of competencies. Reflectiveness involves not just the ability to apply routinely a formula or method for confronting a situation, but also the ability to deal with change, learn from experience and think and act with a critical stance. (OECD, 2005: 5)

Final thoughts

Mary Whalley discusses a number of different views of leadership and management in the early years in her chapter and most of these conclude that they involve more than taught knowledge and skills. The leader who is a learner and who supports the learning of others is a key emerging theme, as is the leader as an agent of change involved in transformation.

The multiplicity of roles and the situated, context-specific nature of the role are also clearly identified in the literature (Muijs et al., 2004) and in the foregrounding of 'contextual literacy' by Siraj-Blatchford and Manni (2007). The new multi-agency, multidisciplinary ways of working that are currently envisaged call for professionals who can comfortably develop 'contextual literacy' across boundaries, who look to draw on different expertise, who can accept and engage with diversity, and who have 'relational agency' (Edwards, 2010). Edwards defines an aspect of this as the ability to build common knowledge and common language – to seek 'to know enough to be able to talk'.

Developing professionalism at an individual level and the professionalization of a group therefore needs to be seen as a process, not an end product, because change and complexity are central aspects of life. As Jan Peeters and Michel Vandenbroeck suggest, the process of professionalization needs to be considered as a social practice and as a result of complex interactions between social evolutions involving individuals and groups. It involves practitioners in meaning making and the active construction of knowledge. It also requires an understanding that experience shapes knowledge – people will have different experiences – it isn't (or shouldn't be) possible to standardize experience or regulate what people choose to foreground or learn from.

The notion of the learning self developed by Iris Duhn, drawing on the work of Hannah Arendt (1958) together with the concept of the reflective, reflexive and responsive practitioner who seeks to understand her own actions and engage with others in creating new meanings, goes beyond narrow definitions of competence or imposed views of professionalism. Those leading and managing provision and practice in the early years need to be ready, willing and able to engage with new ideas, learn from others, accept that there are multiple ways of seeing and doing – to recognize that expertise is constantly developed and redefined and that it is more than a body of specified knowledge and skills.

 Summary

- Traditional ways of viewing professionalism are being challenged.
- New and multiple ways of viewing professionalism in the early years are emerging which take account of practitioner subjectivities.
- 'Spaces' formed or created by and with practitioners enable the exploration of meanings and the development of reflective, reflexive and responsive practitioners.
- The importance of an ethics of care and emotional labour in work with young children and their families is being revisited and highlighted.
- Early years practitioners do not act in isolation and professionalism involves practitioners in developing relational agency – the ability to learn from, learn about and learn with others.
- It is time to review, broaden and deepen our understanding of the competences or capabilities that are needed for work and leadership in the early years.

 Questions for discussion

1. What does professionalism mean to you? Have you changed your views as a result of reading chapters in this book? Can you identify one or two key ideas that you want to consider further?
2. What do you consider are essential competences or capabilities for work in the early years?
3. Do you think that others in your setting share your views of professionalism? What opportunities do you have to create 'spaces' where you can consider different views and work with others to explore different understandings? (*Higher level questions*)

Further reading

Levels 5 and 6

Cable, C. and Goodliff, G. (2010) 'Transitions in professional identity: women in the early years workforce', in S. Jackson, I. Malcolm and K. Thomas (eds) *Gendered Choices: Learning, Work, Identities in Lifelong Learning*. London: Springer.

This chapter explores the impact of Foundation Degree study on the changing professional identities of women and considers some of the challenges early years students face in becoming reflective and reflexive practitioners within a strongly regulated environment.

Muijs, D., Aubrey, C., Harris, A. and Briggs, M. (2004) 'How do they manage? A review of the research in early childhood', *Journal of Early Childhood Research*, 2(2): 157–69.
This article provides a review of the literature on leadership in the early years. The authors note that much of the existing research focuses on the roles of leaders and highlight the lack of specific leadership training.

Levels 6 and 7

Dahlberg, D. and Moss, P. (2005) *Ethics and Politics in Early Childhood Education*. Abingdon: Routledge.
This book explores a number of the themes raised by the authors of chapters in this book. Drawing on discussions from philosophy, ethics and politics, the authors suggest different ways of conceptualizing work and ways of working in the early years. They suggest that recent developments open up possibilities for new discourses which emphasize participation and democracy.

Fenech, M. and Sumsion, J. (2007) 'Early childhood teachers and regulation: complicating power relations using a Foucauldian lens', *Contemporary Issues in Early Childhood*, 8(2): 109–22.
In this article, the authors engage with and problematize reconceptualist thinkers who see regulation as repressive. Drawing on teacher perceptions of regulation, they argue that it should not be perceived as inherently constraining or enabling. They suggest that through engaging in critical reflexive processes, teachers can explore and enhance their own understandings and agency with respect to regulation.

Websites

www.cwdcouncil.org.uk/index.asp
This is the website for the Children's Workforce Development Council.

www.earlychildhoodaustralia.org.au
This website is for early years practitioners working in Australia. Among other things, it provides a version of a code of ethics agreed with and by the profession.

References

Anning, A. and Edwards, A. (2006) *Promoting Children's Learning from Birth to Five*, 2nd edn. Maidenhead: McGraw-Hill/Open University Press.
Arendt, H. (1958) *The Origins of Totalitarianism*, 2nd edn. New York: Meridian Books.
Cable, C., Goodliff, G. and Miller, L. (2007) 'Developing reflective early years practitioners within a regulatory framework', *Malaysian Journal of Distance Education*, 9(2): 1–19.
Cannella, G. (2005) 'Reconceptualising the field (of early care and education): if "western" child development is the problem, then what do we do?', in N. Yellard and A. Kiderry (eds) *Critical Issues in Early Childhood Education*. Maidenhead: Open University Press/McGraw-Hill Education.

Children's Workforce Development Council (CWDC) (2007) *Early Years Professional Status: Handbook*. Leeds: CWDC.

Children's Workforce Development Council (CWDC) (2008) *One Children's Workforce – A Journey to the End of the Rainbow*. Available from: www.cwdcouncil.org.uk?whats-new/news/1126 (accessed 31 March 2010).

Children's Workforce Development Council (CWDC) (2010) *Integrated Qualifications Framework*. Available from: www.cwdcouncil.org.uk/iqf (accessed 30 March 2010).

Dahlberg, D. and Moss, P. (2005) *Ethics and Politics in Early Childhood Education*. Abingdon: Routledge.

Department for Education and Skills (DfES) (2003) *Every Child Matters: Green Paper*. Nottingham: DfES.

Department for Education and Skills (DfES) (2005) *Common Core of Knowledge and Skills for the Children's Workforce*. Nottingham: DFES.

Department for Education and Skills (DfES) (2007a) *The Early Years Foundation Stage: Setting the Standards for Learning, Development and Care*. Nottingham: DfES.

Department for Education and Skills (DfES) (2007b) *National Standards for Leaders of Sure Start Children's Centres*. Nottingham: DfES.

Edwards, A. (2010) 'Relational agency and common knowledge at boundaries between professional practices', paper presented at the Activity Theory and Practice Learning Conference, The Open University, 10 March.

Ellsworth, A. (2005) *Places of Learning: Media, Architecture, Pedagogy*. New York: RoutledgeFalmer.

Fleer, M. (2006) 'A socio-historical analysis of the formation of everyday knowledge and schooled knowledge in economically disadvantaged communities – cognitive blocks and pedagogical gaps', paper presented at the European Early Childhood Education Research Association Conference, Democracy and Culture in Early Childhood, 30 August–2 September, Reykjavik, Iceland.

General Teaching Council for England (GTCE) (2009) *Code of Conduct and Practice for Registered Teachers*. Available from: www.gtce.org.uk/teachers/thecode/ (accessed 31 March 2010).

Hughes, P. and Mac Naughton, G. (2000) 'Consensus, dissensus or community: the politics of parent involvement in early childhood education', *Contemporary Issues in Early Childhood*, 1(13): 241–57.

Lansdown, G. (2010) 'Promoting children's welfare by respecting their rights', in L. Miller, C. Cable and G. Goodliff (eds) *Supporting Children's Learning in the Early Years*. Abingdon: Routledge/David Fulton.

Mac Naughton, G. (2005) *Doing Foucault in Early Childhood Studies: Applying Poststructural Ideas*. Abingdon: Routledge.

Miller L. (2008a) 'Developing professionalism within a regulatory framework in England: challenges and possibilities', *European Early Childhood Education Research Journal*, 16(2): 255–68.

Miller L. (2008b) 'Developing new professional roles in the early years', in L. Miller and C. Cable (eds) *Professionalism in the Early Years*. London: Hodder Education.

Miller, L. and Cable, C. (2008) *Professionalism in the Early Years*. London: Hodder Education.

Moss, P. (2007) 'Bringing politics into the nursery: early childhood education as a democratic practice', *European Early Childhood Education Research Journal*, 15(1): 5–20.

Moyles, J., Adams, S. and Musgrove, A. (2002) *SPEEL Study of Pedagogical Effectiveness in Early Learning, Research Report RR363*. London: Department for Education and Skills.

Muijs, D., Aubrey, C., Harris, A. and Briggs, M. (2004) 'How do they manage? A review of the research in early childhood', *Journal of Early Childhood Research*, 2(2): 157–69.

OECD (2005) *The Definition and Selection of Key Competencies: Executive Summary*. Available from: www.oecd.org/dataoecd/47/61/35070367.pdf (accessed 30 March 2010).

Ofsted (2007) *Framework for the Regulation of Childminding and Day Care*. London: Ofsted.

Simpson D. (2010) 'Being professional? Conceptualising early years professionalism in England', *European Early Childhood Education Research Journal*, 18(1): 5–14.

Siraj-Blatchford, I. and Manni, L. (2007) *Effective Leadership in the Early Years Sector: The ELEYS Study*. London: Institute of Education, University of London.

Stronach, I., Corbin, B., McNamara, O. Stark, S. and Warne, T. (2002) 'Towards an uncertain politics of professionalism: teacher and nurse identities in flux', *Journal of Education Policy*, 17(1): 109–38.

Sylva, K., Melhuish, E.C., Sammons, P., Siraj-Blatchford, I. and Taggart, B. (2004) *The Effective Provision of Pre-School Education (EPPE) Project: Final Report*. London: DfEE/Institute of Education, University of London.

Thompson, B. and Calder, P. (1998) 'Early years educators: skills, knowledge and understanding', in L. Abbot and G. Pugh (eds) *Training to Work in the Early Years*. Buckingham: Open University Press.

Training and Development Agency (TDA) for Schools (2006) *Professional Standards for Higher Level Teaching Assistants*. London: TDA. Available from: www.tda.gov.uk

Training and Development Agency (TDA) for Schools (2008) *Professional Standards for Qualified Teacher Status and Requirements for Initial Teacher Training*. London: TDA. Available from: www.tda.gov.uk

Urban, M. and Dalli, C. (2008) 'Editorial', *European Early Childhood Education Research Journal*, Special Edition on Professionalism, 16(2): 131–3.

Wenger, E. (1998) *Communities of Practice: Learning and Meaning*. Cambridge: Cambridge University Press.

INDEX